The Evolution of Sanātana Dharma

A Bird's Eye View

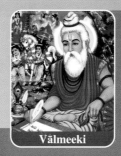

Vālmeeki

Vedavyāsa

Shankarāchārya

Tulasidāsa

ॐ पूर्णमदः पूर्णमिदं पूर्णात्पूर्णमुदच्यते । पूर्णस्य पूर्णमादाय पूर्णमेवावशिष्यते ॥

Om ! poornamadah poornamidam poornāt poornamudachyate.
Poornasya poornamādāya poornamevāvashishyate.

Om ! That is perfect. This is perfect. Out of perfect only perfect comes.
Even after taking perfect out of perfect, that is perfect which remains.

MAY THE WORLD BE PEACEFUL!
MAY THE WICKED BECOME GENTLE!
MAY ALL CREATURES THINK OF MUTUAL WELFARE!
MAY OUR MINDS BE OCCUPIED WITH WHAT IS SPIRITUAL AND ABIDING!
MAY OUR HEARTS BE IMMERSED IN SELFLESS LOVE FOR THE LORD!
OM! PEACE, PEACE, PEACE BE UNTO ALL

- Vedic Prayer

Yugābda 5110   **Shaka Samvat 1930**   **Vikrama Samvat 2065**

Special Publication 2008

The Evolution of Sanātana Dharma
A Bird's Eye View
A Timeless Ocean of Knowledge, Strength, Wisdom and Spiritual Freedom for All

Shardanand
Ashok K. Sinha

PUBLISHED BY
VISHWA HINDU PARISHAD OF AMERICA, INC.
P.O. Box 441505, Houston, TX 77244-1505
Website : http://www.vhp-america.org

This publication, *The Evolution of Sanātana Dharma : A Bird's Eye View* has been compiled from earlier publications of many authors, religious scriptures and material available on the internet.

First Edition, 2008
2000 copies

Copyright © 2008
Vishwa Hindu Parishad of America, Inc.

ISBN-13: 978-0-9793501-0-8
ISBN-10: 0-9793501-0-7

Published by

Vishwa Hindu Parishad of America, Inc.
P.O. Box 441505
Houston, TX 77244-1505
USA

Web URL : http:/bookstore.vhp-america.org
Email : bookstore@vhp-america.org

Correspondence Address

Vishwa Hindu Parishad of America, Inc.
Metropolitan Washington, D.C. Chapter
301 Saybrooke View Drive, Gaithersburg, MD 20877-3780
U.S.A.

Printed in India

Unprecedented progresses in Science, astonishing development in technical knowledge, and a great variety in the means of communication have brought the world closer. The world, in a way, has become contracted and small. No wonder the present age is called the "Age of Globalization". The basic cause of this Globalization is not some noble human ideal or great thought. All countries in the world wish to get some economic benefit from this growing mutual and virtual closeness. They are all in search of markets for their goods — the developed countries in the developing ones and the developing countries in the undeveloped ones. Globalization has given us a new way of life — that of viewing the whole world as a market and to earn maximum profit from it with a minimum expense. However, Indian Culture and Hindu Dharma does not look at the world as a market, rather it regards the whole world as one family

"वसुधैव कुटुम्बकम्" । *All men are members of this global family.*

The gospel of the Hindu Dharma prominently and tirelessly exalts such a global family and basic human values.

"आत्मवत् सर्वभूतेषु य पश्यति सः पंडितः"
He who views all living beings as his ownself is indeed a learned person.

"आत्मनः प्रतिकूलानि परेषां न समाचरेत्"
One should not treat others in a way not favorable for his ownself.

"सर्वे भवन्तु सुखिनः" - *May all be happy.*

We must make one more important observation in this context. Hindu Dharma is an ancient, universal and all-inclusive way of life. When a religion dictates the worship of only one person; declares only one scriptural book exclusively as authentic, divine and trustworthy; and commands all its followers to follow only one restricted way of worship; that religion becomes too narrow, and its followers at best assume the form of a parochial community. Indeed, depending on the degree of its narrowness and intolerance, the followers of such a religion could be, or may become, extremely dogmatic, dictatorial, conceited fanatic and even inhuman.

On the other hand, the basis of Hindu Dharma is not just one single chosen prophet, nor is there just one restricted way of worship. You may worship the Formless Abstract Ultimate Reality and you are also free to worship your ideal of divinity in a specific form, you might personally choose or cherish. You may follow the path of *'Bhakti-Yoga'* (Devotion) or may also realize your desired goal through the path of *'Karma-Yoga'* (righteous action). Many are the ways of achieving salvation. Here a devotee is completely free to choose his or her favorite god and goddess (symbolic personification of divine characters; or mythological and historical ideal characters) as one's spiritual ideals or ways of worship may differ, but still one does not obstruct others in following their own ideals. Tolerance and mutual co-operation are the hallmarks of Hindu Dharma, keeping it ever-new, through thousands of years.

Hindu Dharma tells us that all of us are children of One God and our souls are parts of the same Supreme Soul. We may worship God by any name or in any form. Despite the variety in names and forms, we worship that one *'BRAHMAN'* Who is Almighty, Omniscient and Omnipresent. He is One, but His Names and Forms are many "एकम् सद्विप्रा बहुधा वदन्ति" .

Contemplation, meditation and other Yoga-Practices, as well as pure devotion and other forms of worship — all these are means for achieving spiritual purity and salvation and are paths for leading the soul towards the Supreme Soul. It is said :

यथा नद्यः स्यन्दमानाः समुद्रेऽस्तं गच्छन्ति नामरूपे विहाय।
तथा विद्वान् नामरूपाद् विमुक्तः परात्परं पुरुषमुपैति दिव्यम्।। —*Mundaka Upanishad (3/2/8)*

Just as rivers, giving up their names and forms, merge into the sea, so does a learned person, giving up his name and form, merges his identity in the Supreme, the Highest, Most Effulgent, Soul — God.

The main aim of Hindu Dharma is to guide a person towards salvation by merging in that Supreme Soul. It does not negate worldly needs and comforts, yet the highest aim of life according to Hindu Dharma is *MOKSHA* (salvation). Hindu Dharma is an individual's journey from the natural to the super-natural, from materialism to spiritualism. It is also a happy social journey in life as a continuous and joyful celebration, embodied in myriads of festivals with utmost care for the welfare of one and all.

The two authors of **THE EVOLUTION OF SANĀTANA DHARMA**, Dr. Shardanand and Dr. Ashok K. Sinha, have very ably given expression to these generous, noble and glorious aspects of Hindu Dharma. I am sure this book will be very popular among interested Hindu and, hopefully, even non-Hindu readers, and especially among young readers who wish to obtain a brief introduction of the simple elements of this vast and deep religion at one place. I consider it a splendid book which has depicted Hindu Dharma in a very simple and down-to-earth manner.

The book has seven chapters. In Chapter I the authors have discussed the basic features of Hindu Dharma. It also refers to the great connection of Jain, Buddha and Sikha Dharmas with Hindu Dharma. Gods and goddesses of Hindu pantheon, such as Brahmā, Vishnu, Mahesha, Ganesha, Lakshmi, Saraswati, Gāyatri, etc, have been briefly described in Chapter II. Chapter III deals with Avatāras (Incarnations) of Lord Vishnu, with special reference to the four prominent Incarnations who have made permanent imprints on the Hindu society through millennia, and continue to do so even today. Main Hindu temples in India and abroad have been described in Chapter IV. Chapter V refers to the most sacred of Hindu pilgrim centers in India. The authors highlight the underlying spiritual unity with the unity of India as a nation throughout the known history. Chapter VI introduces some of the numerous personalities — scholars and saints and others — of India whose lives reflect the ideals of Hindu Dharma evolving through the ages. Study of this chapter brings before our eyes the glorious past of our country. Chapter VII presents a brief introduction of several miscellaneous topics including the Divine Incarnations of Lord Vishnu; Sixteen Samskāras followed in Hindu Dharma; the divine love of Rādhā and Krishna; importance of the Swastika symbol; and various yogic postures (*Āsanas*), breathing techniques (*Prānāyāma*) and meditation (*Dhyāna*) in the practice of yoga. Āyurvedic system of medicine has also been briefly discussed in this chapter. A brief introduction of Hindu System of Time Measurement and Shaka Calendar is also given.

The book draws a life-like picture of Hindu Dharma. The two authors have dealt with the subject in a very lucid and colorful way with the help of a number of pictures. I heartily congratulate them in their commendable efforts to undertake this task. I believe that this book will play a useful role in the noble task of exposition of Sanātana Dharma (Hinduism) to those young and inquisitive minds not yet familiar with its common principles and practices in India and abroad. The artistic and attractive presentation of the book should go a long way toward serving this purpose. This introduction will be incomplete without an appreciation of the publishers for their selection of a wonderful set of pictures to accompany the text.

The exposition of the Hindu Dharma is a noble and holy '*Yajna*' and I am obliged to the authors for giving me the opportunity to make my little offering in the form of this Introduction.

Swami Avdheshanand Giri

THE
E
V
O
L
U
T
I
O
N

OF

SANĀTANA DHARMA
A
Bird's Eye View

****

हरि ओ३म्

CONTENTS

ॐ सर्वे भवन्तु सुखिनः। सर्वे सन्तु निरामयाः। सर्वे भद्राणि पश्यन्तु। मा कश्चिद् दुःखभाग्भवेत्॥
ॐ शान्तिः शान्तिः शान्तिः।

(गरुड़ पुराण-२/३२/२९)

Om sarve bhavantu sukhinah; sarve santu nirāmayāh;
Sarve bhadrāni pashyantu; mā kashchit-duhkh-bhāg-bhavet.
Om Shāntih Shāntih Shāntih.

Om! May all be happy; May all be free from afflictions; May all see the goodness of others and in everything; May no one suffer sorrow.

ॐ सह नाववतु । सह नौ भुनक्तु । सह वीर्यं करवावहै । तेजस्वि नावधीतमस्तु । मा विद्विषावहै ।।
ॐ शान्तिः शान्तिः शान्तिः
(कठोपनिषद्)

Om saha nāvavatu; saha nau bhunaktu; saha veeryam karavāvahai;
Tejasvi nāvadheetamastu; mā vidvishāvahai
Om Shāntih Shāntih Shāntih

*Om! May the Lord protect us; May He give us joy; May we exert together;
May our efforts be successful; May we never be jealous of each other.*

DEVANAGARI SCRIPT (SANSKRIT-HINDI)
TRANSLITERATION INTO ENGLISH
PRONUNCIATION GUIDE

अ	आ	इ	ई	उ	ऊ	ओ	औ	ए	ऐ
a	aa, ā	i	ee	u	oo	o	au	e	ai

क	ख	ग	घ	ङ	च	छ	ज	झ	ञ
ka	kha	ga	gha	nga	cha	chha	ja	jha	nja

ट	ठ	ड	ढ	ण	त	थ	द	ध	न
ta	tha	da	dha	na	ta	tha	da	dha	na

प	फ	ब	भ	म	य	र	ल	व	श
pa	pha	ba	bha	ma	ya	ra	la	va, wa	sha

ष	स	ह	क्ष	त्र	ज्ञ	ऋ
sha	sa	ha	ksha	tra	jna	ri

Remove alphabet 'a' after each letter, the letter becomes half.
Examples :

क्	ख्	र	घ्	ङ्	च्	छ्	ज्	झ्	ञ्
k	kh	g	gh	ng	ch	chh	j	jh	nj

MATRA

ा	ि	ी	े	ै	ो	ु	ू	ौ	ृ	ं	ें
a	i	ee	e	ai	o	u	oo	au	r	m	ein

BCE is the abbreviation of <u>B</u>efore <u>C</u>urrent <u>E</u>ra
CE is the abbreviation of <u>C</u>urrent <u>E</u>ra

AN OBEISANCE

ॐ कराग्रे वसति लक्ष्मीः करमध्ये सरस्वती।
करमूले तु गोविन्दः प्रभाते करदर्शनम्॥

Om Karāgre vasati Lakshmeeh karmadhye Saraswati;
Karamoole tu Govindah prabhāte karadarshanam.

Om ! The front of the hands (palms and fingers) is the abode of Lakshmi (goddess of wealth), the middle of hands, of Saraswati, and the root (part of the hands near to the shoulders), of Govinda. Every morning one should respectfully have a look at one's hands (which symbolize remembrance of mentioned gods and goddesses and receiving blessings and inspiration for leading a life of truthful earning, learning and godliness.)

ॐ असतो मा सद् गमय। तमसो मा ज्योतिर्गमय । मृत्योर्मा ऽमृतम् गमय॥

Om asato mā sad gamaya ! Tamaso mā jyotirgamaya ! Mrityormā-amritam gamaya

Om ! Lead me from the unreal to the real; from the darkness (ignorance) to the light (knowledge); and from the death to immortality.

* * * * *

ॐ शान्तिः शान्तिः शान्तिः

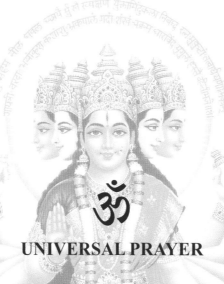

UNIVERSAL PRAYER

Gāyatri and Mrityunjaya Mahāmantras are considered more potent of the ancient Sanskrit mantras. They are for enlightenment and purifying our actions (*karmas*) and beneficial for mental, emotional, and physical health.

गायत्री महामंत्र
Gāyatri Mahāmantra

ॐ भूर्भुवः स्वः तत्सवितुर्वरेण्यं।
भर्गो देवस्य धीमहि धियो यो नः प्रचोदयात्।।

Om bhoor-bhuvah-svah tat-savitur-varenyam;
Bhargo devasya dheemahi dhiyo yo nah prachodayāt.

—Yajura-Veda (Ch. 36, Mantra 3)

Om! *Let us meditate upon the glory of Ishwara, Who has created this earth, the space and the universe; Who is worthy of being worshipped; and Who is the fountainhead of wisdom. May He enlighten our intellect?*

महामृत्युन्जय मंत्र
Mahāmrityunjaya Mantra

ॐ त्र्यम्बकं यजामहे सुगन्धिम् पुष्टि वर्धनम्।
उर्वारुकमिव बन्धनान्मृत्योर्मुक्षीय मामृतात्।।

Om tryambakam yajāmahe sugandhim pushti vardhanam,
Urvārukamiva bandhanān-mrityormuksheeya māmritāt.

-Rig-Veda (Mantra 7, Shukti 59, Mantra 12)

Om! *We meditate on the Three-eyed reality (Lord Shiva) who permeates and nourishes all like a fragrance. May we be liberated from death for the sake of immortality, even as the melon is severed from its bondage (to the creeper)?*

✴ ✴ ✴ ✴ ✴

ॐ शान्तिः शान्तिः शान्तिः

Hinduism is at the crossroad of an unimaginably difficult situation, and so is India, because of their intertwined relationship. The organized onslaughts of the adverse forces of Christianity and Islam are relentlessly trying to eradicate the ancient, rich heritage of the Hindu Dharma and to destabilize the very fabric of the Hindu society and India that may lead to fragmentation of the country. We, the Hindus — the custodian of this rich heritage — are searching for solutions and in doing so, blame others. In fact, we are responsible for all the problems. We, at the best, have become helpless lambs to be butchered at the altar of '*Punyabhoomi*' Bhārata. We must stop finding excuses. The solution to our problems lies in the 'Hindu Unity' and 'Social Justice.' This is the challenge we must embrace. Let us be worthy of this challenge.

Often we are bombarded with sermons by the Hindu preacher-cum-religious pundits that all religions are the same. In principle, any religion is ideally supposed to lead people to higher level of consciousness and spirituality, and induce in them genuine love and adoration towards the Ultimate Reality (God) as well as mutual brotherhood among all men. However, in practice, different religions vary tremendously in their overall motivation, dogmatic beliefs, agenda and historic evolution. Thus the concept of equivalence of different religions creates confusion among the young generation of Hindus in India as well as abroad. The leaders of the so-called revealed religions find the resulting attitude of indifference of many Hindus towards the Hindu values conducive to their mission of religious conversion. An organized global campaign of religious conversion to Christianity is going on in the name of freedom of religion. Similarly, forceful suppression and conversion of the 'non-believers' is a basic tenet and hallmark of Islam. As such, Islam achieves the same results by creating fear, intimidation and acts of violence and terror. The religious teaching must not be for religious conversion. It is meant only to understand other religious philosophies to avoid misconceptions that may become the obstacle to peace.

The religious conversion in India is blatant aggression against Hinduism. The religious conversion, in any pretext, form or means of temptation, including the lure of salvation in the name of freedom of religion, leads to the obliteration of the inherent culture. Even providing the social service with the intent of conversion is inherently evil. The crime of religious conversion must stop for the good of the humanity.

In Hinduism the process of synthesis and integration of new ideas is an ancient tradition. New ideas are not only welcome but encouraged. The emergence of Buddhism, Jainism and Sikhism are the testimony to this tradition. Even elements of religions of foreign origin became assimilated in India with no opposition. Christianity has not adopted this route but for the public relations it seems to be opening to discussion. In the cover of this openness and freedom of religion, the Christian missionaries are proselytizing others by hook or by crook. It may be noted that Hinduism and Judaism are the only religions which do not proselytize others.

The present unrest and blood-bath in the world is primarily due to Islamic Jihād, literally interpreted by radical Islam as extreme terrorist violence, mostly against innocent people and organizations. By design, it has retarded the progress made by the civilized world in the last few decades. The mentality of Jihād has to give way to reason. As a first step, sane Islamic leaders and scholars have the great responsibility of setting radical Islam for a critical examination. Moderate Muslims can best accomplish this goal. They must throw the light of reason on radical Islamic theology and its history of ruthless expansionism and imperialism. All extremist ideologies have been scrutinized and exposed, including slavery, the inquisition, apartheid, fascism, Nazism, colonialism, imperialism and, recently communism. They all have given way to reason or fallen flat on their faces. Only radical Islam avoids exposition. Now is the turn of radical Islam to give way to reason for the good of humanity.

The Hindu Dharma and its Sanātana vision to rejuvenate itself in all its glory to serve the humanity remained vibrant and dynamic all through the history, and survived all obstacles in the past. Now, once more, it is under attack. Hindus must arise and awake! You know the glorious past of the Sanātana Dharma — the source of inspiration — and take the present conditions as the challenge to your 'purushārtha,' and make the future of the Hindu Dharma as glorious as it was in the ancient times. As a primary first step, the solution to this problem lies with the parents, who need to explicitly appreciate and practice the basic tenets of the Hindu Dharma, and then pass on that knowledge to their children. The role of the temples is doubly important. They have to educate the people about the meaning, latent significance, and purpose of rituals and how they are related to the real life. They have to serve as centers of religious education, culture, heritage and ancient rich history, for the children and the parents alike. The invigorating sound of 'Pānchajanya' emanating from the temples would be the death-bell to the obstacles. The proactive role of the temples and other Hindu organizations would safeguard our beliefs, assets and heritage, not only from the organized onslaughts of adverse forces, but also from those who are misguided within the Hindu fold. The temples and the Hindu organizations have hard work ahead.

The present publication is a humble effort to provide some basic information to the parents and the young generation of Hindus about some important facets of the Sanātana Dharma (Hinduism.)

The First chapter contains the salient features of the Hindu Dharma including the very concept of formless (*Niraguna*) God and the personal (*Saguna*) God. The basic teachings of Buddhism, Jainism and Sikhism are also presented since these derivative religions of Hinduism emerged at the crucial times of the Hindu history, as timely reformation of certain degradation in practice of the Hindu Dharma, or against Islamic attacks and tyranny, or as a development for protection of the Dharma. However, over the centuries, these denominative or derivative religions have attained the status of world-religions in their own right.

The Second chapter is devoted to brief introductions of the prominent male and female manifestations of God, that is, of gods and goddesses (*Devi* and *Devatā*) of the celebrated and familiar Hindu pantheon. From the vast Hindu pantheon and mythology, only twelve such forms or manifestations most commonly worshipped by the Hindus are presented. They represent specific 'Saguna' (personal) aspect of '*Brahman*' the Ultimate Reality (God).

The Third chapter introduces the Four selected Incarnations of Lord Vishnu; namely, Maryādā Purushottama Shri Rāma, Yogeshwara Shri Krishna, Maharshi Vedavyāsa, and Bhagawāna Buddha, who have left permanent imprint on Hinduism by their teachings and exemplary lives.

The Fourth chapter depicts the most celebrated temples, the popular abodes of selected figures or forms of personal (*Saguna*) gods and goddesses. Among these temples, eleven are the ancient ones and three are newly built. The temples help keep our faith and provide public places for congregation and for performing poojā as well as imparting essential 'Samskāras.' In this age, the temples representing various aspects of gods and goddesses can be chosen to serve as strategic places for peaceful, defensive, and collective planning and for awakening and unifying the Hindu populace, habitually a sleeping giant. The temples of the 'offshoot' (derivative) religions are also highlighted, since they represent the inherent unity with their Mother religion: the Sanātana Dharma.

The Fifth chapter describes the important places of pilgrimage (teerthasthānas) which are also the symbols of Hindu unity. These centers of pilgrimage are located throughout India, upholding the underlying unity of the holy land of Bhārata (India). People travel to, and assemble at, these places as centers of congregation, and celebrate the pertinent Hindu festivals and also the specific historical culture and mythology unique to that place. The Twenty-three teerthasthānas including those of religions derived from Hindu Dharma (Buddhism, Jainism and Sikhism) constitute a highlight of this brief presentation.

The Sixth chapter is the largest. It describes the lives and legacy of a great many men, women, and youth in the Hindu history, spanning the eras of Sat-Yuga, Tretā-Yuga, Dwāpara-Yuga and the present Kali-Yuga. These are the people who dedicated their lives for upholding the basic, humanitarian principles of the Hindu Dharma and traditions of culture, and also for achieving the noble goals they set for themselves. Many of these illustrated characters sacrificed their lives for the safeguard of the Dharma and the country. They are the heroes and heroines, and the sources of inspiration to us, for all times to come. By their lives these heroes and heroines have enriched the Hindu culture and history. We all owe eternal gratitude to them.

The Seventh chapter, labeled miscellaneous, offers the sub-topics for selected material discussed briefly in the preceding chapters. Also are given the great achievements, namely, the concepts of time measurement in the field of Cosmology and Astronomy including the 'Shaka Calendar'. In the end bibliography is given. The sponsors of this publication are gratefully acknowledged.

The main source of material presented in this publication is some of earlier publications, teachings of many mentors and authors, scriptural texts, and open literature available on the 'Internet.' In many cases, the compiled material is simply a 'cut and paste' from the original source. We are thankful to those who used the electronic media for the dissemination of valuable information on the Sanātana Dharma. The materials have been largely compiled by one of us (Shardanand); and their presentation has been generally edited for length-constrain and somewhat improved for coherence and linguistic correction, by the second author (Ashok Sinha) of this publication. We are thankful to Dr. Liladhar Viyogi, a renowned scholar and former Head, Post-Graduate Department of Hindi & Sanskrit of S. D. College (Lahore) Ambala, India and Mr. S.K. Jain for their valuable suggestions and comments.

Finally, we are grateful to Swāmi Avdheshanand Ji Giri of Prem Pukār Āshrama, Kankhal, Haridwāra, India for his blessings in writing the Foreword with his inspiring wisdom.

Shardanand
Ashok K. Sinha

जय सीताराम ❖ जय राधेश्याम

> **I slept and dreamt that life was joy.**
> **I woke up and saw that life was service.**
> **I acted and behold service was joy.**
> *- Rabindranath Tagore*

SANĀTANA VISION
A peaceful, prosperous and humane Society

We Hindus believe that men are born of divine nature — having no prejudice, no malice and no vice of any kind — full of compassion and love for all humans and even for the animal and plant lives. Our spirituality is simply defined in terms of a human nature of man for peaceful co-existence with animate and inanimate species. The divine nature envisions a person, to be of free will, free to think and evolve in time and abide, by consensus, by the rule of law unopposed to Dharma for the good of the society at large. This humane nature is a link of commonality among all as if something inherent within everyone is the same. This something is the soul. If the soul in everyone is inherently the same, it must have a common origin — the storehouse of all the souls. The soul is immortal and cannot be destroyed even as a person dies. The birthless and deathless soul simply immigrates to assume another body. This is one of the truths propounded in Geetā and Upanishads: the paramount scriptures of Sanātana Dharma. It is an absolute truth.

However, when we look around we find that people are apparently different, most likely as a result of the influence each one of us is subjected to by the various thoughts, upbringing and exclusive doctrines. If we focus on the peace and prosperity of the society as the goal, then we have to overlook and accommodate even those who do not believe in God and Heaven, what to speak of religious doctrines. After all, such people are also a part of the society. Any view that makes a person an honest citizen of the society should be welcome. Accepting this basic fact, the different approaches mentioned in the doctrines of so-called revealed religions become fallacious. The present conflict and unrest in the world that are tearing apart the very fabric of civilized society are the results of one doctrine's attempts to gain supremacy over others. What we must focus on in the world is the welfare of all people! We do not have to accept a particular God and Heaven and Hell for maintaining peace in the society in which no one is hurt physically or mentally or deprived of the basic freedom and, above all, every one advances on the path of spirituality. Spirituality doesn't require the sanction of any religion. The spirituality is a path of moving forward towards achieving the calmness of mind, developing the warmth of heart and absence of ego, all leading to the service of others in need. This is the path of social justice and peace — the making of the world we live in itself a 'Heaven'.

Peace, and peace, alone is the supreme basis of human endeavor. Let this be the 'human-mission' of our existence — the mission of 'Borderless World' — the beautiful garden enriched with flowers of different colors, sizes and smell. The flowers are the men and women with ideas supporting each other; ready to serve those in need; and ennobling each other in peace.

ॐ PEACE, PEACE, PEACE BE UNTO ALL

SANĀTANA DICTUM
There is no virtue like helping others and there is no sin like giving sufferings to others.

-Sant Tulasidāsa

To do good deeds to others is 'Punya', and to cause sufferings to others is sin.

- Rishi Vedavyāsa

Chapter 1

श्रीपरमात्मने नमः

A Few Basic Elements of
THE SANĀTANA DHARMA AND ITS EVOLUTION IN TIME

Among all the *'Mantras',* the most powerful and sacred one is the single-syllable incantation called the *'Pranava Mantra'*. It is written symbolically as ॐ which is a letter (called *'Akshara'*—the imperishable) of the Sanskrit alphabet. Let us begin with this symbol, that represents the 'Creation and Creator' in the Sanātana Dharma. This symbol and the pronunciation of the associated sound (OM) are known to embody profound significance. Traditionally, in Sanātana Dharma this symbol and sound precede all ritualistic and formal worship, recitation of Sanskrit verses (*Mantras — Shlokas*), and study of the scriptures. This symbol and its sound also accompany spiritual practices in vogue, such as meditative concentration and yoga, on individual as well as collective manner. In ancient times it was a common practice of the Rishis to focus the mind on the symbol ॐ to remain engaged in *'tapasyā'* (austerities and penance) and yoga and to achieve the state of *Samādhi* (deep meditation) where the intellect and consciousness embrace the whole cosmos. It is believed that sustained practice of such spiritual exercises enable one to acquire power to extend the longevity to hundreds of years. With the power so achieved the Rishis were able to travel back and forth in time and know the past and foretell the future and were, therefore, called *'drashtā'* — seers. Also, it is believed by most Hindus that the symbol ॐ and the associated sound were actually envisioned and realized by ancient *Rishis* who, by virtue of their supreme meditative power, were able to transcend Time, traveling mentally backward in time to the point of origin of the universe. In this process the objective involved was to focus the mind (consciousness) on the essence of all the creation — the entirety of the universe with all its limitless splendor and expanse in Time (past, present, future) — as well as the loving glory of the Creator, the Ultimate Reality behind this panorama of matter and energy. Indeed, ॐ symbolizes the very Creation (and Creator) of the universe starting from a single point of potently infinite mass and energy (referred in scriptures as the "*Hiranyagarbha*"), and continually expanding into present and future states of the universe. This phenomenon is now universally accepted by the scientific community actively engaged in the forefront of modern physics (the so-called Big Bang Theory). This is an illustrious example of the superhuman achievements of the Sanātana Dharma, confirmed by science thousands of years later.

In reference to the Hindu religion and spirituality, this most elemental and transcendental syllable is regarded by Hindus to be the manifest 'Word of God'. It is a unique holy symbol displayed on all auspicious occasions, such as, invocation, benediction, ritual worship, festivals and religious ceremonies, not only of Hinduism but also of all religions that originated in Bhārata (India). Thus, it is a universally accepted important binding thread of Hinduism, Buddhism, Jainism and Sikhism. The use of this symbolic divine icon dates back to the very origin of the Sanātana Dharma, from prehistoric times. One of the first scriptural references and explanation of ॐ appears in the *Mundaka Upanishad*, as follows :

ओमित्येतदक्षरमिदं सर्वं तस्योपव्याख्यानं भूतं भवद्भविष्यदिति सर्वमोङ्कार एव।
यच्चान्यत् त्रिकालातीतं तदप्योङ्कार एव।।

Oumityetadaksharamidam sarvam tasyopavyākhanam bhootam,
Bhavadbhavishyaditi sarvomomkāra eva, yachchānyat trikālāteetam tadapyomkāra eva.

–मुण्डकोपनिषद् (खण्ड ४/१)

ॐ is Akshara or the imperishable syllable, the eternal Godhead Brahma. This entire universe is the evidence of its glory. The Past, the Present and the Future (of the entire universe) are all encompassed in ॐ. Even that which is beyond the three Folds of Time is also ॐ.

As mentioned, this sacred symbol ॐ is also referred to as the '*Pranava*' word. Literally the word *pranava* means: "That by which God is effectively praised." It also means: "That which is ever new." Its sacred sound is identified with '*Brahman*' — the Ultimate Reality. *Pranava* has been extolled highly in the Vedas, the Upanishads and the Geetā, as also in other scriptures. In the Upanishads, ॐ is the symbol of '*Nirguna Brahman*', which has no attributes and is beyond human consciousness and duality? The *Yajur-Veda* exhorts us to try to realize *Brahman* through repeating and remembering ॐ. The *Kathopanishad* declares that ॐ is *Pārabrahman* (The Absolute). The *Mundaka Upanishad* advises the spiritual aspirant to meditate on the unity of the ātman (the Self) with *Brahman* (God) using ॐ for *Japa* (chanting). Shri Krishna declares in the Geetā that He is sacred ॐ among words :

पिताहमस्य जगतो माता धाता पितामहः।
वेद्यं पवित्रमोंकार ऋक् साम यजुरेव च।।

Pitāhamasya jagato mātā dhātā pitāmah;
Vedyam pavitramomkāra rik sāma yajureva cha.

- *Shrimad Bhagavad Geetā (Ch. 9, Shloka 17)*

*I am the Father of the universe; I am the Mother, the Sustainer, as well as the Grandfather. I am the goal of the Vedic knowledge. I am the sacred **Om**, and I am verily the Rik, the Yajur and the Sāma (Vedas).*

महर्षीणां भृगुरहं गिरामस्म्येकमक्षरम्।
यज्ञानां जपयज्ञोऽस्मि स्थावराणां हिमालयः।।

Maharsheenām bhriguraham girāmasmyekamaksharam;
Yjnānām japayajnao'smi sthāvarānām himālayah.

- *Shrimad Bhagavad Geetā (Ch. 10, Shloka 25)*

*I am Bhrigu among the great sages, I am the one lettered **Om** among words, I am Japa-Yajna among sacrifices, and the Himālaya among the immovable (mountains).*

ओंतत्सदिति निर्देशो ब्रह्मणस्त्रिविधः स्मृतः।
ब्राह्मणास्तेन वेदाश्च यज्ञाश्च विहिताः पुरा।।

Omtatsaditi nirdesho brahmanastrividhah smritah;
Brāhmanaastena vedāshcha yajnāshcha vihitāh purā.

- *Shrimad Bhagavad Geetā (Ch. 17, Shloka 23)*

The three syllables — ॐ तत् सत् (Om Tat Sat) — have been used to indicate the Supreme Absolute Truth (Brahman) in three ways. Brāhmanas uttered them while chanting the Vedic hymns during Yajnas for praising the Supreme.

All Hindu religious rites are started with the repetition of ॐ. Also, if anyone succeeds in chanting ॐ at the time of his death, simultaneously thinking of God, he would attain the highest Truth. The Yogasootras of

Patanjali declare that *pranava* is the symbol of God and that one can attain *Samādhi* by its repetition, and meditation on Him. Finally, it may be said: **The word manifesting God is ॐ.**

The Sanātana Dharma, literally meaning the Timeless or Eternal Religion as it is based on Eternal spiritual principles and Truth, provides mankind the guiding principles of living together in peace with all beings and in harmony with Nature. Its beginning and the source of origin cannot be traced to any one person or any one book or scripture. It is said that it has no beginning and no end: it is Eternal. *Certainly, it is known to be in existence since prehistoric times or since as far back as one can trace. In its long history ranging over many millennia, various saints, sages and divine incarnations have enriched Hinduism by teaching its universal and eternal principles.* By interpreting the earlier scriptures, they have made the religion relevant to the changing times. In this evolutionary process it has taken many names: the Vedic Dharma (based on the teachings enunciated in the Vedas and their expositions — the Upanishads), the Ārya Dharma (the religion of the Nobles or the Āryans), the Mānava Dharma (being nonsectarian and universal — applicable to entire humanity) and, presently, the Hindu Dharma or, simply, Hinduism. The Eternal Truth enunciated in the Sanātana Dharma revealed to ancient sages of Bhārata forms its foundation. These sages, most of whom preferred to remain anonymous, realized that the Truth must have existed at all times and must have come from God — the Creator, the Ultimate Reality, the Absolute Being, the Source of Everything in the universe. As the **Truth** was revealed by God, the sages called it *'Apaurusheya'* — not man-made. Later on, this Truth was recorded in the *'Vedas'* — which means 'knowledge' in Sanskrit. These Vedas are the original basis of Hinduism.

A galaxy of such illumined seers and sages have provided versatility to the Truth expounded in the scriptures and proclaimed to the world that the cause of everything in this universe is only God who is called by various names by different people: ***Ekam Sad Viprā Bahudhā Vadanti*** (एकं सद् विप्रा बहुधा वदन्ति). In the Hindu scriptures, the word ***'Brahman'*** denotes this Ultimate Reality, also described as the ***'Supreme Spirit'*** or ***'Absolute Truth'*** or ***'Consciousness'*** or ***'Infinite Bliss,'*** and is beyond all the limitations of time, space and causation. In the Sanskrit language the word for God is also ***'Ishwara.'***

Thus, transcending the time and space, ***'Brahman'*** is infinite, eternal and changeless in its formless aspect — ***'Nirguna Brahman.'*** The same Brahman has been realized and experienced as God with form — **'Saguna Brahman'** or *Bhagawāna*. *Bhaga* implies six attributes: *Absolute Fame, Absolute Dharma, Absolute Riches, Absolute Knowledge, Absolute Beauty and Absolute Detachment (yet remaining engaged in actions).* One possessing these attributes is *Bhagawāna.* In simple words, One personified as Truthful, the most Powerful (Almighty) and Perfect — par excellence — is Bhagawāna and commonly connoted by the word 'God'. The One who is Virtue-Incarnate is God. The One who has lived to the ultimate limit of righteousness and all positive attributes is God.

In any form, God is omniscient, omnipresent and omnipotent. He manifests in various forms by His own will. He has created, He sustains, and He will dissolve this ever-changing world. The foremost concept of the 'Trinity' in Hinduism embraces this absolute principle that any part or aspect of Existence is first *born*, then it is *sustained* for some length of time, and ultimately it perishes. This principle of Universal Existence is expressed as the *'Trinity'* where **Brahmā** embodies or represents the Creator (of the physical universe); **Vishnu**, the Sustainer; and **Shiva** or **Mahesha**, the Annihilator. They are addressed as *'Trimoorti'* or *'Trinity'*. Hindus believe that this Cycle of Universal Existence — Creation, Sustenance and Dissolution — is periodically repeated on an endless cosmic Time scale. Clearly, *Trimoorti* as well as all other gods and goddesses of the Hindu pantheon are symbolic personifications of the Forces and Elements of Nature, and their 'Saguna' representations are devised by the Rishis to help the devotees — especially those who have limited capacity for abstract thinking — to focus their minds in a simple and accessible manner. Most of the gods have their consorts who are goddesses in their own right. This unique feature of the Hindu pantheon is a representation of giving equal importance to the divinity and power of the male and female elements of the Nature as well as of human society. The figurative representation of each god and goddess is designated to embody the corresponding attributes.

Brahmā

Lord Brahmā is the God Supreme in the creative aspect in the Hindu Trinity. He is the Creator of the universe and of all animate and inanimate beings in it. Space, time and causation originate from Him. He is *Pitāmah*, the patriarch; *Vidhātri*, the ordinator; and *Lokdesha*, the master of the universe. His consort is Saraswati, the goddess of Knowledge and Arts.

Lord Brahmā has four heads, representing the four Vedas; He holds the books of the Vedas in His hand. Goddess Saraswati is depicted with a white garment representing purity. She holds a Veenā (Indian musical instrument) as the originator of music, and sits on a lotus, an emblem of beauty.

Vishnu

Lord Vishnu is the Second deity of the Hindu Trinity, though in later scriptures He is regarded as the Supreme Godhead. He incarnates in every age or cosmic cycle to save Dharma and to vanquish the power of *Adharma* (Anti-dharma) as Shri Krishna reaffirmed:

यदा यदा हि धर्मस्य ग्लानिर्भवति भारत।
अभ्युत्थानमधर्मस्य तदात्मानं सृजाम्यहम्।।

Yadā yadā hi dharmasya glānirbhavati Bhārata;
Abhyutthānamdharmasya tadatmānam srijāmyaham.

-Shrimad Bhagavad Geetā (Ch. 4, Shloka 7)

O Arjuna! Whenever there is a decline of righteousness, then I manifest Myself for emancipating and glorifying Dharma.

He represents *Sattvaguna* responsible for sustenance, protection and maintenance of the created Universe. He pervades everything and everywhere in the universe. He provides the inherent power for existence. He is also known as Nārāyana — the One who is the abode of all human beings, whose abode is the heart of all human beings. Lord Vishnu has a blue complexion, *Neelameghashyām*, like that of the rain clouds. His color stands for all-pervasiveness like the infinite, deep blue space. His consort is Lakshmi, the goddess of wealth and happiness.

Mahesha (Shiva)

Lord Shiva is the Third deity of the Hindu Trinity. He is responsible for the dissolution of the universe at the end of each cosmic cycle. He is the embodiment of the tendency towards dispersion and annihilation of all (material) Existence. Shiva literally means the One in whom the universe 'sleeps' after the dissolution of the last cosmic epoch and before the next Creation. He is worshipped in human form as well as the Shiva-*Linga*. Shiva has Pārvati as His consort and Ganesha and Kārtikeya are their two sons.

Avatāra : Incarnation and Personification of God

For common masses with limited spiritual and intellectual facility, worship of a personal form of God with sincere devotion (*Bhakti*) has been said to be of the highest value and is the most accessible way. An average person may attribute any of the God's qualities that are most appealing to him or her and may meditate upon it with full concentration. As already mentioned, most of the elements and forces of Nature are also personified and worshipped as gods and goddesses. This concept has given rise to many symbolic forms attributed to God; each with a distinct virtue, leading to a rich galaxy of gods (*devatā*) and goddesses (*devi*).

Hindus look upon God as the Ultimate mother and father; and conversely, they are to regard their mother and father as goddess and god. Depending upon this common mental attitude, the devotees can establish other relationships with God as well. As mentioned above, **Ishwara** (*Nirguna*, Absolute formless God) or Bhagawāna (*Saguna* representation of God, with form and attributes) has endless aspects or powers. As indicated, Bhagawāna and specific manifestation of the same are personified as myriads of 'deities' forming the large pantheon of Hinduism. For example, Saraswati is the goddess in the knowledge aspect of God.

Matsya (Fish)

Kachchhapa (Tortoise)

Varāha (Boar)

Narasimha

Vāmana

Parashurāma

Rāma

Krishna

Buddha

Kalki

Dashāvatāra (Ten Incarnations) of Bhagawāna Vishnu

Lakshmi is the personification of wealth and opulence, and so on.

One of the basic belief system of Hinduism includes the concept of incarnation, according to which, when the practices of Dharma (virtuous principles) decline, God incarnates on Earth to reestablish Dharma and to protect righteousness, so that His creation may live and thrive in peace. An incarnation of God is known as *"Avatāra."* There have been several Avatāras in the history of the Earth (in the Hindu mythology). The **'Saguna Brahman'** — God with Form — has been experienced by many saints from time immemorial. Revelation and veneration of this personal aspect of God is the beauty of Hinduism. Earlier Avatāras — at various epoch's of the Earth's history — include non-human forms such as Kachchhapa (Tortoise), Matsya (Fish), Varāha (Boar), followed by Narasimha (Half-human, Half-Lion), as well as human-forms Avatāras (Vāmana, Parashurāma, Rāma, Krishna, Buddha). This fairly well parallels the evolutionary history of Life on the Earth. Thus, two examples of recent human Avatāra in Hinduism are Maryādā Purushottama Shri Rāma and Yogeshwara Shri Krishna, in the *Tretā-Yuga* and *Dwāpara-Yuga* (epoch), respectively. Shri Rāma battled with Rāvana, an evil king, and showed supreme qualities of human perfection, guiding the Hindu society toward righteous conduct of living; so He is regarded as the Incarnation of God (Vishnu). Shri Krishna killed an evil king Kamsa and later played a central role in the Mahābhārata war in eradication of the evil forces and persons of the time. He is also regarded as an Incarnation of God. These two human Incarnations appeared on the earth at different epochs to play guiding roles to humanity, and left permanent marks in history for people to emulate. We are the beneficiaries of this great heritage and worship them as *Bhagawāna* who appeared for the benefit of mankind in specific forms and as exemplary personalities. They are immortalized by sage-poets Vālmeeki and Vedavyāsa who wrote the Sanskrit epics the Rāmāyana and the Mahābhārata, respectively, glorifying their lives and deeds.

In short, on one hand, many saints and sages have emphasized the worship of, and meditation upon, the One formless God, the Infinite, Absolute and Ultimate Reality. In contrast, there are people who worship God in different forms to which they impart particular symbolic personalities, attributes and qualities, based on their own intellectual capacity, personal tastes and preferences. These personal forms of God are helpful for visualization and concentration. It can be said that either mode of worship can lead to *Moksha* (Salvation) if practiced with a true and sincere heart.

The tenet of Incarnation (*Avatāra*) is unique in the Hindu Dharma, according to which, in every cosmic epoch (Yuga) God appears in a human or other form to guide the humanity in the proper path and to remove tyranny and evil from the Earth. In the *Shrimad Bhāgavatam*, written by sage Vedavyāsa, twenty-two Divine Incarnations are cited. These Incarnations are listed elsewhere in this publication. Among them ten Incarnations of God, referred to as the *'Dashāvatāra,'* are the most celebrated ones — each marking a particular epoch (*Yuga*) in the cosmological evolution of the Earth or historical development of the human society (in India). Among them the Incarnations in the form of Kachchhapa, Matsya, Varāha, Narasimha, Vāmana and Parashurāma are called *Ansha-Avatāra* (Partial Incarnation). The most important Incarnations (*Avatāras)* that have lasting imprints in shaping the Hindu way of life, called the *Poorna Avatāra* (Full Incarnation), are of Rāma, Vedavyāsa, Krishna and Buddha. It may be noted that Vedavyāsa is one of the Incarnations cited in the Shrimad Bhāgavatam but not included in the *Dashāvatāra*. The last of the latter, Kalki-avatāra, is foretold in the Shrimad Bhāgavatam and is expected to take place at the end of the present epoch (Kali-Yuga). A more detailed view of the four *Poorna-Avatāras* is presented separately in this publication.

With the above background, it is useful to summarize the basic code of righteous conduct for human behavior which promotes peace, harmony and the coexistence of all species in the nature (animate and inanimate), the quintessential element of the Sanātana Dharma. Such codes of conduct are the important tenets of Hindu Dharma specified in Vedas and Upanishads and later explained in the Shrimad Bhagavad Geetā and other Hindu Scriptures. These tenets have been practiced for millennia and found to bear the test of time. These tenets are not dogmas or sectarian rules, but universal guiding principles valid for all times and places. In brief, some of these tenets are as follows:

The Goal of the Sanātana Dharma : The goal of the Sanātana Dharma is to ennoble oneself by living righteously. The ancient Rishis also envisioned the dream of

कृण्वन्तो विश्वमार्यम्

Krnvanto vishvamāryam.

Let us ennoble the whole world.

The Hindu scriptures have emphasized : Let there be peace in the universe.

ॐ द्यौः शान्तिरन्तरिक्ष शान्तिः पृथिवी शान्तिरापः शान्तिरोषधयः शान्तिः। वनस्पतयः शान्तिर्विश्वे देवाः शान्ति-ब्रह्मन शान्तिः सर्व शान्तिः शान्तिरेव शान्तिः सा मा शान्तिरेधि।

ॐ शान्तिः शान्तिः शान्तिः।

Om dyauh shāntih, antariksham shāntih, Prithavee shāntih, rāpah shāntih, roshadhayah shāntih, vanaspatayah shāntirvishve devāh shāntih-Brahana shāntih, sarve shāntih, shāntireva shāntih, sā mā shāntir-edhi.

Om ! shāntih, shāntih, shāntih.

-Yajura-Veda (Ch. 36, Mantra 17)

Om! May there be peace in the sky and in space. May there be peace on the earth and in the waters. May herbs and food bring us peace. May celestial beings bring us peace. May God grant us peace. May the peace be peaceful. **Om! Peace, Peace, Peace.**

Path of Dharma : Dharma is derived from the Sanskrit word *'dhri'* (धृ) which means to sustain and support. Dharma is what really sustains an individual and the society in the journey of life. Without Dharma (that is under the prevalence of *'Adharma'* or evil), the individual, society, country or the world is bound to fall apart, degenerate and disintegrate.

Life is a journey and if followed in accordance with Dharma, would foster well-being and continued progress, eradicating evil elements from an individual and the society. Peace would prevail as it directs the life-journey of every one towards goodness and greatness. It would also help a person to be free from physical ailments through the practice of yoga and meditation, an integral part of the practice of the Hindu Dharma.

Indeed, following the path of Dharma is worship by itself.

The Concept of Ishwara : The 'Truth' is only One, but its expressions are many: "Ekam sad viprā bahudhā vadanti (एकं सद् विप्रा बहुधा वदन्ति)." We call the Almighty *'Ishwara'* and others call Him God or Jehovah etc. The whole universe is His manifestation. God is omnipresent; His presence is manifest in every particle of the universe ("ईशावास्यमिदं सर्वं यत्किञ्च जगत्यां जगत्" l). He resides within the soul of every person. Some Hindu philosophers regard Nature (प्रकृति, माया) to be identified with God (अद्वैतवाद — the Principle of Non-Duality), while others regard it to be separate, complementary to God (द्वैत — the Principle of Duality).

The Nature of Soul : The soul is the essence of one's being, manifested as one's highest order of consciousness. It is a part of the Supreme Soul, the Paramātmā or *Pārbrahman*. The soul is immortal.

न जायते म्रियते वा कदाचि-न्नायं भूत्वा भविता वा न भूयः।
अजो नित्यः शाश्वतोऽयं पुराणो न हन्यते हन्यमाने शरीरे।।

Na jāyate mriyate vā kadāchi-nnāyam bhootwā bhavitā vā na bhooyah;
Ajo nityah shāshwatoyam purāno na hanyate hanyamāne shareere.

- Shrimad Bhagavad Geetā (Ch. 2, Shloka 20)

The soul is never born nor does it die; it is not that it was not in existence in the past, nor will it ever cease to exist in the future. For it is unborn, eternal, everlasting and primeval; even though the body is slain, the soul is not.

The Concept of Spirituality : Spirituality really means a relentless pursuit of the Truth. Spirituality is a way of 'live and let live.' It is the true manifestation of the idealized human nature. It requires one to be brave and fearless. Hindu spirituality gets its strength from the Hindu view that man is born free to think and act. Hinduism requires one to be spiritual and thus is often referred to as a 'Way of Life'. A sure sign that a person is advancing towards spirituality is the absence of ego, calmness of mind, and warmth of heart; leading to peace, prosperity, and justice for all.

The Concept of Culture : Man is divine in nature, though this divinity may be only latent, and hence not manifest, in worldly life, due to ignorance. This divinity, the pure nature of human being, often finds expression in the refinement of culture which mirrors in the pattern of thought and behavior on individual as well as collective (societal) basis, including in arts and music, religious songs (*Bhajanas*), dances, literature, social and religious practices, rituals, and institutions, etc. In Hinduism, culture is greatly influenced by spirituality. Even classical music, drama and dance are mostly in the praises of God or form the expressions of God's '*Leelā*' (enactment of human life as various incarnations of Lord Vishnu).

The Concept of Poojā : In general term, the process of showing the highest adoration and respect to a chosen 'ideal' is 'Poojā,' which also means 'worship'. In the realm of religion, the chosen one is usually a deity — the personification of an aspect of *'Saguna Brahman.'* Formal Poojā commonly entails the specific rites and rituals — the offering of flowers and performing of the '*ārati*', etc. The Poojā is generally followed by 'bhajans' (devotional songs) recited in praise of, and expressing love for, and gratitude to, the Lord (इष्ट देवता). However, when we accept the concept of *'Nirguna Brahman',* meditation upon the formless God is itself a mode of poojā, even though no specific rites may be followed.

The Concept of Deity Worship : The practice of MOORTI-POOJĀ (Deity Worship) is the most common mode of worship in Hinduism. However, the worship of God is an integral part of every faith. In the Hindu tradition and philosophy, meditation upon One God as Infinite, Formless and Abstract or Supreme Power, governing the entire universe (this is referred to as *Nirguna Brahman*) was a practice among Rishis (seers and sages). This, perhaps the earliest, form of worship of One Ultimate Reality (God) by mankind, initiated by the Vedic seers (7,000 **BCE**) was, naturally, followed by Vedic hymns and prayers composed by sage-poets dedicated to *Devatās* (literally meaning 'Givers, unconditionally, of divine boons') who freely make life possible, bountiful and blissful on the earth. Foremost among *Devatās* (gods) was Indra (Rain-god), who provided rains to make crops grow. Other divine 'Givers' prayed to and worshipped included Aruna (Sun-god), Varuna (Water-god), Vāyu (Wind-god), and Agni (Fire-god), etc.

Subsequent Vedic and Purānic periods saw the worship of the Hindu Trinity of Brahmā, Vishnu and Mahesha (Shiva) as the universal, symbolic personifications of the Creative, Sustaining and Annihilating powers, respectively, with their consorts — the female aspects of Divinity — Saraswati, Lakshmi and Pārvati, respectively. Later, Vishnu came to be regarded as the Supreme Lord, with recurring Incarnations (*Avatāras*) in various cosmic eras. Eventually a vast array of other gods and goddesses emerged, forming the Hindu pantheon now worshipped. It is easy to visualize that such an evolution of the concept of the Divine is but natural for a people who make it their pious duty to express gratitude to every positive aspect of the Nature that plays a universal role in Life on the planet, without any dogma, stigma or denial. At the same time, it is also obvious that nowhere in such a concept is any trace of negation of One Supreme, Ultimate Reality, The All-Pervading, Absolute Almighty (*Brahman*), as commonly connoted by the English word 'God.' Various gods and goddesses are simply symbolic projections of One Infinite-Dimensional Abstract God onto tangible planes, so to say, focused on specific powers that definitely exist and work under His subordination for the benefit of mankind.

Generally, in the terminology of Sanātana Dharma (Hinduism), the followers of the '*Jnāna Mārga*' (the Path of Knowledge) are intellectually equipped to follow a tradition of meditating upon and venerating an Abstract representation of the Divine ('*Nirguna Brahman*'). However, for common masses not so blessed, the '*Bhakti Mārga*' (the Path of Devotion) is most suitable where worship is of the '*Saguna Brahman*' (God with Form and Attributes). The personified images attributed to various gods and goddesses, specific powers of One Ultimate Divinity, simply facilitate remembrance and contemplation of *THAT* Absolute, otherwise intractable by a human mind of much limited capacity. This all-embracing approach accessible to every member of humanity, ranging from the most enlightened to the most pedestrian, constitutes the framework of the so called 'deity-worship' in Hinduism. The fact that there may be specific religious practices followed for deity-worship that evolved with the passage of time over many millennia and over a large geographical region (India), hardly detracts from the inherent merit of the spiritual system. Since the attributes of God are infinite, there could be (and are) a very large number of deities. Commonly, not surprisingly, the form ascribed to a deity is human. Indeed, the latest Incarnations of Vishnu are human (viz., Rāma and Krishna). In fact, through an admixture of the country's history and mythology, Rāma and Krishna, and many other historical figures, by virtue of their supreme human quality and grandeur, came to be venerated so high as to be identified with divinity. One can say that Hinduism not only aspires to make God more easily accessible to man, but also endeavors to elevate man to Godliness.

In short, the multitude of gods and goddesses worshipped as deities in Hinduism are the personified symbolic representations of Infinite, Absolute, One, Divine Power ('Brahman'), as is supposedly understood by the conventional word 'God' in the West.

Finally, the difference, then, is nothing but that of language — a purely semantic difference. However, there is one important difference that is self-evident. *If any religion* conventionally regards the word 'God' (or any equivalent thereof) to mean *only* a sectarian entity presiding over *only* their own clan *exclusively,* then such an *Exclusive religion* actually prescribes its followers to worship only a finite projection of the All-Inclusive Absolute Divinity. In other words, in fact, any Exclusive religion is actually confining itself to a rather narrow type of 'deity-worship.' In contrast, Hinduism, an Inclusive religion, with respect for all faiths of mankind, however limited, as different paths toward the same goal of God-realization, ultimately aims for the realization of and devotion to *THAT* Almighty, All-Pervading, Universal Power, embracing not only all humanity without bounds, but also the whole universe — All Existence, for all Past, Present and Future and also beyond all Space and Time; the entirety of Nature in all its splendor — ought to be considered as the only true and creditable religion of mankind at large. If God, by definition, is Omnipresent, how could any thing, or any one, not already be a reflection of His presence within? Expectedly, a realization of this simple contrast would dawn in the world all over, full of turmoil primarily due to sectarian strife filling the pages of history. Perhaps the new millennium would offer the requisite enlightenment, with advancing knowledge in all fields and dimensions, including the inner vistas, of genuine imagination and endeavor man is capable of, by the grace of God.

The Doctrine of *Moksha* and Rebirth : This doctrine is unique to Hinduism. Every physical being that comes into existence has to decay and die. This is the absolute Truth. The body is born, grows old and finally dies. However, the soul is immortal, and is reborn in a different body. Life consists of relentless action, referred to as *Karma*, which is an essential feature of existence; ceasing of action is a form of death. To transcend the transient nature of the body or even the miseries of earthly life may be looked upon as liberation. The doctrine of rebirth is a logical belief that explains the disparity with which each one of us is born and is subjected to the consequence of the *Karma* or action of the previous life or lives. Life invariably entails suffering, disease and death. Liberation of the soul from the cycle of birth and death is called '*Moksha.*' However, modern science ascribes the disparity among the attributes of different individuals at birth to the biological genes that each one of us carries when born. It may be argued that the predisposition of the reborn soul, in terms of the inheritance of the genes, is itself the result of the actions of the past life or lives. It is of interest to point out that some individuals are born with especial faculties and facilities, while others with opposite attributes. What is the cause of such inherent disparities and differentiation? It is desirable that, apart from providing spiritual guidance, the philosophy of a religion provide satisfactory explanation for such inherent inequities into the mysterious nature of 'fate' as well. In Hinduism such inborn variations are ascribed to the law of *Karma*, that is, the result of the actions in the previous birth(s) of the individual in a simple cause-and-effect relationship; whereas most other religions ascribe such variations to inexplicable or blind destiny.

It has been explained in the Shrimad Bhagavad Geetā that a possible way for attaining *Moksha* is to follow the system of '*Yoga,*' comprising of the *Karma-Yoga* (Self-realization through selfless work), the *Jñāna-*

Yoga (Self-realization through knowledge), the *Rāja-Yoga* (Self-realization through disciplining the mind by performing meditation and breath-control exercises), and the *Bhakti-Yoga* (Self-realization through devotion to God). Any one of the four Yogas, or any combination of these, if followed sincerely, would lead one — that is, one's soul — to the path of spiritual ascension and to a freedom from the cycle of rebirth. Yoga teaches us to attain real freedom through mastery of the 'Self,' instead of being enslaved by our ego. The word 'Yoga' originates from the Sanskrit word 'yoke' meaning 'to join' or 'to control', that is, to join the soul of man with the supreme Soul or God. The four types of *'Yogas'* mentioned above are briefly described below.

The Karma-Yoga : The Law of Karma

Everyone is engaged in action throughout life. Even Bhagawāna is relentlessly engaged in actions, said Shri Krishna to Arjuna :

न मे पार्थास्ति कर्तव्यं त्रिषु लोकेषु किंचन।
नानवाप्तमवाप्तव्यं वर्त एव च कर्मणि।।

Na me Pārthāsti kartavyam trishu lokeshu kimchana;
Nānavāptamavāptavyam varta eva cha karmani.

- Shrimad Bhagavad Geetā (Ch. 3, Shloka 22)

O Pārtha! I have no duty to fulfill in the Three Worlds, because there is nothing to be attained by Me. Yet I keep Myself engaged in action.

However, the '*Law of Karma*' propounds that every action yields a corresponding good or bad consequence that its doer must bear sooner or later, in this life or even in the next. The Geetā also recommends that any action should be performed without overly attachment to, or expectation of, the fruits of action. Thus, appropriate actions should be undertaken with a sense of righteous duty, and surrender to God in regard to the resulting outcome. There are five key factors that should constitute the guiding principles of our actions: Knowledge, Sacrifice, Service, Valor, and Renunciation-in-action. We call them the 'Five Truths.' The first four are interdependent and self-explanatory. But the principle of renunciation-in-action recommends that we do our duty without express attachment to, or even want for, the fruits of action. Shri Krishna said in the Geetā :

कर्मण्येवाधिकारस्ते मा फलेषु कदाचन।
मा कर्मफलहेतुर्भूर्मा ते सङ्गोऽस्त्वकर्मणि।।

Karmanyevādhikāraste mā phaleshu kadāchana;
Mā karmaphalaheturbhoormā te sangostvakarmani.

- Shrimad Bhagavad Geetā (Ch. 2, Shloka 47)

Your jurisdiction is only over performing your duty, not over the fruit thereof. Let the fruit of action not be your primary objective, nor let your attachment be to inaction (non-performance of duty or action.)

The performance of duty is a reward in itself. This doesn't mean we should have no goals or no motivation for beneficial results. In fact, we must not leave any stone unturned in our efforts to perform our duty. A desired result may not always materialize, however. But this should not cause being disheartened or a loss of faith in God. The principle of renunciation-in-action keeps one free from disappointment, keeping the spirit of being duty-bound regardless. Thus, any undue focus on success or failure must not be our motivation for action, but the basic sense of duty by itself must be the prime motivation.

The Jnāna-Yoga : Self-Realization through Knowledge :

A realization of one's Higher-Self pursuing the path of knowledge is called Jnāna-Yoga. Pursuit of knowledge which is uplifting intellectually and spiritually can help one shed one's ego and awaken closeness to God. The knowledge acquired could be in one or more of the multifarious fields of human endeavor; such as, the origin of the Universe, the structure of chemical bonds in molecules, the wonders of the Golden Rule, ways to cure a disease, the communication pattern of neurons, etc., etc. Of course, the most elevating knowledge is the nature of the soul (Self) and its relationship to God, which takes one to the threshold of *moksha*.

Knowledge is a very general term. Every idea that comes to the mind is knowledge. But every idea doesn't lead one to the Self-Realization. We provide a few guidelines of the process that enable us to understand that knowledge which is helpful in the realization of the Self. According to Swāmi Vivekānanda, One needs to analyze everything that comes to the mind by the sheer will power. Next, assert what we really are — *Existence*, *Knowledge*, and *Bliss*. Meditation is the means of unification of the subject and object. True knowledge brings the realization that *of one being in all beings, and all beings in oneself. Then the true realization follows : **Om Tat Sat** — Om is the only Reality. I am existence above mind. I am the one Spirit of the universe. I am neither pleasure nor pain. The body drinks, eats, and so on. I am not the body. I am not the mind. I am the witness of all. When health comes I am the witness. When disease comes I am the witness. I am Existence, Knowledge and Bliss **(Sachchidānanda)**. I am the essence and nectar of knowledge. Through eternity I change not. I am calm, resplendent, and unchanging.* I am He (सोऽहम्)."

The Rāja-Yoga: Self-Realization through the Control of Mind :

It is said that all our Self-Knowledge resides within us, within our mind, body, and spirit; and we simply need to awaken the latent energy within us through specific spiritual practices. These practices include meditation, concentration and prāṇāyāma. Our Rishis have indicated that there are seven 'chakras' in our body; e.g., the 'Kundalini Chakra' at the base of our spine, and the 'Sahasrar Chakra' at the zenith of our scalp, representing 'sex energy center' and 'pure enlightenment energy center', respectively. Thus, each 'chakra' represents a nerve and energy center formed by concentration of a set of important veins and arteries, and corresponds to enhancement of a specific character in one's nature when activated or 'awakened,' similar to the case of the central nodes of a complex electrical or communications network. By the mentioned yogic practices intensely, gradual ascension of the 'chakras' toward the final goal of submerging the 'Kundalini' into the 'Sahasrar' is said to be achievable, bestowing pure joy and light within the yogi's whole existence permanently.

Of Rāja-Yoga, Swāmi Vivekānanda said: Rāja-Yoga is a science of analysis of the mind, a gathering of the facts of the super sensuous world and thereby building up of the spiritual world. All the great spiritual teachers of the world have said, 'I see and I know.' They claimed actual perception of the spiritual truths they taught. This perception is obtained by yoga. Meditation and yogic practice lead one to control the centers of internal energy (*"chakras"*), a gradual ascension of the lower *"chakras"* to the upper most level, thereby revealing the divine light ("*Sahsrar*") making one realize the identity of the "self" with the Supreme Self.

Neither memory nor consciousness can be the limitation of existence. There is a super conscious state. This life of ours covers just a little consciousness and vast amount of unconsciousness, while over it, and mostly unknown to it, is the super-conscious plane. Through sincere practice, layer after layer of the mind open before us leading to enhanced consciousness. Each layer of consciousness reveals new facts, which will ultimately take us to realize God. To achieve this goal, three things are necessary. **First** is giving up all ideas of enjoyment in this world and care only for God and Truth. Man is a thinking being and must struggle on until he conquers death, not be able to express it. We have to go beyond sense-limit and transcend even reason until we sees the light — the enlightened vision. **Second**, is an intense desire to know the Truth and God. Be eager for them, long for them as a drowning man longs for breath. **Third**, restrain the mind from going outward; restrain the senses; turn the mind inward; suffer everything without murmuring; fasten the mind to one idea; think constantly of your real nature until you realize your oneness with God.

Without these disciplines no results can be gained. We can be conscious of the absolute, though we may not express it. We have to go beyond sense limit and transcend even reason. We have the power to do it.

The Bhakti-Yoga: Self-Realization through Devotion to God :

Bhakti-Yoga is the path of Self-realization or Union with God through pure devotion to God. Again, a primary step here as well as in other paths mentioned is to dissolve the ego which stands in way of identification with God, since a sense of egoistic 'I' and 'my' always separates one from everyone else, what to speak of an identification and merger into the Supreme Power of the Universe — God. Dissolution of the lower 'self' toward recognition of the higher 'self' is most simply possible through a total surrender to God, which is the hallmark of Bhakti. A person may not be capable of following the above mentioned paths (Jnāna -Yoga, Rāja-Yoga) since they require particular capabilities and faculties; and may be too rigorous for everyone to follow. However, Bhakti is within the reach of everyone — all that is required is full love for God, and a sense of surrendering oneself to His Will. This simplest of the yoga has also been characterized by Shri Krishna in the Geetā as most preferred — He loves His devotees even more than yogis following other paths. He also indicates, however, that in the end, all paths are equivalent; following one path, one achieves the results of other paths as well.

According to Swāmi Vivekānanda, the best definition given of Bhakti-Yoga is perhaps embodied in the verse through which Prahlāda prayed to Lord Vishnu: *"May that undying love which the non-discriminating have for the fleeting objects of the senses never leave this heart of mine as I seek after Thee!"*

We observe that men have a strong love and longing for earthly relations and sense objects — family members, friends, and possessions. So in the above prayer, Prahlāda says, *"I will have that attachment — that tremendous clinging — but only to Thee."* This love of God is Bhakti — the eagerness to surrender to God, to be one with God. It is when the love of God becomes a necessity like breathing without which we cannot live. Bhakti in reality is a series of efforts at religious realization, beginning with ordinary worship and ending in a supreme intensity of love for God.

However, Shri Krishna repeatedly emphasized the interdependence and equivalence of the various types of 'Yogas.' He said in the Geetā :

सांख्ययोगौ पृथग्बालाः प्रवदन्ति न पण्डिताः ।
एकमप्यास्थितः सम्यगुभयोर्विन्दते फलम् ॥

Sānkhy-yogau prathagvālāh pravadanti na panditāh;
Ekamapyāsthitah samyagubhayorvindate phalam.

- Shrimad Bhagavad Geetā (Ch. 5, Shloka 4)

The learned do not speak of Karma-yoga and devotional service as being different from the Jnāna-Yoga or analytical study (Sānkhya). Those who are actually learned say that he who applies himself well to one of these paths achieves the results of both.

यत्सांख्यैः प्राप्यते स्थानं तद्योगैरपि गम्यते ।
एकं सांख्यं च योगं च यः पश्यति स पश्यति ।

Yatsānkhyaih prāpyate sthānanm tadyoagairapi gamyate;
Ekam sānkhayam cha yogam cha yah pashyati sa pashyati.

- Shrimad Bhagavad Geetā (Ch. 5, Shloka 5)

One who knows that the position reached by means of renunciation can also be attained by works in devotional service and who therefore sees that the path of works and the path of renunciation are one, sees things as they are.

यं संन्यासमिति प्राहुर्योगं तं विद्धि पाण्डव ।
न ह्यसंन्यस्तसंकल्पो योगी भवति कश्चन ॥

Yam samnyāsamiti prāhuryogam tam vididha pāndava;
Na hyasamnyastasamkalpo ygee bhavati kashchana.

-Shrimad Bhagavad Geetā (Ch. 6, Shloka 2)

What is called renunciation is the same as yoga, or linking oneself with the Supreme, for no one can become a yogi unless he renounces the desire for the sense-gratification.

Any one who sincerely commits himself to the practice of yoga becomes a Brāhmana, a completely detached person from the worldly affairs. Such a person has equipoise in sorrow and happiness. Here, Brāhmana refers to the virtuous person, and not to the person identified with 'Varna Vyavasthā'. These qualities referred to as 'Brāhmanness' can be acquired by any one while remaining engaged in performing his duties in any of the four varna-categories, namely, Brāhmana, Kshatriya, Vaishya and Shoodra.

Principle of Harmony and Evolution of Thoughts : The Hindu Dharma is open to new ideas: It declares, "*Let noble thoughts come to us from all sides — Aa no bhadrāh kratavo yantu vishwatah* (आ नो भद्राः क्रतवो यन्तु विश्वतः). In Hinduism it is rather common to embrace new progressive ideas and centrically synthesize and integrate them in the existing system. This contributes to the process of evolution and thus meets the needs and challenges the society in particular, and the world at large, face in changing times. The overriding consideration is to maintain the peace and harmony necessary for the advancement of humanity.

The Doctrine of the Whole World as One Family : Hinduism treats the entire world as one family, "*The whole world is one Family—Vasudheva kutumbakam* (वसुधैव कुटुम्बकम्)." This concept encourages one to develop an attitude of a kith-and-kin relationship necessary for a harmonious living of all human beings regardless of religious or other differences. Then all can share the resources of the world equitably and enjoy together, fulfilling the directive — *Sah nau bhunaktu* (सह नौ भुनक्तु). The principles, "*Look upon all being as your own self —Ātmavat sarvabhuteshu* (आत्मवत् सर्वभूतेषु)," and "Use resources with sacrifice for others — *Tena Tyaktena bhunjeethāh* (तेन त्यक्तेन भुञ्जीथाः)" also underscore the paramount importance of mutual harmony and peace. All this becomes easy when we accept the dictum: "*Eashāvāsyam idam sarvam* (ईशावास्यं इदं सर्वम्) — The presence of God is manifested in every particle of the universe.*" If God resides within everything and in every person, there is little chance one would feel maligned to another person or indifferent to one's environment.

Nature of Human Beings : Every one is born of divine nature (*Amritsya Putrah*). The divinity is within all of us: "सोऽहम् (Soauham — I am He)." Everyone has full freedom to choose his or her *Ishta Devatā* (Personal god). Such total freedom of thoughts and spirit is the hallmark of Hinduism.

The Concept of Happiness : True human nature is 'to be happy', which is really possible only when one becomes free from incessant worldly desires, said our saints and sages, even thousands of years ago. According to the teachings of Buddhism and Jainism, a happy person is the one who has attained 'Enlightenment' or 'Nirvāna' through cessation of desires, leading to a state of 'Liberation' of the soul from the earthly bondage of life. Likewise, one's aspirations may be limited or boundless depending on one's attitude and knowledge.

More specifically, happiness is a subjective characteristic representing the degree of harmony between one's inner and outer worlds. The conscious or subconscious innermost reality of an individual is the inherent divinity, the soul (*Ātmā*). The outer reality is the surrounding environment and one's interactions with it. The Ultimate Reality is *THAT*: Timeless, Omnipresent and Omnipotent God or Absolute, Supreme Soul (*Paramātmā*). Happiness, then, is a measure of the harmony of the soul (*Ātmā*) with God (*Paramātmā*). This harmony can be enhanced by the understanding and following of the true human Nature (Dharma), through the path(s) of proper knowledge, action and devotion to God. Once such harmony is achieved, a person attains the state of *Sachchidānanda* (*Sata, Chita, Ānanda*), which is the state of Supreme Happiness where the self is perfectly identified with God.

ॐ नमः सच्चिदानन्दरूपाय परमात्मने।
ज्योतिर्मयस्वरूपाय विश्वमाङ्गल्यमूर्तये।।

Om*! Salutations to the Supreme Self — Paramātmā, Who is 'Truth - Consciousness - Bliss' - Incarnate, Perfect Light - Incarnate, and Universal Auspiciousness - Incarnate*

- A Hindu Prayer

Nature of Wealth : The Hindu scriptures delineate different types of wealth — material, intellectual, and spiritual. Material wealth is recognized as necessary for livelihood, but indulgence in the same becomes the source of problems and conflicts. The wealth of knowledge and of spirituality is regarded to be of progressively higher grades.

The wealth of knowledge is the most intriguing:
The more of it one gives to others; the more it grows !

Way of Living : Formally, there are Sixteen *Samskāras* as per the Hindu traditions, namely, Birth, Initiation of formal education, Marriage, Death, among others — which form the most important and common episodes of life. These *samskāras* are described in more detail elsewhere in this publication. Furthermore, a system of four stages or phases called *'Āsharamas'* (*Brahmacharya, Grahasthya, Vānaprastha and Sanyāsa*) has been prescribed. *Brahmacharya* is the phase of student-life when pursuit of knowledge, learning, character-building and self-discipline including celibacy prior to marriage, among other virtues, are to be observed. *Grahasthya* is the stage of married life and family-building when one is also responsible for earning the livelihood for the family. *Vānaprastha* is the period of life when a person retires from professional occupation but still continues to be engaged with guiding the younger generation and with performing social service, and so on. Finally, *Sanyāsa* is the stage of life highlighted with spiritual pursuits including a renunciation of worldly ties, for seeking the union of *Ātmā* with *Parmātmā* — the realization of God. Following the righteous path is at the heart of the Hindu Dharma and way of living at every stage and each moment.

The principle of the four basic elements of *'purushārtha'* — *Dharma, Artha, Kāma and Moksha* — is also at the heart of the Hindu way of life. One is supposed to pursue these basic elements in a balanced and timely fashion. If the material requirements (*Artha*) and legitimate desires (*Kāma*) are satisfied according to the rules of the righteous code of conduct (*Dharma*), then only salvation (*Moksha*) is plausible. In particular, use of vegetarian diet and avoidance of toxic food and drinks are highly recommended.

Principle of Freedom for Harmony in the Society : Freedom to think and act is the most precious in human life. The total freedom of thoughts and spirits is the hallmark of the Hindu Dharma and philosophy. It is also said that life without freedom is not worth-living. But we need to emphasize the idea of interdependent freedom which is necessary for a harmonious living. To a large extent, the interdependence of every one affects, and is affected by, others in the society, from birth to death. The societal norms of morality and the laws of democratic nations are developed with a consideration of such mutual interactions and interdependence. Thus, freedom can be defined only in terms of respecting wisely the extent of independence of others. In Hinduism, it is recognized that:

न स्वातन्त्र्यसमं सौख्यम्।

Na swātantryasamam saukhyam.
No joy is greater than that of freedom.

Freedom can be truly and wisely enjoyed by those who are physically, mentally and spiritually healthy. Even for the performance of religious duties, a healthy body is necessary.

शरीरमाद्यं खलु धर्मसाधनम्।

Shareeramādyam khalu dharmasādhanam.
One's body is the most important instrument for religious observances.

Nature of Speech : Honesty, truth, simplicity and openness in one's speech is valued as one of the key-factors in harmonious social interactions, as it is said:

स्पष्टवक्ता न वञ्चकः।

Spashtavaktā na vanchakah.
A person who speaks clearly can never be a cheat.

However, one is advised to keep in mind the effect of one's speech on others.

सत्यस्य वचनं श्रेयः सत्यादपि हितं वदेत्।

Satyasya vachanam Shreyah satyādapi hitam vadet.

Truth in speech is commendable, but even more commendable is speech that is virtuous (to others).

Wisely designed interdependent freedom is the key to a harmonious living.

The Ideal of Equality : As mentioned in the Isopanishad, Hinduism declares that God lives in every thing: "*Ishāvāsyam idam sarvam* (ईशावास्यं इदं सर्वम्) —*The whole Creation is the abode God.*" Thus, every life, even the animal or the plant-life is considered sacred, to be protected and supported by all. All are equal in God's eyes. As such, there should be no discrimination based on social order, religion, race, skin-color, gender, etc. The principle of equality must be universally applied; each one of us should be accorded equal privilege and opportunity to become a productive member of the society.

The Doctrine of Inclusiveness : Hinduism is unique in according full respect to all religions. Hinduism has always been receptive and open to new and diverse ideas. Even a view totally opposed to the accepted norms is not rejected outright but is given full consideration. An example is the doctrine of hedonism advanced by Chāravaka who did not accept the Vedic philosophy and even rejected the concept of God, Moksha and rebirth. In spite of his non-conventional views, Chāravakas was considered a great thinker and philosopher in his own right, of his time, and addressed as a great '*Rishi.*' His views are respected by some Hindus even today.

This openness to new ideas created many *Sampradāyas* (sects) with different approaches to realize the 'Ultimate Truth', but without any inherent malice or animosity toward one another.

Sampradāyas (Sects) in Hinduism

As mentioned, as a unique feature, Hindu Dharma has always been open to new ideas and new reinterpretation of the existing principles. This has led to enrichment of Hinduism and, at the same time, has enabled it to meet the challenge of time. As a part of this tradition, it has freely permitted the inner voice of everyone to be heard and the curiosity of the seeker to be satisfied. Accordingly, many '*Sampradāyas*' (schools of thoughts and philosophy) emerged over the long history of the Hindu Dharma. Some of them developed their own elaborate traditions and attracted a sizable number of followers, even though they all retained their identity as integral parts of the Hindu Dharma. Over time, the synthesis and integration of these schools led some of them to join each other. This process helped to broaden their appeal, leading, in turn, to the establishment and acceptance of broad-based *Sampradāyas* that even now are practiced as part-and-parcel of Hindu Dharma. The followers of some of the main *sampradāyas* are known as the **Vaishnava,** the **Shaiva,** the **Shakta** and the **Smārtha**, respectively. Each *sampradāya* has its own particular rituals, beliefs, traditions and personal god(s) and goddess(es), and has its own philosophy for achieving the ultimate goal of life — *Moksha.* Each may usually follow a different method of self-realization and worships a different aspects of the One Supreme God. However, each *sampradāya* commonly respects other ones as well. Among the Hindu as a whole, there is a strong belief, '*There are many paths leading to the One God, whatever one chooses to call that Ultimate Reality.*' In time, many sub-sects within a *sampradāya* came into existence with adherence to one teacher or another. There is an often healthy cross-pollination of ideas and logical *samavāda* (debate) serving to refine each school's philosophy, in keeping with the unique tradition of the umbrella of Hindu Dharma.

The Vaishanava Sampradāya

The followers of the Vaishnava Sampradāya worship Lord Vishnu or His *Avatāras* (Incarnations). Consequently, Krishna and Rāma are its supreme godheads. The sub-sampradāyas are:

- Shri Vaishnavas : Followers of Rāmānujāchārya
- Madhavās or Sad-Vaishnavas : Followers of Madhavāchārya
- Rudra Vaishnavas : Followers of Vallabhāchārya
- Gaudiyā Vaishnavas : Followers of Chaitanya Mahāprabhu and close to those of the Madhava Sampradāya.

More Recent Vaishnava Sampradāyas include the following:

- **The Swāmināryana Samsthā :** Initiated by Shri Swāmināryana in the last century. The followers of Swāmināryana have many things in common with the teachings of Rāmanujāchārya. They also believe in a few of the *Smārtha* teachings, for example, in the *panchdevatā* (Five forms of God). They believe that the teachings of this organization would continue through unbroken chain of successive Gurus (Teachers) and this *Guru-paramparā* would thus remain 'Akshara' (imperishable). The gurus are considered the main source through whom *Moksha* (salvations) is possible. As a mark of such a high reverence for the gurus, ornate images of the Gurus are enshrined in their temples, called Akshardhāma temples.

- **International Society of Krishna Consciousness (ISKCON) — Madhava / Gaudiyā Vaishnava Sampradāya :** ISKCON was established in 1966 by A.C. Bhaktivedānta Swāmi Prabhupāda in the USA who primarily propagated it among Western disciples. It follows the *Guru-paramparā* established by the previous āchāryās, starting from Chaitanya Mahāprabhu.

- **The Shaiva Sampradāya**

Shaivites are those who primarily worship Shiva as the Supreme God, both Immanent and Transcendent. Shaivism embraces both the Monoism and Dualism. It focuses on yoga, meditation and love for all beings. The major theological schools of Shaivism are **Shaiva Siddhānta** and **Virasaivism**. To Śhaivites, God Śhiva is both with and without form. He is the Supreme Dancer, Natarāja. He is the 'Linga' (Procreator) without beginning or end.

The Shakta Sampradāya

This *Sampradāya* is perhaps the oldest in Hinduism. **Shaktas**, the followers of this group, worship '***Shakti***,' the Divine Mother, in her many forms, like Kāli, Durgā, Lakshmi, Saraswati, etc. Shaivism and Shakata forms have many things in common and in some respects they are inseparable, as is the description of Shiva and Satee—Pārvati. Shakta philosophy has also connections with Vaishnavism as goddess Durgā is called Nārāyani. The followers of Shakta are generally identified with the main stream of the Hindus and worship all forms of '*Ishwara*' as worshipped in Hinduism. They do not believe in a separate identification from Hindus as is clear from the fact that Devi-poojan (goddess-worship) is widespread among all the Hindus all over India and abroad.

The places of reverence for Shaktas are called Shakti Peethas, located all over India. They are fifty-one in number. Most celebrated are the Kālighāta Mandir at Kolkata, the Kamākhya Mandir at Assāma and the Vaishno Devi Shrine in Jammu.

Various Hindu Philosophers, such as Rāmakrishna Paramhansa and Swāmi Vivekānanda, who guided the Hindus with their depth of understanding of humanity and religion, in fact, were Shaktas. They celebrate the Hindu festivals like Diwāli, Janmāshtami, Shivarātri, etc. The Rāmāyana, the Mahābhārata, the Shrimad Bhāgavatam and the Shrimad Bhagavad Geetā are the revered texts. As such, the Shaktas are identified as the main stream of the Hindus.

The Smārtha Sampradāya

Although the **Smārthas** are free to worship any deity of their choice, usually, they accept and worship the six manifestations of God, namely, Ganesha, Shiva, Shakti, Vishnu, Soorya and Skanda. It is the Smārtha view that dominates the view of Hinduism in the West as this belief includes the '*Advaita*' philosophy. Swāmi Vivekānanda, who brought Hinduism to the West, was an adherent of *Advaita*. Later, A.C. Bhaktivedānta Swāmi Prabhupāda introduced and propagated Vaishnavism in the West.

Freedom of Choice for One's Own Path for Worship and Moksha : In Hinduism, the individual is afforded the greatest possible degree of freedom of choice as regards beliefs, mode of worship, personal gods and goddesses to worship, routine in connection with religious observances, and so on. In this respect, Hinduism inherently embodies the concept of 'democracy' of religion, in contrast to most other religions where strict 'Autocratic' adherence to prescribed beliefs, modality of worship, conformance to dogmas, etc., is a prerequisite.

The Concept of Charity : The noble concept of charity is prevalent in almost all cultures of the world. However, in Hinduism the idea of charity is associated with very living: *A life giving to others in need is the life worth-living.* Giving education, devoting time in the service to others (volunteering), and giving donation to meet the basic necessities of others, are the most basic virtues envisioned in Hinduism. Giving should be with no expectation for a return. Giving is a reward by itself. It is considered a part of the performance of duty. It is emphasized that the donor and receiver both should be deserving candidates for this noble task. It takes an added dimension when giving involves the material possessions that need to be acquired by the donor by following the guidelines of Dharma. At the same time the receiver must also be in need and would utilize the donation for the purpose it is intended.

Use of Nature's Resources : Our Hindu Rishis have repeatedly cautioned about the exploitation of 'Natural Resources.' The caution is expressed, for example, in the Upanishadic words : *Tena Tyaktena bhunjeethāh* (तेन त्यक्तेन भुञ्जीथाः) — enjoy, but with a sense of sacrifice (some also interpret this to mean: *Accept only necessary things that are set aside for you by God*). It is accepted that the world resources are limited and we require great care in their use. All need to share the resources equally and as per need. This becomes easier if we accept that the Nature's resources belong to the humanity and follow the principle, '*The whole world is one family*' that requires of us to treat others as one of our own.

Principle of Non-Violence (Ahimsā अहिंसा) : One of the foremost ideals propounded in Hinduism is non-violence as the supreme observance of religion (अहिंसा परमो धर्मः). Ideally, to refrain from inflicting injury to others in deeds, thoughts and words is non-violence. Vedavyāsa stated:

परोपकारः पुण्याय पापाय परपीडनम् ।।
Paropakārah punyāya pāpāya parapeedanam.
To do good deeds to others is 'Punya' (spiritual credit) and to inflict suffering on others is sin.

This view was reinforced thousands of years later by Sant Tulasidāsa:

परहित सरिस धर्म नहीं भाई। पर पीड़ा सम नहि अधमाई।।
Parahita sarisa dharma nahein Bhaaee, Para peeraa sama nahi adhamaaee.
There is no virtue like helping others, and there is no sin like giving sufferings to others.

A clear distinction should be made between non-violence versus cowardice and valor. The non-violence practiced by a brave and powerful is worth-emulating. Cowardice has no place in a civil society. The non-violence backed by power can be sustained and thus the valor is a virtue. However, in reality when an evil-doer cannot be persuaded to mend his ways, even an elimination of such a person is justified although it may constitute even killing. Here it is asserted that non-violence cannot be sustained so long the evils persist. A society free from evils can be peaceful and prosperous. This principle was followed by Shri Rāma when all His efforts failed to redeem Seetā from the evil king Rāvana. In doing so the army of Rāvana was routed and Rāvana killed. Shri Krishna even helped Pāndavas to win the Kurukshetra war in which the evil-minded Kauravas and their supporters were totally annihilated. In both cases the aim was to eliminate the evil and to sustain peace and prosperity of the virtuous.

War and Peace : In general terms, war of any kind that causes loss of life and property is undesirable. But the war waged for eliminating evil and establishing a peaceful civil society is justified when all attempts for a peaceful resolution have failed. In the long Hindu history ranging over many millennia, there were many justifiable wars. In every case after such a war, peace and prosperity was established and sustained for a long time.

The Concept of Self-Government and Public Administration: Ideal of Democracy : Principle of Consensus (सर्वमत) : The concept of democracy, a voting system of majority consent, as presently practiced is the process of making choices by the majority where minority views play a very little or no part. It is a better system than the unautocratic one, but certainly not the most ideal. In ancient Hindu tradition the ideal is not the majority views but the views arrived at by full consensus (सर्वमत). It is a unique concept in

Hinduism. Shri Rāma followed this ideal and set an example for others to follow. We call this tradition of administration 'Rāma-Rājya' — the rule by consensus. Mahātma Gāndhi had this dream for the 'Independent India'. In the Hindu tradition the ruler always sought the guidance of Dharmāchārya (spiritual teachers). There was no hue and cry of the separation of Dharma in guiding the administration. In fact the tenets of Dharma were at the roots of administration. Although the rulers were called the kings and emperors, but they had to abide by the wishes of the people. In fact, a king had to take an oath of loyalty to the people who had the power to dethrone the king. This system has suffered ups and downs during a long Hindu history. The rule of the Mauryan-dynasty and the Gupta-dynasty that lasted for over 1,000 years (300 **BCE**-700 **CE**) is a testimony to such a system of Hindu ideals and is called the 'Golden Period' in the Indian history, just preceding barbaric Islamic invasions that virtually destroyed the nation.

Righteous Code of Human Conduct : To follow the path of Dharma is a journey of life that each one of us has to undertake. The path of Dharma is to follow the righteous code of conduct in daily life. The righteous conduct is broadly dependent on what a person or a group of persons need to do under the-then prevailing circumstances in order to maintain peace and tranquility in the society, by eliminating the evil within us and around us, leading to prosperity. The yard-stick is to follow the course of non-violence in order to arrest the tendencies responsible for the evil actions. It is often not the successful course of action. In such circumstances a hard course may have to be adopted, to eradicate the evil, as required for maintaining the peace. For this purpose many of the tenets discussed in this publication need to be acquainted with, taking help of our scriptures and the lessons from the lives of great many historical figures who by their actions had succeeded in their mission of peace. To remain engaged in action is a life worth-living. But our actions require the following general considerations :

The actions **(i)** should be non-violent; **(ii)** should not have selfish motives; **(iii)** should not adversely affect innocent; **(iv)** should be in conformity with the just wishes of the people; **(v)** must promote peace and harmony; and finally **(vi)** should be appropriately planned to successfully serve Dharma.

The key to success is to dissolve the division between action and thought, practice and theory and silence and speech.

Women in the Hindu Society : Hindu tradition has always accorded great respect for women. The Hindus worship gods and goddesses with equal reverence, and also introduced the unique representation of godhead in the form of half-man-and-half-woman (*Ardhanāreeshwara*). Sage Manu declares :

यत्र नार्यस्तु पूज्यन्ते रमन्ते तत्र देवताः।
यत्रैतास्तु न पूज्यन्ते सर्वास्तत्राफलाः क्रियाः।।

Yatra nāryastu poojyante ramante tatra devatāh;
Yatreitāstu na poojyante sarvāstatrāphalāh kriyāh.

- Manusmriti (Chapter 3, Verse 56)

Gods reside where women are respected and worshipped. Every endeavor becomes futile where women are not worshipped.

The relation of man and woman is the expression of duality, each being complementary to the other. The division of the sexes is only a biological phenomenon. Male and female constitute a fundamental unity. In Hinduism the ideal of womanhood is Seetā, the consort of Shri Rāma, and Sāvitree, among others.

The Doctrine of Classification of the Society : Varna Vyavasthā (वर्ण-व्यवस्था) : The concept of classification of people based on the needs of peaceful and prosperous society was envisioned by the Hindu sages in the ancient time. The society was divided into four groups, namely, *Brāhmana, Kshatriya, Vaishya* and *Shoodra*. In those days the crossover of one belonging to one *Varna* to another was very common and was based on the aptitude and qualification of the person involved, and not by birth. The system worked well for some time. However, in the long Hindu history, the system became distorted as one's *Varna* started to be determined only by birth, leading to a divisive caste-system. It is a real tragedy. It even became the cause of a down-fall of the Hindu society. The sooner the caste system is eradicated, better will be the future of the

Hindu society. Again, the Hindu Dharma will flourish. Let us work to achieve this goal for our future generation in particular and the world at large.

It should be remarked that the Government of India, after Independence in 1947, introduced laws to abolish discrimination based on the caste-system.

The Concept of Marriage and Family : Family is a basic unit of a civil society. In the Hindu tradition, a family consists of a husband, a wife and the children. Usually, father, mother, brothers and unmarried sisters also are the part of the (extended) family. The responsibilities are shared by all members of the family and resources are equally enjoyed as per individual needs. In a Hindu family the parents make great sacrifice to provide a good education to their children and hope to raise them to a level higher than them. The children, in turn, may curtail their freedom and luxury when parents grow old and infirm and need support from the younger generation. This is an ideal system requiring no help from the government through the systems like 'Social Security' and 'Medicare' presently prevalent in the Unites States of America. And of course, there is no need for the 'Nursing Homes'.

Clearly, marriage between a male and female becomes an important factor in making of the family unit. Marriage is an institution and an important component of the Sixteen samskāras. In ancient times, the parents of the girl used to search for a suitable boy belonging to a compatible family with similar traditions, and invite the boy to meet the girl who had the final say in the matter. There was no such thing as the present-day dating system. When the boy and the girl agreed to get married, the marriage was solemnized, taken as an act of the divine will. This system worked quite well for a long time. Now, under the cover of unrestrained freedom, the system of arranged marriage may not work as well as expected. Moreover, in ancient times gifts were exchanged but no demand of wealth was ever made. Now a monetary demand has become very common on the part of the boy's family. It is called dowry. It has become a curse to the society that is beleaguered under this prevailing system. The ill of dowry needs to be abolished. The institution of marriage should seek the purity and benefits of its ancient roots, and especially strengthen in the belief of one marriage for life. This will keep the family together and the children would be raised in a healthy family environment guaranteeing the progress of the society.

However, in spite of the mentioned shortcoming, the Hindu marriage system is relatively stable as compared to the Western system where divorce is more common and has become an accepted norm. In Hinduism, the institution of marriage is a social system and not a legal one as in the West. Even then, once a marriage is performed there is rarely a case when either party has denied its validity. This is the strength of the institution of the Hindu marriage.

HINDU UNITY AND SOCIAL JUSTICE

Presently, Hinduism is facing organized onslaughts by the adverse forces of Christianity and Islam which are relentlessly trying to eradicate the ancient rich heritage of Hindu Dharma and to destabilize the very fabric of the Hindu society. This may lead to further fragmentation of India. There are two main reasons posing such a grave risk for India and the Hindu Dharma: Lack of unity among the Hindus and certain problems of social justice within the traditional Hindu society.

Lack of Hindu Unity : The Hindu religion is decentralized and doesn't follow a formal central authority, as is the case in most other religions. Various Hindu *sampradāyas* are often self-centered, self-righteous and even arrogant, pre-occupied in their own affairs and less aware of the wider interest of the Hindu Dharma at large. Often the Hindu youth educated in the western institutions forget that they are the custodian of an ancient rich heritage and as such have the responsibility to carry it forward and pass it on to the next generation. Powerful individuals in various walks of life including many religious leaders are absorbed in their own parochial and petty interests. The result is that there is no effective unified effort and co-operation to safeguard the interests of the pristine Hindu culture and heritage. The adversaries are quick to take advantage of this pathetic situation and are succeeding in proselytizing Hindus to their faith. The solution of these problems for the Hindus is to unite and face the adverse forces working against the Hindu culture and heritage.

Social Justice : The caste-system, an outgrowth and distortion of the division of labor based *Varna Vyavashthā* of the ancient Hindu tradition, has led to a large social as well as economic divides among the Hindus. The privileged Hindus are often insensitive about the poor plight of the under-privileged and poor masses, who have been discriminated for ages. The caste-system, still prevalent in most of India, is at the root of many of the problems, forcing many to remain at the bottom range of the society. This situation also hampers the cause of Hindu Unity. We should meet this menacing discrimination head-on and improve the lives of all Hindus, to be worthy of calling ourselves Hindus.

YOGA AND ĀYURVEDA

Hindu Dharma encourages all of us to be physically and mentally healthy and spiritually wise so that one may live a holistic life. For this, the technique of yoga has been developed and perfected. However, a person may still suffer from diseases caused by impure environment due to the occurrence of harmful natural events and human activities. For this, the science of *Āyurveda* (science of the longevity of life) has been developed. It is a medical science mainly based on natural treatment using herbal resources.

Yoga — A Technique for Healthy Living : Yoga is a multidimensional system of physical, mental and spiritual practices that originated in India, as an integral part of the Hindu Dharma, some 7000 years ago. The Sanskrit word 'yoga', meaning union, is a noun derivative of the (Sanskrit) verb 'yuj' meaning 'to add' or 'to unite'. The Hindu scriptures (the Vedas, the Upanishads, the Geetā) signify 'Yoga' as the Ultimate Union of the *Ātma (individual soul)* with *Paramātma (the Universal or Supreme Soul, that is, God)*. This Union is commonly referred to as *Moksha* or *Mukti (Liberation of the Soul),* the Ultimate aim of the human life as mentioned above. The four yogas, namely, Karma-Yoga, Rāja-Yoga, Bhakti-Yoga and Jnāna-Yoga are helpful for such a union (*Ātma* with *Paramātma*).

However, the technique of yoga, as known all around the Western world just connotes healthy living. Thus, it envisions a person to be physically fit and mentally alert, free from stress. In the Hindu religion, this is only the first requirement for advancing towards spirituality. This technique of integral yoga of physical, mental and spiritual well-being was developed and perfected by Rishi Patanjali, and is described in his famous treatise, 'Patanjali Yoga Darshana'. The knowledge contained in this treatise is so valuable that it is considered to be another Veda. For achieving good physical and mental health, the complete yoga system comprises of eight steps, of which the following three steps are most common :

- Yoga-āsana (physical postures and exercises)
- Prānāyāma (breathing exercises)
- Dhyāna or Sādhanā (meditation)

It may be pointed out that the specific techniques of yoga as taught in different schools vary somewhat depending on the emphasis on one or more of the above factors. However, scientific studies have revealed all these practices to be beneficial and they yield fruitful results, namely, reducing the stress and helping in controlling and even preventing many diseases. Among the 'Yoga-āsanas (physical postures and exercises), the *'Sooryanamaskāra'* is the most effective and is recommended for the busy life of modern times. It is described elsewhere in this publication, along with a short account of 'Āsanas', 'Prānāyāma' and 'Meditation'.

Āyurveda — Science of Longevity of Life : In the Hindu mythology, Dhanvantri is considered as the divine physician who, along with the Ashwini twins, discovered the medical science of Āyurveda. It is a holistic system of medicine rooted in the Vedic culture originated in India. It is a science of healthy living, natural medicine and prolong longevity. However, Rishi Charaka is known to have perfected this system long before the advent of Current Era, and his findings are contained in his treatise 'Charaka Samhitā'. Āyurveda deals with the measures of healthy living, along with therapeutic measures that relate to physical, mental, social and spiritual harmony. Āyurveda is probably the earliest traditional systems of medicine including disease-preventing guidelines, medication, as well as surgery. Āyurveda views a healthy individual whose mind, body and spirit are in harmony with each other and has specific methods for keeping the balance between them. For the diagnosis of the imbalance that causes diseases, it postulates and divides the constitution of a person into three categories — *Vāta* (ether/air), *Pitta* (fire) and *Kapha* (water/earth). According to this system, *Vāta* rules mental mobility; *Pitta* governs digestion and assimilation of food; and *kapha* governs the substance within the body and is responsible for weight, cohesion and stability. These three factors, in various combinations of two, create six sub-types. A seventh sub-type also exists, which is a combination of all the three categories. The Āyurvedic medicines are extracted mainly from herbs and minerals for possible treatment of the diseases, which are the result of the imbalance between *Vāta, Pitta* and *kapha*. Because of its paramount importance, the Āyurveda is referred to as another Veda. A short account of Āyurveda is given elsewhere in this publication.

The Hindu Dharma provides a tool for living a holistic life.

OTHER RELIGIONS THAT ORIGINATED FROM THE SANĀTANA DHARMA

The Sanātana Dharma is like a banyan tree that has many roots emanating from its branches, nourishing and allowing them to have their own identity and at the same time remain an integral part of the mother-tree. The eternal nature of the Sanātana Dharma lies in the fact that it has stood the test of time millennia after millennia. It emphasized time and again that the various aspects of its guiding tenets are open to meet the challenges of time. Naturally, several schools of thought emerged that formed the basis of various teachings, which later became recognized as Dharma (religion) in their own right. We describe, in nutshell, three religions that have their roots in the Sanātana Dharma, namely, Buddha Dharma (Buddhism), Jain Dharma (Jainism) and Sikha Dharma (Sikhism).

THE BUDDHA DHARMA
(BUDDHISM)

Siddhārtha Gautama, the son of King Shuddhodana, was born about 600 **BCE.** He became Buddha (the Enlightened One) on the 49th day of his meditation (*tapasyā)* beneath a Pipala tree in Bodha Gayā (in Bihar, India), now known as the *Bodhivriksha* (Tree of Enlightenment). From that day on he also became known as *Tathāgata*, the one who experienced Truth. After experiencing Truth, he delivered his first sermon to his five disciples at Sāranātha, near Kāshi (Vārānasi) in India. The embodiment of love and compassion, Buddha was an ethical teacher and reformer who envisioned the entire humanity as ONE. In this sermon he propounded the *Four Noble Truths*:

1. Life in the world is full of suffering;
2. There is a cause of suffering;
3. It is possible to stop suffering;
4. There is a path, which leads one to free oneself from suffering.

Buddha pointed out that every one is burning in the fires of desire, passion, hatred, sorrow, old age and death, which are responsible for human suffering. The cause of suffering is the ignorance of the path that can free one from suffering. He did not discuss the origin of the universe or about any supernatural power (God) that would help to achieve the pain-free life. One has to achieve liberation from the suffering through one's own efforts.

Buddha showed a way consisting of an eight-step process, known as the *Eight-Fold-Path*, that can minimize and ultimately eliminate suffering, and help attain the ultimate goal of human life — *Nirvāna* or *Moksha* (Liberation). These steps are :

1. Right Knowledge of the Four Noble Truths
2. Right Resolve to reform life in the light of the Truth
3. Right Speech
4. Right Conduct

5. Right Means of livelihood
6. Right Efforts
7. Right Mindfulness
8. Right Concentration or meditation

BUDDHA: THE ENLIGHTENED — THE AWAKENED
BUDDHA : THE TATHĀGATA —THE ONE WHO REALIZED THE TRUTH

THE JAIN DHARMA
(JAINISM)

Lord Mahāvira, the 24th *Teerthankara* — the liberated soul, a contemporary of Lord Buddha (600**BCE**), organized the teachings of all the previous *Arihantas* (Venerable Ones) in a systematic way, which led to the establishment of the Jain Dharma or Jainism. Like Buddhism, it does not focus on a belief in God as a super entity. It teaches that every soul has the potentiality to reach the state of perfection — the goal of each human being. By the practice of the five fundamental tenets that are really interdependent, one may achieve perfection and become a Self-realized soul. These tenets are briefly outlined below :

1. Ahimsā (Non-violence)

The Jain philosophy is virtually synonymous with the principle of *ahimsā* (non-violence),

Ahimsā parmo dharmah — Non-violence is the supreme religion.

"There is nothing so small and subtle as the atom, nor any element as vast as space. Similarly, there is no quality of soul more subtle than non-violence and no virtue of spirit greater than reverence for life."

All the Arihantas in the past, present and future discourses and counsel proclaim, propound and prescribe thus in unison:

**Do not injure, abuse, oppress, enslave, insult, torment, torture or kill any creature or living being.*

The teaching of *ahimsā* refers not only to physical acts of violence but to violence in the hearts and minds of the human beings, their lack of concern and compassion for their fellow humans and for the animate and inanimate entities of the world. Even the intention to harm or the absence of compassion that tends to make one's action violent is against the principles of Jainism.

2. Parasparopagraho Jivānām (Interdependence)

Mahāvira proclaimed a profound truth for all times when he said: "One who neglects or disregards the integrity of earth, air, fire, water and vegetation jeopardizes his own welfare that is entwined with the former." Jain philosophy recognizes the fundamental truth that all lives are bound together by mutual support and interdependence. Life is viewed as a gift for togetherness, accommodation and assistance in a universe teeming with interdependent constituents.

3. Anekāntavāda (the Doctrine of Manifold Aspects)

The concept of universal interdependence extends to the principle known as *anekāntavāda* or the doctrine of manifolds aspects. *Anekāntavāda* describes the world as a multifaceted, ever-changing reality with infinite viewpoints depending on the time, place, nature and state of the viewer and the viewed. This leads to the doctrine of *syādavāda* or relativity, which states that truth is relative to different viewpoints *(nyāsa)*. What is true from one point of view is open to question from another. Absolute truth cannot be grasped from any particular viewpoint alone, because absolute truth is the sum total of all the different viewpoints that make up the universe.

4. *Samyaktavāda* (Equanimity)

The discipline of non-violence, the recognition of universal interdependence and the logic of the doctrine of manifold aspects, leads inexorably to the avoidance of dogmatic, intolerant, inflexible, aggressive, harmful and unilateral attitudes towards the world around. It inspires the personal quest of every Jain for *Samyaktavāda* (equanimity) towards both *jiva* (animate beings) and *ajiva* (inanimate substance and objects). It encourages an attitude of give and take, of live and let live. It offers pragmatic peace plan based, not on the domination of nature, nations or other people, but on equanimity of mind devoted to the preservation of balance in the universe.

5. *Jiva-dayā* (Compassion)

Ahimsā is an aspect *of dayā* (compassion, empathy and charity), described by a great Jain scholar as "the beneficent mother of all beings" and the "elixir for those who wander in suffering through the ocean of successive rebirths."

Jiva-dayā means caring for and sharing with all living beings, and tending, protecting and serving them. It entails universal friendliness (*maitri*), universal forgiveness (*kshamā*) and universal fearlessness (*abhaya*).

These five tenets are considered to be the viable route for humanity's common pilgrimage for holistic environmental protection, peace and harmony in the universe.

JAIN — ARIHANTA: THE PERFECT — THE REALIZED SOUL

THE SIKHA DHARMA
(SIKHISM)

The Sikha religion (Sikhism) teaches a strict monotheism and the brotherhood of humanity. There is no concept of deity worship and no division of society based on birth. Sikhism teaches the devotion and remembrance of God at all times. Truthful living, social justice and equality of mankind are its hallmarks. It rejects superstitions and blind rituals.

Sri Guru Grantha Sahib is the Sikha Holy Book and Living '11th Guru' where the teachings of its previous Ten Gurus are enshrined. Sikha Code of Conduct requires a person to abide by the following rules to be a Sikha:

    (i)   One Immortal Being,

    (ii)   Ten Gurus, from Guru Nanak Dev to Guru Gobind Singh,

    (iii)   The Guru Grantha Sahib (as the scripture and 'Guru' after Guru Gobind Singh),

    (iv)   The utterances and teachings of the ten Gurus, and

    (v)   The baptism bequeathed by the Tenth Guru.

Philosophy and Beliefs of Sikhism

♦ There is only One God. He is the same God for all people and of all religions.

♦ The soul goes through many cycles of births and deaths before it reaches the human form. The goal of a human life is to lead an exemplary existence so that one may merge with God (*Moksha*). A Sikha should remember God at all times and practice living a virtuous and truthful life while maintaining a balance between the spiritual obligations and temporal obligations.

♦ The true path for achieving salvation and merging with God does not require renunciation of the world or celibacy, but living the life of a householder, earning an honest living, and avoiding worldly temptations and sins.

- Sikhism rejects rituals such as fasting. It does not believe in devils or angels or heavenly spirits. There is no mythology, and blind obedience to an external authority is discouraged.

- Sikhism preaches that people of different races, religions or sex are all equal in the eyes of God. It teaches the full equality of men and women. Women can participate in any religious function or perform any Sikha ceremony or lead the congregation, or *Sangata*, in prayer. The basic Sikha principles are service, humility and equality.

Sikhism is a way of life. Its main virtue is simplicity. It is a faith of hope and cheer. It does not lead to despair and defeatism. Though it affirms Karma, it recognizes the possibility of the modification of one's Karma with the grace of the Guru or God. Sikhism accepts a democratic process in its deliberations. The decisions of the *Sangata* (elected governing body) are regarded as binding, having the force of law (*Gurmatta*). Guru Gobind Singh vested the authority in the organization *(Pantha)*.

SIKHA — AN ENLIGHTENED DISCIPLE OF GOD

ETERNAL HINDU PRAYER

MAY ALL BE HAPPY

MAY ALL BE FREE FROM AILMENTS

MAY ALL PERCEIVE WHAT IS AUSPICIOUS AND ABIDING

MAY NONE BE SUBJECTED TO MISERIES

MAY THE WICKED BECOME GENTLE

MAY THE GENTLE ATTAIN PEACE

MAY THE PEACEFUL BE FREE FROM BONDAGE

MAY THE FREE ONES FREE OTHERS

MAY ALL OVERCOME DIFFICULTIES

MAY ALL ATTAIN WHAT IS GOOD

MAY ALL HAVE ENLIGHTENED INTELLECT

MAY ALL BE JOYFUL EVERYWHERE

MAY ALL BE LED FROM UNTRUTH TO THE TRUTH

MAY ALL BE LED FROM DARKNESS TO LIGHT

MAY ALL BE LED FROM DEATH TO IMMORTALITY

ॐ ! PEACE, PEACE, PEACE BE UNTO ALL

Chapter 2

THE HINDU PANTHEON

It is stated in *Shrimad Bhāgavatam* that, although certain incarnations of Lord Vishnu are most celebrated, in true sense there are innumerable incarnations of God :

अवतारा ह्यसंख्येया हरेः सत्त्वनिधेर्द्विजाः।
यथाविदासिनः कुल्याः सरसः स्युः सहस्रशः।।

Avatārā hyasankhyeyā hareh sattva-nidher dvijāh;
Yathāvidāsinah kulyāh sarasah syuh sahasrashah.

- Shrimad Bhāgavatam (Canto 1, Ch. 3, Shloka 26)

O Brāhmana! The incarnations of the Lord Vishnu, the Ocean of Truth and Ultimate Reality, are innumerable, like thousands of rivers flowing from inexhaustible sources of water.

Many saints and sages have emphasized the worship of, and meditation upon, formless God, the Infinite, Absolute and Ultimate Reality. In contrast, there are people who worship God in different forms to which they impart particular attributes and qualities based on their intellectual capacity, personal tastes and preferences. These personal forms of God are helpful for mental visualization and concentration. Many saints have experienced vision of God with form from time immemorial. Free acceptance of this personally preferred aspect of God is one of the beauties of Hinduism. Obviously, personal form of God can be simply regarded as projection of the One infinite dimensional Absolute God onto a finite — dimensional 'plane' that is more accessible for an ordinary devotee who can identify with, worship the image of, and realize, the almost human-type attributes of one or more personal gods and goddesses.

In the tradition of Avatāras (incarnations), most people relate to specific attribute of God and thus the Hindu mythology presents a rich pantheon of a great number of *Devis and Devatās* (gods and goddesses). A few from among the Hindu pantheon of gods and goddesses include, for example, Brahmā (god of 'Creation'), Vishnu (god of 'Sustainment'), Shiva or Mahesha (god of 'Destruction'), Yama (god of 'Death'), Varuna (the 'Water' god), Agni (the 'Fire' god), Māruti (the 'Air' or 'Wind' god), Soorya (the 'Sun' god), Chandra (the 'Moon' god), Ganesha (the god of 'Success'), Satyanārāyana (the god of 'Truth'), Lakshmi (the goddess of 'Wealth' and 'Prosperity'), Saraswati (the goddess of 'Learning' and 'Knowledge'), Gauri, Durgā, Kāli (the goddesses of 'Strength'), Gāyatri Mātā, Vaishno Devi, Hanumāna, Bālāji and Āyyappā, etc. The most celebrated gods and goddesses are briefly characterized in this Section.

BRAHMĀ

Lord **Brahmā** is the Lord Supreme in the creative aspect in the Hindu Trinity. He is the Creator of the universe and of all animate and inanimate beings in it. Space, time and causation originate from Him. He is *Pitāmah*, the patriarch; *Vidhātri*, the ordinator; and *Lokesha*, the master of the universe. He performed the first "*Yajna*" in the holy place of Prayāga after creating the universe.

According to the Purānas (Hindu Scriptures), Brahmā is self-born, sitting upon the lotus flower which emanates from the navel of Lord Vishnu. This explains His another name *Nabhijā* (born from the navel). Another legend says that Brahmā was born in the celestial water, and hence Brahmā is also called *Kanja* (born in water). He created a seed that later became the golden egg (*Hiranyagarbha*) which eventually expanded into the 'Brahmānda' (the Universe). Brahmā is said also to be the son of the Supreme Being, called *Ishwara* or *Brahman*, and the godly female energy known as *Prakrti* or *Māyā*.

At the beginning of the process of creation, Brahmā sequentially created ten *Prajāpatis* who are believed to be the successive 'Administrators' of the created universe and the ultimate fathers of the human race. The *Manusmriti* by Sage Manu enumerates them as *Marichi, Atri, Angirā, Pulastya, Pulaha, Kratu, Vasishtha, Prachetas* or *Daksha, Bhrigu*, and *Nārada*. He is also said to have created the seven great sages or the *Saptarishi* to help him create the universe. However since all these sons of His were born out of His mind rather than from body, they are called '*Mānas-Putras*' or mind-sons.

Brahmā's consort is Saraswati, the goddess of Knowledge and Arts. However, there is an interesting legend that Lord Brahmā had a second consort, Gāyatri. According to this legend, once Saraswati was late to arrive at the time when Brahmā was to perform 'Yajna' (ritual and purifying grand-worship). Brahmā became angry because His consort's presence was indispensable to complete the sacred ceremonies. Brahmā asked the priest to fetch a woman to wed Him to complete the *Yajna*. It so happened that in the neighborhood was found a very lovely shepherdess. In reality she was Gāyatri, the most sacred Vedic hymn, incarnated as a beautiful woman. Brahmā married her. However, Saraswati, angry over this act, cursed Brahmā that He would not to be worshiped by His devotees any more. Consequently, among the 'Hindu Trinity,' Lord Brahmā is not worshiped whereas Lord Vishnu and Lord Mahesha (Shiva) are universally worshiped.

Lord Brahmā is depicted as having four heads, representing the Vedas; He holds the Vedas in His hand. Goddess Saraswati is depicted with a white garment representing purity. She holds a *Veenā* (Indian musical instrument) representing her as being the originator of music, and sits on a lotus, an emblem of beauty.

Although Brahmā is prayed to in most of the Hindu religious ceremonies, there are only three temples dedicated to Him in India; the most prominent one being at Pushkar, near Ajmer in Rājasthāna, India. Once a year, on the full moon night (*Poornimā*) of the Hindu lunar month of Kārtika (October - November), a religious festival is held in Brahmā's honor. There is also a famous statue of Lord Brahmā at Mangalwedha, 52 km from Solāpura district in Mahārāshtra; and another one being in Angkor- Vat in Cambodia, in South East Asia.

* * * * *

'Brahman' is the Supreme Cosmic Spirit of the Hindu Philosophy.
'Brahmā' is one of the gods in the Hindu Trinity.

'Brāhmana' is a particular class in the Hindu social structure,
devoted to spiritual knowledge, practices and rituals.

VISHNU

Bhagawāna Vishnu is the second deity of the Hindu Trinity and regarded as the Supreme Godhead. He is the Supreme Being in the Vaishnava Sampradāya (sect), and the principal manifestation of 'Brahman' in the Advaita or Smārtha traditions. The 'Vishnu Sahasranāmā' describes Vishnu as the All-Pervading essence of all beings, the master of and transcendent to Time and the One who supports, sustains and governs the Universe.

He represents *Sattvaguna* responsible for protection and maintenance of the created Universe. He provides the inherent power for existence. He is also known as Nārāyana — the One who is the abode of all human beings, and whose abode is the heart of all human beings. Lord Vishnu has a blue complexion like the clouds (*Neelmeghashyām*) which also stands for all-pervasiveness like the infinite, deep blue space. In the Purānas, Vishnu is symbolically described as having four arms, holding a *lotus*, a *mace*, a *conch*, and the *Sudarshana-Chakra* (Celestial Discus).

Most often, Vishnu is depicted in two forms: standing upright on a lotus flower by Himself or with His consort, Lakshmi, beside Him, on a similar pedestal; or reclining on the coiled-up, thousand-hooded Sheshanāga (celestial king of serpents), with His consort, Lakshmi seated at His feet, in the "Ksheera-Sāgara" (celestial Ocean of Milk). Vishnu is also depicted as having a '*Vishwaroopa*' (Cosmic Universal Grand Form), containing the entire cosmos, beyond the limits of ordinary human vision, as mentioned in the Bhagavad Geetā.

It is mentioned in the Shrimad Bhāgavatam that Vishnu incarnates in every '*Yuga*' (cosmic era) to rejuvenate Dharma and to vanquish the evil. Shri Krishna reaffirmed :

यदा यदा हि धर्मस्य ग्लानिर्भवति भारत ।
अभ्युत्थानमधर्मस्य तदात्मानं सृजाम्यहम् ।।

Yadā yadā hi dharmasya glānirbhavati Bhārata;
Abhyutthānamadharmasya tadatmānam srijaamyaham.

-Shrimad Bhagavad Geetā (Ch. 4, Shloka 7)

O Arjuna! Whenever there is a decline of Dharma (righteousness), I recreate Myself for the re-emergence of Dharma.

In the Purānas, Bhagawāna Vishnu is said to have incarnated on the earth Twenty-two times. As cited in the *Shrimad Bhāgavatam* (not to be confused with the Shrimad Bhagavad Geetā), in the present *Chaturyugi*, comprising four *Yugas*, namely, *Sata-Yuga, Tretā-Yuga, Dwāpara-Yuga and Kali-Yuga*, there have been so far Twenty-one *Avatāras* (Incarnations) and the Twenty-second ('*Kalki*') Iincarnation is foretold at the end of the present Kali-Yuga, in 43,006 **CE**. Out of these 22 *Avatāras*, the ten incarnations (*Dashāvatāra*), namely, the incarnations as *Varāhā* (Boar), *Matsya* (Fish), *Koorma* (Tortoise), *Narasimha, Vāmana, Parashurāma, Rāma, Krishna, Buddha* and *Kalki* are the most-cited ones in connection with the evolutionary aspect of life on earth and of the human society. Among these ten, two incarnations, namely, Shri Rāma in the Tretā-Yuga followed by Shri Krishna in the Dwāpara-Yuga, the most celebrated ones, have permanent imprint in the Hindu psyche, and are worshiped by Hindus all over the world.

✠　　✠　　✠

श्री ओंकारेश्वर   श्री त्र्यम्बकेश्वर   श्री घुश्मेश्वर   श्री वैघनाथ   श्री नागेश्वर

श्री महाकालेश्वर   श्री केदारनाथ   श्री रामेश्वर

श्री मल्लिकार्जुन

श्री सोमनाथ

श्री भीमाशंकर

श्री विश्वेश्वर

SHIVA

Lord **Shiva** is one of the Godheads in the Hindu Trinity. He is also known by many other names : Shankara, Mahesha, Mahādeva, Chandramauli, Shashidhara, Mahāyogi, Pashupati, Natarāja, Bhairavanātha, Vishwanātha, Bholenātha, Neelakantha, Gangādhara, etc. Shiva also appeared in five forms, namely, Bhairava (भैरव), Natarāja (नटराज), Dakshinamurthya (दक्षिणमुर्थ्यं), Somaskandha (सोमस्कन्ध) and Pitkchadanara (पित्क्वदनर). He also manifests Himself as the cosmic power behind the '*Pralaya*' (periodic annihilation) of the cosmos at the end of a '*Mahāyuga*' (the great cosmic era consisting of four yugas), as propounded in the Hindu mythology. His consort, Pārvati, symbolizes creative energy (*Shakti*).

In many temples, Shiva is represented and worshipped as the *linga* (the sacred phallic symbol symbolizing life-generating energy). Also popularly worshipped is His image of the Yogi with total renunciation. A crescent moon adorns His matted hair from which the river Gangā ensues in her journey from the Heaven to the Earth. The legend has it that Bhageeratha, an ancestor of Rāma, performed penance to bring the Gangā from the Heaven and Shiva held the sacred river in His mats before releasing it gently to the Earth, lest the latter should become pulverized under momentous current from a direct descent of the great celestial river (Gangā). A coiled serpent representing the tamed spiritual energy girdles Shiva's neck. He sits on a tiger skin, His body smeared with ashes symbolizing total renunciation. His throat is blue (hence the name Neelakantha) because of the fatal poison — that came out from the mythological '*Samudra Manthana*' (churning of the sea) — He captured in His throat to save the world from being scorched.

Mahā-Shivarātri, the special night for the worship of Lord Shiva, occurs on the Fourteenth day of *Phālguna Krishna Paksha*, when Hindus offer special prayer to Lord Shiva. Shivarātri is considered especially auspicious for women. Married women pray for the well-being of their husbands, sons and daughters, while unmarried women pray for an ideal husband like Shiva. It is believed that anyone who utters the name of Shiva during Shivarātri with pure devotion, becomes free from all sins and achieves *Mukti* (liberation from the cycle of birth and death). The devotees keep severe fast, chant the sacred *Panchākshara* mantra **"Om Namah Shivāya,"** and make offerings of flowers and incense to the Lord amidst sonorous ringing of temple bells.

There are twelve especially celebrated Shiva temples, each with a '*Jyotirlinga*' enshrined, located in various parts of India. The most famous among them is the Somanātha Temple. These temples are among the main centers of Hindu pilgrimages.

ॐ नमः शिवाय ✠ ॐ नमः शिवाय ✠ ॐ नमः शिवाय

GANESHA

Lord Ganesha is the son of Lord Shiva and his consort, Pārvati. Kārtikeya is his brother. Lord Ganesha has four hands, an elephant-like head and a big belly. He carries a symbolic rope to lead devotees to the truth and an axe to cut devotees' negative worldly attachments. Devotees offer him sweets — especially 'laddoos', and Lord Ganesha also holds a *laddoo* in one of his hands as a symbol of a sweet for reward to the devotees for spiritual upliftment. His fourth hand has its palm extended to bless people.

Lord Ganesha is also called Vināyaka, the One who is the storehouse of knowledge and fountainhead of wisdom. He is also worshipped as '**Vighneshwara.**' the remover of all obstacles. Therefore, on all occasions his presence is invoked by reciting the following prayer at the start of any ceremony or project for a successful completion and conclusion of the same.

गजाननं भूतगणादि सेवितं कपित्थ जम्बूफल चारु भक्षणम् ।
उमासुतं शोक विनाश कारकं नमामि विघ्नेश्वर पादपंकजम् ।।

Gajānanam bhootaganādi sevitam kapittha jamboophala chāru bhakshanam,
Umāsootam shoka vināsha kārakam namāmi vighneshwaram pādapankajam.

I bow to 'Lotus-feet', Elephant-headed, Lord Ganesha, son of goddess Umā (Pārvati), who is served by the 'bhootaganas,' (all beings), who eats the sweet 'Jamboophal,' and who is the remover of all sorrows and obstacles.

शुक्लाम्बरधरं विष्णुं शशिवर्णम् चतुर्भुजं ।
प्रसन्नवदनं ध्यायेत् सर्व विघ्नोपशान्तये ।।

Shuklāmbaradharam Vishnum shashivarnam chaturbhujnam;
Prasannavadanam dhyāyet sarva vighnopashāntaye.

I meditate upon Lord Ganesha, who wears a white garment, has a bright complexion, has four arms and has an ever-smiling face, for removal of all obstacles.

Other popular prayers for Lord Ganesha are as follows :

जय गणेश जय गणेश जय गणेश देवा ।
माता जाकी पार्वती पिता महादेवा ।।

Glory to Lord Ganesha, the god whose mother is Pārvati and father Mahādeva (Lord Shiva).

जय गणेश जय गणेश जय गणेश पाहि मामू
श्री गणेश श्री गणेश श्री गणेश रक्ष मामू ।।

Glory to Lord Ganesha, Protect us (from all evils and obstacles) and ennoble us.

✠   ✠   ✠

SATYANĀRĀYANA

Shri Satyanārāyana is Lord Vishnu Himself. He is worshipped by Hindus, with family and friends joining the worshippers. The story of Shri Satyanārāyana (*Shri Satyanārāyana Kathā*), once told by Lord Vishnu Himself to sage Nārada for the benefit of humankind, is narrated in the Purānas. Between the splendid valleys, amidst the two hill-tops on the banks of Alakanandā, Bhagawāna Vishnu was meditating in the form of Nārāyana Rishi. Goddess Lakshmi was present there in the form of 'Badrikā' (Bera) tree. This area is, therefore, called 'Badree Forest' and Bhagawāna Vishnu is worshipped as Badreenārāyana or Badreenātha. The *Satyanārāyana* poojā means the worship of Nārāyana (Vishnu) as the incarnation of **SATYA** (Truth). It is performed usually on a full moon (*Poornimā*) day of the month.

He is shown in *Chaturbhuja* (four-armed) like Lord Vishnu. However, His fourth hand does not hold a lotus flower; rather it is extended upward to bless people. In his two upper hands he holds a discus (a symbol of power) and a conch shell (a symbol of Existence), respectively. With his third hand holding a mace (to vanquish the untruth) extended downward, He asks devotees to have faith and to surrender to Him for protection.

His Poojā bestows all the desired opulence, glory and well-being to the devotees.

श्रीसत्यनारायण जी की आरती जो कोई गावे।
भगतदास सुख सम्पत्ति मनवांछित फल पावे।।

Shree Satyanārāyana jee kee ārati jo koee gāve.
Bhagatadāsa sukha sampatti manavānchhita phala pāve.

One, who recites with devotion the prayer of Shri Satyanārāyana, gets all the desired opulence and happiness.

✦ ✦ ✦ ✦ ✦

सगुण ब्रह्म
SAGUNA BRAHMA
The concept of a 'Personal God' is the highest concept envisioned by man.

HANUMĀNA

Shri Hanumāna is the foremost devotee of Shri Rāma. He symbolizes one with a perfectly steady mind (*sthitapragya*) as conceived by the Hindus. Hanumāna is the epitome of service to God, nobility, humility, truthfulness, egolessness and righteousness — the essential qualities of a perfect man. His worship brings strength, wisdom and knowledge to the devotees.

Hanumāna was born of *Anjani* and *Pavana*, the wind-god, at the most auspicious hour of the morning of *Chaitra Poornimā,* on a *Mangala* day (Tuesday). Therefore, *Mangala* (Tuesday) is the Hanumāna-Day and the Hindus worship him on that day. Also, the '*Hanumāna Jayanti*' (Anniversary) is celebrated each year on the full-moon-day (Poornimā) in the month of Chaitra (the first month of the Hindu calendar). Hanumāna's body was as powerful as Bajra (lightning) and hence also the name Bajarangabali for him. He is also known by many other names: Mahāvira, Pavansuta, Anjaniputra, Mārutinandan and Sankatamochana.

He was a great scholar who learnt the scriptures from Sun-god. He was the wisest of the wise, strongest of the strong and bravest of the brave. It is believed that one who meditates upon him and chants his name attains strength, courage, hope, knowledge, intellect, devotion, glory, prosperity and success in life. He was steady, firm and successful in all his actions; failure was not known to him.

Hanumāna is pictured as a robust monkey-god holding a '*gadā'* (mace), a sign of bravery. He has an image of Lord Rāma impressed on his chest, a sign of his devotion to Lord Rāma.

The legend has it that when Shri Rāma ascended to Heaven, His Supreme Abode, Hanumāna also wished to follow Him. But the Lord asked him to remain in this world as His representative and attend all the assemblies of men where discourses on His deeds are held, and help the devotees in cultivating even higher devotion.

Hanumāna is one of the seven Chiranjeevis (who live forever). He is believed to be present everywhere.

अश्वत्थामा बलिर्व्यासः हनुमांश्च विभीषणः।
कृपः परशुरामश्च सप्तैते चिरजीविनाः।।

Ashwatthāmā bālirvyāsah hanumānshcha vibheeshanah,
Kripah parashurāmashcha saptaite chirajeevināh.

Nityakarama Poojā Prakāsha (Geetā Press) - Page10

Ashwatthāmā, Bālee, Vyāsa, Hanumāna, Vibheeshana, Kripāchārya and Parashurāma are in all the seven Chiranjeevis.

He who has eyes and devotion to behold him receives his blessings. It is said that wherever Hanumāna is present, there are Shri Rāma and Seetā as well; and wherever Shri Rāma and Seetā are praised and the story of their deeds recited, there is present Hanumāna, too.

Hymns to Hanumāna, the blessed devotee of Lord Rāma, are recited in the Hanumāna Chāleesā, written by Sant Tulasidāsa, who wrote the *Rāmacharitamānasa* (Rāmāyana) in *Awadhi* (a dialect of Hindi). May his blessings be upon all! Let us sing his glory in unison in the following lines :

जय हनुमान ज्ञान गुन सागर। जय कपीस तिहुँ लोक उजागर।।
रामदूत अतुलित बल-धामा। अंजनि-पुत्र पवनसुत नामा।।

* * * * *

मंगल मूरती मारुति नंदन। सकल अमंगल मूल निकंदन।।
पवनतनय संकट हितकारी। हृदय विराजत अवधबिहारी।।

जय जय जय हनुमान गोसाई।
कृपा करहु गुरुदेव की नाई।।

श्री हनुमतेः नमः

ĀYYAPPĀ

Lord Āyyappā is the manifestation of the combined energy source of Lord Vishnu and Lord Shiva. The devotees of Āyyappā call him by several favorite names: Dharma Shasta (the One who secured Dharma); Manikānta (the One who wears bell in his neck); Bhoothanātha (Master of the spirits, Lord Shiva's entourage).

The legend of Āyyappā is described in the 'Brahmānanda Purāna' and the 'Skanda Purāna.' Āyyappā, also called Hari-Hara-Puthra, is regarded as the incarnation born from the union of Vishnu's Mohini avatāra and Lord Shiva, in order to destroy the demon Mahishi and to save the Devas (gods). Baby Āyyappā was found on the shores of the holy Pampa river by the heirless king of Pandalam, Rajasekara, when he was out on a hunting trip. As the divine child was wearing a golden bell around his neck, the king named him Manikānta and adopted him as his son. Soon the queen had her own child. As the children grew up, young Manikānta was loved and admired by all. A jealous and scheming minister persuaded the queen to feign a strange ailment which required tiger's milk, and Manikānta took up the task of getting it for his mother. He ventured boldly into the forest, caught up with Mahishi and fulfilled the purpose of the avatāra by killing the demon. The divine child returned home triumphantly riding a tigress and the queen realized the divine nature of her foster son. Prince Manikānta explained to his foster parents his divine mission, helped install his younger brother on the throne, told the King to build a temple in the Sabari Hills, and then he disappeared.

The pilgrims visiting the Sabari Mala Āyyappā temple undertake strict and rigorous austerities. They start with a '*vratham*' (pledge for religious observance) lasting for forty-one days. All wear black, blue or saffron clothes and tulasi beads. Three strict austerities prescribed and observed include that of the body, of the mind and of the speech, combined with strict vegetarianism, *Brahmacharya* (continence, to help conserve the physical energy into spiritual energy), *Samarpana* (total surrender toward Self realization) and the prayer 'Swāmiye Saranam (I Surrender to Thee Completely).' Before starting the pilgrimage to the Sabari Hills, each devotee prepares an '*Irumudi*' (A bag with two separate compartments and with two knots) for the long and strenuous journey through the jungles. The front compartment contains a coconut filled with ghee (purified butter) and the other one, food and personal belongings. The devotee walks on foot from the shore of the Pampā river to Swāmi Sannidhanam, climbs the 18 steps to the Sanctum-sanctorum, and offers the ghee to the deity.

The forty-one days of '*vratham*' is to force the mind to withdraw from attachments to worldly possessions and to direct it towards the Absolute Truth. The pedestrian walk through the jungle symbolizes adopting the path of spirituality that requires a great effort. The coconut symbolically represents the human body: the outer shell of the coconut symbolizes the ego, and the ghee, the ātman (soul). A coconut shell bears three eyes: two eyes represent the intellect and the third one, the spiritual eye. The deity represents Brahman (God). The rear compartment of the '*Irumudi*' symbolizes 'Prārabdha Karma' (destiny arising from the accumulated karma). The devotee exhausts all the worldly possessions during the journey and reaches the Sanctum-sanctorum with the ghee-filled coconut. The devotee opens the spiritual eye of the coconut, breaks the coconut and pours the ghee on the deity (surrenders or submerges the ātman into Brahman). At this time, the devotee has detached himself from the ego and worldly possessions. He or she attains symbolic unification (Yoga) of the ātman with Brahman. The devotee realizes the true meaning of the Hindu Mahāvākyam (Great Saying): "*Tat Twam Asi*" (Thou Art That)!

This text is written by C.K. Dhananjayan of Sri Siva Vishnu Temple, Lanham, Maryland.

LAKSHMI

Lakshmi is the goddess of fortune. Being the consort of Lord Vishnu, the preserver of the universe, she represents the power of opulence and prosperity, necessary elements for preservation. She is worshiped by householders for the health and welfare of their families; business men and women offer her prayers toward the success of their endeavors. Most Hindus perform Mahālakshmi poojan on the auspicious day of Deepāvali. She is frequently shown standing on her lotus-throne and holding lotus-buds, which are symbols of beauty and riches. Lakshmi is said to have many incarnations as the consort of Lord Vishnu, two most popular are of the divine couple being as Rāma and Seetā, and Krishna and Rādhā. However, goddess Lakshmi is commonly portrayed in eight forms (स्वरूप), namely, Ādya Lakshmi, Vidyā Lakshmi, Sobhāgya Lakshmi, Amrita Lakshmi, Kāma Lakshmi, Satya Lakshmi, Bhoga Lakshmi, and Yoga Lakshmi..

Image of Lakshmi is usually shown in pink complexion symbolically reflecting prosperity. The pinkish complexion also reflects her motherly compassion. Her four hands signify the power to grant four *Purushārthas*, namely, Dharma (righteousness), *Artha* (wealth), *Kāma* (worldly pleasure) and *Moksha* (liberation from the cycle of birth and death and thus from all pain and suffering.) She is prayed as :

नमस्तेऽस्तु महामाये श्रीपीठे सुरपूजिते।
शंखचक्रगदाहस्ते महालक्ष्मी नमोऽस्तु ते।।

Namastestu mahā-māye shreepeethe surapoojite;
Shankha-chakra-gadā-haste Mahā-lakshmi namostu te.

Salutations to you, O Mahālakshmi, who is all powerful, who is the source of wealth, and who is worshipped by the gods and who has a conch, a disc and a mace in her hands.

आरती लक्ष्मी जी की जो कोई नर गाता।
उर आनन्द अति उमगे पाप उतर जाता।।

Ārati Lakshmi jee kee jo koee nara gātā;
Ura ānanda ati umage pāpa utara jātā.

Whoever pays homage to goddess Lakshmi, he or she gains great bliss in his or her heart and becomes free from any sin.

✴ ✴ ✴ ✴ ✴

Every good thought has Dharma as its foundation.

SARASWATI

Saraswati, the consort of Brahmā, is the goddess of *Vidyā* (learning and knowledge). *Hansa* (swan) is her vehicle. She represents the power and intelligence without which the creation is impossible. She is commonly depicted seated on a lotus holding the string-instrument, the *veenā*. Devotees, particularly children starting school and students of all ages, worship Saraswati as the source of knowledge. As the goddess of music, she is particularly sacred to those who pursue the art of music in the form of singing or playing musical instruments. She is also known as Shārada, the storehouse of wisdom. The *Hansa* symbolically represents *Vivek*, the wisdom and power to discriminate goodness from evil.

Buddhist and Jains, whose faiths place emphasis on knowledge as the means to liberation, also worship Saraswati. The following prayer is recited before the start of the studies :

SARASWATI-VANDANĀ

O Divine Virtuous Goddess Saraswati, we bow to your feet;

O Goddess of Speech, all-pervading with cosmic vibrations, we surrender at your divine feet;

O Goddess, shelter to the seeker, giver of blessing in the Three Worlds, worshipped by divine seers, your melody is with nine aesthetic senses and divine poetry, adorned with the varied taste of learning;

O the One seated on the throne of a swan;

O the One endowed with white complexion, pure as snow and the moon, the One seated on the white lotūs, remove from us lethargy and expand our horizon of vision;

O Goddess, you are embodiment of artistic skills and store of knowledge;

O the One holding the divine book of learning and the *veenā,* we submit ourselves in entirety at your lotus-feet;

O Goddess, remove from our minds the poison of hatred.

या देवी स्तूयते नित्यं विबुधैर्वेदपारगैः।
सा मे वसतु जिह्वाग्रे ब्रह्मरूपा सरस्वती।।

Yā devi stuyate nityam vibudhairvedapāragaih
Sā me vasatu jihvāgre Brahmaroopā Saraswati.

Saraswati, the goddess of knowledge, who is praised by the wise, who have mastered the shastras, who is the consort of the Creator, May she live on the tip of my tongue.

PĀRVATI

Pārvati is the consort of Lord Shiva and mother of Lord Ganesha and Lord Murugan (Kārtikeya). The followers of '*Shakti*' philosophy consider her the goddess supreme (above all other goddesses). Pārvati is variously also known as Umā, Lalitā, Gauri, Aparnā, Shivakāmini, Girijā, Shailajā, Dakshayāni, Bhavāni, etc. The *Lalitā Sahasranāmā* contains all her names recited by her devotees. The name Pārvati is derived from a Sanskrit word '*parvata,*' meaning mountain. It is believed that her parents were Parvatarāja Himavata (personification of the Himālaya Mountains) and the apsarā Mainā. The devotees also recite the names of Shiva and Pārvati as Shambhu-Bhavāni. Just as Shiva is the presiding deity of Destruction, the couple jointly symbolizes the power of renunciation and asceticism.

Pārvati symbolizes many noble virtues esteemed by the Hindu tradition, such as marital felicity, devotion to the spouse, asceticism, power, and fertility. It is said in the Saundarya Lahiri, a famous literary work on the goddess, composed by Ādi Shankarāchārya, that she is the source of all power in this universe and that she empowers Lord Shiva as well. Thus, Hindus often worship Shiva and Pārvati in the form of '*Ardhanārishwara,*' a deity depicted as half-male (Shiva) and half-female (Pārvati). Kālidāsa's epic *Kumārasambhavam* details with matchlessly lyrical beauty the story of the maiden Pārvati: her devotion aimed at gaining the favor of Shiva; the annihilation of Kāmadeva (the god of love) as a wrathful Shiva opens His Third Eye; the universe turning into a total lifelessness; the nuptial of the two partners; the immaculate birth of Subrāhmanya; and the eventual resurrection of Kāmadeva after intercession by Pārvati to Shiva in his favor.

Kāli and Durgā are also incarnations of Pārvati. As her devotees believe, Pārvati assumed all these forms to kill the wicked and to protect the virtuous in the world at different mythological epochs.

As Pārvati is the source of all auspicious things to those who faithfully follow the path of virtue, she is '*Sarvamangala.*' Since her childhood, she was a devotee of Lord Shiva. She would constantly engage herself in meditation and worship of Shiva. Her mother, Mainā, out of exasperation, would say, "Pārvati, don't do this *tapasyā* (meditation)." In Sanskrit 'U' is a word of address and 'ma' means 'don't', hence her name 'Umā.'

Affection for and obedience to the elders, loyalty to good traditions, determination, steady devotion to Shiva, kindness towards those in distress, perseverant till the completion of a good deed — these are the traits of Pārvati.

There are several famous temples, for instance, Meenākshi temple at Madurāi, Kāmākshi Amman temple at Kānchipuram, Kāmākhya temple near Gawahāti (Assam) and Akilāndeshwari temple at Thriuvanaikaval, where the presiding deity is Pārvati.

जगदेश्वरी ✠ जगदेश्वरी ✠ जय मात तू महेश्वरी

GĀYATRI MĀTĀ

Gāyatri Mātā is known as Veda-Mātā, the mother of all Vedas and thus the mother of all the spiritual knowledge and storehouse of wisdom. As per legend, she is another consort of Lord Brahmā. According to this legend, Saraswati was late to arrive at the time when Brahmā was to perform 'Yajna.' Brahmā became angry because His consort's presence was indispensable to complete the ceremonies. Brahmā asked the priest to fetch a woman and to wed Him to her on the spot. It so happened that in the neighborhood was found a very lovely shepherdess. In reality she was no other person than the Vedic hymn of Gāyatri incarnated as a beautiful girl. Brahmā married that girl and kept her as His other consort together with Saraswati. However, in an instantaneous anger, Saraswati cursed Brahmā so He would not be worshipped thereafter. Consequently, among the 'Hindu Trinity' Lord Brahmā is the only one who is not worshipped, whereas the other two — Lord Vishnu and Lord Mahesha — are worshipped universally.

In the Hindu tradition, Gāyatri Mata is also the personification of all the pervading *Pārabrahman*, the ultimate unchanging Reality that lies behind all phenomena. She is shown having five heads and is shown seated upon a lotus. Four heads of Gāyatri represent the four Vedas and the remaining one represents the Almighty Lord Himself. In her ten hands she holds all the symbols of Lord Vishnu, including mace, lotus, axe, conch, sudarshana, etc. It is said, "the Gāyatri is Brahmā, the Gāyatri is Vishnu, the Gāyatri is Shiva, and the Gāyatri is the Vedas."

It is said that our ancient Rishis selected the words of various *mantras* from the Vedas and arranged them in such a way that not only resulted in another mantra (now known as Gāyatri Mantra) conveying an important meaning, but also the chanting creates specific energies. The Gāyatri mantra inspires righteous wisdom. It conveys the meaning that may the Almighty God illuminate our intellect so as to lead us on the righteous path. This Gāyatri mantra is regarded as the most important prayer. It is called *'Mahā-Mantra'*. For the Hindus, the Gāyatri is seen as a divine awakening of the mind and soul, and a way to reach the most supreme form of existence, and the way to union with Brahman.

It is commonly accepted that this mantra cultivates righteous wisdom when the '*japa*' (chanting) of this mantra is taken up as '*Sādhanā*' (spiritual practice). It is ordained that repeating this hymn leads to *Moksha* (spiritual liberation).

In essence, Gāyatri Mātā represents the most sacred 'Gāyatri Mahā-mantra', a hymn recited by the Hindus on all auspicious occasions.

ॐ भूर्भुवः स्वः तत्सवितुर्वरेण्यं।
भर्गो देवस्य धीमहि धियो यो नः प्रचोदयात्।।

Om bhoor-bhuvah-svah tat-savitur-varenyam;
Bhargo-devasya-dheemahi dhiyo yo nah prachodayāt.

Yajur-Veda (Ch. 36; Shloka 3)

Om! Let us meditate upon the glory of Ishwara, Who is the Creator of the Earth, Space and the Heaven (the universe), Who is worthy to be worshipped, Who is the source of the intellect of the gods; may He enlighten our intellect!

Worship of Gāyatri Mātā by reciting this mantra brings every kind of fortune
at the physical, mental and intellectual level.

✳   ✳   ✳   ✳   ✳

**It is the renunciation of the worldly attachments and submission to God that purifies
the human life.
God personifies virtues and strength.**

DURGĀ

The most widely worshipped female aspect of god (*Shakti*) is represented as Durgā. Literally Durgā means the one who is difficult to approach and difficult to know. She is the Supreme Power by which the whole universe is energized. She is the personification of *Yajna* (sacrifice), *Pāravidyā* (highest knowledge), as well as *Apāravidyā* (knowledge of secular sacrifices). She bestows inner power and energy, dispels difficulties, and annihilates the evil ones.

Her places of worship are called *'Shakti Peetha'* or *'Siddha Peetha'*. The total number of these *Peethas* in Āryāvarata (ancient India, i.e., the combined region of undivided India, Tibet, Nepal, Bangladesh, Afghanistan and Sri Lanka) is 51.

A prayer recitation for her is :

या देवी सर्व भूतेषू शक्तिरूपेण संस्थिता।
नमस्तस्यै नमस्तस्यै नमस्तस्यै नमो नमः।।

Yā devee sarva-bhooteshoo   shakti-roopena sansthitā;
Namastasyai namastasyai namastasyai namo namah.

The goddess, who is present in all beings as Power and Energy — I bow to her; I bow to her; I bow to her.

दुर्गे स्मृता हरसि भीतिमशेषजन्तोः।
स्वस्थ्यैः स्मृता मतिमतीव शुभां ददासि।
दारिद्रयदुःख भयहारिणि का त्वदन्या।
सर्वोपकार करणाय सदार्द्रचित्ता।।

Durge smritā harasi bheetimashesha-jantoh;
Swasthyaih smritā matimateeva shubhām dadāsi;
Dāridrya-duhkha bhayahārini kā tvadanyā;
Sarvopakāra karanāya sadārdra-chittā.

O Mother Durgā, whoever remembers you during a difficult situation, is freed of all forms of fear. When remembered by those who are healthy, you grant them the most pure intellect. Who, other than you, is the dispeller of poverty, pain and fear, with a heart forever compassionate for doing good to everyone — but you?

✳ ✳ ✳ ✳ ✳

A sincere aspiration brings its response.
If there is continuity in the goodwill, the results are bound to follow.

आनन्दमयी ✠ चैतन्यमयी ✠ सत्यमयी ✠ परमेश्वरी

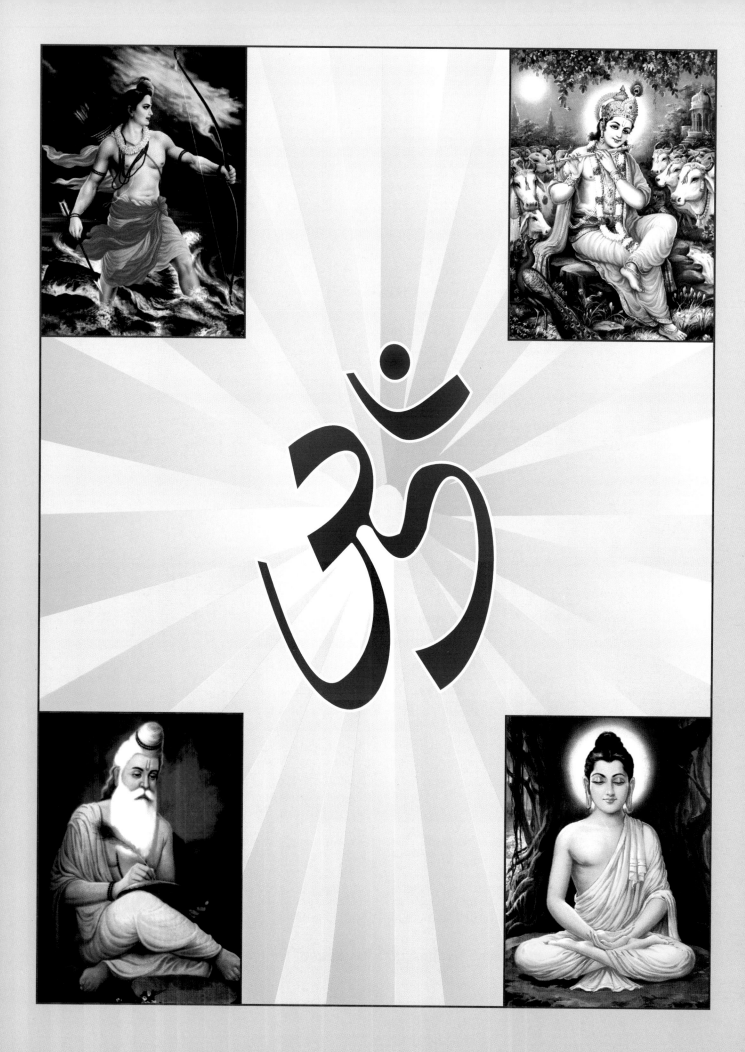

Chapter 3

VISHNU AVATĀRA

Bhagawāna Vishnu, the Sustainer of the Creation, manifests Himself whenever there is a decline in the righteousness. He appeared many times to re-establish Dharma. This manifestation of Godhead is referred to as Avatāra (Incarnation). As cited in the Shrimad Bhāgavatam, in the present *Chaturyugi*, comprising of four *Yugas* (cosmic time periods), namely, *Sata-Yuga, Tretā-Yuga, Dwāpara-Yuga and Kali-Yuga* — there have been so far twenty-one Incarnations and the twenty-second 'Kalki' Incarnation is foretold at the end of the present *Kali-Yuga* — about 43,006 **CE**. Out of these 22 Avatāras, the ten Incarnations *(Dashāvatāra)* — namely, the Incarnations in the form of *Varāha* (Boar), *Matsya* (Fish), *Koorma* (Tortoise), *Narasimha, Vāmana, Parashurāma, Rāma, Krishna, Buddha* and *Kalki* — are the most-cited ones, and appear to be correlated with the evolutionary pattern of life on earth. Among these ten Avatāras, two Incarnations, namely, Shri Rāma in the *Tretā-Yuga* followed by Shri Krishna in the *Dwāpara-Yuga*, are the most celebrated ones and have permanent imprint in the Hindu psyche, as evidenced by their being worshipped by all Hindus. During their appearance, they personified the highest levels of godly as well as human characters and showed the path of idealism, peace and harmony to all. In their dealing with others, they also showed that for righteousness to prevail, the enforcement of power (physical, spiritual and ethical) is essential. In their teachings and actions as narrated in the great Sanskrit epics, the Rāmāyana and the Mahābhārata by the concurrent sage-poets, Vālmeeki and Vedavyāsa, respectively, it was emphasized that an evil person understands only the language of force. They never hesitated to use force against the evil persons and powers when all persuasive actions for peaceful resolution failed.

Two other Incarnations, Shri Krishna Dvaipāyana Vyāsa (the Organiser of the Four Vedas — hence also the name Vedvyāsa — and the author of the great epic, the Mahābhārata) and Bhagawāna Buddha (Originator of Buddhism), also have lasting imprint on the humanity. Therefore, brief accounts of the lives of these four celebrated Incarnations, namely, Rāma, Krishna, Vyāsa and Buddha, are presented in this Section.

* * * * *

विष्णुध्यानम्

शांताकारं भुजगशयनं पद्मनाभं सुरेशं
विश्वाधारं गगन सदृशं मेघवर्णं शुभाङ्गम्।
लक्ष्मीकान्तं कमलनयनं योगिभिर्ध्यानगम्यं
वन्दे विष्णुं भवभयहरं सर्वलोकैकनाथम्।।

Shāntākāram bhujagashayanam padmanābham suresham
Vishvādhāram gagana sadrisham meghavarnam shubhāngam;
Lakshmee-kāntam kamal-nayanam yogibhir-dhyāna-gamyam
Vande Vishnum bhava-bhaya-haram sarva-lokaika-nātham.

I adore Lord Vishnu who has a pacific stature; who lies on the (divine) serpent; whose navel is the (symbolic) origin of the lotus (on which Lord Brahmā, the Creator sits); who is the king of all gods; who is the sustainer of the entire world; whose complexion is swarthy like the clouds; whose body shines with heavenly beauty; who is the beloved of goddess Lakshmi; whose eyes are charming like a pair of lotus flowers; who is meditated upon by the yogis; who is the remover of worldly fear; and who is the singular Master of the whole universe.

ॐ शान्तिः शान्तिः शान्तिः।

MARYĀDĀ PURSHOTTAMA SHRI RĀMA

The life and the ideals of Shri Rāma have been described in the Sanskrit epic 'The Vālmeeki Rāmāyana.' His virtues are mirrored in a question posed by the Sage Vālmeeki to celestial Sage Nārada, "Is there anyone in the present world who is full of virtues and at the same time possessed great prowess; who is well versed in Dharma; who is grateful, truthful and of firm resolve; who is possessed of right conduct; who is friendly to all living beings; who is a man of knowledge and also powerful; who has subdued his own-self; who has conquered anger; who is possessed of splendor; and whom the very gods dread when his wrath has been provoked in battle?"

To this question, sage Nārada replied, "Yes! There is one, born in the line of Ikshvāku, and known by the name of Rāma."

Shri Rāma, an incarnation of Lord Vishnu, was born as the eldest son of Dasharatha, the king of Ayodhyā, a kingdom in the present State of Uttara Pradesha (UP) in India, and of mother Kaushalyā, during the period of the *Tretā-Yuga*. He was the prince of the 'Suryavamsha' (the 'Sun' Dynasty), and a descendant of great kings such as Ikshvaku, Raghu, and Bhageeratha. He had three younger brothers: Bharata, the son of Queen Kaikeyi; and Lakshmana and Shatrughna, twin sons of Queen Sumitrā.

Rāma and His three brothers received their education in the scriptures (Vedas, Upanishads etc.) and in the art of warfare under the guidance of Maharshi Vashishtha. Rāma and Lakshmana were later ushered by Sage Vishwāmitra to protect the sages performing 'Yajna' (ritualistic worship to please gods and also to purify the environment) against the demons (godless, wicked tribes). During this period, Shri Rāma and Lakshmana received training in the use of special weapons. Vishwāmitra also escorted the two princes to the 'Swayambara' (a ceremony in which a princess chooses her own husband from among many aspiring princes attending the ceremony) arranged by the king Janaka of Mithilā in order for his daughter Jānaki (Seetā) to select her husband. She selected Shri Rāma. As it came to pass, all four brothers were married at the same ceremonial occasion. Lakshmana was married to Urmilā, the younger sister of Seetā; and Bharata and Shatrughna were married to Māndavi and Shrutikirti, respectively, the daughters of Kushdhawaja, the younger brother of king Janaka.

For the sake of upholding his father's word to Queen Kaikeyi, Rāma gave up the throne and took an exile for fourteen years in the forest. Brother Lakshmana and Seetā accompanied Him. First they stayed at Chitrakoota forest as advised by Sage Bhāradwāja and then moved to the forest named Panchavati in the present-day Mahārāshtra. There Seetā was abducted by the demon king Rāvana of Lankā. During a long and arduous search for Seetā, Rāma and Lakshmana met Hanumāna and Sugreeva, the 'vānara' (monkey) king, who helped in this search. Hanumāna discovered that Seetā was a prisoner of Rāvana and was kept at

Ashoka-Vātikā (Garden) in Lankā. Rāma's army of 'vānaras' and 'reechhas'(bears), under the supervision of Nala and Neela, built a long bridge over the Indian ocean over which the army crossed the ocean and the colossal battle against Rāvana began. The warriors of Shri Rāma's army destroyed the army of Rāvana who was slewed by Rāma. Thus, Shri Rāma won the war and Seetā — ever devoted to her loving husband — was liberated. After the victory, a proposal was made to make Shri Rāma as the king of Lankā, which was the most prosperous and was called the 'Golden-Lankā'. Shri Rāma refused the proposal, saying:

जननी जन्मभूमिश्च स्वर्गादपि गरीयसी।

Janani Janma-bhoomishcha swargādapi gareeyasi.

One's mother and motherland are superior even to heaven.

His love for His mother and motherland (Bhāratavarsha) was the uppermost in His mind. Vibhishana, Rāvana's pious brother devoted to Rāma, was crowned the king of Lankā.

By this time the fourteen-year exile was completed. Flying on the 'Pushpaka Vimāna' (a plane lent by Kubera, the god of wealth), Shri Rāma, Seetā and Lakshmana, along with Hanumāna, returned to Ayodhyā and, to the great delight of the people of Ayodhyā, Shri Rāma was crowned the king of Ayodhyā. He remained the king for a very long time, an era of perfect happiness, peace, prosperity and justice, known as the 'Rāma Rājya'. Such a perfect harmony — '**Rāma Rājya**' — is still the dream of the Hindus. Mahātmā Gāndhi enunciated this dream to be his goal for Free India.

The fourteen-year period of exile was not without events in Ayodhyā. When Shri Rāma left for the exile, brothers Bharata and Shatrughna had gone to their maternal uncle's home. Mahārājā Dasharatha could not bear the shock of separation from Rāma and passed away. The curse of Shravana Kumāra's parents — that Dasharatha would die as a result of separation of his son — was fulfilled. He was bound by the tradition of the 'Raghukula' (the Raghu- Dynasty) :

रघुकुल रीति सदा चलि आई, प्रान जाहुँ बरु बचनु न जाई।

Raghukula reeti sadā chali āyee, Prāna jāhun baru bachanu na jāyee.

It has been the eternal tradition in the Raghu-dynasty — One would forsake one's life, but not one's word.

Bharata and Shatrughna were immediately summoned back to Ayodhyā. Bharata performed the last rites of his father. He was very much in distress because of his father's passing away and at the exile of Shri Rāma who was dear to him more than his own life. He rebuked mother Kaikeyi for causing this entire calamity for her desire to make her own son the king instead of Rāma. Bharata then embarked on his mission to persuade Shri Rāma to return to Ayodhyā and be crowned the rightful king. But Rāma bade him to return without him, so he could carry out his father's promise. Bharata reluctantly returned, but led an ascetic's life while keeping Rāma's 'Pādukā' (Sandles) on the throne as His symbolic representative. The youngest brother, Shatrughna, looked after the affairs of the State. As an ideal brother, the example of Bharata is unsurpassed.

In Shri Rāma's rule, the views of every citizen were heard and respected. A washer-man happened to question the chastity of Seetā when she was a prisoner of Rāvana. Shri Rāma, knowing fully well that Seetā was chaste and innocent, adhered strictly to His Dharma of a king to keep every citizen satisfied and happy, and exiled his beloved wife, Seeta, to the forest where she lived in the āshrama of Rishi Vālmeeki. There she gave birth to twin sons of Shri Rāma who were named Lava and Kusha, respectively. When they grew up, the Rishi narrated the story of Rāma to Lava and Kusha, who memorized the entire text and were able to recite the epic poems in a melodious voice.

Eventually, Shri Rāma performed the 'Ashwamedha Yajna' at Ayodhyā. In course of this 'Yajna', Rishi Vālmeeki brought Lava, Kusha and Seetā to Ayodhyā to be reunited with Shri Rāma. However, there Seetā wished to return to her original mother, the Mother Earth, and was accordingly engulfed by the 'Mother Earth.' Shri Rāma's rule lasted for a long period. In time, entrusting the kingdom to 'Yuvarāja' — crown-prince Lava — Shri Rāma followed the injunction of Dharma and finally departed to His celestial abode, leaving His mortal body by taking 'Jalasamādhi' (being eternally submerged in water) in the Sarayu river.

The day Shri Rāma returned to Ayodhyā from Lankā after completing His exile, the entire city of Ayodhyā was lighted with lamps and fireworks were displayed. It was the *Amāvasyā* of *Kārtika Krishna Paksha* (the Fifteenth day of the month of Kārtika). The festivity is now commemorated annually and is called '*Deepāvali*' or Diwāli (Festival of Lights). Another festival associated with Shri Rāma is *Vijayadashami* (*Dussehrā*). It is the celebration commemorating the day when Shri Rāma killed Rāvana and Seetā was redeemed. It was the Tenth day of *Āshwina Shukla Paksha*. On this day, the effigy of Rāvana is burnt with great celebration of the Victory of Rāma. These festivals are celebrated even today by the Hindus all over the world as symbols of 'Victory of good over evil.' This tradition is in practice for the last many millennia.

Shri Rāma's images are usually shown holding a bow and arrow, indicating his readiness to use force to eliminate the evil-doers. More commonly, He is pictured as a king with His consort Seetā, brother Lakshmana and devotee Hanumāna sitting near Lord Rāma's feet.

The epic, the *Rāmāyana,* describes the life of Shri Rāma and His perfect adherence to Dharma despite the hardships He suffered in His life. The original Rāmāyana was written by Sage Vālmeeki in Sanskrit. A more recent Hindi epic, the *Rāmacharitamānasa*, written by Sant Tulasidāsa in the Sixteenth century, proved to be a savior of the Hindu Dharma and populace during the period of oppressive rule of the Mughals. The life, deeds and divine philosophies of Rāma became the source of strength to bear the hardships perpetuated by the tyrannical Muslim rulers. The *Rāmāyana* is referred to as the wisdom of the Vedas in action. Shri Rāma, an embodiment of Truth and morality, was an ideal son, an ideal brother, an ideal husband, an ideal father, an ideal king, and above all, an ideal keeper and protector of the Dharma (righteousness). Hence He is known as *Maryādā Purushottama Rāma* — an ideal man with the highest human qualities and endeavors. His consort, Seetā, was an *Avatāra* of Lakshmi and virtue-incarnate, an embodiment of perfect wife and womanhood exalted in the Hindu society and culture. According to the *Shrimad Bhāgavatam*, Shri Rāma was the Eighteenth incarnation of Lord Vishnu.

नरदेवत्वमापन्नः सुरकार्यचिकीर्षया।
समुद्रनिग्रहादीनि चक्रे वीर्याण्यतः परम्॥

Nara-devatvamāpannah   sura-kārya-chikeershayā;
Samudra-nigrahādeeni   chakre veeryāny atah param.
- *Shrimad Bhāgavatam (Canto 1, Ch. 3, Shloka 22)*

In the Eighteenth incarnation, the Lord appeared as King Rāma. In order to perform some pleasing work for the demigods, He exhibited superhuman powers by controlling the Indian Ocean and then killing the King Rāvana, who was on the other side of the sea?

> ## THE WATCH WORDS OF HINDU DHARMA :
> ### Emulate the life of Shri Rāma.

ॐ श्रीपरमात्मने नमः

जय रघुनन्दन जय सियाराम। व्रज-गोपी-प्रिय राधेश्याम॥
रघुपति राघव राजाराम। पतित पावन सीताराम॥
सबको सम्मति दे भगवान। जय रघुनन्दन जय सियाराम॥

✱ ✱ ✱ ✱ ✱

YOGESHWARA SHRI KRISHNA

Yogeshwara Shri Krishna, a *Sampoorna Avatāra* of Vishnu, was born on the 8th day of the Hindu Calendar — *Bhādrapada Krishna Paksha* — about five thousand years ago in Mathurā, India, as the son of Vasudeva and Devaki while they were in prison by the orders of king Kamsa, an atheist and an evil king. This day called Janmāshtami is celebrated with great rejoicing by the Hindus all over the world. Shri Krishna's appearance was to eradicate the evils and thus to create an era of peace and prosperity. He explained the essence of the Vedas and the Upanishads to Arjuna in the battlefield of Kurukshetra in the Mahābhārata War. His message is in fact applicable to all, for all times. According to *Shrimad Bhāgavatam*, He was Twentieth incarnation of Lord Vishnu.

एकोनविंशे विंशतिमे वृष्णिषु प्राप्य जन्मनी।
रामकृष्णाविति भुवो भगवान हरद्भरम्॥

Ekonavimshe vimshatime   vrshnishu praapya janmanee;
Rāmakrishnāviti bhuvo bhagawāna haradbharam.

-Shrimad Bhāgavatam (Canto 1, Ch. 3, Shloka 23)

In the Nineteenth and Twentieth incarnations, the Lord (Vishnu) took birth as Lord Balarāma and Lord Krishna respectively, in the family of Vrishni (the Yadu dynasty); and by so doing, He removed the burden of the world.

However, among the most cited incarnations called *Dashāvatāra* (दशावतार), Shri Krishna is the Eighth Avatāra of Lord Vishnu; other Avatāras being that of *Varāha* (Boar), *Matsya* (Fish), *Koorma* (Tortoise), *Narasimha, Vāmana, Parashurāma, Rāma, Buddha* and *Kalki,* the last to appear at the end of the **Kali-Yuga** — about 43,006 **CE**.

Shri Krishna preached, among other things, the philosophy of Karma-Yoga, according to which one must perform one's duty, but without attachment to its results; the immortality of the soul; and the meaning of Yoga of various types for the attainment of 'moksha' or union with God. The complete sermon of Shri Krishna to despondent Arjuna is contained in the *Shrimad Bhagavad Geetā*. He annihilated all the demons and evil-doers of the time. He slew Kamsa, reinstated Ugrasena on the throne of Mathurā, but He Himself remained as the sentinel at the court entrance. On another occasion He took upon Himself the menial service of cleaning after meals in the great *Rājasuya Yajna* of Yudhishthira, where He was the person honored with *Agrapoojana* — an essential part of the *Yajna* ceremony. Such was the ideal of Shri Krishna.

The manifestation of God as Shri Krishna is intended to demonstrate the perfection of God in full glory. Spiritual laws are manifest in the life and gospel of Shri Krishna. This is why His ethics, teachings and philosophy are rather difficult to grasp. Shri Krishna and Arjuna were Nārāyana (Vishnu) and Nara (human), respectively, and their association was invincible. The last verse of the Geetā is the testimony to this truth :

यत्र योगेश्वरः कृष्णो यत्र पार्थो धनुर्धरः।
तत्र श्रीर्विजयो भूतिर्ध्रुवा नीतिर्मतिर्मम।।

Yatra Yogeshwarah Krishno yatra Pārtho dhanurdharah;
Tatra shreervijayo bhootir dhruvā neetir matir mama.

—*Shrimad Bhagavad Geetā (Ch. 18, Shloka 78)*

Sanjaya says, *"Wherever Shri Krishna, the Lord of Yoga, and Arjuna, the wielder of the bow, are together, there victory, propriety and glories are certain to follow, that is my opinion."*

Divine grace and human endeavor towards righteousness go together. Proper knowledge and action go together in perfect blend. God and man, the Creator and the creation, respectively, are inseparable. Further, it is emphasized in the Geetā :

यदा यदा हि धर्मस्य ग्लानिर्भवति भारत।
अभ्युत्थानमधर्मस्य तदात्मानं सृजाम्यहम्।।

Yadā yadā hi dharmasya glānir bhavati Bhārata;
Abhyutthānamadharmasya tadatmānam srijāmyaham.

—*Shrimad Bhagavad Geetā (Ch. 4, Shloka 7)*

O Arjuna! Whenever there is a decline of righteousness, then I manifest Myself for the revival of the Dharma.

परित्राणाय साधूनां विनाशाय च दुष्कृताम्।
धर्मसंस्थापनार्थाय संभवामि युगे युगे।।

Paritrānāya sādhoonām vināshāya cha dushkritām;
Dharma samsthāpanārthāya sambhavāmi yuge yuge.

—*Shrimad Bhagavad Geetā (Ch. 4, Shloka 8)*

For the protection of the virtuous, for the annihilation of the miscreants, and for reestablishing Dharma (righteousness), I appear (take birth) in every Yuga (cosmic era).

Through these verses of the Bhagavad Geetā, Shri Krishna proclaims the meaning of His descent for the ascent of the spirit of man. There are various facets in the life of Shri Krishna: the spiritual or the supremely transcendent metaphysical aspects, the cosmic aspect, the human aspect, the family aspect, the national aspect and the ethical, moral, social, economic and even political aspects. Could anyone comprehend all these aspects of His personality ? Can anyone — even a Yogi or Rishi — excel the knowledge and power of Shri Krishna? He was at once the greatest householder, the greatest Sanyāsi, the greatest Yogi, the source of all knowledge and love, supreme embodiment of duty and power. He could speak to Brahmā and Rudra at the same time, and yet wash the feet of guests who attended the Rājasuya Yajna of Yudhishthira. He preached the highest spiritual knowledge of the Geetā while acting as a charioteer of Arjuna in the battlefield of Kurukshetra ! He was behind the Pāndavas' victory in the Mahābhārata war, making Yudhishthira the emperor of the Hastināpura Empire.

The life of Shri Krishna was full of miracles beyond human capacity to comprehend. Even when He was a child, many miraculous occurrences demonstrated His godly and human 'Leelā' (make-believe play), such as crossing the river Yamunā in full furry as He was taken to be cared for by Nanda and Yashoda when He was only hours old; playing with *gopies* (cowherd girls) and entertaining them with His flute; lifting the Govardhana Hill on His little finger to protect the people of Vraja Mandala against the cataclysmic rain by an angry Indra (god of rain); and killing of demon Pootanā and killing the tyrannical and evil king Kamsa.

After killing Kamsa and reinstating Ugrasena on the throne, Shri Krishna and His brother, Balarāma, moved to Dwārakā. Hereafter, His actions were that of a warrior and wise statesman, ready to take arms, if required, for the protection of the virtuous. He was a messenger of peace; and yet, when His peace-mission failed due to the evil Kauravas, He assumed the role of the champion of the 'Mahābhārata War' for the destruction of the evil and for the vindication and victory of the righteous Pāndavas.

Among the many of His feats, Rukamini *Harana* was the first of its kind. From the events that happened from the start to finish between the Pāndavas and Kauravas, it is evident that He did foresee all that was going to happen. Whether it was the wedding of Draupadi that He attended unidentified-uninvited and later presented the gifts to the Pāndavas living incognito; or being far away in Dwārakā during the game of dice leading to *Draupadi-cheera-harana* by Dushāsana and still saving the honor of Draupadi — all these were myriad of miracles He performed. Evil Duryodhana drew many schemes for killing the Pāndavas: going to the forest to kill the Pāndavas; burning the Pāndavas and Kunti alive in the palace of wax; having Sage Durvāsa, known for his short temper, curse the Pāndavas; and so on. Shri Krishna Himself went to the royal court to seek justice on behalf of the Pāndavas in order to avoid war. But His peace-mission remained fruitless due to the blind arrogance of wicked Duryodhana. The Mahābhārata war that followed, leading to an absolute victory of the Pāndavas, is a most momentous part of history of Bhārata (India).

Shri Krishna revealed still another side of His personality when he met His old school-mate Sudāmā, saying :

यस्याहं अनुगृह्णामि तस्य विपत्तिं हराम्यहम्।

Yasyāham anugrihnāmi tasya vipattim harāmyaham.

Whenever I bestow my grace upon a person, I absolve him of all misery.

Shri Krishna treated emperors and paupers alike, with love, provided their hearts were pure. His life was full of miraculous deeds, beyond the capacity of men to comprehend. Yet, with all the glories of Shri Krishna described above, His life-story is incomplete without an understanding of the spiritual love of Rādhā for Him. The relationship of Rādhā and Krishna is described elsewhere in this publication.

Apart from the Shrimad Bhāgavatam written by the great sage-poet Vedavyāsa, the epic of the 'Mahābhārata,' by him contains a description of many of the glorious deeds of Shri Krishna, including His sermon to Arjuna (the Bhagavad Geetā, which forms a part of one chapter of the Mahābhārata, tiltled ' the Bheeshma Parva').

* * * * *

Prayer to Bhagawāna Krishna

वसुदेवसुतं देवं कंसचाणूर मर्दनम्।
देवकी परमानन्दं कृष्णं वन्दे जगद्गुरुम्॥

Vasudevasutam devam Kamsachānoora mardanam;
Devakee parmānandam Krishnam vande jagadagurum.

I bow to Lord Krishna, the supreme guru, son of Devakee and Vāsudeva, and the conqueror of Kamsa and (demon) Chānoora.

* * * * *

GLORY TO SHRI KRISHNA !

VEDAVYĀSA

Vedavyāsa was the son of Sage Parāshara. His mother was Satyavati. Parāshara was a great Rishi and the author of the Parāsharasmrithi, which is a treatise on the rules of righteous human conduct. Satyavati was the daughter of Dasharāja, the king of the fishermen. One day she was rowing the boat carrying Parāshara to cross the river Yamunā. Parāshara, by Divine will, was captivated by the beauty of Satyavati, and they fell in love. From their union, Satyavati gave birth to a boy she named Krishna Dvaipāyana — 'Krishna', because he had dark complexion; 'Dvaipāyana,' because he was born on an island *(dweepa)* in the Yamunā river. Later, 'Vedavyāsa' was added to his name because he compiled and classified the existing spiritual knowledge into four branches known as the four Vedas. It is said that Vyāsa does not signify the name of any one person — it is a title; every *Dwāpara-Yuga* witnesses the birth of a Vyāsa. He bears the title till the next *Dwāpara-Yuga* comes and the next Vyāsa is born.

Shri Krishna Dvaipāyana was raised up in the care of his father, Sage Parāshara, receiving education in the Scriptures. He grew into manhood and acquired wisdom at an early age. He became well-versed in the Vedas, the Shāstras, the Purānas etc., poetry, history and other branches of learning. He had a long life and became an eye-witness to the happenings in the *Dwāpara-Yuga*, including the Mahābhārata war .

Rishi Parāshara passed away. Eventually, Satyavati married Emperor Shāntanu, the-then '*Chandravanshi*' (also called the 'Kuru' dynasty) king of Hastināpura (present-day Delhi), who already had a son Devavrata (also called Gangāputra or Bheeshma) from Gangādevi. Satyavati gave birth to two sons, Chitrāngada and Vichitravirya. Chitrāngada died young. Vichitravirya had two wives, Ambikā and Ambālikā. Vichitravirya also died but left no heir to the throne. Satyavati was unhappy because the dynasty itself would come to an end. She called her son Vyāsa to bless her two daughters-in-law, each to have a son. Ambikā gave birth to Dhritarāshtra and Ambālikā to Pāndu. A maid serving the queens also had a son, named Vidura. The sons of Dhritarāshtra and Pāndu were called the Kauravas and the Pāndavas, respectively. Thus, Vyāsa was the elder in the Kuru family.

Vedavyāsa, one of the greatest sages of India, played a very significant role in the growth of Sanātana Dharma. He was the most prolific author and gifted poet. He made a lasting contribution to the development of the Hindu culture.

According to the legend, when the Mahābhārata war, to which Vyāsa was an eye-witness, was over, Lord Brahmā appeared before sage-poet Vyāsa and asked him to write the story of the Mahābhārata. It would be good for the mankind. Lord Brahmā advised Vyāsa that he take the help of Lord Vināyaka (Ganesha) in this mammoth task. Vyāsa accepted the challenge and wrote 'the Mahābhārata,' the vastest epic (1,00,000 shlokas or verses) known to mankind. It still remains a storehouse of wisdom and a marvel in the literature of the world. It is sometimes also called the Fifth Veda. It should be noted that the Shrimad Bhagavad Geetā is a part of the great epic of the Mahābhārata.

Vyāsa played an active role in the affairs of the Kuru-dynasty. He tried to lead the Kauravas and the Pāndavas princes on the path of virtue and Dharma.

After the death of king Pāndu, Dhritarāshtra became the king and the ultimate cause of the family conflicts. He was unable to control the evil designs of his wicked son, Duryodhana, who hated the Pāndavas and made many attempts to kill them. Having failed in doing so, Duryodhana and his uncle Shakuni cheated the Pāndavas in the game of dice. The eldest of the Pāndava, Yudhishthira, who was playing against Duryodhana, lost everything — his kingdom, his brothers and even wife Draupadi, who was deeply humiliated in the presence of king Dhritarāshtra. This led to an exile of the Pāndavas for thirteen years. Vyāsa, by the power of his austerities, could see the impending crisis and came to Hastināpura to warn Dhritarāshtra, "You are a fool and your blind love for wickedest Duryodhana is responsible for all the problems. Your sons are destined to bring ruin to themselves. What a pity! You all forget that Lord Krishna Himself is on the side of the Pāndavas. The Pāndavas are on the path of Dharma. If you want the welfare of your children, restore the kingdom of Indraprastha to the Pāndavas. Remember my words." With these words of advice, he left the palace.

Vyāsa then went into the forest looking for the Pāndavas. After a warm hospitality accorded to Rishi Vyāsadeva, they described their harsh life in the forest. When they were talking, Draupadi could not hold back her tears. Vyāsa was deeply touched. He said, "Daughter, don't grieve. These hardships won't last long. Dharma will triumph. The Pāndavas are pious and heroic. The very purpose of their lives is to uproot the evil Kauravas. Do not weep."

After the death of Duryodhana, Vyāsa visited and comforted Dhritarāshtra who was in extreme grief. In the end, Yudhishthira and his brothers came to seek the blessings of Gāndhāri. However, she was enraged at the death of her sons and was about to curse the Pāndavas. Vyāsa then again appeared and said, "Daughter, check your anger. How are the Pāndavas to blame? Let bygones be bygones. Think that now the Pāndavas are your own children." She was comforted and she blessed the Pāndavas.

When Mahābhārata war was over and most of the warriors, friends and relatives on both sides were killed, everyone in Hastināpura was grieving. Vyāsa again came to console them by his sermon: "Whatever happened had to happen as a result of the people's 'karma.' Grieve no more."

Yudhishthira was crowned the king of Hastināpura. He was deeply touched by the suffering and the blood-bath the war had caused. He grew weary. He thought of giving up his kingship. He wanted to become a 'sanyāsi' and to live in the forest, performing 'tapasyā' (austerities and penance). Vyāsa could foresee this and came to see Yudhishthira and said to him, "Do not be a fool. You are a 'kshatriya' (a person of the brave-ruler and warrior-class). You ought to know your duty. Do not behave like a coward." While this dialogue was going on, Uttarā, the wife of Abhimanyu, came. She was also grieving at the death of her husband. Vyāsa told her, "Abhimanyu did not die a coward's death; he fought like a hero and is in heaven with the great heroes. His very name lends glory to your dynasty." Vyāsa thus consoled Uttarā and foretold, "Your son, Parikshita, would be a great emperor, bring glory to 'Bhārata-Varsha' and the dynasty of Pāndavas will survive."

Dhritarāshtra and Gāndhāri lived for some time in the care of Yudhishthira. Vyāsa returned to his hermitage at Badrikā. Dhritarāshtra, Kunti and Gāndhāri accompanied by Vidura, seeking solitude, left the palace for penance and meditation.

This way, time and again, Vyāsa guided one and all with words of wisdom. He showed everyone the path of duty and finally returned to his hermitage. He is indeed living-in-soul* even today. Vedavyāsa had a number of disciples. The four great 'Rishis'; called Vaishampāyana, Paila, Jaimini and Sumantu, respectively, were his main disciples. They propagated the knowledge of the Vedas in different parts of Bhārata.

Thus, Vyāsadeva appeared at a critical time when humanity was on the road of decline. It was the time of the end of the *Dwāpara-Yuga* and the advent of *Kali-Yuga*, the period of vices like ignorance and hypocrisy. People were having difficulty in grasping the knowledge revealed to seers and sages that was being passed over orally generation after generation. Vyāsadeva organized and compiled that knowledge for the benefit of people into four branches called *the Sāma-Veda; the Yajura-Veda; the Rig-Veda* and *the Atharva-Veda*, respectively. Then Vyāsa wrote the *Brahmasootras* in order to explain the meaning of the Vedas. To explain the main background of the *Brahmasootras*, he wrote the eighteen Purānas; in these he wrote about the great men connected with the *Brahmasootras* and also told a number of moral tales. Finally, Vyāsa wrote the *Harivamsha*, the life history of Lord Krishna. He wrote a total of 24,00,000 *Shlokas*, the most monumental literary work ever accomplished. We honor Sage Vedavyāsa by celebrating Guru (Vyāsa) Purnimā on the 15th day of *Āshāda Shukla Paksha of the Vikram Era*.

It is stated in *Shrimad Bhāgavatam* that :

तततः सप्तदशे जातः सत्यवत्यां पराशरात् ।
चक्रे वेदतरोः शाखा दृष्ट्वा पुंसोऽल्पमेधसः ।।

Tatah saptadashe jātah satyavatyām parāsharāt
Chakre vedataroh shākhā drishtvā pumso'lpamedhasah.

—*Shrimad Bhāgavatam (Canto 1, Ch. 3, Shloka 21)*

In the Seventeenth incarnation of Godhead, Shri Vyāsadeva appeared in the womb of Satyavati through Parāshara Muni, and he divided the Vedas into several branches and sub-branches, knowing that the people lacked comprehension (of the original Vedic knowledge).

✶ ✶ ✶ ✶ ✶

ॐ नमो भगवते वासुदेवाय । ॐ नमो भगवते वासुदेवाय । ॐ नमो भगवते वासुदेवाय ।
ॐ नमो भगवते वासुदेवाय । ॐ नमो भगवते वासुदेवाय ।
ॐ नमो भगवते वासुदेवाय ।

---

*Vedavyāsa is one of the seven Chiranjeevis (Living-in-Soul - believed to be living forever).

अश्वत्थामा बलिर्व्यासः हनुमांश्च विभीषणः ।
कृपः परशुरामश्च सप्तैते चिरजीविनाः ।।

Ashwatthāmā bālirvyāsah hanumānshcha vibheeshanah,
Kripah parashuhrāmashcha saptaite chirajeevināh.

Nityakarama Poojā Prakāsha (Geetā Press) - Page10

Ashwatthāmā, Bālee, Vyāsa, Hanumāna, Vibheeshana, Kripāchārya and Parashurāma are in all the seven Chiranjeevis.

BHAGAWĀNA BUDDHA

Siddhārtha Gautama was born in 623 **BCE** as the son of King Shuddhodana and mother Māya (Anjanā) in the famous gardens of Lumbini* near the city of Kapilavastu situated on the bank of river Rohini at the foot of Mount Palpa in the Himālayana ranges of Nepal, about one hundred miles north-east of Vārānasi, India. His mother passed away soon after his birth. Gautama was brought up by his foster-mother, Mahāprajāpati, who was his mother's sister.

In the history of India, it was the period when the original teachings of the Vedas and the basic instructions of non-violence were forgotten. Violence — in the form of animal-sacrifice as a part of ritualistic worship in Hindu temples dominated by the pretentious priests — was the norm rather than exception. At such a critical period of cruelty, degeneration and hypocrisy, Buddha appeared to eradicate such non-Vedic practices and to disseminate the message of equality, unity, compassion and love.

At the birth of Siddhārtha, the astrologers predicted, "This child, on attaining adulthood, would become either a great king or would become a Buddha — a perfect, enlightened soul, for the salvation of mankind." The astrologers told king Shuddhodana that the child would renounce the world on seeing an old man, a diseased man, a dead man and a monk. The king took every possible precaution to avert any situation where any of these four predicted signs might come in the view of Prince Gautama. Siddhārtha was kept surrounded with all kinds of luxury and indulgence, in order to cultivate an attachment for worldly pleasures and to prevent him from becoming a *sanyāsi*. Gautama got married at the age of sixteen with princess Yashodharā and had a son named Rāhula. Gautama was kept in a walled palace with gardens, fountains, music and dance to make him cheerful and happy.

However, one day Gautama went out of the palace, taking a ride on his chariot. He moved around in the town along with his attendant Channā, to see how the people were getting on with their lives. As destiny would have it, he saw a decrepit old man, a sick man, a corpse and a monk. The sites induced him to renounce the world. He realized that he, too, would be a prey to old age, disease and death; that his mundane life, despite all its luxuries and comforts, was full of miseries; and that worldly happiness was transitory and meaningless. What struck him the most was the serenity of the monk? He resolved to become an ascetic.

---

* *Lumbini is a place of pilgrimage where stands one of the commemorative pillars built by Emperor Ashoka. The site, where the archaeological remains associated with the birth of the Lord Buddha have been found, is now being developed as a Buddhist pilgrimage center.*

Unable to reconcile the suffering of others with his own privileged life, Prince Gautama, at the age of twenty-nine, renounced his kingdom and worldly pleasures. He left his palace, wealth, dominion, power, and family. Thereafter, Siddhārtha devoted himself entirely to spiritual pursuits. He practiced severe 'tapasyā' (austerities) for years in search of inner peace and knowledge, often foregoing even food. He had little success by adopting this method, however. He was reduced to a skeleton. He became exceedingly weak, unable even to walk.

While pondering over his condition, he saw a troupe of girls passing by, singing joyfully a melodious song, which carried the following meaning :

> *The Sitar's musical gift imparts a lesson*
> *Of the Middle Path, to men, for wisdom:*
> *The instrument's strings ought to be tuned right,*
> *To make melodious music; for, if slack, the strings*
> *Wouldn't yield a note, and, if too tight,*
> *They would snap, and a shattered Sitar no music brings.*

In the song, Buddha found a real message of profound spiritual significance. He realized then that he should not go to extremes, torturing the body by starvation; and he should generally adopt the Middle Path.

Siddhārtha remained relentless in his pursuit to attain inner peace and Self-realization. He was spiritually hungry. One day he sat in a meditative posture underneath a *Pipala* tree, plunging himself into deep meditation, 'Samādhi'. Ultimately, he attained enlightenment, becoming a seer of the true nature of human life and its predicament, and full of profound compassion. He thus became the Buddha — **An Enlightened One**. The tree under which he sat meditating has now become famous as the 'Boddhi-Tree.' It is located in the city of Bodha Gayā in the Province of Bihār, India. Bodha Gayā is the birth-place of the Buddha Religion (Buddhism) and, therefore, is the most important Buddhist pilgrimage in the world.

Buddha said of the Samādhi-Experiences, "I thus behold my mind released from the defilement of earthly existence, released from the defilement of sensual pleasures, released from the defilement of heresy, released from the defilement of ignorance."

In the emancipated state arose the knowledge: "I am emancipated, rebirth is extinct, the religious walk is accomplished, what had to be done is done, and there is no need for the present existence. I have overcome all foes; I am all-wise; I am free from stains in every way; I have left everything and have obtained emancipation by the destruction of desire. Myself having gained knowledge, whom should I call my Master? I have no teacher; no one is equal to me. I am the holy one in this world; I am the highest teacher. I alone am the absolute omniscient one (सम्बुद्ध). I have gained coolness by the extinction of all passion and have attained 'Nirvāna.' To establish the kingdom of Dharma I will go to Vārānasi. I will beat the drum of immortality in the darkness of this world." *

Lord Buddha then went to Vārānasi. He delivered his first sermon at the 'Deer-park' now called Sāranātha, situated a few miles from the city of Vārānasi. At Sāranātha, Buddha preached what he realized, namely, *Chatvari Ārya Satyani* (The Four Noble Truths) and the *Āryāshtānga Mārga* (the Eightfold Path), to his first five disciples. His most notable disciple among them was Ānanda. He preached to all without exception: men and women, the high and the low, the ignorant and the learned.

The four Noble Truths that Buddha propounded are: ***dukha*** (misery), ***dukha samudāya*** (advent of misery), ***nirodha*** (restraint of misery), and ***mārga*** (the way that liberates from misery). Buddha pointed out that what causes sorrow or misery is desire (*Trishnā*) — the endless craving. Abjuring desire is imperative for *nirvāna* — a complete cessation from the cycle of death and rebirth and the miseries of life. To achieve *nirvāna* is the supreme goal of the Buddhists. To attain this goal, Buddha prescribed the Eightfold Path that laid emphasis on the **Right Conduct, Right Views, Right Intentions, Right Action, Right Effort, Right Mindfulness, Right Recollection and Right Contemplation.** Also, righteousness and compassion ***(Karunā)*** are deemed fundamentally important. The main scriptures of Buddhism include the

Dhammapada, the Vinaya Pittaka, the Sutta Pittaka and the Abhidhamma Pittaka. Buddhists practice a life of total non-violence and live in peace and harmony based on Buddha's teachings.

In consonance with Buddha's first sermon, the Buddhist Sangha (Assembly of Buddhists) was established where the members take the oath of joining the Sangha, pronouncing:

Buddham Sharanam Gachchāmi	*	*I come under the shelter of Buddha*
Dhammam Sharanam Gachchāmi	*	*I come under the shelter of Righteousness*
Sangham Sharanam Gachchāmi	*	*I come under the shelter of Sangha*

This oath is referred to as the *tri-ratna* (Three Gems). A Buddhist monk is expected to be non-violent, celibate, austere and conscientious.

Buddhist monks went far and wide to spread the teachings of Buddhism. Later, when Emperor Ashoka adopted Buddhism, the religion was propagated beyond the boundaries of India through his ambassadors of love and peace, invited by kings of China and Lanka. Presently, it is one of the major religions of the world.

Buddha delivered his last sermon at Vaishāli and announced his departure (*nirvāna*) from earth. He passed away at the age of eighty.

Lord Buddha's preaching of non-violence succeeded in curtailing the practice of animal-sacrifice by orthodox Hindus of the time. He did not preach the tenets of the Vedas. *Lord Buddha taught not to be unnecessarily concerned with the question of the origin of the world or the existence of God.* Because of his silence regarding these questions, Buddhism is considered an atheist religion by some. However, Buddhism primarily stresses morality, self-discipline for spiritual progress, and absolute non-violence. Buddhists have absolute faith in Lord Buddha as a divine spiritual soul. However, most Hindus consider Buddha as an incarnation of Lord Vishnu. This acceptance of Lord Buddha paved the way for continued spread of the Vedic teaching in the centuries that followed. Thus, now Buddhism remains a minority religion in India, the country of its birth.

Subsequently (a few centuries later), many regions of the world where Buddhism (and Hinduism) was a major religion (e.g. present-day Afghānistāna, Malaysia, Indonesia, etc.) came under Islamic attacks and domination, the sword of Islam finding little resistance due to the creed of non-violence of the meek Buddhists (and Hindus) who were butchered barbarically.

It is said in Shrimad Bhāgavatam:

तत: कलौ सम्प्रवृत्ते सम्मोहाय सुरद्विषाम्।
बुद्धो नाम्नांजनसुतः कीकटेषु भविष्यति।।

Tatah kalau sampravratte sammohāya sura-dvishām;
Buddho nāmnānjana-sutah keekateshu bhavishyati.
— *Shrimad Bhāgavatam (Canto 1, Ch. 3, Shloka 24)*

Then, in the beginning of Kali-Yuga, the Lord will appear** as Buddha, the son of Anjanā, for charming those who are envious of the faithful theist.

---

* SOURCE : *Swāmi Sivānanda: http://www.dlshq.org*
**NOTE: *The Shrimad Bhāgavatam was compiled just prior to the beginning of the age of Kali-Yuga, about 5000 years ago, and Lord Buddha appeared about 2400 years later. Thus, in the Bhāgavatam, the appearance of Lord Buddha is foretold. Therefore, the text of this Shloka is in future tense.*
***NOTE : *Megalithic statues of Buddha in Afghanistan were destroyed recently by Talibāna.*

Jagannath, Subhadra, Balabhadra

Lord Buddha at Mahabodhi Temple

Stupas at Mahabodhi Temple Garden

Chapter 4

CELEBRATED HINDU TEMPLES
The Centers of Glorious Vision of Hindu Dharma, Culture and Heritage

India has been the home of a great civilization for more than 8,500 years. Hindu temples have played a pivotal role in the development, promotion, and preservation of the Hindu heritage and culture through the ages.

Hinduism is the origin of, and largely encompasses, Buddhism, Jainism and Sikhism. The concept of Hindu temple is an extension of the concept of a personal God. The temple is *Devālaya* or a Residence of god. They are built to enshrine the images of gods or goddesses or saints, except for the Sikha *Gurudwāras* where the only object of veneration is the Sacred Book — *Guru Granth Sāhib*, and the *Ārya Samāja Mandirs* where God is worshiped as formless (*Nirākāra or Nirguna*). If it is a Buddhist temple, the object of worship is invariably a relic mound called the *Stupa* or an image of Buddha. In Jain temples any of the twenty-four *Teerthankaras* is enshrined as the deity.

The temples sustain higher values of culture; inspire a higher way of life; teach us to respect one another; and are sanctuaries for worshipping and realizing God. The temples are places of paramount peace.

The temples promote scholastic learning and intellectual pursuits. In ancient times, discussions and discourses used to be held in the temple premises to conduct debate (शास्त्रार्थ) among proponents of alternative philosophies and to define the way of life for peaceful living. Attached to the temples were schools where pupils learnt literature, theology, philosophy, and codes of righteous conduct, etc. The local village assembly (*Panchāyata*) or social or religious groups congregated there to perform poojā (worship), to hold functions, to discuss community affairs, or to adjudicate personal disputes. The very fact that elections to local bodies or the hearing of civil disputes were conducted in the presence of the deity gave these proceedings an atmosphere of solemnity and righteousness.

Many of these temples became centers of pilgrimage and the pilgrims often traveled from temple to temple to complete their pilgrimage. In this way these temples, more than any other artifacts of the society or history, contributed significantly to cultural unity of the country. The temples are also associated with religious festivals that are occasions of great social rejoicing.

All through the evolution of the Hindu Dharma, new temples were constructed, while old temples were remodeled to meet the need of the time. This has become a tradition of Hinduism. Many times in the long history of this vast country (India), Hindu temples in thousands were demolished by tyrannical Islamic invaders, conquerors and rulers. Some of these temples were rebuilt again and again.

In this publication an attempt is made to present the historical background and other pertinent details of some of the ancient temples and of some of the recently constructed ones, representing the ever-expanding glorious vision of the Hindu Dharma. They provide inspiration and hope for the preservation of the Hindu culture and heritage.

* * *

धर्मो रक्षति रक्षितः
Dharmo rakshati rakshitah
One who protects Dharma is protected by Dharma.

73

Jagannātha, Subhadrā, Balabhadra

A 'Mandir' is an ocean of spiritual energy, which preserves and protects culture and tradition.

JAGANNĀTHAPURI TEMPLE

Jagannāthapuri is the abode of Lord Jagannātha (the Lord of the Universe). The deities of Lord Jagannātha, Subhadrā and Balabhadra are enshrined in the temple. The temple has a curvilinear tower on a *Pancha-Ratha* (five-chariot) plan. It was built by Ananta Barma Chodaganga Deva during the 12th century **CE** and was completed by his grandson Ananga Bhima Deva. The temple has four gates, one in each direction: East, South, West and North — called the Lions Gate, Horse Gate, Tiger Gate and the Elephant Gate, respectively. The temple has four big halls in a row. The *Vimāna hall* is for deity worship; *Jagamohana hall* is for the audience; *Natamandapa* is for spiritual dance, and the *Bhoga Mandapa* is for serving the *prasādama* (sanctified food).

Lord Jagannātha, the symbol of universal love and brotherhood, is worshipped in the Temple along with Balabhadra, Subhadrā, Sudarshana, Mādhava, Sridevi and Bhoodevi on the *Ratnavedi,* the bejeweled sacred platform.

It is one of the four holy centers (*Dhāmas*) of India; the other three centers are at Dwārakā, Badreenātha and Rāmeshwarama, respectively. The annual Chariot Festival (*Ratha Yātrā*) at Puri is the high point of all festivals and has been attracting hundreds of thousands of devotees and pilgrims since time immemorial. To see the Lord on the Chariot on the *Ratha Yātrā* day — 2nd day of *Vikrama Āshādha Shukla Paksha* — is to secure '*moksha*' (salvation from the cycle of birth and death), as believed by most devotees. When the '*Malamāsa*' (an additional month according to Vikram Samvat — based on the relative motion of the earth and the moon) falls in the month of *Āshādha*, the deities are replaced with new ones carved of the sanctified-wood. The ceremony is called '*Navakalevarna*'. The previous celebrations were held in the years 1950 **CE**, 1969 **CE**, and 1996 **CE**, respectively, and the next such event will be held in 2015 **CE**. This period is an added attraction of celebration drawing huge gathering of the devotees from around the world.

Puri is a great center of *Vaishnavism* (a sect of Hinduism worshipping Vishnu as the supreme godhead). This is the place where Chaitanya Mahāprabhu — the incarnation of Lord Vishnu in *Vaishnava* tradition — spent a good part of his time. The temple is situated in a huge complex, and the 214-feet high temple dominates the Puri skyline.

Jagannāthpuri Dhāma, or Puri as it is called, is situated on the sea-shore of the Bay of Bengal in the State of Orissā, Eastern India. It is served both by air and railways.

Glory to Lord Jagannātha

Golden Lotus Tank

Temple Gopurama

The Outer View

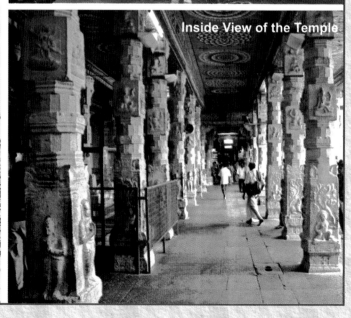
Inside View of the Temple

A 'Mandir' is an ocean of spiritual energy, which preserves and protects culture and tradition.

MEENĀKSHI TEMPLE

The Meenākshi temple is dedicated to goddess Meenākshi (another name for Pārvati), the consort of Lord Shiva. The temple, as splendid as it is, was built by the Nāyaks who ruled Madurāi from the 16th to the 18th Century and left a majestic imprint of their rule in this Meenākshi-Sundareshwara Temple.

The temple complex is within a high-walled enclosure, at the core of which are the two sanctums for Meenākshi and Sundareshwara, surrounded by a number of smaller shrines and grand pillared halls. Especially impressive are the twelve temple *Gopuramas* (towers). The outer towers, each nine storey tall and facing each of the four directions, are the landmarks of Madurāi.

A visitor entering the temple through the eastern gateway first enters a hall —'*Ashta Shakti Mandapama.*' The scriptures on the pillars of the hall relate some of the Lord Shiva's miracles and also the story of Meenākshi's birth and her life as the princess of Madurāi.

There is an ancient tank '*Potramaraikulama*' (Golden Lotus Tank) where devotees take bath in the holy water. On the western side of the tank are the *Oonjal* (swing) and *Killikoontu* (parrot cage) *Mandapama*. The 28 pillars of the hall exhibit excellent sculptures of figures from the Hindu history. Sundareshwara shrine dedicated to Lord Shiva is to the north of *Killikootu Mandapama* where the deity of Lord Vināyaka (Ganesha) is enshrined.

Another attraction is 'The Thousand Pillar Mandapama', each pillar of which is a monument of the Dravidiana sculpture. There is an Art Museum in this hall where 1200 years of history is exhibited through the icons, photographs and drawings.

There are two famous festivals attracting devotees in large numbers:

Teppama Festival : It is the annual Float Festival wherein the images of Meenākshi and Lord Sundareshwara are mounted on an illuminated raft embellished with flowers, and taken to Mariammana Teppakkulam Tank. The float is pulled back-and-forth across the water in the middle of the tank for several days.

Meenākshi Kalyānama : The annual solemnization of the marriage of Meenākshi with Lord Sundareshwara (Shiva) is one of the most spectacular temple festivities. This continues for twelve days.

This temple is the most holy pilgrimage center where Hindus from all over the world come for blessings of goddess Meenākshi. It is located at Madurāi in the State of Chennai, South India.

✳ ✳ ✳ ✳ ✳

VISIT THE TEMPLE
BRING HAPPINESS IN LIFE.

The Main Temple

Lord with Lakshmi and Padmāvati

Footprints of Lord at Nārāyangiri Hill

Sacred Golden Altar Balipeetam

Illuminated Temple

A 'Mandir' is an ocean of spiritual energy, which preserves and protects culture and tradition.

BĀLĀJI VENKATESHWARA TEMPLE

The ancient and sacred temple of Shri Venkateshwara is located on the seventh peak, Venkatachala (Venkata Hill) of the Tirupati Hill, and lies on the Southern banks of Shri Swāmi Pushkarini in Chittoor district, Āndhra Pradesh, India — 120 Kilometers from Chennai and 18 Kilometers northwest of Tirupati. Tirumala, the seat of Lord Venkateshwara, is surrounded by seven hills; thus he is known as Lord of the Seven Hills.

Lord Venkateshwara, popularly also known as Bālāji, is the presiding deity of Shri Venkateshwara Temple. He is one of the manifestations of Lord Vishnu, who incarnated in a previous Kali-Yuga at the request of Sage Nārada. Lord Vishnu as Venkateshwara is worshipped at Tirupati temple that is believed to be the richest of all the Hindu shrines in the world. It is a masterpiece of South Indian architecture. The temple has its origin in Vaishanvism, which advocates the principles of equality and love, and prohibits animal sacrifice. Over millennia, many saints had visited the shrine and offered worship to Lord Venkateshwara. Notable among them was Shri Rāmānujāchārya who installed *chakra* and *conch* on the deity. Several devotees had composed beautiful *keertanas* (devotional songs and hymns) in praise of Lord Venkateshwara, most notable amongst them being Tyāgaraja and Annamācharya.

The temple of Shri Venkateswara has acquired unique sanctity in Hindu religious lore. The Purānas, *Sthala Mahātyams* and *Alwara hymns* unequivocally declare that, in the *Kali-Yuga*, one can attain 'mukti' (salvation) by worshipping Shri Venkateswara. The benefits acquired by a pilgrimage to Venkatachala are mentioned in the Rig-Veda and the Asthādasa Purānas. There are year-round celebrations of festivals. Among these, *Brahmotsavam* celebration is the most elaborate and auspicious. This temple draws millions of pilgrims and is believed to be the busiest pilgrimage center in the world. The elaborate rituals and mode of worship in the temple prescribed by the saint Rāmānujāchārya are being followed even today.

Shri Venkateshwara Suprabhātam, written by one of Shri Rāmānuja's disciples, is recited during the early hours (*Brahma Muhurta*) every morning to wake up the Lord from his sleep. It is believed that Lord Venkateswara will bestow prosperity in abundance to the devotees who recite Lord's *prārthanā* (prayer) every morning.

All great dynasties of rulers of the Southern Peninsula — Pallavas of Kānchipurama (9th century **CE**), the Cholas of Thanjavura (10th century **CE**), the Pandyās of Madurai, and the kings of Vijayanagara (14th-15th century **CE**) — have paid homage to Lord Venkateshwara. Such is its glorious past. Presently, it is managed by Charitable and Religious Endowments Act of 1966.

There is a wonderful uniqueness associated with Lord Venkateswara, and His Abode, Venkatādri.

वेंटकाद्रि सममु स्थानमु ब्रह्मांडे नास्ति किञ्चन।
वेंकटेश समो देवो न भूतो न भविष्यति।।

Venkatādri samam sthānam brahmānde nāsti kinchana,
Venkatesha samo devo na bhooto na bhavishyati.

There is no place like 'Venkatādri' (The Venkata Hill) in the whole universe. A god like 'Venkatesha,' there never was in the past, nor will ever be in the future.

❀   ❀   ❀

Mahākāli Mahālakshmi & Mahāsaraswati

Bhawan (The Temple Complex) at Trikuta Mountain

The Entrance Gate

The Passage to the Shrine

The Sānjhi Chhat

A 'Mandir' is an ocean of spiritual energy, which preserves and protects culture and tradition.

VAISHNO DEVI SHRINE

This cave-temple has a very popular following from people of all faiths. It is one of the most revered shrines and the oldest in the region situated on the Trikuta Mountain. The legend is that Vaishno Devi took the cave for her abode upon being chased by a demon named Bhairon, whom she slew outside the shrine. A visit to the temple is also dedicated to Bhairon who was absolved of his sin before he died. It is an obligatory part of the pilgrimage. An important temple, midway at Ardhkunwāri, marks a major center of obeisance where the goddess is believed to have spent nine months on her journey up the mountain.

The cave shrine is narrow and pilgrims have to walk through a running stream of cold water of Charana Gangā to get to the sanctum sanctorum. Inside, three rock-cut deities of the goddesses, Mahākali, Mahālakshmi and Mahāsaraswati, are venerated. Canopies of silver and gold adorn the deities.

Vaishno Devi temple is an extraordinary structure that was built at an altitude of 6000 feet. The temple was in existence in the cave since the primeval days. It is known to have been built by the Pāndava brothers. Icons of several Hindu deities are inscribed on it. While creeping through the narrow tunnel, the devotees get *darshana* of sculpted Ganesha, Sooryadeva, Chandradeva, Brahmā, Vishnu, Maheshwara, Kāmadhenu, Hanumāna and the Pāndava brothers. The emblem of *Shankha* (Conch), *Chakra* (Disc), *Gadā* (Mace) and *Padma* (Lotus) are engraved as well.

In course of time, the devotees of the goddess Vishno Devi have transformed the old structure into a beautiful temple. Inside the temple compound, there is a provision for comfortable accommodation in which thousands of pilgrims can rest and stay. Most of the usual facilities are available at this place. For the use of the pilgrims, all necessary items like blankets, bed-covers, quilts, torches, lanterns, cooking items and even kitchens are available. There are restaurants and hotels, open round-the-clock.

There is a general belief that the visiting pilgrims to this shrine get relief from distress, and attain peace and happiness. There is another popular belief that the persons who go there never come empty-handed. Vaishno Devi is believed to be the bestower of wealth, bravery, health, and wisdom to her devotees and also to annihilate internal and external fears. The Shrine remains jam-packed with devotees standing in queue, fervently waiting to have a *Darshana* of the All-giving deity. It is customary for the people to offer to the goddess coconut, *Mauli* (sacred thread), *Lāla Chunni* (red scarf) with gold/silver trimming, vermilion, incense, *Mehandi* (henna), *Supāri* (beetle-nut), dry fruits and *Chhattra* (umbrella). These paraphernalia can be obtained from the near-by shops.

In Katrā, there are many trusts that perform elaborate *Yajnas* and *Havanas*. They distribute *poories* and *halwā* as *prasādama* to the pilgrims. This shrine is visited by the people from different parts of the world at different times of the year. Most people walk-up the hill chanting Jai Mātā Di. Due to a heavy inflow of devotees, the *pilgrim-yātrā* is continued round-the-clock with unending queues.

✴ ✴ ✴ ✴ ✴

JAI MĀTĀ DI ✠ JAI MĀTĀ DI
आनन्दमयी ✠ चैतन्यमयी ✠ सत्यमयी ✠ परमेश्वरी

**Ādi Jyotirling
at Somanātha**

**Ādi Jyotirling
Shri Somanātha
Mahādeva**

Sculptures at Somanātha Mandir

A 'Mandir' is an ocean of spiritual energy, which preserves and protects culture and tradition.

SOMANĀTHA — THE SHRINE ETERNAL
The Abode of Lord Someshwara

Somanātha Temple is the home of the first of the 12 *Jyotirlingas* of Lord Shiva worshiped as Kālabhairava Shivalinga or Bhairavanātha, as mentioned in Prabhāsa Kānda chapter of the Skanda Purāna. The legend is that Brahmā, one of the Trinity, installed the *Brahmashilā* that paved the way for the construction of the Somanātha temple — The Shrine Eternal. This ancient temple of Pashupata Shaivism is located on the Southern sea-coast of Gujarāta, at Somanātha city formerly famous as *Prabhāsha* — a very prosperous city. Prabhāsha was traditionally a sacred place even in the days of Mahābhārata. It was situated at a holy spot where the river Saraswati, now extinct, flowed into the sea. The shrine dates back to prehistoric times.

The glory and wealth of Somanātha was legendary. The original temple was decorated with gold and silver. In ancient times the temple was earning the produce of ten thousand villages. The deity of the temple is regarded as *Swayambhu* (self-born). Hundreds of thousands devotees visited this temple and considered themselves blessed and to have achieved piety in their lives. Offerings of the devotees amounted to millions of rupees each day. Additionally, the Sun- worshipping foreigners and traders (including Zoroastrian Pārsis) also contributed a part of their profits to the temple treasury. Thus, the treasury of the temple remained abundantly full at all times.

However, the Somanātha temple passed through a very tragic phase of history. In 1026, this fabulously wealthy temple was sacked and plundered by the Muslim invader Mahmud of Ghazani. The Shivalinga was smashed and 50,000 Brāhmanas were slaughtered. The temple was demolished and a mosque was erected at its site. In fact, this state of affairs was repeated seventeen times by tyrannical Mahmud. But of all the shrines in India, there is perhaps none other that symbolizes the undying devotion and aspiration of an overwhelmingly large majority of the people of India as Somanātha does. Each time the temple was captured and demolished; it was regained by its devotees and restored in its full glory. In 1701 the temple was once again demolished and a mosque built on its site by the Mughal Emperor Aurangazeb. Still, the remains of the temple withstood the ravages of time and survived the attacks of its destroyers. Even aged and desecrated, the temple weathered the Islamic assaults for centuries.

The mosque, a symbol of humiliation to the Hindus till 1951, was finally replaced and the temple resurrected after India gained Independence in 1947. A new grand Somanātha temple was built at the original site under the direction of Sardāra Vallabhbhai Patel. On May 11, 1951, Dr. Rajendra Prasad, the-then President of India, re-installed the Jyotirlinga of Lord Shiva upon the same Brahmashilā on which the earlier temples were repeatedly rebuilt and destroyed. It was the day of great pride and rejoicing to the Hindus all over the world.

श्री महारुद्राय सोमेश्वर ज्योतिर्लिंगाय नमः।
GLORY TO LORD SOMESHWARA

* * * * *

The history of Somanātha is the history of undying devotion and commitment to the Hindu Dharma.

Lord Krishna lifting the Govardhana Hill

Entrance to the Temple

A 'Mandir' is an ocean of spiritual energy, which preserves and protects culture and tradition.

SHRINĀTHJI MANDIR

Shrināthji is a deity form of Shri Krishna, with arms upraised to lift the Govardhana Hill, situated in the temple town of Nāthadwāra near Udaipur, Rājasthāna, India. Shrināthji specifically refers to the story in the Bhāgavata Purāna wherein Lord Krishna lifts the Govardhana Hill to protect the inhabitants of Vraja Mandala (Mathurā-Vrindāvana area) from the downpour of rain sent by Indra, the king of Devatā (gods). Lord Krishna in His form of Shrināthji is worshipped throughout India by the followers of the Bhakti-Movement, especially by those of the Vaishnava tradition, mostly within the state of Gujarāta. The town of Nāthadwāra is often referred to as 'Shrināthji' and Shrināthji as the Lord of Nāthadwāra.

The priests and servants working for the temple are not paid any cash salaries; they only receive *prasādam* (Blessed food) as recognition for their duties. The *prasādam* is distributed to the devotees who visit the temple for *darshana* of Shrināthji.

Presently, Nāthadwāra enshrines Shrināthji — the deity of Lord Krishna — that was originally enshrined at Govardhana in Vrindāvana. The deity was brought to Mewāra for protecting it from being desecrated by the Seventeenth century Mughal emperor, Aurangazeb, who was destroying the Hindu temples ruthlessly. It is said that the chariot carrying the deity stuck here whilst traveling and hence the temple was established with the permission of Rānā of Mewāra at the location presently called Nāthadwāra. According to one legend, the deity of Shrināthji was originally self-manifested from a stone. In the beginning Shrināthji was worshipped in a humble shrine and then the deity was moved to a larger temple in its vicinity. Vallabhāchārya set up the mode of worship of the deity. The tradition was followed by his son Vitthalesh Goswāmi and is continuing even today.

गोविन्द जय जय गोपाल जय जय ।
राधा रमण हरि गोविन्द जय जय ।।

Mainsource : Wikipedia — the free encyclopedia

✳   ✳   ✳

The Deities and Carvings at the Temple

A 'Mandir' is an ocean of spiritual energy, which preserves and protects culture and tradition.

KANDARIYA MAHĀDEVA TEMPLE
A Glorious Architecture and Wonder of the World

Among the wondrous Khajurāho temples, the Kandariya Mahādeva Temple is the most glorious. These temples were built during the reign of Chandella dynasty that ruled the Central India from the 9th through 13th Century **CE**. Out of the eighty-five original temples, thirty survive even today, and are mostly known for the exquisite sculpture covering the exterior walls. To the north of Khajurāho is the Kandariya Mahādeva Temple, the largest in Khajurāho group of temples. It is considered to be the best representation of the Khajurāho style of Indo-Āryan temples.

The whole Khajurāho temple complex is dedicated to the wedding of Lord Shiva and Pārvati, and the Kandariya Mahādeva celebrates the occasion with erotic figures on its outer walls. The Kandariya Mahādeva temple is one of the largest and architecturally and sculpturally the most impressive of all the temples at Khajurāho, with over 900 sculptures carved into sandstone stacked without mortar. The vibrantly carved exterior contrasts with a very plain interior space that enshrines a Shiva-lingam in the innermost chamber (*griha*) of the temple located beneath the main *'shikhara'* (spire). It has a 5-part plan with an *ardhamandapa*, *mandapa*, a *mahāmandapa* supported with pillars, the *garbhagriha* and the *pradakshinā* passage around it. This ornately carved temple depicts various gods and goddesses in elaborate details. The temple is a culmination of the design seen earlier in Lakshmana and Vishwanātha temples. Its *shikhara* rises about 100 feet above the platform which it shares with the Devi Jagadambi temple. The name 'Kandariya Mahādeva' echoes the Purānic description of Shiva — the ascetic residing in a mountain cave.

In ancient times, Khajurāho was known as Khajuravāhaka. The legend has it that the city gates were adorned with two golden *Khajura* (date-trees). It is also believed that the name was derived from the numerous date-trees that thrived in the vicinity.

There are three groups of temples at Khajurāho. The Western group has temples dedicated to Lords Shiva and Vishnu. The northern group has Vaishnava temples for the most part, and the southeastern group consists of Jain temples. These temples are outstanding illustrations of the well-developed Indo-Āryan Nagara style of temple architecture.

Khajurāho is served by air from major cities of India. It is at a distance of 175 miles from Gawālior, 110 miles from Jhānsi, and 75 miles from Satanā. All three places are major railway stations.

✦ ✦ ✦ ✦ ✦

Om Namah Shivāya ❖ *Om Namah Shivāya* ❖ *Om Namah Shivāya*

Lord Buddha at Mahābodhi Temple

Stupas at Mahābodhi Temple Garden

A 'Mandir' is an ocean of spiritual energy, which preserves and protects culture and tradition.

MAHĀBODHI TEMPLE

The Mahābodhi Temple is located at Bodhagayā in the State of Bihār, India, seven miles south of the city of Gayā. It is believed that 250 years after the Enlightenment of Lord Buddha, Emperor Ashoka (Third century **BCE**) visited Bodhagayā and built the Mahābodhi temple where a gilded image of Buddha is enshrined. The temple consists of an elongated spire crowned by a 'Stupa' containing the relics of Buddha and a *chhatrāvali* on a platform. The temple has a beautiful stone railing around it. Depicted on the walls of the temple are scenes from Buddha's life. A museum in the vicinity has gold-bronze and stone-images of Buddha. The mouldings on the spire contain Buddha's images in niches. The temple was renovated in the First century during the reign of the Kushana dynasty. With the decline of Buddhism in India, the temple was abandoned and forgotten, buried under deep layers of soil and sand, and enveloped by trees. In the Nineteenth century, the temple was rediscovered by Sir Alexander Cunningham as a part of his work for the British Archaeological Society. In 1883, he, along with J.D. Beglar and Dr. Rajendralal Mitra, excavated the site. Extensive renovation work was carried out restoring Bodhagayā to its former glory.

Inside the temple is an enormous statue of Buddha. In front of the Buddha image is a Shiva-Linga said to have been installed by the great Hindu sage Ādi Shankarāchāraya. The Hindus believe that Lord Buddha was one of the Incarnations of Lord Vishnu. Thus, the Mahābodhi temple is a pilgrimage shrine for Hindus as well. Behind the temple are the two most venerated objects of the Buddhist world, namely, a seat of Buddha's meditation called *Vajrāsana* that is now adorned with diamonds, and a Bodhi-Tree, sitting underneath which Lord Buddha attained enlightenment. The present tree is a sapling of the Mahābodhi-Tree at Anurādhāpura in Sri Lanka, itself a sapling of the original Bodhi-Tree.

The followers of Buddhism visit this place on Buddha Poornimā, the 15th day of *Vikram Samvat Vaishākha Shukla Paksha* — the day when Buddha attained enlightenment.

As of 2002, Mahābodhi temple is chosen a UNESCO World Heritage Site and specifically nominated for the international 'World Heritage Program.'

卐 बुद्धं शरणम् गच्छामि 卐
卐 धर्मं शरणम् गच्छामि 卐
卐 संघं शरणम् गच्छामि 卐

Northern Gateway

Eastern Gateway

Southern Gateway

The Monastery Ruins

Stupa Carvings

Ashoka Pillar

A 'Mandir' is an ocean of spiritual energy, which preserves and protects culture and tradition.

THE SĀNCHI STUPA

The Great Stupa at Sānchi city is one of the most celebrated Buddhist pilgrimages. It has four elaborate gateways surrounding it from the four directions. The panels of each pillar unfold Buddha's life in intricate details. Though all four gates are similar in shape, the stories they narrate are different. The southern gate has a scene of Buddha in one of his previous incarnations. The northern gate is the best preserved and considered the most elaborate. It has a fragmented *'Dharmachakra'* (the wheel of the Dharma) and two tridents symbolizing the Buddhist trinity. On the eastern gate, panels depict scenes from the life of Buddha, including his mother's dream about her conception — that Buddha entered her womb in the form of a white elephant. It is amazing that these sandstone pillars have stood the test of time for more than two millennia.

Sānchi city was a bustling Buddhist center once used by the monks of yore and was among the most important centers of Buddhism. Today, a few attendants, camera-clicking tourists, and inquisitive students of art, architecture and archaeology populate the remnants of Sānchi. What is unique about Sānchi is that this site has no known connection with the life of Buddha, unlike other Buddhist pilgrim centers in India and Nepal. The origin of the stupa can be traced back to Emperor Ashoka who built the first stone-pillar during the mid-3rd Century **BCE**. Subsequent dynasties enlarged the site, adding many more stupas and other religious structures till the 12th Century. With the decline of Buddhism in India, Sānchi was forgotten and left to be covered by a thick jungle, protecting it from marauding armies and invaders, until it was rediscovered in 1818 by a British Army General. A century later, Sir John Marshal, Director General of Archaeology, and the Buddhist scholar, Albert Foucher, devoted seven years in restoring and repairing the stupas and the temples.

Stupas, hemispherical mound of stone and earth, are endemic to stronghold of Buddhism. It is believed that first stupa was designed by Lord Buddha himself as a symbol for disseminating his teachings after his death. Apart from the stupa and the four gateways, one can also see the stump of an Ashoka-pillar that has four lions (one hidden from view in the picture), which is the emblem of India symbolizing peace through strength. It is a reaffirmation of India's ancient commitment to world peace and goodwill.

The Sānchi Stupa is situated in Sānchi city, which is about 60 km northeast of the capital of Madhya Pradesha, Bhopal, India.

* * * * *

FOLLOW THE TEACHINGS OF LORD BUDDHA
BUDDHA : THE TATHĀGATA — THE ONE WHO REALIZED THE TRUTH

Lord Ādinātha Temple

Carvings on the Pillars and Ceiling

A 'Mandir' is an ocean of spiritual energy, which preserves and protects culture and tradition.

DILWĀRĀ JAIN TEMPLES

The Jain Temples at Mount Abu, built in the Nagara Style, are among the finest monuments of India. The first of these ornate temples dates back to 1032 **CE**, approximately the period in which the grand Brihadishwara Temple at Thanjavura in Tāmilnādu (South India) was built in the Dravidian architecture. The Dilwārā Jain temples have been described as a dream in marble. Other attractions are the Adhar Devi temple, Achalagarh Shiva temple and the Gau Mukha Shiva temple.

In every phase of Indian history, art & architecture found supporters in rich merchants and princes who spent lavishly on the commemoration of their religious beliefs. Gujarāta and Rajasthāna, the traditional centers of merchants and princes, also became centers of great architectural activity, in which *Vimala Shah*, *Vastupāla* and *Tejapāla* contributed immensely to Jain art and architecture.

According to the inscriptions, Mount Abu was basically a seat of Shaivism; and Jainism made its appearance only in 11th century. The first Jain temple of Dilwārā, the Vimala Vasahi, was built in 1032 **CE** by Vimala Shah, minister of Bhimadeva.

The Vimala Vasahi Temple is dedicated to the first Jain Teerthankara, Rishabhadeo, one of the incarnations of Lord Vishnu. It stands in an open courtyard defined by 58 subordinate cells which contain small icons duplicating the saint's image in the main shrine. The plan of the temple resembles that of Kashmiri Sun-Temple at Martand. The entire temple is carved out of white marble.

It is believed that when the intricate carvings were finished, Tejapāla asked the carvers to add greater delicacy to the floral patterns by more chiseling, offering them reward in silver weighing as much as the marble filed. Later Tejapāla offered gold in equal weight to the marble if it could be chiseled further. Whatever the truth, there is no doubt that it must have taken a good deal of artistic mastery and encouragement to complete a monument of such beauty and refinement.

The Tejapāla Temple, although resembling the architectural plan of Vimala Vashi temple (built nearly 200 years earlier), nevertheless stands as the last of the monuments built in the Solanki style, which came to an end with the occupation of Gujarāta by the Muslims towards the end of 13th Century. The striking feature of the Tejapāla Temple is its dome which stands on 8 pillars. The pendant of the dome is a perfect gem; as it drops from the ceiling, it looks like a cluster of half-open lotuses.

From the dome, one's attention is diverted to the '*Garbhagriha*' (principal cell) which, when lighted, reveals the massive image of Naminātha. The representation of the marriage pavilion in one of the panels identifies the scene and graphically portrays the cause of the conversion of Naminātha who was betrothed to Rājimati, the daughter of the king of Girnāra.

In the *Hāthikhānā* (the elephant room), there are 10 elaborately carved elephants. Behind the elephants are 10 slabs, each bearing a male and female figure on it, believed to be the figures representing the members of Vastupāla's family.

At the northern end, the 7th and 8th slab carry the figures of Vastupāla with Lalitā Devi, and Viryta Devi and Tejapāla with Anupama Devi, the guiding spirit behind this venture of Tejapāla and rightly described in the inscription as a 'flower of celestial beauty', whose whole family was distinguished for prosperity, modesty, wisdom, decorum and talent.

Mount Abu : *A popular hill station, located in Rajasthāna, is on the Ahmedabad - Jaipur - New Delhi railroad, off Abu Road, the nearest railhead.*

❀   ❀   ❀

Originally written by S. K. Jain, India

The Main Temple

Guru Granth Sāhib
(The Holy Book)
at the Temple

A 'Mandir' is an ocean of spiritual energy, which preserves and protects culture and tradition.

THE GOLDEN TEMPLE

Hari Mandir, famous as 'The Golden Temple', is situated in the ancient city of Amritasara in the State of Punjab, India. It is the holiest shrine of the Sikha religion. The Sikha devotees from all over the world come to the Golden Temple to enjoy its blissful environs and to offer their prayers. This sacred shrine is increasingly becoming a tourist attraction for visitors from all over the world.

The history of the temple starts with Guru Amar Dāsa, who took the first steps towards building a shrine. His successor, Guru Rāma Dāsa, came to live near this tranquil and peaceful site, and started building the pilgrimage center around the small pool, which later became a *Sarovara*. Guru Arjun Deva envisioned the sanctum. The sanctum today stands as the hallowed symbol of the indestructibility of the Sikha faith. He designed it to have four entrances, one on each side, symbolizing that the temple is open to people of all four *Varnas*, namely, Brāhmana, Kshatriya, Vaishya and Shoodra, and to other people irrespective of their religion, color, creed or gender. The only restrictions are that the person must not drink alcohol, eat meat, smoke cigarettes or take narcotic drugs while in the shrine. All Sikha temples (Gurdwārās) in the world follow the traditional rule that everyone is welcome to enter. One must cover one's head as a sign of respect, and wash feet in the small pool of water as one enters the Hari Mandir Sāhib premises.

The temple construction was completed in 1601 during the time of the fifth Guru, Guru Arjun Deva (1581-1606). The Grantha Sāhib, the holy book of the Sikha, was installed in the sanctum in 1604, three years after its completion. The presence of the Grantha Sāhib adds to the sanctity and reverence of the sanctum. The temple was later sacked by a Muslim army General, Ahmed Shah Abdāli, and had to be rebuilt in the 1760s. All the gold and exquisite marble work was conducted under the patronage of Mahārājā Ranjit Singh.

The festival of Diwāli that falls on 15th day of *Vikram Samvat Krishna Paksha* is celebrated by the Hindus, Sikha and Jains alike. The Sikha celebrate Diwāli to commemorate the laying of the foundation stone for the Hari Mandir in 1588. It is also the joyous day when the sixth Guru, Guru Har Gobindji, returned to Amritasara after his release from the prison by Jahāngira — a Muslim ruler of that time.

In the early morning of this auspicious day, Sikha and Hindu pilgrims take a dip in the sacred tank surrounding the Hari Mandir while reciting the '*Japaji Sāhib*', and then pray at the temple. Circumambulation of the tank (*Parikramā*) is also a tradition. In the evening, the Hari Mandir Sāhib is illuminated with *Diyās* (earthen oil lamps) or candles. There is *Ātishbāzi* (fireworks display) in the evening.

✶　✶　✶　✶　✶

सत् श्री अकाल

A 'Mandir' is an ocean of spiritual energy, which preserves and protects culture and tradition.

SHRI SWĀMINĀRĀYANA MANDIR OF LONDON

The **Swāminārāyana Mandir** of London is the first ever traditional Hindu Mandir of stone to be constructed in Europe. Carved and created in 1995, it is constructed entirely according to ancient Hindu *Shilpashāstras* (architecture). This magnificent temple is the largest one outside India. It is a masterpiece of exotic design and workmanship that rises above London's skyline. Replete with luminescent white pinnacles and glittering marble pillars, the Mandir continues to attract over half-a- million visitors annually.

Deities and motifs spring from the walls, ceilings and windows, representing the sacred faith and beliefs of a people that date back over 8,500 years. The huge dioramas and panels lead one through a journey of discovery of the origins, science and beliefs of Hinduism. The adjoining cultural complex is entered through a richly hand-carved wooden courtyard that opens into a magnificent foyer with soaring wooden columns and panels. The dancing peacocks, delicate lotus flowers and royal elephants beckon greetings.

There are several ornate shrines which are the focal points of the Mandir and house the sacred deities: Harikrishna Mahārāja and Rādhā Krishna Deva, Dhāma, Dhāmi, Muktā, Ghanshyāma Mahārāja, Shiva and Pāravati, and Rāma and Seetā, replete with lavish thrones and royal attire.

The Exhibition *'Understanding Hinduism'*, on the ground floor, is a concise, yet comprehensive study of the Hindu religion — its origins, beliefs, growth, glory and what Hindu values can contribute to the individual, the society and the world at large. The exhibition systematically portrays the contribution of Hindu seers and scholars in the field of mathematics, astronomy, medicine, education and religion. The illustrious heroes of faith and culture such as Nachiketā, Shravana Kumar, Rantideva, Seetā, presented in colorful 3-D miniature dioramas, eloquently reflect the core of Hindu ethics and culture. The Video Presentation explains how the Mandir was built, and traces the various stages of construction and how the 'Moortis' were installed. The significance of the Mandir and its various activities are explained in a very systematic way.

The creator and organizers of 'The Swāminārāyana Hindu Mandir' in Neasden, London are the Bochasanwāsi Shri Akshar Purushottam Swāminārāyana Sansthā (BAPS). The BAPS, a socio-spiritual organization with its roots in the Vedas, was revealed by Bhagawāna Swāminārāyana in the late 18th Century and established in 1907 CE. The hallmark of the Swāminārāyana devotee is that he or she devoutly begins the day with poojā and meditation, works or studies honestly and donates regular hours in serving others. No Stealing, No Adultery, No Alcohol, No Meat, No Impurity of body and mind — these are the five principal vows. Such moral purity and spiritual commitment surety add a deeper brilliance to all the hundreds of social services performed for better Life

Shri Swāminārāyana Mandir is located at 105-119 Brentfield Road, Neasden, London NW108JP, United Kingdom. *Web: www.swaminarayan.org   Telephone: (020) 8965-2651 Fax: (020) 8965-6313 Email: shm@swaminarayan-baps.org.uk*

A 'Mandir' is an ocean of spiritual energy, which preserves and protects culture and tradition.

BARSĀNĀ DHĀMA — SHRI RĀSESHWARI RĀDHĀ RĀNI TEMPLE

Established in 1990 by His Divinity Swāmi Prakāshānanda Saraswati, Barsānā Dhāma* is the main U.S. Center of the Jagadguru Kripālu Parishat. It provides the rare opportunity to experience the true devotional environment that prevailed in the āshrams of the historic saints of Vrindābana and Barsānā 500 years ago. The 200 acres of wooded ground is a representation of the holy land of Vraja, India, where Shri Rādhā Rāni and Shri Krishna appeared some 5,000 years ago. Areas of Barsānā Dhāma have been developed to be the places of devotional inspiration and meditation. Important places of Vraja, namely 'Govardhana,' 'Rādhā Kunda,' 'Prem Sarovara,' 'Shyām Kuti' and 'Mor Kuti', are represented in Barsānā Dhāma of the United States of America where the natural stream of water, named Kālindi, represents the Yamunā River of Vrindāvana.

The Shri Rāseshwari Rādhā Rāni Temple represents the ultimate Divine truth of the Upanishads and the true vision of Rādhā - Krishna Leelās (called *Nikunja Darshana*) as described in the *Rādhikopnishad* and in the writings of the Great Masters of Vrindāvana — which makes it one of the most special temples in the world. A unique feature of the *Satsanga* hall of the temple is that it depicts the essence of the entire Bhārtiya philosophy. The themes of the most important scriptures are described in a continuous panel on the sides of the hall.

Barsānā Dhāma, the abode of Rādhā-Krishna, radiates the Divine Love of God. It has become a place of pilgrimage for Hindus living in the Western world.

The temple is a unique blend of North and South Indian architecture, and of ancient and modern styles. The native Texas landscape has been incorporated into intricate designs of floral patterns on the entrance doors and the shrine itself. There are 85 columns and five levels in the building with covered area of 35,000 square feet. On both sides of the shrine there are large glass windows overlooking the hill, the native flowers, Rādhā Kunda (the holy pool), Mahārasa Mandala and the garden. It appears as if the shrine is situated in a true 'Nikunja' — a blossoming garden of a beautiful hilly area under the early morning sky where the fragrant breeze is caressing the temple of Shri Rāseshwari Rādhā Rāni. The adjoining guest rooms, wedding hall and community hall serve as a center of religious and cultural activities and provide overnight accommodation for out-of-state and international visitors.

जय श्रीराधे

Barsānā Dhāma, established by His Divinity Swāmi Prakāshānanda Sarswati, is managed by Jagadguru Kripālu Parishat— a non-profit, charitable, religious and educational organization registered with the IRS as a 501 (c) 3 tax-exempt one in the United States of America. Barsāna Dhāma is located at 400 Barsānā Road, Austin, TX 78737 U.S.A. **Phone:** *(512) 288-7180* **Fax:** *(512) 288-0447* **Web:** *www.BarsanaDham.org*

The Main Temple

The Ornate Mandovar - Outer Wall
decorated with moortis of
divine Incarnātions, sages and āchāryas

The artistic Entrance Gates

Spectacular Musical Fountain
at the Temple

Gajendras - Out of 148 stone elephants
at the Temple

A 'Mandir' is an ocean of spiritual energy, which preserves and protects culture and tradition.

SWĀMINĀRĀYANA AKASHARADHĀMA MANDIR OF NEW DELHI

"Delhi is the throne. The flag should fly high in Delhi. A pinnacled monument will rise. The land which has been performing penance shall be acquired. Now Yamunāji is waiting. She has become restless. The land on the banks of Yamunāji will be acquired. The Lord will fulfill this in His divine way."

- Yogiji Mahārāja, 1969

The above prophesy of Yogiji Mahārāja became a reality on November 8, 2000, when the foundation stone was laid down on a thirty-acre land on the banks of river Yamunā, New Delhi, India. After the due poojā-ceremony, Swāmiji blessed the Shilānyāsa assembly thus :

"A mandir is a place that calms the wavering mind. Although there is great material progress due to science and technology, there is no inner peace. The mandir provides inner peace by reducing greed, lust, jealousy and ego and brings a person closer to God. We need to follow the guidance of great rishis, Bhagawāna Swāminārāyana, Āchāryās Ādi Shankara and Rāmānuja. Inner peace will be attained. In preserving our values and our culture, we protect ourselves. Whoever comes to the mandir will be redeemed."

The pink sandstone cultural complex is a show-case of the grandeur of Indian history, art, culture and values. It took over 7,000 master craftsmen and thousands of volunteers from all over the world almost five years to complete the marvel. It was inaugurated by the President of India on November 6, 2005, in the presence of the Prime Minister. The monument, depicting ancient Indian *'vāstushāstra'* and architecture, is a marvel in pink sandstone and white marble that is 141 feet high, 316 feet wide and 370 feet long, with 234 ornate pillars, over 20,000 sculptures and statues of deities, eleven 72-foot-high huge *'mandapams'*, and decorative arches. A double-storied *'parikramā'* of red sandstone encircles the monuments with over 155 small domes and 1,160 pillars like a necklace. The whole monument rises on the shoulders of 148 huge elephants with eleven-feet-tall *'panchdhātu'* statue of Bhagawāna Swāminārāyana presiding over the structure.

The other attractions of the complex are three exhibition halls, 'Sahajānanda Darshana,' 'Neelkantha Darshana' and 'Sanskriti Vihāra,' spaced around two huge ponds, one serving as a venue for light-and-sound show. In the Sahajānand Darshana, the life of Swāminārāyana is displayed through robotic shows, while Neelkantha Darshana has a huge I-Max theatre screening movie based on the life of the Lord. Another amazing presentation takes place in the Sanskriti Vihāra, with a 12-minute boat ride providing a unique experience of India's glorious heritage. The Swāminārāyana Akshardhāma successfully combines ancient heritage of India and modern technology under one roof, offering an enlightening experience to a visitor.

This new temple represents the ever-expanding glory of the Hindu Dharma.

* * * * *

Glory to Bhagawāna Swāminārāyana

The famous Ratha Yatra of Jagannathpuri

The Temple

Hindu monk taking a bath

Durgiana Temple Main

Akal Takhat

First Sermon of Lord Buddha at Sárnáth

A Glimpse of some Teerthsthānas

Chapter 5

हिन्दू तीर्थस्थान
HINDU TEERTHASTHĀNA
(Places of Hindu Pilgrimage)

Hindu Dharma is the most ancient religion in the world. It has evolved over the period of many millennia in India. It is generally accepted that the time of composition of the Mahābhārata, the greatest epic the world has known, is about 3000 **BCE**. The Vedas were compiled by Sage Vedavyāsa, the author of the Mahābhārata, around the same time-frame. However, the evolution of Vedic thoughts and traditions took place much earlier. While Shri Krishna, regarded as the human incarnation of God, appeared in the era of the Mahābhārata, Shri Rāma, another human incarnation, preceded Him by a Cosmic Era (*Yuga*) supposedly consisting of hundreds of thousands of years. Whether this chronology is absolutely historical or symbolically mythological, there is no doubt that the practice of Hinduism in India has continued over vast time-spans. Its earliest name, Sanātana Dharma (Sanātana meaning eternal), is very much alive even now. It has taken other names — Vedic Dharma, Ārya Dharma, Mānava Dharma, over its long history. The most recent name is Hindu Dharma (Hinduism).

It may be remembered that passage of time builds history which, combined with the rich and diverse spiritual philosophies and traditions of Hinduism, has given rise to a plethora of mythological stories involving pantheon of gods and goddesses. The ancient sages (Rishis) brought forth these stories entailing gods and goddesses as symbolic representations and personifications of various attributes of the Ultimate Reality (God). These interconnected stories contain not only the finest and mind-staggering reaches of human imagination, but also the outcome of deepest meditative insight of human nature and existence, bordering on divine vision. Figuratively, the web of these stories is indeed like the outcome of churning of the ocean. Extensive collections of such stories are contained in the Purānas — treatises composed millennia ago. Most famous among the Purānas are the Vishnu-Purāna, the Shiva-Purāna, the Skanda-Purāna, and the Bhāgavata-Purāna.

This excursion in the mythological and Purānic literature serves as a background behind the existence of Hindu *Teerthasthānas* (Pilgrimages) throughout India. Each Teerthasthāna is generally associated with one or more gods and goddesses and, often, with specific episodes of some Purānic story. For instance, Ayodhyā in the Uttara Pradesha is a celebrated Teerthasthāna as the birth-place of Lord Rāma; Dwārakā in Gujarāta is a venerated Teerthasthāna as the capital of the kingdom Lord Krishna ruled. Many Teerthasthānas are associated with Lord Vishnu, while numerous ones are dedicated to Lord Shiva. In the extreme north, in the Himālayana region is Amaranātha where a Shivalinga of ice naturally appears for a limited period each year. At the Southern tip of India, there is Rāmeshwarama where Lord Rāma started construction of the bridge across the ocean to attack on Lankā's King Rāvana who had abducted Seetā.

Then there are untold numbers of sacred rivers of India harboring a large number of Teerthasthānas, foremost among them is the river Gangā. Near the origin of the Gangā in the Himālayana range is the Gangotree (the source of Gangā), in the planes is the famed holy city of Vārānasi (Benārasa). Examples of Teerthasthānas at the bank of rivers or atop hills and mountains are, literally, numberless. Hinduism teaches to revere elements of Nature as well, as the manifestation of the Divine.

The rishis who contributed to the Purānic stories and directly or indirectly led to the establishment of these Teerthasthānas millennia ago were indeed inspired with profound vision. For the masses, the realization of an Abstract Ultimate Reality is no easy task. Association of a specific attribute and personality, especially with the help of a story, temple, statue and image is often helpful, even though such an approach is only symbolic. It may serve primarily only as an auxiliary means for ascending to a higher plane of spirituality. Also, if the story entails specific dates or time-periods, large congregations of people from different parts of the country assemble at the place of the pilgrimage, forging national identity. India is a vast country, and travels to near and far places of pilgrimages are bound to uplift the physical, social and spiritual health of the pilgrims. Ādi Guru Shankarāchārya, in fact, established four Teerthasthānas in the four corners of India, namely, Jagannāthapuri in the east, Dwārakā in the west, Badreenātha in the north, and Shringeree in the south. Hindus, broadminded as they naturally are, make pilgrimage to holy places of other faiths as well — Bodha Gayā of Buddhist, Golden Temple at Amritasara of Sikhas, Ajamer of the Muslims.

Often Hindus reserve the old age for visiting distant holy shrines and pilgrimages. Although sometimes it is more convenient to undertake such journeys after retirement, younger age is no less suitable for this purpose. Indeed, the youth, including those from a foreign country, may find it a most rewarding experience to visit one or more of the numerous Teerthsthānas of Bhārata (India).

To keep in memory and revere the sacred land of India, Hindus recite
'Bhārata Ekātmatā Stotram' (भारत एकात्मता स्तोत्रम्)
where important Teerthasthānas are mentioned.

अयोध्या मथुरा माया काशी काञ्चि अवन्तिका । वैशाली द्वारिका ध्येया पुरी तक्षशिला गया ।।
प्रयागः पाटलीपुत्रं विजयानगर महत् । इन्द्रप्रस्थं सोमनाथः तथाऽमृतसरः प्रियम् ।।

Ayodhyā, Mathurā, Māyā (Haridwāra), Kāshi (Vārānasi), Kānchi, Avantikā (Ujjain), Vaishāli, Dwārakā, Dhyeyā, Puri, Takshashilā, Gayā, Prayāga, Pātaleeputra, Vijayānagara, Indraprastha, Somanātha and Amritasara are the great and favorite (Teerthasthānas).

The above Teerthasthānas are like the beads of a garland, uniting the whole of India into an ideal nationhood. Historically and geographically, India's spread is uncommonly expansive. Even within the framework of Hinduism, there exists staggering diversity in the professional background, language, thought-pattern, and life-style of the followers of the faith. A gathering of devotees at the Teerthasthānas is not only spiritually uplifting, but also beneficial for gaining familiarity of the nation at large.

Here, a few Teerthasthānas are briefly introduced. The most popular Teerthasthānas are Prayāga, Haridwāra, Nāsika and Avantikā (Ujjaina), where the 'Kumbha Melā' (Fair) festivals are celebrated. It is believed that the elixir of life is filled in a kumbha (pitcher) in '*Swarga*' (Heaven). With a certain combination of the Sun, the Moon, the Jupiter, the elixir falls from heaven to earth, and the Kumbha Melā is held at those locations. Also, presented are concise descriptions of the four Mathas — Badreenātha, Dwārakā, Shringeree and Jagannāthapuri, which were established by Ādi Shankarāchārya and are the symbols of Hindu National Identity. The remaining places of Hindu pilgrimage described here include Ayodhyā, Mathurā, Vārānasi(Kāshi), Somanātha, Gayā, Kānchi, Rāmeshwarama, Takshashilā, Kurukshetra, Indraprastha, Bodha Gayā, Vaishāli, Sāranātha (of the Buddhist religion), Amritasara (of the Sikha religion), and Pālitānā (of the Jain religion).

The huge gatherings of the people from all walks of life at these Teerthasthānas to pay their obeisance to the Almighty and to commit them to follow the tenets of Sanātana Dharma are the testimony of strong bonds of faith in Hinduism. The pilgrims use this opportunity to repent for the wrong-doings they might have committed and pledge to renew the vows of Dharma-based life, righteousness and truthfulness. This is an unbroken tradition of Hindu Dharma since time immemorial. The people do swarm at these places at the scheduled time, even without being informed via a wide-spread public-information media. This shows the inherent strength that keeps Hindus united, a visible evidence of their faith. However, if people are properly organized for a greater level of nation-wide 'Hindu Unity' and 'Social Justice', the future history of India would be even more glorious, as the adversary forces that are working to weaken Hinduism would not dare do so.

＊　＊　＊　＊　＊

धर्म की जय हो ❖ अधर्म का नाश हो ❖ प्राणियों में सद्भावना हो

After visiting the Kumbha Melā of 1895, Mark Twain wrote*:
"It is wonderful, the power of a faith like that, that can make multitudes upon multitudes of the old and weak and the young and frail enter without hesitation or complaint upon such incredible journeys and endure the resultant miseries without repining. It is done in love, or it is done in fear; I do not know which it is. No matter what the impulse is, the act born of it is beyond imagination marvelous to our kind of people, the cold whites."

---

* Mark Twain, "Following the Equator : A journey around the world"

PRAYĀGA
A Holy Place of the Kumbha Festival

Prayāga, in the state of Uttara Pradesha, India, is an ancient city dating back to the Vedic period. It is located at the confluence (*Sangama*), called Triveni, of the three holy rivers: the Gangā, the Yamunā and the legendary but now extinct river Saraswati. When the river Yamunā merges with Gangā, the water of Yamunā becomes that of Gangā. The water of Gangā can be kept for years without being spoiled, a unique feature of the Gangā river water. The water of the Gangā is considered holy and is used on all occasions of the Hindu Samskāras such as birth, marriage, death etc. Prayāga in Sanskrit means a 'place of sacrifice', and is believed to be the site where Lord Brahmā performed His first *yajna* after creating the universe. In the times of the Rāmāyana, Prayāga was inhabited by great saints (Rishis). Lord Rāma spent some time here, at the hermitage of Sage Bhāradwāja, before proceeding to nearby Chitrakoota during His exile to the forest.

It is important to note that as the solar eclipses in Prayāga occur exactly 5 hours and 30 minutes ahead of those at Greenwich, the city is the reference point for **Indian Standard Time** maintained by the city's observatory. Also, it is a famous center of higher education. Notable points of attraction include a fort built of red stone that houses deities of the Hindu gods and goddesses, and an Ashoka pillar (242 **BCE**) with inscriptions, among others.

Besides being a center of literary geniuses, Prayāga has also been a center of political activities during the pre-independence period. However, it is most famous as '*Teertharāja*' for the Hindus. The most famous and the holiest event that takes place here is the Kumbha Melā.

It is believed that the elixir of life (*amrita*) is filled in a '*kumbha*' (pot) in '*Swarga*' (heaven). With certain combination of the orbital position of the Sun, the Moon and the Jupiter, the elixir falls from heaven to the earth, and the Kumbh Mela is held on those locations.

The legend has it that the primeval ocean was churned by gods and demons, out of which emerged divine physician, Dhanvantri, holding the *kumbha* (pitcher) of *amrita* (nectar). As devatās (gods) and the asurās (demons) both lunged for the pot, Dhanvantri, transforming himself into a rook, flew off to the sky with the pitcher. On his journey that lasted for 12 days, he rested at four places — Prayāga, situated at the Triveni, Nāsika, Avantikā (Ujjaina) and Haridwāra, which were consequently consecrated by the drops of nectar that fell there. Hence Hindus consider these places sacred and believe that a dip in the sacred waters at these places, especially on an auspicious day, will cleanse them and their ancestors, back to eighty-eight generations, of all evil and sin, ensuring their salvation (freedom from the cycle of death and rebirth). The festival of Kumbha is celebrated at these four places after every three years in cyclic rotation; for example, at Prayāga in 2001**CE**, at Nāsika in 2004 **CE**, at Avantikā/Ujjaina in 2007 **CE**, at Haridwāra in 2010 **CE**, and **Poorna (Full) Kumbha at Prayāga in 2013 CE.**

The most auspicious day for a bath at Kumbha is the day of the new moon day. In Prayāga, the Kumbha falls in the month of Māgha (January-February) when Jupiter is in Taurus and the sun and the moon are in Capricorn.

In Prayāga, every year there is an annual festival on the 'Sangama,' where the "*Kalpavāsees*" spend the entire month on the bank of the Gangā, meditating, performing rituals and bathing thrice a day. Equally important is Ardha-Kumbha (Half-Kumbha) that comes every six years apart. In addition, there is Poorna-Kumbha, the most auspicious, that falls once every 12 years and is celebrated at Prayāga. Then there is a 'Mahākumbha', which comes every 144 years when special configuration, the sun in Capricorn and the Jupiter in Aries, falls on Monday, the Somāvatee Mauni Amāvasya. The last Mahākumbha at Prayāga was in 1989. It is believed that bathing on this day brings supreme spiritual blessing. According to the Vishnu Purāna, the merit bestowed by a bath during the Kumbha at Prayāga is greater than the merit which may be earned by a thousand *Ashwamedha Yajnas* or one lākha circumambulations of the earth :

अश्वमेध सहस्राणि वाजपेय शतानि च।
लक्षप्रदक्षिणा भूमि कुम्भ स्नानेन तत्फलम् ।।

Source : Kumbha Melā — wikipedia, the free encyclopedia.

Hari Ki Pauri

Mahā Kumbha at Haridwāra

The Temple at the Ghāta

HARIDWĀRA
A Holy Place of the Kumbha Festival

Mayāpuri in Uttara Pradesha, India, is the ancient town now called Haridwāra, literally meaning the Gateway to Bhagawāna Vishnu. Haridwāra is situated on the bank of the holy river Gangā. It is the point where the Gangā, descending on its long and winding journey through the Himālayas, spreads over the northern plains of India. Associated with both Lord Shiva and Lord Vishnu, Haridwāra is among the seven sacred cities of India. It is also one of the four venues for the Kumbha Melā, held every twelve years. It is a religious center which is said to hold promise of salvation (*Mukti*) for the devotees. Also, it is on the main route to the holy shrines of Badreenātha and Kedārnātha, and is called the gateway to Hari, the presiding deities in these shrines.

There are six main sacred bathing areas (*ghāta*) in Haridwāra, namely, *Gangādwāra, Kankhala, Neela Parvata, Vilvakeshwara Teertha, Kusavarta and Hari-Ki-Pauri*. It is believed that bathing on these spots washes away sins as it is said to be endorsed by the foot-prints of Lord Vishnu on a stone near by. Of these, the '*Hari-ki-Pauri — the feet of Lord Vishnu*' is the most important. Religious ceremonies are performed here round-the-clock. As the twilight hour draws near, the place assumes a more religious look. Huge oil lamps are lit in preparation for the evening ***ārati***. Hundreds of burning wicks, one each for the numerous temples lining the shore, lend a mystical mood. However, this place is most famous for the Kumbha Melā.

It is believed that the elixir of life (*amrita*) is filled in a '*kumbha*' (pot) in '*Swarga*' (heaven). With certain combination of the orbital position of the Sun, the Moon and the Jupiter, the elixir falls from heaven to the earth, and the Kumbh Mela is held on those locations.

The legend has it that the primeval ocean was churned by gods and demons, out of which emerged divine physician, Dhanvantri, holding the *kumbha* (pitcher) of *amrita* (nectar). As devatās (gods) and the asurās (demons) both lunged for the pot, Dhanvantri, transforming himself into a rook, flew off to the sky with the pitcher. On his journey that lasted for 12 days, he rested at four places — Prayāga, Nāsika, Avantikā (Ujjaina) and Haridwāra, situated at the river Gangā, which were consequently consecrated by the drops of nectar that fell there. Hence Hindus consider these places sacred and believe that a dip in the sacred waters at these places, especially on an auspicious day, will cleanse them and their ancestors, back to eighty-eight generations, of all evil and sin, thus ensuring their salvation (freedom from the cycle of death and rebirth). The festival of Kumbha is celebrated at these four places after every three years in cyclic rotation; for example, at Prayāga in 2001 CE, at Nāsika in 2004 **CE**, at Avantikā/Ujjaina in 2007 **CE**, at **Haridwāra in 2010 CE**, and Poorna (Full) Kumbha at Prayāga in 2013 **CE**.

The most auspicious day for a bath at Kumbha is the day of the new moon. In Haridwāra the Kumbha falls in the month of Phālguna (February-March) or Chaitra (March-April) when the Sun passes through the Aries and the Moon is in Sagittarius and Jupiter is in Aquarius.

Hinduism's preoccupation with refinement and purification, physically as well as spiritually, leads to a great importance being accorded to the bath. The bathing, being a spiritual rejuvenation and reaffirmation, is a public act, performed in the open and by flowing water, ideally on the banks of a river or a stream, and includes a complete submergence of the body under water and an oblation to the sun.

Source : Kumbha Mela — wikipedia, the free encyclopedia.

Main Altar at
Harsiddhi Temple

Shiprā River Ghāta
at the Temple

Mahākāleshwara Temple

AVANTIKĀ
A Holy Place of the Kumbha Festival

Avantikā, an ancient city presently called Ujjaina, is situated in Madhya Pradesh, India, on the bank of the Shiprā River. In Astrology, its location is unique: on the Tropic of Cancer, the prime meridian of India. The system of Hindu calendar referred to as the 'Vikrama Samvat' originated in this city. It is one of the seven sacred cities referred to as the 'Moksha-puris' or 'Sapta-puris' of the Hindus, and one of the four sites of Kumbha festival that is held there every twelve years. It is a home to Mahākāleshwara Jyotirlinga, one of the twelve Jyotirlinga shrines dedicated to Lord Shiva.

Ujjain was the traditional capital of King Chandragupta II, also known as Vikramāditya, at whose court the nine scholars known as the Navaratna (the Nine Jewels) of Sanskrit literature are said to have flourished. Most of the temples and bathing areas (ghāta) of Shiprā River are located in the old part of the city. The well known temples are:

Gopāla Mandir, a Krishna temple with two-feet tall silver Deity of Gopāla Krishna enshrined on an altar made of inlaid marble with silver-plated doors;

Mahākāleshwara Temple of Lord Shiva is the home of one of the twelve Jyotirlingas. The temple has a deity of Omkāreshwara Shiva consecrated in the sanctum along with the images of Ganesha, Pārvati, Kārtikeya and Nandi (Shiva's conveyance). It is open to non-Hindus as well;

Sandipani Muni's Āshrama, where Lord Krishna, Balarāma and Sudāmā studied under Guru Sandipani;

Navagraha Mandir is situated at the Triveni Ghāta on the Shiprā River and dedicated to the nine planets. However, Avantikā is most famous for the Kumbha Melā.

It is believed that the elixir of life (amrita) is filled in a 'kumbha' (pot) in 'Swarga' (heaven). With certain combination of the orbital position of the Sun, the Moon and the Jupiter, the elixir falls from heaven to the earth, and the Kumbh Mela is held on those locations.

The legend has it that the primeval ocean was churned by gods and demons, out of which emerged divine physician, Dhanvantri, holding the kumbha (pitcher) of amrita (nectar). As devatās (gods) and the asurās (demons) both lunged for the pot, Dhanvantri, transforming himself into a rook, flew off to the sky with the pitcher. On his journey that lasted for 12 days, he rested at four places — Prayāga, Nāsika, Avantikā (Ujjaina), situated at the bank of the Shiprā river, and Haridwāra, which were consequently consecrated by the drops of nectar that fell there. Hence Hindus consider these places sacred and believe that a dip in the sacred waters at these places, especially on an auspicious day, will cleanse them and their ancestors, back to eighty-eight generations, of all evil and sin, thus ensuring their salvation (freedom from the cycle of death and rebirth). The festival of Kumbha is celebrated at these four places after every three years in cyclic rotation; for example, at Prayāga in 2001 CE, at Nāsika in 2004 CE, at Avantikā/Ujjaina in 2007 CE, at Haridwāra in 2010 CE, and Poorna Kumbha at Prayāga in 2013 CE.

The most auspicious day for a bath at Kumbha is the day of the new moon. In Ujjain, the Kumbha is held in the month of Vaishakh (May), when other planets are in Libra, the Sun and Moon are in Aries and Jupiter is in Leo.

Hinduism's preoccupation with refinement and purification, physically as well as spiritually, leads to a great importance being accorded to the bath. The bathing, being a spiritual rejuvenation and reaffirmation, is a public act, performed in the open and by flowing water, ideally on the banks of a river or a stream, and includes a complete submergence of the body under water and an oblation to the sun.

Source : Kumbha Mela — wikipedia, the free encyclopedia

Gondeshwara Temple

Triyambakeshwara Temple

Devotees at Lord Shiva Shrine at Triyambakeshwara

Hindu monk taking a bath

Devotees offering prayers

NĀSIKA
A Holy Place of the Kumbha Festival

Nāsika is an ancient city predating the Vedic period. It is situated in the State of Mahārāshtra, India, on the banks of the Godāvari River, which is considered as holy in South India as the Gangā River. The land around Nāsika is of exquisite grandeur where Bhagawāna Rāma, Seetā and Lakshmana had spent most of the time of fourteen years of exile. Nearby is a famous pilgrimage center — Shirdi where thousands of people come to receive the blessings of Shri Sāi Bābā.

The river Godāvari descends here from a hill called 'Brahmagiri.' Nearby there is the 'Gangāsāgara' bathing pool into which the river Godāvari dribbles in, from its source. A bath in these waters is supposed to wash away sin. This is a city of temples. The most famous temples are:

Triyambakeshwara Temple near Nāsika is an ancient shrine dedicated to Lord Shiva where one of the twelve Jyotirlingas is enshrined. There is a belief that anybody who visits Triyambakeshwara attains salvation;

Someshwara Temple of Lord Shiva and Hanumāna is standing on the bank of the Godāvari River;

Sundaranārāyana Temple is standing on the west bank of the Godāvari. This Vaishnavite temple has three black Vishnu images. There are small carvings of Hanuman, Nārāyana and Indra on the walls;

Kālārāma Mandir has a deity of Lord Rāma in black color (hence the name Kālārāma Mandir). The temple is made of black stones and has a twenty-five meter high 'Shikhara' (tower). There are great festivities during Rāmanavami (the birth anniversary of Lord Rāma) and Vijayadashami (the anniversary of Rāma's victory over Rāvana).

It is believed that the elixir of life (*amrita*) is filled in a '*kumbha*' (pot) in '*Swarga*' (heaven). With certain combination of the orbital position of the Sun, the Moon and the Jupiter, the elixir falls from heaven to the earth, and the Kumbh Mela is held on those locations.

The legend is that the primeval ocean was churned by gods and demons, out of which emerged divine physician, Dhanvantri, holding the *kumbha* (pitcher) of *amrita* (nectar). As devatās (gods) and the asurās (demons) both lunged for the pot, Dhanvantri, transforming himself into a rook, flew off to the sky with the pitcher. On his journey that lasted for 12 days, he rested at four places — Prayāga, <u>Nāsika, situated at the banks of the Godāvari river</u>, Avantikā (Ujjaina) and Haridwāra, which were consequently consecrated by the drops of nectar that fell there. Hence Hindus consider these places sacred and believe that a dip in the sacred waters at these places, especially on an auspicious day, will cleanse them and their ancestors, back to eighty-eight generations, of all evil and sin, thus ensuring their salvation (freedom from the cycle of death and rebirth). The festival of Kumbha is celebrated at these four places after every three years in cyclic rotation; for example, at Prayāga in 2001 CE, at **Nāsika in 2004 CE**, at Avantikā/Ujjaina in 2007 **CE**, at Haridwāra in 2010 **CE**, and Poorna Kumbha at Prayāga in 2013 **CE**.

The most auspicious day for the bath at Kumbha is the day of the new moon. In Nāsika, it is celebrated in the month of Shrāvana (July-August), when the Sun and Moon are in Cancer and Jupiter is in Scorpio.

Hinduism's preoccupation with refinement and purification, physically as well as spiritually, leads to a great importance being accorded to the bath. The bathing, being a spiritual rejuvenation and reaffirmation, is a public act, performed in the open and by flowing water, ideally on the banks of a river or a stream, and includes a complete submergence of the body under water and an oblation to the sun.

Source : Kumbha Mela — wikipedia, the free encyclopedia

Rāmanāthaswāmi Temple

An overview of the Island

RĀMESHWARAMA
A Holy Place for Both the Vaishnavites and Shaivites

Rāmeshwarama is an island situated at the very tip of the Indian peninsula in the State of Tamil Nadu. This island is in the shape of a conch. From the prehistoric period, it is a center of the Hindu pilgrimage. Rāmeshwarama is the place from where Lord Rāma had built a bridge across the sea to rescue His consort Seetā, abducted by Rāvana, ruler of Lankā. According to the Purānas, Rāma, along with Seetā and Lakshmana, installed and worshipped the Shivalinga here to expiate the sin of *Brahmahatyā* (killing Rāvana who was a Brāhmana). It is one of the four *Dhāmas* (The Greatest of all Pilgrimages), other ones being Badreenātha, Dwārakā and Jagannāthapuri. The Hindu pilgrimage is considered incomplete without the visit to Rāmeshwarama. It is also the place where one of the twelve Jyotirlingas, called Rangalingama, dedicated to Lord Shiva, is enshrined as the presiding deity. Owing to these facts this place is a 'Teerthasthāna' (place of pilgrimage) for both the Vaishnavites and Shaivites. There are many places of worship here.

Rāmanāthaswāmi Temple: It was built and rebuilt over the period by many rulers. The present structure was completed in the 17th century. This temple is famous for its 1200 gigantic granite columns. The 54 meter tall 'gopurama' (tower), 1220 meter of magnificent corridors and the flamboyant columns embellish and render fame to the temple. It is interesting that the water in each of the 22 sacred wells in the temple has a different taste;

Agniteertham: One hundred meters away from the temple is Agniteertham, where Lord Rāma worshipped Lord Shiva, to absolve himself from the killing of Rāvana;

Gandamadana Parvatham: The imprint of Lord Rāma's feet placed on a *Chakra* (wheel) is found in this shrine, which is at the highest point on the island at 2 km from Rāmeshwarama;

Shri Anjaneya Temple: It is a celebrated temple of Shri Anjaneya (Hanumāna) from where Shri Rāma built a bridge to Lankā;

Kothandaramaswāmy Temple: It is the only salvaged part of the 1964 cyclone. It holds the deities of Rāma, Seetā, Lakshmana, Hanumāna and Vibheeshana who surrendered himself to Rāma at this place.

Tiruppullani: Outside the island, there are three other sites traditionally connected with Shri Rāma's expedition to Lankā. A big temple in Tiruppullani commemorates Lord Rāma's acquiring a bow and arrows to use in the impending war from its presiding deity; and also Varun's (Lord of the Ocean) submission to Rāma toward the bridge-building to reach Lankā.

* * * * *

Blessed are those who make their pilgrimages to all the four Dhāmas :
Badreenātha, Dwārakā, Jagannāthapuri and Rāmeshwarama.

The Main Temple

The Tapta Kunda

BADREENĀTHA
Abode of Lord Badreenārāyana — The Home of Jyotirmatha

Badreenātha, one of the holiest pilgrimages (Dhāma) for Hindus, is situated in the Uttarānchala Pradesha, India. It is regarded as a seat of Lord Vishnu in His aspect of Badreenārāyana. The shrine is located at an altitude of 11,248 ft, at the feet of two mountains named Nara and Nārāyana, with the Neelkantha peak providing a spectacular backdrop in the Himālayana range on the bank of *Alaknandā*, a tributary of the Gangā River. It is considered the most important of the four Dhāmas — other ones being Jagannāthapuri, Dwārakā and Rāmeshwarama, of the Hindu pilgrimages.

Badreenātha temple is the most important Vaishnava temple. It is believed that there is no other place that is as sacred as Badreenātha, nor shall there be. The temple has three parts — the *'garbha griha'* (sanctum), the *'darshana mandapa'* where the rituals are conducted, and the *'sabhā mandapa'* where devotees assemble. The complex features fifteen deities. Especially attractive is the one-meter high image of Badreenātha, finely sculpted in black stone. It represents Lord Vishnu seated in a meditative pose. The present Badreenātha temple was rebuilt by Ādi Shankarāchārya who also established the Jyotirmatha (also called Joshimatha) located nearby.

Badreenātha shrine evokes the most intense religious feelings. It is an abode of seers, saints and yogis from time immemorial. A devout Hindu makes pilgrimage to this place in his lifetime to attain *'moksha.'* Badreenātha is known as *'Tapobhoomi'* (तपोभूमि), a land of meditation and penance, and also as *'Bhoobaikuntha,'* heaven on the earth. Facing the Badreenātha temple is a hot water spring, known as *'Tapta Kunda.'* Other famous springs are the Nārada Kunda and the Soorya Kunda.

Other sites of interest are the temples of Nava Durgā and of Lord Narasimha. Apart from its paramount religious importance, this place is also unparalleled for its scenic beauty.

✳   ✳   ✳   ✳   ✳

**Blessed are those who make their pilgrimage to all the four Dhāmas:
Badreenātha, Dwārakā, Jagannāthapuri and Rāmeshwarama.**

Jagata Mandir at Dwārakā

The Main Temple

Rukamini Mātā Mandir

A brighter sky-view of the Temple

The Deity

Lord Shiva at Nāgeshwara Temple

Entrance Gate

Gomati River at Dwārakā Temple

The Temple Ghāta

DWĀRAKĀ
The Eternal Place
The Home of Dwārakā Matha

Dwārakā is one of the seven ancient holy cities situated on the banks of the Gomati River in the State of Gujarāta, India. This legendary city was the dwelling place of Lord Krishna till He ascended to heaven. Mathurā and Vrindāvana were the places of His childhood-days. Dwārakā has acquired multifarious names down the ages: Dwārakā — the gateway to eternal happiness, and Swarnapuri — the city of gold, as it was quite prosperous. Dwārakā is mentioned in the Mahābhārata, the Harivansha-Purāna, the Bhāgavata-Purāna; the Skanda-Purāna; and the Vishnu-Purāna. It is believed that, due to damage and destruction by the sea, Dwārakā over time has been submerged six times into the water and modern Dwārakā is the seventh city built in the area. The recent underwater studies conducted by the Archeological Survey of India reveal the existence of a city dating back to the 2nd millennium **BCE**.

It is one of the four Dhāmas along with Badreenātha, Puri and Rāmeshwarama. Dwārakā is also the site of Dwārakā Matha (also known as Kālikā Peetha), one of the four cardinal mathas established by Ādi Shankarāchārya, the other ones being those at Badreenātha, Puri and Shringeree. The Dwāraka Matha harbors extensive research work in Sanskrit and is home to many renowned scholars.

There are many temples in Dwārakā. Most of the temples and pilgrimage spots around Dwārakā are associated with Shri Krishna and the Vaishnava tradition. The Dwārakādheesha temple, dedicated to Lord Krishna, is the focal point of all pilgrimages. Some parts of the temple date back to the 12th-13th century and others to the 16th century. But the Jagata Mandir, its sanctum sanctorum, is estimated to be 2,500 years old. Here, the visitors enter through the 'Swarga-Dwāra' and exit through the 'Moksha-Dwāra.' However, the temple of Somanātha, which is not far from this place, is dedicated to Lord Shiva as Nāganātha or Nāgeshwara Mahādeva, and enshrines 'Nāgeshwara Jyotirlinga,' one of the twelve 'Jyotirlingas'. The present magnificent temple that was built in 1951 is a replica of the original temple, which was destroyed seventeen times by the Islamic invaders. Each time the devotees rebuilt it.

There are shrines to Rukmini, Trivikrama, Devaki, Jambāvati, Lakshmi Nārāyana and other deities as well. The Gomati Kunda is the most sacred pool where pilgrims take bath to complete the pilgrimage at Dwārakā.

✦　✦　✦　✦　✦

Blessed are those who make their pilgrimage to all the four Dhāmas :
Badreenātha, Dwārakā, Jagannāthapuri and Rāmeshwarma.

The famous Ratha Yātrā of Jagannāthapuri

The Temple

JAGANNĀTHAPURI
Abode of Lord Jagannātha, Brother Balarāma and Sister Subhadrā

Jagannāthapuri is an ancient city located 60 km from the city of Bhubaneshwara in the State of Orissā, India. It is said that the Hindu pilgrimage is incomplete without making a journey to this holy city. This place is called *Shri Purusottama Dhāma or Martya Vaikuntha*, the abode of Lord Vishnu in His form as Jagannātha on the earth. It is one of the four major Dhāmas, other ones being at Badreenātha, Dwārakā and Rāmeshwarama. It is also the home of Govardhana Matha (Peethama) established by Ādi Shankarāchārya. Jagannāthapuri is of special significance to *'Gaudiyā Vaishnava Sampradāya'* because the revered Vaishnava saint, Chaitanya Mahāprabhu, spent much of his time here. The famous āchāryās like Ādi Shankarāchārya, Rāmānuja, Nimbārka and, recently, in January 1977, Srilā Prabhupada, have made their pilgrimages to this holy city.

There is also a Gaudiya Matha established by Srilā Saraswati Thakura at Cataka-parvata where he resided and performed bhajana for some time. Here there are deities of Vyāsadeva and Madhvāchārya as well of Sri Sri Gaura Gopi Gopinātha.

Among the hundreds of temples located here, '**The Jagannātha Temple**' is the most sanctified one. The King Anangabheema Deva built the present temple in 12th century, replacing an original temple that might have been constructed about two thousands years earlier. There are three deities in this temple, namely, Lord Jagannātha, brother Balarāma and sister Subhadrā, whose images adorn the shrine. Since the deities are made of wood, the *'Navakalevarana'* — the ritual of deity transformation with new sanctified pieces of wood — is held in the month of *Malamāsa* (additional month) when falls in the month of *Āshādha* as per Vikram Samvat of the Hindu Lunar calendar. The previous such celebrations were held in the years 1950 **CE**, 1969 **CE**, and 1996 **CE**, respectively, and the next such event will be held in 2015 **CE**. The *Ratha Yātrā* during this special ceremony draws millions of people from all over India and abroad. There is also a sanctum of Satyanārāyana, Rāmachandra, and Narasimhadeva in the temple.

Jagannāthapuri is most famous for the annual *Ratha Yātrā* (chariot-trip) festival that attracts more than a million people from all over India. Images of Lord Jagannātha, Balarāma and Subhadrā travel on three gigantic chariots, pulled by devotees, over a short distance of three kilometer in a grand procession, to the Gundeecha Temple, and stay there for nine days before returning to Their Abode on the tenth day. The *Ratha-Yātrā* is a visible-living embodiment of socio-cultural-religious ethos of the Bhāratiya civilization. A glimpse of Lord Jagannātha on the chariot is considered to be very auspicious. The saints, poets and scriptures have repeatedly glorified the sanctity of this festival. Also, this event symbolically commemorates Shri Krishna's visit from Dwārakā to Vrindāvana. The concept of the chariot has been explained in the Kathopanishad in the following words :

आत्मानम् रथिनं विद्धि शरीरम् रथमेव तु।
बुद्धिं तु सारथिं विद्धि मनः प्रग्रहमेव च॥

Ātmānam rathinam viddhi shareeram rathameva tu
Buddhim tu sārathim viddhi manah pragrahameva cha.

—Kathopanishad (*Ch.3, Shloka 3*)

The body is the Chariot and the soul is the deity installed in the chariot. The wisdom acts as the charioteer to control the mind and thoughts.

✶ ✶ ✶ ✶ ✶

**Blessed are those who make their pilgrimage to all the four Dhāmas :
Badreenātha, Dwārakā, Jagannāthapuri and Rāmeshwarama.**

Vidyāshankara Temple

Shārdaṁbā Temple

The Goupuram of the Temple

Dhyāna Mandir

Vidyāsāgara Temple

Deity Shārdā

SHRINGEREE
Abode of Gods
The Home of Shāradā Peethama and the Āchāryās

Shringeree is a town on the banks of the river Tungā, in the Chikmagalura district of the Karnātaka State, India. It is 190 kilometers from the city of Mangalore. It is the home of the Advaita Vedānta Matha — Shāradā Peethama — one of the four mathās established by Ādi Shankarāchārya. The Advaita Vedānta philosophy is subscribed to the Vedic phrase "*Aham Brahmosmi*" (अहं ब्रह्मोऽस्मि), which means: "I am the Universal Spirit." The material world is considered as '*māyā*,' that is temporary and illusory. In Advaita tradition Shiva and Vishnu are one and the same. It is important to mention that Vishwarupa, assuming the name Sureshvarāchārya, became the successor of Śhankarāchārya before the latter resumed his tour to found other three peethamas at Puri, Dwārakā and Badreenātha, respectively.

Profoundly holy, scenic, peaceful and serene, this place is associated with Ādi Shankarāchārya, who left an indelible impact of his impassioned intellect and universality on Indian philosophy, poetry and ethics. Shankarāchārya enshrined here the goddess of learning, Shāradā. Since the inception of the 'Peethama', it is a home of intellectualism, humanity and grace. Shāradā Temple and Shāradā Peethama suffered mutilation at the time of Islamic invasion, but were rejuvenated since then.

There are many shrines and temples in and around Shringeree. Ādi Shankarāchārya established four temples for four deities as the protector of the Shāradā Peetham. They are Kālabhairava temple to the east, Durgā temple to the south, Anjaneya temple to the west, and Kāli temple to the north. The Janārdana temple and the Harihareshwara temple are also beautiful and well known. A grand '*gopurama*' is built to Shāradā temple. Every year during Navarātri, a grand festival is observed here. The goddess Shāradā is taken out in procession through the streets of the town. Thousands flock to the temple to witness this ten-day festival.

Shringeree overflows with life and brisk activities. Everyday one can find a celebration of some kind. Celebrations on a grand scale take place on days like Shankara Jayanti, Ganesha Chaturthi, Shivarātri, etc. The Rathotsavas (the chariot festival) of Shāradādevi, Vidyāshankara and Malahanikāreshwara present a grand spectacle of religious congregation.

The Ancient Ayodhyā

The Proposed Rāma Janambhoomi Temple

AYODHYĀ
The Birth Place of Maryāda Purushottama Shri Rāma

Ayodhyā is a very holy city and is an important pilgrimage site of the Hindus. This ancient city, the birth place of Bhagawāna Shri Rāma — an incarnation of Lord Vishnu — is situated on the banks of the holy river Sarayu in the Faizabad district of Uttara Pradesha, India. The Atharvaveda describes it as "a city built by gods and being as prosperous as paradise itself." The illustrious *Ikshvāku* of the *Soorya-Vamsha* was the first ruler of this region. Ikshvāku was the eldest son of Vaivasvata Manu, who established himself at Ayodhyā. The earth is said to have derived its name *'Prithivi'* from Prithu, the 6th king of the line. A few generations later came Māndhāta, in whose line the 31st king was Harishchandra, known widely for his love of truth. Emperor Sāgara of the same dynasty performed the *Ashvamedha Yajna* and his great-grandson, Bhageeratha, is known to have brought the holy river Gangā on earth by virtue of his penance. Later came the great Raghu, after whom the dynasty came to be called as *'Raghuvamsha.'* His grandson was King Dasharatha, the illustrious father of Shri Rāma, with whom the glory of the Raghu dynasty reached its pinnacle. The story of Shri Rāma has been immortalized by Sage Vālmeeki in the great Sanskrit epic Rāmāyana, and later by Sant Tulasidāsa in Hindi, and by many others in other Indian languages.

Several religions have grown and prospered here in the past. According to the Jain belief, five Teerthankaras were born at Ayodhyā, including Ādinātha (Rishabhadeva), the First Teerthankara. Skanda Purāna and some other Purānas rank Ayodhyā as one of the seven most sacred cities of India. In this city of Hindu temples, the most popular temples are as follows:

Hanumāna Garhi: Situated in the center of the town, this temple is accessible by a flight of 76 steps. Legend has it that Hanumān lived here in a cave and guarded Rāma's Janmabhoomi (Rāmkota). The main temple has the deity, Mātā Anjani, with baby Hanumāna seated on her lap. The faithful believe that all their wishes are fulfilled with a visit to this holy shrine. This is a massive structure in the shape of a four-sided fort, with circular bastions at each corner housing a temple of Hanumāna.

Rāma Janmabhoomi Temple: The oldest temple was renovated by King Vikramāditya some 2000 years ago. It was destroyed by the Islamic invader Bābar in around 1526 **CE** and a mosque was constructed on that very site — a visible sign of humiliation to the Hindus. Many attempts were made to reclaim the temple site but in vain. In 1992 some devotees of Lord Rāma demolished the mosque. Now a temporary temple structure stands and the worship of Shri Rāma Lalā is continuing. Presently, the plan to build a grand temple is bogged down in the bureaucracy of the Government of India.

Rāmkota: The chief place of worship in Ayodhyā is the site of the ancient citadel of Rāmkota which stands on an elevated ground in the western part of the city. Although visited by pilgrims throughout the year, this sacred place attracts devotees from all over India and abroad on the day of festival of `Rāma Navami' that falls on the *Vikram Chaitra Shukla 9*, the birthday of Lord Rāma.

Swarga Dwāra: Lord Rāma is said to have ascended to His Heavenly Abode at this site.

Tretā ke Thākura: This temple stands at the place where Rāma is said to have performed the *Ashvamedha Yajna*.

Nāgeshwaranātha Temple: This temple was established by Kush, the son of Shri Rāma. Legend has it that Kush lost his armlet while bathing in the Saryu River, which was picked up by a Nāga-Kanyā who fell in love with him. As she was a devotee of Lord Shiva, Kush erected this temple for her. This has been the only temple to have survived till the time of Vikramāditya; the rest of the city had fallen into ruins and was covered by dense forests. It was by means of this temple that Vikramāditya was able to locate Ayodhyā and the sites of different shrines. The festival of Shivarātri is celebrated here with great pomp and splendor.

❀   ❀   ❀

जय रघुनन्दन जय सियाराम ✳ जानकी वल्लभ सीताराम

The Dwārikadheesha Temple

A Ghāta of Vrindāvana

MATHURĀ
The Birth Place of Yogeshwara Shri Krishna

The city of Mathurā, situated on the banks of the holy river Yamunā in the State of Uttara Pradesha, India, is the nucleus of 'Vrajabhoomi,' the land associated with the pastime of Lord Krishna. It was founded by Shatrughana — the youngest brother of Lord Rāma. Every square-inch of this city is wrapped in timeless devotion to Lord Krishna, His brother Balarāma and His beloved Rādhā. The entire region resonates with Krishna's childhood and youthful adventures. The little towns and villages are still alive with the tales of His mischievous childhood, still seeming to echo with the sound of His flute. Each and every phase of Lord Krishna's early life, up to the age of twenty-eight when he moved to Dwārakā, is rooted in this region.

Once, this was a very prosperous region. It suffered heavily at the hands of invading armies. Mahmud of Ghazni in 1017, Sikandar Lodi in 1500, the Mughal Emperor Aurangzeb and finally Ahmad Shah Abdali, all plundered and looted the city. First Buddhist sites, then Hindu temples and other religious sites were destroyed. As a result, Mathurā went into oblivion until the resurgence of the 'Bhakti-Movement.' During this period, the Hindu rulers and rich merchants built temples, riverfront ghātas and other structures to revive the Krishna legend. Today, Mathurā is geared to the needs of pilgrims and tourism services, heavily steeped in the Hindu tradition.

Shri Krishna Janmabhoomi : This is the spot where Lord Krishna was born in Mathurā. A marble slab marks the original spot of birth in the Katrā Keshav Deo Temple at the site. The main shrine is inconspicuous; a narrow passage leads into a small room with a raised platform where beautiful pictures of the child Krishna adorn the platform and the story of his birth is written and also illustrated on the walls. A narrow set of marble steps lead to a terrace through a walled corridor, creating the effect of a prison while leading out.

Adjoining the Janmabhoomi complex is the Katrā Masjid, erected around 1656 on the site of the once-famous Keshava Deo Temple, which was destroyed by the Mughal Emperor Aurangzeb. This mosque is the visible sign of humiliation to the Hindus and is the cause for tension among the Hindus and the Muslims.

The Dwārikādhisha Temple : Built in 1814, with its temple carvings and fine paintings, it is Mathurā's most visited shrine and is beautifully decorated during the festival of Shri Krishna Janmāshtami.

The Geetā Mandir : Recently built on the Mathurā-Vrindāvana road — this temple has a magnificent image of Lord Krishna in its sanctum. The complete Bhagavad Geetā is inscribed on a pillar called the *Geetā Stambha*.

The Rangbhoomi : It is the site where Lord Krishna killed King Kamsa.

The Vraja Mandala Parikramā : This circumambulation of all the important religious and cultural places is undertaken in the rainy month of Bhādrapada when Lord Krishna was born.

There are many other places associated with Lord Krishna which are visited by the devotees. Most famous among them are Vrindāvana, Gokula, Govardhana Hills, Barsānā (famous for the Holi festival) and Nandagāon.

❖ ❖ ❖

मेरो तो गिरिधर गोपाल, दूसरो न कोई।

Shri Kāshi Vishwanātha Temple

Vārānasi Dasheshwamedha Ghāta

Another Vārānasi Ghāta

VĀRĀNASI - KĀSHI
ABODE OF LORD VISHWANĀTHA AND HIS CONSORT ANNAPOORNĀ
A Place of Divine Light and Moksha

Vārānasi is the oldest city, with recorded history of over 3000 years, and the holiest of holy cities in India. It is located on the banks of the river Gangā. This is the only city where Gangā flows from south to north. Once it was the great center of education and culture. This is the place where Ādi Shankarāchārya debated and defeated a renowned scholar, Pundit Mandana Mishra, on the interpretation of Vedānta, bringing a revival of the Sanātana Dharma.

The bathing in the river Gangā is a holy ritual. Therefore, for the convenience of the pilgrims, a number of ghātas have been built with long rows of stone steps on the banks of the Gangā, from the Assi ghāta to the Pancha ghāta. These ghātas have a great number of Yogis and Mahātmās meditating there. Thousands of people use these ghātas daily to take an early morning bath in the holy river Gangā as a sacrament. It is believed that any one dying on the banks of the river Gangā in Vārānasi attains *Moksha* (Liberation).

Vārānasi is the home of most ancient and holy temples in India. Each temple is unique and has a story to tell. The most famous among these temples are :

- ★ Sankata Mochana Temple
- ★ Kāshi Vishwanātha Temple
- ★ Rāma Mandir at Tulasee Ghāta
- ★ Tulaseemānasa Temple
- ★ Kedāra Ghāta Temple
- ★ Pancha Gangā Ghāta Temple
- ★ Vishwanātha Temple at Banārasa Hindu University

Sankata Mochana Temple: It is one of the most ancient temples. The legend has it that Pavana-Putra Hanumāna meditated at this spot. Hundreds of people visit this temple every Tuesday — the birthday of Shri Hanumāna — and offer their prayers.

Vishwanātha Temple: There are two Vishwanātha temples in Vārānasi. One is an ancient Kāshi Vishwanātha Temple, which was destroyed by Islamic zealots and a mosque stands on that spot, a conspicuous sign of humiliation for the Hindus. The relics of destroyed temple also stand side by side. It is believed that one's visit to Vārānasi is incomplete without visiting this temple, along with two **Bhairava Temples** that are regarded as the doorkeepers of the city. The second Vishwanātha Temple is built recently in the campus of Banārasa Hindu University. On the eve of Mahāshivarātri, thousands of devotees throng these temples for the Darshana of Lord Shiva.

There are many other celebrated temples where countless Hindu devotees worship and show their reverence to the Almighty.

हर हर महादेव ❖ हर हर महादेव ❖ हर हर महादेव

The Main Temple

Illuminated Somanātha

Pilgrims at Somanātha Mandir Sea Shore

Dehotsarg Teertha

Bhalka Teertha

Balrāmji Ki Guphā

SOMANĀTHA
The Seat of Jyotirlinga of Lord Shiva

Somanātha is an ancient pilgrimage held in great reverence throughout India. It is situated near Veravala on the Southern Sea-coast of Gujarāta formerly famous as *Prabhāsha* — a very prosperous city. It is the seat of the first of the twelve *Jyotirlingas* of Lord Shiva worshiped as **Kālabhairava Shivalinga** or **Bhairavanātha,** as mentioned in Prabhāsa Kānda chapter of the Skanda Purāna. The legend has it that Brahmā, one of the trinity, installed the *Brahmashilā* that paved the way for the construction of the Somanātha temple. Thereafter, the story of the city is the story of the Somanātha Temple — The Shrine Eternal.

Of all the shrines in India there is perhaps none other that symbolizes the undying devotion and aspiration of overwhelming large majority of the people of India as Somanātha does.

The glory and wealth of Somanātha was legendary. The original temple was decorated with gold and silver. In ancient times the temple was earning the produce of ten thousand villages. The deity of the temple is regarded as *Swayambhu* (Self-born). Hundreds of thousands devotees visited this temple and considered themselves blessed and to have achieved piety of their lives. Offerings of the devotees amounted to millions of rupees each day. Additionally, the Sun-worshipping foreigners and traders (including Zoroastrian Pārsis) also contributed a part of their profit to the temple treasury. Thus the treasury of the temple remained abundantly full at all times.

However, the Somanātha temple passed through a very tragic phase of history. In 1026, this fabulously wealthy temple was sacked and plundered by the Muslim invader Mahmud of Ghazni. The Shivalinga was smashed and 50,000 Brāhmanas slaughtered. The temple was demolished and a mosque was erected at its site. In fact, this state of affairs was repeated seventeen times by tyrannical Mahmud. But each time the temple was captured and demolished, it was regained by its devotees and restored to its full glory. In 1701 the temple was once again demolished and a mosque built on its site by the Mughal emperor Aurangazeb. Still, the remains of the temple withstood the ravages of time and survived the attacks of its destroyers. Even aged and desecrated, the temple weathered the Islamic assaults for centuries. The mosque, a symbol of humiliation to the Hindus till 1951, was finally replaced and the temple resurrected after India gained Independence in 1947. A new grand Somanātha temple was built at the original site under the direction of Sardāra Vallabhai Patel. On May 11, 1951, Dr. Rajendra Prasad, the-then President of India, re-installed the Jyotirlinga of Lord Shiva upon the same Brahmashilā on which the earlier temples were repeatedly rebuilt and destroyed. It was the day of great pride and rejoicing to the Hindus all over the world.

Somanātha will teach you volumes of wisdom: *Some of these old temples of Southern India, and those like Somanātha of Gujarāta, will teach you volumes of wisdom, will give you a keener insight into the history of the race than any amount of books. Mark how these temples bear the marks of hundred attacks and hundred regenerations, continually destroyed and continually springing up out of the ruins, rejuvenated and strong as ever! That is the national mind; that is the national life-current. Follow it and it leads to glory. Give it up and you die; death will be the only result, annihilation the only effect, the moment you step beyond that life-current.*
- Swāmi Vivekānanda

Vaikuntha Perumal Temple in Kānchi

Devrājaswāmy Temple at Kānchi

Kailāshnātha Temple at Kānchi

Kāmākshi Amman Temple Gate in Kānchi

KĀNCHI
The Seat of Shri Kānchi Kāmakoti Peethama

Kānchi is a city situated 74 Kilometers southwest of Chennai, India. This place is associated with Ādi Shankarāchārya who propounded the philosophy of Advaita-Vedānta (Monism) and with his successors who are keeping the torch of enlightenment ablaze even today.

More than 2500 years ago, an avalanche of non-Vedic religious practices threatened to wipe away the Sanātana Dharma when Ādi Shankara was born on the fifth day of *Vaishākha Shukla Paksha of Yugābda* 2593 (509 **BCE**) at Kaladi in Kerala, India. It is believed that Shankara was a partial incarnation (अंश-अवतार) of Lord Shiva to eradicate *Adharma* and to redeem *Bhāratavarsha* (India) from the clutches of *non-Vedic* practices. Also, in this city of Kānchi, Shri Shankara Bhagavatpada settled down at the end of his peregrinations and spent the evening years of his life in the *'Kānchi Peethama'* that he established on *Vaishakha Shukla Purnima* of the Yugābda 2620 (482 **BCE**). It is this city where this world-preceptor, Shankara, desiring to leave for his own abode, sitting in the *'Moskhapuri'* (Kānchi) attained eternal bliss *Sat-Chit-Ānanda*.

Thus the story of the city is the story of Ādi Shankarāchārya and the *Shri Kānchi Kāmakoti Peethama* that he established and helped build three principal temples, namely, of Shri Ekamranatha, Devi Kāmākshi and Shri Varadarāja Shankara. Also, the Shrichakra was consecrated before Devi Kāmākshi, thereby securing her bounteous grace for the devotees. *Shri Kānchi Kāmakoti Peethama* has a very distinguished record of propagating the Advaita discipline and alleviating the sufferings of the people. The Peethama runs hospitals at different places, which includes the Kāmakoti Child Trust Hospital in Chennai, Eye Hospitals at Coimbatore and Guwahati, hospitals at Madhubani (Bihār), Rathura for tribals (Uttrānchala), Berhampura (Orissa) and Hindu Mission Hospitals in many places in Tamil Nadu. The Matha runs shelter for the cows. A significant event in the history of the city is his occupying the *'Sarvajnanpeetha'* - the Throne of Omniscience at Kānchi.

Shankarāchārya mastered the Vedas, Upanishads and other Vedic scriptures before the age of sixteen, accepted the order of Sanyāsa and began his sojourn of India. During this sojourn he debated and defeated the scholars of that time, finally debating with the renowned scholar Pundit Mandana Mishra at Vārānasi. Thereafter, he was known as the greatest authority on Vedic-dharma, eulogized by later scholars as the greatest philosopher of his time. He was a discerning dialectician, a consummate commentator and celebrated poet. During the course of his peregrination he established four centers of spiritual awakening (*Mathas*) in four corners of India. These are *Jyotira Matha* at Badreenātha in the North, *Shāradā Peethama* at Shrigeree in the South, *Dwārakā Matha* at Dwārakā in the West, and *Govardhana Matha* at Jaganāthapuri in the East. These centers stand even toady as the symbol of national identity and unity. His miraculous achievements, within a short span of life of thirty-two years, speak of his super-human stature.

Kānchipurama is a celebrated pilgrimage. It is a city of temples. It is one of the seven sacred cities (*Mokshapuris)* by living in which or by death therein man gets liberation from rebirth. Five important sacred places in South India are collectively called "*Panchabhoota-Kshetras*" where Lord Shiva is worshipped in the Linga form. The Ekambareshvara temple of Kānchi enshrines the *Prithvi* (Earth-Linga), Jambukeshvara temple at Tirruvanaikava houses the *Apas* (water-linga), Arunachaleshvara temple at Tiruvannamalai has the *Jyotira* (fire-linga), Kalahastināthar temple at Kālahasti has the *Vāyu* (air-linga) and the Natarāja temple at Chidāmbarama enshrines *Ākāsha* (ether-linga). Kānchi is a center of literary pursuits and advanced learning.

* * *

The Buddha Stupa and the Ashoka Pillar

Vishwa Shanti Stupa

Buddha in Vishwa Shanti Stupa

Abhisheka Pushkaran (Coronation Tank)

Vaishāli Museum

VAISHĀLI
A Holy Site of Buddhist Pilgrimage

Vaishāli is a place of pilgrimage of the Buddhist, situated about 60 Kilometers from Patnā, the capital city of Bihār, India. It is bound by the hills of Nepal in the north and the river Gandaka in the west. Lord Buddha visited here after five years of his enlightenment and preached the *'Ratna-Sutra'* to the eighty-four thousand people who embraced Buddhism as the new teachings. Also, here the first woman — the foster mother of Lord Buddha, Mahāprajāpati Gautami — was admitted to *'Sangha-Order'* as a bhikshuni (nun).

Nearby is *'Kutagarshālā Vihāra'* where archaeological excavation revealed a Buddha-Stupa and the remains of Buddha monastery with an open courtyard and verandah. Among the precious archaeological finds is the relic casket containing the ashes of Buddha, now preserved in the Patnā museum?

It is in Vaishāli where, following a severe illness, Lord Buddha asked his disciple, Ānanda, to summon all the *bhikshus* (monks) for the last sermon. The Enlightened One told the gathering that his *Mahāparinirvāna* (departure from the mortal world) was imminent. He instructed the gathered monks to spread the *Dharma* in order to cultivate happiness among the people. Vaishāli also finds its mention in the Hindu epic, *Rāmāyana*.

A kilometer away is *Abhisheka Pushkarini* (the coronation tank). Next to it stands Vishwa Shānti Stupa (World Peace Pagoda). A small part of Buddha's relics found in Vaishāli have been enshrined in the foundation and *'chhatra'* of the Stupa. It has an excellent collection dating from 3rd century **BCE** to 6th century **CE**.

One hundred years after the *Mahāparinirvāna*, the second Buddhist Council was held in Vaishāli. The momentous results of this Council were the dispatch of missionaries to different parts of the world to spread the teachings of Lord Buddha.

Numerous references to Vaishāli are found in texts pertaining to both Jainism and Buddhism, which have preserved much information on Vaishāli and the other *Mahā Janapadas*. Based on the information found in these texts, Vaishāli was established as a republic by the 6th century **BCE**, prior to the birth of Gautama Buddha in 563 **BCE**, making it the world's first republic.

The republic of Vaishāli is the birth place of Lord Mahāvira (6th Century **BCE**) who spent 22 years of his initial years here. Vaishāli is also renowned as the land of Ambāpali (also spelled Āmrapāli), the great Indian courtesan, who appears in many folktales, as well as in Buddhist literature. Ambāpali later adopted Buddhism.

Ānanda, the favorite disciple of the Buddha, attained *Nirvāna* in the midst of the Gangā River outside Vaishāli.

Other sites of historical importance in Vaishāli include Chaumukhi Mahādeva, a lingama carved with four faces of Lord Shiva; and the Bhawan Pākhara Temple, where a large number of Hindu deities are enshrined at one place and are worshipped together.

Great Buddha Statue in Bodha Gayā

Mahābodhi Temple in Bodha Gayā

Thai Buddha Temple in Bodha Gayā

Bhutanese Buddha Temple in Bodha Gayā

Japanese Buddha Temple in Bodha Gayā

Tibetian Buddha Temple in Bodha Gayā

Inside view of Chinese Buddha Temple

Bodhi Tree at Bodha Gayā

BODHA GAYĀ
A Place Where Lord Buddha Attained Enlightenment

Bodha Gayā is the birthplace of the Buddhist Religion and is the most important Buddhist pilgrimage destination in the world. It is situated in the State of Bihār, India, about 65 miles south of the capital city of Patnā and about 7 miles from the city of Gayā. About 2,500 years ago, Prince Siddhārtha Gautama (born in 566 **BCE**) sat down under a '*Pipal Tree*' (now known as the Bodhi Tree) and received the ultimate knowledge of spiritual **Enlightenment** that would inspire one of the world's greatest religions. The followers of Buddhism recognize the tree as sacred. It was officially revered by the first great Indian Buddhist Emperor, Ashoka (268-232 **BCE**), who marked it off with a railing. The story of the city is the story of Lord Buddha and his teachings.

Guided by visionary dreams and following the ancient Hindu traditions in the footsteps of Krakucchanda, Kanakamuni, and Kashyapa, the Buddhas of three previous ages, Siddhārtha sat beneath the Bodhi Tree. Touching the earth, thereby calling it to witness the countless lifetimes of virtue that had led him to this place of enlightenment, he entered into a state of deep meditation. Three days and nights passed and his dream was realized. Siddhārtha became the Buddha, meaning the "Enlightened One."

There are four places known as *Chaturmahāpratihārya* — which are associated with Lord Buddha: Lumbini — the birthplace; Bodha Gayā — the place where he realized Enlightenment; Sāranātha — the place where he gave the first sermon, '**Setting in Motion of the Wheel of Truth,**' to his first five disciples and presented the Four Noble Truths and the Noble Eightfold Path — the basic tenets of Buddhism; and Kushinagara — the village where he achieved *parinirvāna* — leaving the mortal world, at the age of eighty.

Three months after the *parinirvāna*, five hundred of his chief disciples met in a cave at Rājagriha and, by common consensus, agreed upon what were to be considered the main teachings of the Buddha. The teachings were collected together into what came to be known as the **Tripittaka**, and they were handed down almost wholly by word of mouth till they were finally committed to writing in Ceylon (Sri Lankā) in the first century **BCE**.

From the very inception, Buddhism tended to be a proselytizing religion. As per the Second Buddhist conference after 200 years of the *parinirvāna* of Lord Buddha, the missionaries were sent far and wide for spreading the teachings of Buddhism.

This site is traditionally believed to be the holy place where the Buddhisatvas (meaning who achieved Enlightenment) of the three previous ages had also attained enlightenment. It is also the city of temples. The most famous is the Mahābodhi temple that is crowned by a Stupa containing relics of the Buddha. Inside the temple is an enormous statue of Buddha. In front of the Buddha image is a Shiva-Linga said to have been installed by the great Hindu sage Ādi Shankarāchāraya. The Hindus believe that the Buddha was one of the incarnations of Lord Vishnu. Thus, the Mahābodhi temple is a pilgrimage shrine for Hindus as well as for Buddhists. Behind the temple are the two most venerated objects of the Buddhist world, namely, the Bodhi Tree and the seat of Buddha's meditation, called *Vajrāsana*, which is now adorned with diamonds.

⌘ ⌘ ⌘

Durgiānā Temple

Durgiānā Temple Deity

Mātā Temple

Akāla Takhata

Jalliānwālā Bāgha

Death Well in Jalliānwālā Bāgha

AMRITASARA
The Home of Holy Shrine of the Sikha Religion — The Golden Temple

Amritasara is an ancient and legendary city. It is the home of the *'Swarn Mandir'* — The Golden Temple — the most celebrated pilgrimage for the followers of Sikha religion. The origin of the place where the Golden Temple stands is traced to the Vedic period in the form of *'Amrita Kunda'* (Pool of Nectar). According to popular belief, Sage Vālmeeki wrote his celebrated epic, the Rāmāyana, near this site. It was here that Seetā, the consort of Lord Rāma, stayed during the period of her *vanavāsa* (residence in forest). Here again, the twin sons of Shri Rāma were taught the Rāmāyana by Sage Vālmeeki. Yet another legend identifies the site of this pool with the place where the army of Shri Rāma was defeated by his sons, Lava and Kusha, and relates how at that time a jug of nectar descended from the heaven to restore the soldiers to life.

Vālmeeki's āshrama was within a short distance of the "Pool of Nectar." There were many more pools with historical significance. One such hexagonal pool, Rāma Teertha, is at a distance of about 1.1 kilometers from Amritasara. Other nearby pools include Rāmasara, Santokhsara, Rāma Talāi and Durgiānā. Guru Rāma Dāsa must have known the legendary importance of the place when he sanctified the 'Pool of Nectar' in the Sixteenth century.

The history of the Sikha religion is a turbulent one. Faith in One God, ten Gurus and the casteless fraternity of *Khālsā Pantha* are the hallmark of the Sikha religion. The Sikhas have a zeal for living. It is said that every Sikha looks upon himself as Savā Lākha, that is, equal to 125,000 enemies, in might.

Sikhas observe all important festivals celebrated by the Hindus of Northern India, namely Vasanta Panchami, Holi and Deepāvali, etc. Among the Sikha festivals, the birthdays of Guru Nānak Deva and Guru Gobind Singh, and the martyrdoms of the 5th Guru Arjun Deva, the 9th Guru Tegh Bahādura, and the two sons of Guru Gobind Singh — Fateh Singh and Jorāvar Singh — are celebrated with full zeal. The founding day of *Khālsā* has a special significance. One of the prominent features of Sikha celebrations is the *Guru Kā Langara* — the mass-kitchen of the worshippers.

The Sikha temple is known as a *Gurudwārā* — the gateway to the Guru. It is a binding duty of each Sikha to perform *Kara-Sewā* — selfless volunteer service. This endeavor represents the spirit of community service, which is considered very important in the Sikha religion.

The Golden Temple at Amritasara is the most revered site. The 'Pool of Nectar' surrounds it and taking bath in it is considered holy. Periodically, the pond is cleaned by performing *Kara-Sewā*. The entire community joins hands in the periodical cleaning of the Sacred Pool, a noble concept of service and community involvement.

First Sermon of Lord Buddha at Sāranātha

Dharamaraja Ka Stupa in Sāranātha

Sāranātha Ruins

Sāranātha Ruins

SĀRANĀTHA
A Place of Pilgrimage for the Buddha Religion

Sāranātha, six miles away from Vārānasi in India, is a holy place for the followers of the Buddhist religion. There is a 'Dhammeka Stupa" at Sāranātha where the relics of Lord Buddha are enshrined.

Although Siddhārtha Gautama attained the 'Enlightenment' — became the Buddha — on the 15th day of *Vaishākha Shukla Paksha* (*Poornimā*) in Vaishāli earlier, he chose Sāranātha to deliver his first sermon to the first group of five persons. They later became his first disciples. It was about 2500 years ago, he spoke of *nirvāna* (final liberation from the bondage of rebirth). This event is referred to as the *Dharma Chakraprivartana* — setting in motion the Wheel of Dharma. First, he preached that self-torture (extreme austerities) is as unworthy as a life of luxury for the seeker of the Noble Truth. Then he preached the knowledge of being un-reborn, ageless, diseaseless, deathless, sorrowless, undefiled, supreme liberation from earthly bondage. He declared "This is the last birth; now there is no more becoming, no more rebirth."

At Sāranātha, Buddha preached what he realized, namely, *Chatvari Ārya Satyanee* (The Four Noble Truths) and the *Āryashtānga Mārga* — the Eightfold Way.

The four Noble Truths that Buddha propagated are : **dukha** (misery), **dukha samudāya** (advent of misery), **nirodha** (restraint of misery) and **mārga** (the way that liberates from misery). Buddha pointed out that what causes anguish is desire (**Trishnā**) — the craving for possession and sensual pleasure. Abjuring desire is imperative for *nirvāna*, which is a complete cessation of Being and the supreme goal of the Buddhist endeavor. To attain this goal, Buddha prescribed the Eightfold Way that laid emphasis on **right conduct, right views, right intentions, right action, right effort, right mindfulness, right recollection and right contemplation.** Also, righteousness and compassion — **Karunā** — are deemed fundamentally important.

In consonance with Buddha's first sermon, the Holy Order, the Buddhist Sangha, was established where the members — monks — take the oath of joining the Sangha as :

Buddham Sharanam Gachchāmi
Dharmam Sharanam Gachchāmi
Sangham Sharanam Gachchāmi

I take refuge in the Buddha, the True Path and the Holy Order.

It is referred to as *tri-ratna* (three gems). Each monk is expected to be non-violent, celibate, austere and conscientious. A monk is a free member of a free community.

These basic norms were preached at Sāranātha which is, hence, a place of reverence and pilgrimage for the followers of the Buddhist religion.

❖   ❖   ❖

Vishnupada Temple Gate

Vishnupada Temple Main Hall

Another Gayā Temple Ghāta

Foot Prints at Gayā Temple

Women Performing Chhat Poojā

The Temple Ghāta

GAYĀ
The Ancient City for Performing the Last Rites

Gayā is an ancient city mentioned in the Purānas, Mahābhārata and in the Buddhist literature. It is situated on the bank of river Phalgu in Bihār, India. In the Purānas, it is said that this place of pilgrimage has been named Gayā after a good and great Asurā devotee of Lord Vishnu, by the name Gayā, who once lived there. It is accepted that one whose *Shrādha* (last rites) is performed in Gayā, he, after being freed of all blemish, goes to the *Brahmaloka*. Bhagawāna Rāma and Dharmarāja Yudhishthira performed the *Shrādha* of their forefathers at Gayā. It is a place for the paternal rites. The **Vishnupada** Temple is the principal place for the worship and worth-seeing. At a place not very far from this city sat Siddhārtha in meditation under a tree and received Enlightenment (bodhi) and became the Buddha, more than 2500 years ago. That place became known as Bodha Gayā. Thousands of Buddhists from within India and from abroad visit this place of pilgrimage every year to see this tree (Bodhi Tree) and the magnificent Mahābodhi Temple enclosing it.

Of Hindu pilgrims it is said :

जो गया को गया, वह गया।

Jo **Gayā** ko gayā, voha gayā.

One who pays homage to this holy city of Gayā, attains moksha, liberation from the cycle of birth and death.

Such is the acceptance (मान्यता) for this holy city.

✴ ✴ ✴ ✴ ✴

OUR SUPREME GOAL
ATTAIN MOKSHA — LIBERATION FROM THE CYCLE OF BIRTH AND DEATH

Ruins of Takshashilā

TAKSHASHILĀ
The Ancient Center of Learning and the First World University

Takshashilā was an ancient historical city in the North-Western Frontier Province of India. It was established by Bharata, the brother of Shri Rāma, in the name of his son, Taksha. Situated between the rivers Sindhu and *Vitastā* (Jehalama), it served as the second capital of the *Gāndhāra Janapada*. The ruins of Takshashilā can be found even today at a distance of about 30 km on the western side of the present day Rawalpindee and about 30 km northwest of Islamabad. Although the site of Takshashilā lies in modern-day Pakistan, it is revered most in India, especially by the Hindus and the Buddhists. It is revered by Hindus because the great strategist-intellectual, Chānakya, who consolidated and united the most of India into one empire, was a senior Āchāryā (professor) there. It is also revered by the Buddhists because it is believed that the Mahāyāna form of Buddhism was founded there.

It may be emphasized that the history of the city of Takshashilā is the history of the Takshashilā Vishwa-Vidyālaya (World University). This university was a well-known center of higher learning in ancient India. In the known history, world's longest lasting university that remained in operation continually for 1200 years was the Takshashilā University, established about 2700 years ago. It was the world's first university. The student body consisted not only of Indians but students from Greece, Syria, Arabia and China. Sixty-eight different streams of knowledge were on its syllabus. The minimum entrance age was 16 and there were some 10,500 students. Wide ranges of subjects (Vedas, Sanskrit language, grammar, philosophy, medicine, surgery, archery, politics, warfare, astronomy, astrology, accounting, music, dance, etc.) were taught. In that university, such great professors as Pānini (the great Grammarian of the Sanskrit language), Jeevaka (the great physician finding a great deal of mention in the Buddhist tradition) and Kautilya (Chānakya, the well-known author of *Arthashāstra* — a great work on economics — and a great political statesman who helped establish the kingdom of Chandragupta Maurya and the Magadha Empire) studied and taught at that university. Takshashilā did serve as a great center of ancient India's political and business affairs. The Greek historians Ariyan and Straton and the Chinese pilgrim Fāhiyān have described the excellence of Takshashilā.

Being in the Frontier area, Takshashilā shared a great deal of political importance. It had also to bear the brunt of foreign invaders' attacks from the North-West again and again. The attackers included Alexander the Great in 325 **BCE** and the Middle Eastern Islamic forces about 1500 years later. After the partition of India in 1947 **CE,** this unique center of Hindu culture and learning became a part of Pakistan.

* * * * *

Education is the most superior wealth.
The more one spends this wealth (by giving it to others), the more it grows.

NOTE IN HISTORY : *Pakistan is the country in the history of the world which was created by the partition of India on religious ground, causing death and destruction of millions of people. May God let such a tragic event never happen again!*

Ruins of Lālkot

Ruins at Mehrauli

Lakshmi Nārāyana Temple

Chhatarpura Temple

Red Fort

Jantar Mantar

Parliament House

India Gate

Present Day (Indraprastha - Hastināpur) Delhi

INDRAPRASTHA
The Capital of the Pāndavas

Indraprastha was an ancient city, about 5000 years old, of great historical importance, and situated on the banks of the Yamunā River. It was very close to the modern capital of India, New Delhi. It served as the capital of the kingdom of the Pāndavas, as narrated in the epic Mahābhārata. It came into existence as a result of a family dispute between Pāndava brothers and their cousins, the Kauravas, on the question as to who should inherit the kingdom. As a compromise, to avoid enmity, the kingdom of *Khandavaprastha*, a region northwest to the city of Hastināpura, was created for the Pāndavas. Indraprastha city was named as its capital. This was done so that peace might prevail. However, this peace was fragile and short-lived. In fact, the division between the Pāndavas and the Kauravas became the cause of the Mahābhārata War at Kurukshetra in which the Kauravas were summarily annihilated.

Following the Mahābhārata war in which the Pāndavas were victorious, the regions ruled by the Pāndavas and the Kauravas were united and Yudhishthira, the newly crowned emperor, retained Hastināpura as the capital. Since much of the historical record of ancient India was destroyed by the Islamic invaders, it is not known exactly what happened to Indraprastha after the Mahābhārata period. However, Indraprastha remained a major city for many centuries, from the time of the Maurya Empire to that of the Gupta Empire in India. But its importance steadily became less significant with the subsequent rise of cities like Pātaliputra that became the seat of India's two most powerful empires. Indraprastha did not play any significant role to leave any imprint in Indian history in the Middle Ages.

147

The Brahma Sarovar

कर्मण्येवाधिकारस्ते मा फलेषु कदाचन। मा कर्मफलहेतुर्भूर्मा ते सङ्गोऽस्त्वकर्मणि।।

Karmanyevādhikāraste mā phaleshu kadāchana; Mā karmaphalaheturbhoormā te sangostvakarmani.

You have control only over performing your own duty, but never over the fruit thereof.
Let the fruit of action never be your object, nor let your attachment be to inaction.

KURUKSHETRA
A Battlefield for the Establishment of the Dharma

Kurukshetra is situated in the present-day state of Haryānā in India. It is the most famous place where the battle of Kurukshetra took place between the Pāndavas and the Kauravas. Just before the battle started, Dhritarāshtra inquired from his charioteer Sanjaya :

धर्मक्षेत्रे कुरुक्षेत्रे समवेता युयुत्सवः। मामकाः पाण्डवाश्चैव किमकुर्वत सञ्जय।।

O Sanjaya, after assembling in the place of pilgrimage at Kurukshtra, what did my sons and the sons of Pāndu — desirous of a battle — do?

-*Shrimad Bhāgavad Geetā (Ch. 1, Shloka 1)*

Sanjaya narrated that a dialogue ensued between Shri Krishna and warrior Arjuna at the outset of the war. At the end of this dialogue, forming a crucial part, called the Geetā of the great epic the Mahābhārata, Sanjaya conluded this narration by saying:

यत्र योगेश्वरः कृष्णो यत्र पार्थो धनुर्धरः। तत्र श्रीर्विजयो भूतिर्ध्रुवा नीतिर्मतिर्मम।।

Wherever there is Krishna — the Lord of Yoga — and Pārtha (Arjuna) — the great archer there shall indeed reside prosperity, victory, glory and righteousness — that is my firm conviction.

-*Shrimad Bhāgavad Geetā (Ch. 18, Shloka 78)*

Such is the story of this great battlefield, Kurukshetra.

The narration of the great 18-day battle of the Mahābhārata, fought here in the ancient past between the Kauravas and the Pāndavas for the cause of the Dharma, brought Kurukshetra into great prominence. It was a war between the good and the evil, in which the righteous Pāndavas were victorious. It is the birth-place of the Shrimad Bhagavad Geetā, the Song Celestial — a divine message which Lord Krishna delivered to Arjuna on the eve of the Great War when He saw Arjuna wavering from his duty. It epitomizes all that is the best and noblest in the Hindu philosophy of life. The lakes called Jyotisara and Thanesara are near the spot where the sermon of the Geetā was delivered. In addition, many geographical names and personalities connected with Kurukshetra are found in the earliest Sanskrit literature, and many of the opening scenes of the drama of Indian history were enacted around this region. Most of the Vedic literature was composed here, and most of the social, religious and political traditions of this country arose in this region. It is, therefore, regarded as the cradle of Indian civilization and culture.

According to the Matsya Purāna, Kurukshetra flourished and became a sacred region of the Dwāpara age, eventually transforming into one of the sixteen *Mahājanapadas* of *Jambudvipa* — an ancient name for India. It was the region of lakes and lotus-beds, a feature seen even now. The great Sage Manu praised the prowess of the people of Kurukshetra. The Sanskrit poet, Bāna, describes it as the Land of the Brave. This place was visited by Lord Buddha and it appears to have been favored by his masterly discourses. Kurukshetra also finds mention in *Pānini's Ashtadhyāni*. It was also visited by nine out of the ten Sikha Gurus, Guru Angad Dev being the only exception. The place where Guru Nānak stayed during his sojourn at Kurukshetra is known as Gurudwārā Sidhbati. The gurudwārā dedicated to Guru Har Gobindji stands near Sannihit tank. Another gurudwārā near the Sthāneshwara tank marks the spot sanctified by the visit of the Ninth Sikha Guru, Guru Tegh Bahādura. Nearby stands the Gurudwārā Rājaghāta, built in the memory of the visit of the Tenth Guru, Guru Gobind Singh.

This region saw the rise and fall of many empires through centuries. The reign of King Harsha was the golden age in the history of India. The brave sons of this soil fought foreign invaders in the battlefield of this sacred land from time to time, and their exploits fill the pages of India's history.

Eradicate Evil * Establish Dharma Rajyā

PĀLITĀNĀ
A Pilgrimage Center for Jains

The Shatrunjaya Hill in Pālitānā, a small town in the state of Gujarāta, India, is famous for the beautifully-carved Jain temples. The architecture of the temples and the elaborate carvings on them are unique and an envy of the world. The town is an important pilgrimage for the followers of Jainism. It is a town of temples. From the base of Shatrunjaya Hill to the peak there are 863 temples. Each temple is a rival to the next for beauty and magnificence, presenting an awe-inspiring spectacle to the devotees and the visitors alike. The multitude of temples, little palaces and fortresses — all made of splendid marble, with their spires aiming the skies — present a spectacular view unmatched in scale and beauty. These were built in two phases during the 11th and 12th centuries as a part of the resurgence of temple building all over India. However, these temples could not escape the attacks of Muslim invaders and were desecrated in the 16th century.

The temples of Pālitānā were constructed in the north Indian architectural style, following the *Vāstushāstra* system of design. As the Jains often walk barefoot to their temples and cover their mouths with a piece of cloth to prevent inhaling tiny insects, the temples were built in groups making the pilgrimage easier and to give each temple an identity of its own despite being a part of a cluster. The Jains consider white color symbolic of purity; their temples too are usually white, embellished with a combination of plaster and marble. As a show of devotion to their Twenty-four Teerthankaras (Jain spiritual leaders), the temples were built depicting their lives in elaborate detail. The Jain temples are known for the artisan and the stone carvings. The most important is the *Chaumukha* Temple that has a four-faced deity of Ādinātha enshrined on a marble pedestal open on all four sides. It was built in early 17th century and is located on the northern edge of the hill.

Climbing on an ascending path to reach the summit of pilgrimage is an ancient Hindu and Jain tradition. This is why many of the holiest temples are located over hills and mountain ranges. The Jains have five separate hill locations for their holiest clusters of temples, Shatrunjaya Hill at Pālitānā being the most important among them. The temples at Pālitānā might not be more beautiful than the Ranakpura and the Dilwārā temples in Rājasthāna, but they have their own architectural style. Nothing can match the vision of a hillside covered with the spires of hundreds of temples, each stretching higher still, as if anxious to establish communion with the skies.

The peak of Pālitānā temple cluster is reached through a jig-jag route of 3 ½ km that has 3500 steps to climb. The cluster of over 800 temples is divided into groups. Throughout the cluster one can see beautiful and jeweled statues of deities in intricate detail. The sight of Sunrise behind the temples is a spectacular one. From summit one can enjoy views of the hills and the river Shatrunjaya below.

Every devout Jain aspires to climb to the top of the mountain at least once in his or her lifetime, because of its sanctity. The journey is arduous. For those unable to bear the strain, sling-chairs are available. The code for the climbers is rigorous in keeping with the spirit of the Jain faith. The descent must begin before evening, for no one is supposed to remain atop the sacred mountain during the night. No one, including the priest, is allowed to sleep overnight because the temple city has been built as an abode for the gods. Pālitānā temples are considered to be the most sacred. Such is the mystique of Pālitānā and the summit of Shatrunjaya.

* * * * *

णमोकार महामंत्र
१. णमो अरिहंताणं   २. णमो सिद्धाणं   ३. णमो आयरियाणं
४. णमो उवज्झायाणं   ५. णमो लोए सव्वसाहुणं
एसो पंचणमोकारो,   सव्वपावप्पणासणो।
मंगलाणं च सव्वेसिं,   पढमं हवई मंगलं।।

ॐ शान्तिः शान्तिः शान्तिः।

Chapter 6

सनातन धर्म निर्माता
THE ARCHITECTS OF SANĀTANA DHARMA
Glimpses of a Few Luminaries

A galaxy of luminaries — men, women and youth — worthy of praise and adoration, lived up to the ideals of their predecessors, following the principles enunciated in the Vedic scriptures, standing firm in their resolves to achieve the expected goals. The history of India — the home of the birth of Sanātana Dharma — is illuminated by such great men, women and youth who guided the society as towering light-houses by virtue of their ideal characters and deeds, and thus themselves became the architects of the nation's history and destiny. Many among them shine like stars. It is virtually impossible to recount the lives of all such luminaries, as India has produced them in rather generous profusion indeed. However, we attempt to offer brief glimpse of a select few of them, arranging their stories roughly in chronological sequence, that is, by the *Yuga* (*Sata-Yuga, Tretā-Yuga, Dwāpara-Yuga and Kali-Yuga*) of their appearance in the land we address as Bhāratavarsha. These are the people who are still inspiring millions of Hindus around the world.

A few words are in order to generally characterize the men, women and youth to orient the reader to their special qualities and contributions they made to the Sanātana Dharma and to the task of nation-building. In the following three Parts, each containing an introductory Section, are presented brief life-sketches of such illustrious men, women and youth.

Part I

THE MEN ARCHITECTS OF SANĀTANA DHARMA

From time immemorial, innumerable men have brightened the face of the Hindu nation through the light of their devotion to God, pursuit of supreme knowledge, chivalry in the battlefield, and service to the society at large, among other traits of uncommon nobility and superhuman achievements. In *Sata-Yuga*, first and foremost among such men, Emperor Bharata must be paid homage to. Son of King Dushyanta and Shakuntalā, Bharata, as a young child, showed his incomparable bravery by counting the teeth of lion cubs and grew up to lay the foundation of this nation which took the name 'Bhārata' after him. King Bhageeratha is credited with the great feat of bringing the river Gangā from the heaven to the Earth — a fitting allegory of channeling the sacred river from the Himālayana peaks and valleys down to the northern plains of India — for the salvation of the cursed soul of his forefathers. The sacred river is also called the 'Bhāgeerathi' after him. Then in the *Tretā-Yuga* came Vālmeeki, who was transformed from a wild hunter to a sage and became the very first poet in human history, gave us the first immortal epic, the Rāmāyana. This story of Maryādā Purushottama Rāma — an incarnation of Vishnu — who is popularly and reverently referred to as an embodiment of the epitome of idealism among men, has inspired, and will continue to inspire, every Hindu soul in every age.

Arjuna of the *Dwāpara-Yuga* will also be always remembered as an epitome of a devout person, yet with utmost bravery in war. He represents yoga incarnate under the precept of the Geetā, a precise gist of the universal principles of Dharma and Karma (action), of Bhakti (devotion) and Duty, propounded by the Vedas and the Upanishads and, of course, by the Mahābhārata, the great epic created by the sage-poet Vedavyāsa. Coming to the present age *(Kali-Yuga)*, the luminous characters, Ādi Shankarāchārya, Tulasidāsa, Kshatrapati Shivāji, Guru Gobind Singh, Chaitanya Mahāprabhu, Maharshi Dayānand Saraswati, Swāmi Vivekānanda, Aurbindo Ghosh and Mahātmā Gāndhi, among numerous other luminaries, have left their imperishable imprints on the sands of time. Glimpses of men such as these follow in this Section.

BHARATA
The Emperor of Bhāratavarsha
The Son of Mother Shakuntalā and Emperor Dushyanta

There have been five famous persons with the name Bharata. The first Bharata was a king and a devotee of Lord Vishnu and came during the life of Sage Manu. The second Bharata was also a king and a warrior; he was the son of Rishabhadeva (Ādinātha), the first Teerthankara of the Jain Sampradāya. The third was the son of king Dushyanta and mother Shakuntalā. The fourth Bharata was the brother of Shri Rāma, the son of king Dasharatha. The fifth Bharata was Bharata Muni, the famous pioneer author of *Nātyashāstra,* a basic treatise on music, dance and dramaturgy.

King Dushyanta belonged to the '*Chandra-Vansha*' and the *Puru* dynasty, carrying the name and the lineage of the famous king Puru. Among all the kings of the Puru dynasty, Bharata was the most valiant. His rule was extended in all corners of Bhāratavarsha. The ninth in the line of his descendents was king Kuru, whose descendants came to be known as the Kaurava(s) and Pāndava(s) of the Mahābhārata period.

According to a generally accepted view, the third Bharata, the son of Shakuntalā and king Dushyanta, who became the Emperor of this ancient land, is the one on whose name the country has been named as Bhārata or Bhāratavarsha, now known as Hindusthāna or India. Actually, the name India was derived by the Persians and the Westerners from the word 'Sindhu,' the name of the river on the western flank of the original (undivided) country that was Bhārata.

In childhood, Bharata was very fond of playing with animals. Fighting with ferocious tigers and lions delighted him. Riding on a lion's back had become his favorite game. He was so strong, valiant and fearless that he counted cubs' teeth, defying growling lions. Bharata ascended to the throne after Dushyanta and ruled the country with rare distinction, to the great delight of his subjects. He established rule of the law and unified the whole country and the neighboring regions, particularly in the east, to form the Greater Bhāratavarsha.

Emperor Bharata performed 55 *Ashvamedha Yajnas* on the bank of the river Gangā and 78 *Ashvamedha Yajnas* on the bank of the river Yamunā. He made victory tours in all directions (*digvijaya yātrā*), defeated the tyrants and *Mleksha* hordes (uncivilized and brutal clans), and eradicated the ruling tyrants from the soil.

Thereafter, he followed the Vedic tradition according to which every man, having finished educating his family, marrying his daughters to suitable husbands, arranging his business affairs in order, and establishing his sons, renounces the worldly affairs and retires to the forest in order to devote the remainder of his life in prayer and meditation toward the realization of God. Thus Emperor Bharata, the great nation-builder, too, finally retired to the forest.

BHAGEERATHA
A Legend of Unshakable Resolve and Sacrifice that Brought the Gaṅgā to the Earth

The great sacrifices of Bhageeratha relate to the descent of the holy river Gaṅgā from the heaven to the Earth. Bhageeratha was the grandson of King Sāgara, an ancestor of Lord Rāma, of the Sun-dynasty (सूर्य वंश). During the 100th *Ashwamedha Yajna* performed by King Sāgara, the horse that was sent around the earth as a symbol of victory did not return to his kingdom, as Indra, in an act of jealousy, kidnapped and hid the horse in the hermitage of Kapil Muni. The 100 sons of Sāgara with the entourage of warriors found the horse and, mistaking Sage Kapil to be the abductor, attacked him. An enraged Kapil Muni cursed that all the attackers be burnt to ashes.

Bhageeratha, one of the grandchildren of King Sāgar, hearing about the plight of his father and uncles, came to Kapil Muni and humbly requested how his ancestors' sin could be atoned. The sage advised that the waters of the river Gaṅgā would miraculously bring back the dead princes to life.

Bhageeratha resolved to bring Gaṅgā to the Earth from the Heaven to purify the ashes of his ancestors and bring them back to life. He performed severe austerities to please Lord Brahmā who came to bless him and grant him the desired boon. The Gaṅgā was allowed to come down to the earth. However, the force of its current was too great for the earth to withstand it. Fearing a catastrophe, Bhageeratha prayed to Lord Shiva, who held out his matted hair to catch the river as she descended. Hence, Lord Shiva is also known as Gaṅgādhara.

Thus, the Gaṅgā was then gently following Bhageeratha as he came to the hermitage of Sage Jāhnu's āshrama. Sage Jāhnu, who was in a state of meditation inside the āshrama, became disturbed. Enraged, he swallowed the Gaṅgā in a single gulp.

Now Bhageeratha offered his prayers to Sage Jāhnu who finally released the Gaṅgā. As a result Gaṅgā is also known by the name Jāhnawee. She is also called Bhāgeerathi as her coming to the Earth is due to the continued sacrifices and efforts of Bhageeratha.

Bhageeratha, a man of action, overcoming all the obstacles in the process, patiently led the Gaṅgā down to the sea from the Himālayas and offered salvation to the souls of his ancestors.

✳ ✳ ✳ ✳ ✳

✿ जय गंगा माता ✿

RISHI VĀLMEEKI
The Author of the Immortal Sanskrit Epic — the Rāmāyana

The great sage poet Vālmeeki lived in the *Tretā-Yuga*. He is regarded as the very First poet (*Ādikavi*) and venerated as the author of the immortal Sanskrit epic, the Rāmāyana. He depicted in this epic the life of Lord Rāma. This epic is known as the Shrimad Vālmeeki-Rāmāyana, and became the source of creative inspiration for many later poets and litterateurs. It narrates the victory of virtue over vice through the life-story of its illustrious hero, Rāma. It is believed that Vālmeeki was contemporary to Rāma and, therefore, Rāmāyana is an eye-witness-account, while others say that Rāmāyana is a 'smriti' penned from memory. It is generally accepted that Vālmeeki was also the author of the 'Yoga Vashistha' that discusses a wide array of philosophical issues.

Many interesting episodes of Vālmeeki's personal life have become popular legends. He was a robber and hunter in the early days of his life, known as Ratnākara. Rishi Nārada reformed him by inspiring him to remember, recite and meditate on the name of Rāma. He followed Nārada's advice and started meditating, sitting on one place, without even moving, for a very long time. Ants made a mound of mud-house around him, covering his body completely; hence the name Vālmeeki — meaning mud-mound of ant-house.

Once, as a hunter, he shot his arrow at a couple of curlew birds in loving embrace of each other, killing the male curlew. The female bird made a deep lamentation at the loss of her lover. On hearing this lamentation, compassion poured from the heart of Vālmeeki and sprang forth as a couplet of poetry, the first-ever poetic creation by man. Later, Vālmeeki used the same verse form called the *Anooshtupa Chhanda* in the creation of the Rāmāyana.

मा निषादप्रतिष्ठं त्वमगमयः शाश्वतीसमाः।
यत्क्रौश्चमिथुनादेकं वधीःकाममोहितम्।।

Ma nishādapratishtham tvamagamayah shāshwataeesamāh,
Yatkraushchamithunādekam vadheehkāmamohitam.

May you fall from grace as a hunter, for all the years, for killing one of the mates of the "Kraunch" bird couple, mating under the spell of passionate desire?

Hindus read the Vālmeeki-Rāmāyana all over the world with great reverence, as it gives the most authentic story of God-incarnate Shri Rāma who has left an indelible impression on our lives. It is as fresh and relevant today as it was during the time of Vālmeeki. It is one of the world's most momentous classics and in fact excels all classics in its moral appeal. This oldest epic, unsurpassed for its poetic excellence, inspired the later poets in almost all languages of India who, in turn, created epics depicting Shri Rāma's story in their own respective languages. One can say without the least exaggeration that the Rāmāyana and its versions in different languages, specially the Hindi Rāmāyana by Sant Tulasidāsa, was a great solace to the Hindus and actually saved the Hindu Dharma during the oppressive period of the Muslim rule in India.

✷ ✷ ✷ ✷ ✷

जय श्रीराम ❖ जय श्रीराम

ĀCHĀRYA DRONA
An Embodiment of Knowledge and Loyalty to the King

Drona was the son of Sage Bharadwāja*. Drona learned the scriptures and the use of arms under the guidance of Agni Veshya. Drupada, the prince of Panchāla, was also a student there, and became a close friend of the young Drona. Drona married Kripi, the twin sister of Kripa and the grand-daughter of Sage Gautama. They had a son named Ashwatthāma. But they were utterly poor. When the poverty became unbearable, Drona remembered his childhood friend Drupada, who was now the king of Pānchāla. However, when he went to the court of Pānchāla and tried to remind the king of his friendship, Drupada insulted him, telling him that friendship can occur only between equals.

Stung, Drona was going towards Hastināpura. On the way he found the young Pāndava brothers playing with a ball. By chance, it rolled into a deep hole in the ground. While Yudhishthira was trying to get it out, his ring slipped off his finger. The Pāndavas, having lost both the ball and the ring, were about to give up, when Drona, passing by, approached them. Drona was able to bring the ball out of the hole by making a chain of grass blades, and the ring with an arrow. The Pāndavas were amazed and invited Drona to the palace. On hearing about this episode, Bheeshma realized that this helper could only be the renowned archer Drona. Bheeshma welcomed Drona with open arms and engaged him as the principal teacher (Āchāryā) to teach the Pāndava and the Kaurava princes the art of warfare. Besides, Kripāchārya, Drona's brother-in-law, was already serving as a royal teacher.

As their graduation gift to him, Drona asked the Pāndavas and the Kauravas to conquer and produce Drupada before him as a prisoner. The Kauravas failed, but Arjuna succeeded in doing his bid. It was now Drona's turn to avenge and humiliate Drupada. However, Drona spared his old friend's life and kingdom.

Thirsting for revenge, Drupada performed a Yajna (sacrifice), and obtained a daughter, Draupadi (also called Yajnasenvi as she was born by performing yajna), who would marry Arjuna. King Drupada also had a son, Dhrishtadhyumna, who was to slay Drona during the Mahābhārata war. Despite knowing the purpose of the Pānchāla prince's birth, Drona accepted Dhrishtadhyumna, along with many other princes, as his disciple for teaching warfare.

In the battle of the Kurukshetra, Drona wished to remain neutral, but sided with the Kauravas, for the sake of loyalty to the royalty (King Dhritarāshtra). Because of this, his brother-in-law, Kripāchārya, also fought on the Kaurava side. After Bheeshma fell in the battle, Drona was made the Commander-in-Chief of the Kaurava army. He wreaked havoc on the Pāndava army. It was Drona who arranged the forces in his command in the 'Chakravyuha' formation in which Abhimanyu was entrapped and slain by treachery. Drona was later killed by Dhrishtadhyumna, the Commander-in-Chief of the Pāndava army.

---

* *Rishi Bharadwāja appeared in Tretā-Yuga as well. He advised Shri Rāma to make Chitrakoota as the place of hermitage during the fourteen-year exile.*

BHEESHMA
A Matchless Symbol of Loyalty to the King, to the People and to Others

King **Shāntanu** was a famous Chandravanshi (of the Moon-Dynasty) king of Hastināpura (present-day Delhi) in the *Dwāpara-Yuga*. He was married to the most beautiful lady, Gangādevi, who gave birth to a son Devavrata, also called 'Gangāputra.' However, Gangādevi left for the heaven before Devavrata could come of age. Therefore, he was raised under care of his father. He was taught the Vedas and the Purānas and also archery and learnt from his father how to rule the kingdom following the ideals of Truth and Justice.

One day Shāntanu, out on a hunting expedition, saw a very charming girl, Satyavati, the daughter of the fisherman Dashrāja. The king fell in love with her. He went to her father and offered the proposal of marriage with her. Dashrāja replied that he would agree only if the child born to her would inherit the throne. Shāntanu did not agree as he could not harm his beloved son Devavrata's future. However, in order to keep his father happy, Devavrata went to see Satyavati's father and vowed that for his father's sake he would neither assume the throne himself, nor ever get married, so as to ensure that only Satyavati's son would inherit it. Dashrāja then gladly agreed to his daughter's marriage with the king. King Shāntanu, hearing about his son's vow, was moved by his great sacrifice and said, "My son, yours is a **'Bheeshma Pratijnā'** — a vow of supreme greatness, severity and sacrifice. May you be known as Bheeshma hereafter? I grant you a boon: Death will not touch you until you give it your permission."

Time passed. Duryodhana, the eldest of the Kauravas (the sons of king Dhritarāshtra), was jealous of the Pāndavas, and not willing to yield even an inch of land to them. Even the peace mission of Lord Krishna could not change his mind. The war became inevitable. Bheeshma reluctantly decided to fight on behalf of the Kauravas — knowing fully well that they were on an unjust path — due to his unflinching loyalty to the state and to King Dhritarāshtra, the-then Head of the state. Bheeshma was appointed as the first Commander of the Kaurava army. The battle raged for 10 days without any sight of victory for the Pāndavas. Shri Krishna then advised Arjuna to make Shikhandi stand in front of him. Bheeshma stopped shooting, since Shikhandi was a woman in the previous life, and Bheeshma would not assail anyone so predisposed. Arjuna kept shooting at him till he felled Bheeshma. Arjuna's arrows piercing his entire body became a bed for him; but he still remained alive by virtue of his father's boon.

Within 18 days, all the warriors of the Kaurava army were killed and the Pāndavas became victorious. They went with Shri Krishna to pay their respect to their grandsire, still lying in the battlefield on a bed of arrows. They touched his feet and Bheeshma heartily blessed them, saying to Yudhishthira, "Even though I had to fight against you, I always loved you Pāndava brothers for your righteousness. Indeed, in my heart I always wished for your victory. *Protect Dharma and Truth as you do. Rule in the interests of the subject. May you all prosper?*" He finally chose to leave his earthly body, as per his own wish, when the Sun became '*Uttarāyana*' (north-oriented), an auspicious occasion for a good soul to depart.

VIDURA
A Unique Character Devoted to Total Selflessness for the Good of the People and to Dharma

The period of Mahābhārata dates back in the history of India to more than 3000 **BCE**. It was a period of turmoil that led to the great war of Mahābhārata. Among all the Mahābhārata characters, Vidura has a unique place. He was an embodiment of Dharma. He was the foster son of the king Vichitraveerya and thus the brother of Pāndu and Dhritarāshtra. He was very prudent, wise, polite, religious, and well mannered, and the Minister-Advisor to Dhritarāshtra.

Pāndavas were pious and always followed the path of Dharma. Kauravas led by Duryodhana were cruel, wicked and constantly planning atrocities against the Pāndavas. Dhritrāshtra had a great love for his son, Druyodhana, and, therefore, sided with him, even though the latter made a number of attempts to kill the Pāndavas. But Vidura helped and protected the Pāndavas in a very subtle way. During the course of Mahābharata, Vidura cautioned Yudhishthira repeatedly of the imminent danger and helped the Pāndavas to escape. Vidura tried his best to put his brother Dhritarāshtra on the right track, but in vain.

During the exile of the Pāndavas, Vidura addressed Dhritarāshtra, "O King, Artha, Dharma and Kāma (wealth, righteousness and pleasure) are received through Dharma only. Dharma is the pedestal of the state. Hence, you should protect yourself and the Pāndavas from the evil designs perpetuated by Duryodhana." On one occasion Dhritarāshtra called Vidura and sought the way for solace. The preaching which Vidura delivered at that time is known as '*Vidura Neeti.*' It is relevant even today. His advice was ignored. Alas! If Dhritarāshtra and Duryodhana had heeded to his advice, the terrible bloodbath of Kurukshetra could have been averted. The chance for the environment of peace and harmony worsened after the peace mission of Shri Krishna failed. The war became inevitable. For eighteen days in the battles that ensued, the great warriors on both sides were killed. But the victory of Dharma followed — the Pāndavas were victorious.

After the battle was over, Dhritarāshtra was in pain. Vidura consoled him by saying that events like comforts and miseries, crisis and fortune and misfortune etc. are due to the result of one's own good or bad deeds. Every living being has to bear the fruits of his Karma (deeds).

After the coronation of Yudhishthira, Vidura, accompanied by Dhritarāshtra, Gāndhāri and Kunti, retired to the solitude of the forest for their penance.

DHARMARĀJA YUDHISHTHIRA
An Embodiment of Righteousness

Yudhishthira was the eldest son of king Pāndu and mother Kunti. He was virtuous, righteous and well-versed in Dharma. He practiced all aspects of Dharma without fail and is referred to as Dharmarāja. He was an epitome of righteous conduct. Virtues like patience, stability of mind, humility, tolerance, kindness and love were his characteristic traits. Because of his courteous nature and good conduct, Yudhishthira and his four brothers, called the Pāndavas, were loved by all. But Duryodhana, the eldest of the wicked Kauravas, was jealous of them, always conspiring to discredit and kill them. Finally, the Pāndavas were given a tract of land called Khāndavprastha. Yudhishthira gladly accepted this compromise proposal for the sake of peace, and established a beautiful capital there called Indraprastha. There he organized the Rājasuya Yajna to unite the country. In a bid to humiliate him, the Kauravas invited Yudhishthira to a game of dice, where they cunningly defeated him and snatched everything from him including himself, his brothers and his wife, Draupadi. Later, Duryodhana once again trapped Yudhishthira in a second game of dice. The Pāndavas again lost and were given an exile for twelve years, to live in the forest. While in exile, a dialogue took place between Yudhishthira and a Yaksha (a superior celestian being) — this philosophical dialogue is an illustrious example of Yudhishthira's great wisdom.

Even at the end of the Pāndavas' exile, the Kauravas refused to return their kingdom. Yudhishthira was ready to be content with five villages only. But the Kauravas were not ready to give them even as much land as the size of a needle's point without war. The peace mission of Lord Krishna failed. Thus the stage was set for the great (Mahābhārata) war. The war began at the battlefield of the Kurukshetra and lasted for eighteen days. In the end the Pāndavas were victorious and Yudhishthira became the emperor of the land.

Yudhishthira ruled for many years. Peace and prosperity was established. Thereafter, Yudhishthira renounced the throne, entrusted it to Abhimanyu's son, Parikshit, and began his last sojourn for the Himālayas along with his brothers and wife Draupadi. On the way, Draupadi and all his brothers fell one by one. But he continued on his journey alone. Finally, Indra, the king of gods, appeared before him and offered him a direct passage to the heaven. He accepted the abode of heaven only after his brothers and wife were also granted the same gift, and subject to the condition that the dog, which had followed him from the very beginning, should also accompany him. Actually the dog was Yamarāja, the god of Death, himself, disguised to test his benevolence. Yudhishthira thus finally ascended to the heaven in his earthly body, a rare distinction for mortals of the earth.

* * * * *

धर्म की जय हो
अधर्म का नाश हो
व्यक्तियों में सद्-भावना हो

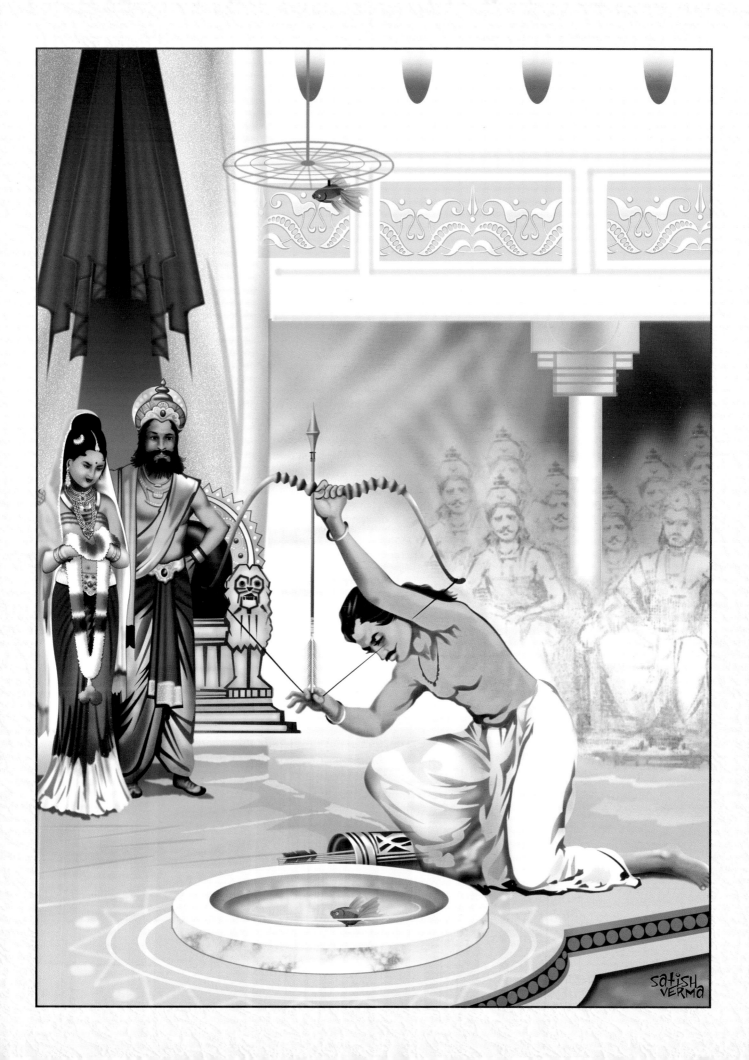

ARJUNA
A Symbol of Valor and Duty

The Emperor Pāndu had two wives, Kunti and Mādri. Kunti was the mother of Yudhisthira, Bheema and Arjuna; and Mādri, of Nakula and Sahadeva. These five princes were called the Pāndavas. Under the guidance of Dronāchārya, they received their education along with the Kauravas, the sons of Dhritarāshtra, learning the scriptures — the Vedas and the Upanishads — and practice of Yoga, Meditation as well as the art of warfare, particularly archery.

Out of all the Pāndavas and Kauravas, Āchārya Drona had greatest love for Arjuna, second to none in archery. This preferential love to Arjuna added to the jealousy and hatred wicked Duryodhana harbored in his heart against the Pāndavas.

Shri Krishna was interested in the marriage of Draupadi, his adopted sister, with Arjuna. But King Drupada, the father of princess Draupadi, put a condition that she would marry the prince who would pierce the eye of the rotating wooden fish atop a pole, just by looking at its reflection in a pool of water below. The *Swayamvara* (the ceremony of the bride herself choosing her husband) for the marriage was arranged. Among all the invited aspirant princes, Arjuna was the only one who succeeded in performing this feat, and Draupadi married Arjuna. Upon reaching home, he beckoned his mother Kunti to see what gift he had brought that day. Kunti, unaware of the incident, and without looking out, responded as usual to divide the gift amongst all the brothers. Her words could not be reversed. Shri Krishna came over and persuaded the Pāndavas to accept their mother's words as destiny and spiritually legitimate. Thus, Draupadi became the wife of all the five Pāndava brothers.

Once, during his self-imposed exile, Arjuna reached Dwārakā. Here, Balarāma wanted to marry sister Subhadrā to Duryodhana against her will. With Shri Krishna's approval, Arjuna eloped with her and they were married. The couple was then blessed with a son, Abhimanyu, who later played a very important role in the war of Mahābhārata. Arjuna also acquired many invincible weapons from gods during his exile that were instrumental in winning the war.

Just before the war was to start, Arjuna became very despondent at the sight of his kins, friends and elders ready to fight and kill one another. Shri Krishna dispelled the *moha* (attachment borne out of ignorance) of Arjuna, teaching him about the immortality of the soul and the paramount importance of performing one's duty following the path of knowledge (*Jnāna-Yoga*), action (*Karma-Yoga*) and devotion to God (*Bhakti-Yoga*). This dialogue is contained in the Shrimad Bhagavad Geetā that forms a part of the vast Mahābhārata epic. This most revered treatise on Dharma and the Hindu philosophy is a universal gift to humanity.

✫   ✫   ✫   ✫   ✫

Authors' Note : All of us have to strive for to be an **Arjuna** in order to grasp the depth of teachings of the **Geetā**. It would require of us to be physically strong and equipped with necessary **ability** to perform the task, mentally firm, optimistic and knowledgeable, and spiritually advanced. Knowledge alone is not enough. Yudhisthira had all the ethical knowledge, but was not adequately equipped in terms of the aptitude of action, in order to win the Mahābhārata war. It was only Arjuna capable of winning the war. But he was disheartened at the sight of friends and relatives in the ranks of the enemy; and **Shri Krishna** chose him as the recipient of the lessons of the Geetā to remind him of his paramount **duty**.

Most of us see an incident of injustice and terror, hear about a case of blatant oppression, read in the news or watch on television events featuring a murder of humanity, and even enjoy a movie on the cinema screen depicting realistic portrayal of ugly characters in politics, the police department and in the social arena, and then go about our life without a second thought or effort in the direction of how to root out these evils from our society and nation. Unless we act in a meaningful and purposeful manner, individually and as a group and people united in the cause of cleaning up the dirt amid us, our indulgence in just learning about them from the media or other sources would do nothing to improve our lives and to help eliminate the evil mentality and injustice.

णमोकार मंत्र

णमो अरिहंताणं

णमो सिद्धाणं

णमो आयरियाणं

णमो उवज्झायाणं

णमो लोए सव्वसाहूणं

एसो पंच णमोक्कारो,
सव्व पावप्पणासणो ।
मंगलाणं च सव्वेसिं,
पढमं हवइ मंगलं ।।

Last Sermon of Teerthankara Mahāvira

TEERTHANKARA MAHĀVIRA
The Apostle of Ahimsa

Lord Mahāvira, the 24th and the last Jain Teerthankara (Spiritual Master), was born in 599 **BCE** in the present State of Bihār, India. At the age of 30, he left his family and royal household, giving up his worldly possessions, including clothing, and became a monk. He devoted the next twelve years in meditation and 'tapasyā' (austerities), conquered his desires and feelings, and acquired knowledge and bliss, a state of perfection. He spent the next thirty years traveling, preaching and narrating his experiences of the Eternal Truth.

He inherited the mantle of Pārasanātha, the most widely acknowledged spiritual leader of his time, and other 22 Teerthankaras. He systematically consolidated the 'Shramana' doctrines which started with the first Teerthankara Rishbhadeva, and re-established the philosophy of ethics and science of life. Mahāvira preached the philosophy of optimism and non-violence (ahimsā) to monks of the Jain Order and the common men alike. He sought to emancipate the Indian society from the shackles of superstition and priest-craft and proclaimed the equality of men and women. He encouraged free discussion and dialogue. He proclaimed, "He who knows his doubts knows the world." He believed in the power of logic and thus reinforced rationality in faith. He allowed women to take 'dikshā' (spiritual initiation). It was a revolutionary step of that time. The tradition of Jain monks and Jain nuns is continuing that sustains the dissemination of Jain philosophy, ethics and religion. Mahāvira was a great social reformer, spiritual leader, and a teacher who built the edifice of Jainism and infused new life and vitality into the 'Arhata' tradition.

Personal equanimity and social equity were the fundamental tenets of Lord Mahāvira's teachings. He taught the people to evaluate and judge their own actions and take responsibility for them; this was his vision of a civil society. Lord Mahāvira did not accept that the world was created by an External Power. However, he believed in the existence of the soul, the importance of one's own actions and the principle of rebirth. He rejected the concept of divine incarnation. He advocated the principle that every soul has the capacity to achieve the highest enlightenment and the ultimate liberation. He believed that there is a higher consciousness within everyone. Those who transcend the limitations of the body and experience enlightenment, attain 'kaivalya'. Thus, in the Jain tradition the 'ātmā' (soul) becomes 'paramātmā' (Supreme Soul). Lord Mahāvira's teachings go beyond denominations and have a universal quality. He did not claim that salvation is possible only through his teachings, nor did he indulge in belittling the teachings of others. His approach was to understand the viewpoints of others in the spirit of seeking the truth in a peaceful, tolerant and non-violent manner.

It is of importance to note Lord Mahāvira's teaching recorded in two ancient Jain scriptures, "Uttarādhyāyana" and "Sutrakrtānga," where he declared, "Penance is my fire. My soul-awareness is the altar. My body, my limbs, my sense, my thoughts, my words and deeds are my instruments and implements for performance of the sacrifice of life for which my karma is the fuel. My vows are my 'shantipātha.' Such is the 'homa' by which I perform my sacrifice; such is the 'homa' which the seers, rishis have approved and extolled.... I bathe in the tranquil and transparent water of my purified soul to remove the dust and soil of my karma."

He taught that human salvation is possible through the *Right Faith, Right Knowledge and Right Conduct.*

✳ ✳ ✳ ✳ ✳

अहिंसा परमो धर्मः

ĀCHĀRYA CHĀNAKYA
The Architect of the Indian Nation, 2350 Years Ago

About 2500 years ago, India was going through a period of great instability. In India's long history, it was the time when the country was being ruled by many kings who did not see eye-to-eye and were fighting among themselves. During this crucial time, Vishnugupta was born as the son of Āchārya Chanaka, who was a great patriot and scholar of Political Science. Later, Vishnugupta came to be known as Chānakya. Āchārya Chanaka was fiercely outspoken about the ills of the reign of the King of Magadha, Dhanānanda, of the Nanda dynasty. He was falsely accused of treason and imprisoned by the king. He later died in the prison. Vishnugupta's mother also died from starvation.

Orphaned and destitute, Chānakya had to go through extreme hardship. He accompanied a caravan of merchants and journeyed from Magadha in the north-east of India to Takshashilā in the north-west. Takshashilā in those days was the greatest center of learning, not only of India but also of the whole world. He received his education in religion and politics at Takshashilā University. After his graduation, he was appointed as a Professor at the university. Chānakya inspired a cadre of dedicated disciples who later worked towards his mission of establishing a strong, united Bhārata (original name of undivided India). During this time, the Greek invader Alexander was attacking Bhārata. The kings in the country, however, were selfish, shortsighted and lethargic, fighting with each other rather fighting together against the foreign invader. Chānakya thus played a pivotal role of organizing the kings and people in the name of a united Bhārata. He tirelessly compaigned so that the nation would not come under the alien rule. In those calamitous times, he performed the momentous task of uniting most of India. He made India free from the alien rule. He visualized the potential of India as a great, prosperous and powerful nation. To achieve this goal, he helped establish a powerful kingdom under his chosen disciple, Chandragupta. In the process, the selfish and arrogant kings, including the king of Maghada, were dethroned and a united empire was established. Thus, Chānakya was instrumental in getting Chandragupta, founder of the Mauryan Dynasty, crowned as the emperor. Chandragupta's success as a king can be ascribed to Chānakya's advice and guidance. According to Chānakya, a king should take an oath of service to the people. If a king did not fulfill the trust and expectation of people, the people had the right to remove and replace him. After the Magadha Empire was firmly established under Chandragupta, Chānakya went back to teaching.

Āchārya Chānakya represents a multifaceted personality, exemplifying greatness in many different aspects of life. We can get guidance from his knowledge of '*Arthashāstra*' (Economics), of *Rāja-Neeti* (Political Science) and *Samāja-Shāstra* (Social Science). He wrote a book on economics and public administration known as Kautilya's "*Arthashāstra*." It discusses the rights and duties of a king, ministers and other authorities in a kingdom. It lays down detailed information and guidance on the various affairs of the State, of trade and commerce, of law, of war and peace, marriage, and of military strategy. Even today this book is considered an excellent treatise on political diplomacy.

✶ ✶ ✶ ✶ ✶

"Preserve with care the key of culture which connects man to man. For, I see that the politics of the states is wrecking man-to-man relationship. Therefore, now culture will have to bear this responsibility of politics. Culture will have to serve as the bridge, since culture is not a language, nor a caste, nor a religion."
- Āchārya Chānakya

The above paradigm holds even today for India and the world at large.

Chandragupta Maurya: The founder of 'Maurya Dynasty' that united and ruled most of India extending from Bengāl, Orissā, and Āssām in the East to Baluchistāna and Afghānistāna in the West. The two-hundred-year reign of the Maurya dynasty is considered as the Golden period in the history of India. In the top corners is the facsimile of postage stamp issued by the Government of India in commemoration of Chandragupta Maurya. In the corners below is the empire of the Maurya dynasty.

CHANDRAGUPTA MAURYA
Emperor of India and Founder of the Maurya Dynasty

*Chandragupta overthrew the Nanda-Dynasty of Magadha in 325 **BCE,** then conquered the Punjab in 322 **BCE,** and expanded his empire west to Iran. He is credited with having united all of India.*

Chandragupta belonged to a poor ethnic family in the present-day State of Bihār. He was intelligent and used to play childhood games dealing with public administration and justice. One day Vishnugupta (Chānakya), a professor of political science at the Takshashilā University, wandering in search of someone for his mission, happened to watch Chandragupta playing the game with other boys acting as the subject with Chandragupta as the king. Vishnugupta was greatly impressed and persuaded the family members of Chandragupta to allow him to take the young boy for his education at Takshashilā. Chandragupta received his education under the guidance of Vishnugupta who prepared him for the mission of uniting the land of Bhārata.

Chandragupta, under the guidance of Chānakya, organized a fighting force and defeated most of the regional rulers including Dhanānanda, the king of Magadha. He established the Maurya Empire with Pātaliputra (present-day Patnā) as its capital. This was the period when Alexander the Great of Greece invaded India. His army was defeated by Chandragupta who, on the advice of Chānakya, concluded a peace treaty with Seleucus, Alexander's Commander-in-Chief. Chandragupta married Seleucus's daughter for the sake of peace and harmony. The most important result of this treaty was that Chandragupta's fame spread far and wide and his empire was recognized as a great power in the western countries. The kings of Egypt and Syria sent ambassadors to the Maurya Court.

Maurya Empire was the largest and most powerful centralized State in the recorded history of India. It was very well governed, with monarchy combined with democracy at the city and village levels. Megasthenes, an envoy of Seleucus, visited the court of Chandragupta Maurya in Pātaliputra, and expressed his admiration for the efficient administration of the empire. His book 'Indica' is a collection of his comments and of other Roman & Greek travelers. Megasthenes wrote at length about the prosperity of the Maurya cities. He further reported that agriculture was well developed, water abundant, and mineral wealth was in plenty. Speaking of the general prosperity, Megasthenes wrote, "The Indians, dressed in bright and rich colors, liberally used ornaments and gems." He also spoke of the division of society according to occupation and the large number of religious sects and foreigners in the empire. Chandragupta died a few years later.

Chadragupta Maurya's son, Bindusāra, became the new Maurya Emperor by inheriting the empire which included the Hindukusha, Narmadā, Vindhyās, Mysore, Bihār, Bengāl, Orissā, Āssām, Baluchistāna and Afghānistāna. The empire lasted until 185 **BCE**, fifty years after the death of Chandragupta's famous grandson, Emperor Ashoka. The reign of Maurya dynasty is considered as the Golden period in the history of India.

✶ ✶ ✶ ✶ ✶

Victorious are those who believe in themselves.

RISHI PATANJALI
A Great Scholar of Many Talents

The biographical details of Rishi Patanjali are not well-established. However, it is said that he was born around 250 **BCE** in Gondā district of Uttara Pradesha in India. Like many other great rishis (sages) of Bhārata, his parental lineage and family life remains unknown.

He was a great scholar of many talents. He was a fountainhead of knowledge for the benefit of men afflicted as they are by time, existence and the workings of cause and effect. Patanjali not only acutely and accurately analyzed and discussed things of the present, but revealed matters of both the ancient past and the immediate and distant futures with accuracy and incisive penetration.

He is known as a great scholar of Sanskrit grammar (*Vyākaranāchārya*), teacher of life science (*Āyurvedāchārya*), and also of the Yoga-Philosophy (*Yogadarshanāchārya*). Patanjali produced his unmatched work on grammar for the sake of standardizing the use of speech (*Vānee-shuddhi*), on life science for the sake of treating the body (*Shareera-Shuddhi*), and on Yoga for the sake of purifying consciousness (*Chitta-Shuddhi*). Patanjali wrote his great commentary (*Mahābhāsya*) on Pānini's *Ashtādhyāni* and propounded the Yoga Philosophy by composing *Yoga-Sootra*. This *Mahābhāsya* is considered to be the most authentic work on Sanskrit grammar. In *Yoga-Sootra* he rendered the complete method of the current *Rāja-Yoga*, its results and its inherent principle (*Siddhānta*), in 194 *Sootras (formulae)*. In the text, the Sootras are presented in such a way that the four subjects usually connected with Yoga-study : **(i)** study concerning *Yoga-Sādhanā*, **(ii)** an acquaintance with the *Yoga-Siddhis* (powers gained through Yoga), **(iii)** discussion and explanation of *Samādhi,* and **(iv)** Yoga-Philosophy, are easily discernible.

According to Patanjali, yoga is a restraint of the tendencies of consciousness (चित्त वृत्ति निरोधः योगः). Without the restraint of mind (*Chitta*), one cannot establish oneself in its own being (*kaivalya*). For the achievement of this goal of yoga, the process called the Eight-Stepped Yoga (*Ashtānga yoga*) was introduced.

It incorporates :

(i) *Yama* (controlling of negative tendencies) **(ii)** *Niyama* (to cultivate positive practices) **(iii)** *Āsana* (regulating the body postures) **(iv)** *Prānāyāma* (controlling and regulating breath) **(v)** *Pratyāhāra* (turning the senses inwards) **(vi)** *Dhārnā* (concentration of thought) **(vii)** *Dhyāna* (meditation) and **(viii)** *Samādhi* (Sublimation to the spiritual Self). This science of yoga is one of the several unique contributions of India to the world. One can discover and realize the Ultimate Reality through yogic practices. The 84 yogic postures invented by Patanjali can enhance the efficiency of the respiratory, circulatory, nervous, digestive and endocrine systems and organs of the body. The Yoga Philosophy is one of the six philosophies discovered in India.

Patanjali was the family preceptor (Kula-Guru) to show the right path to the Emperor Pushyamitra of the Shung Dynasty, who promoted and protected the Vedic culture.

* * * * *

चित्त वृत्ति निरोधः योगः
Chitta Vratti Nirodah Yogah.
Yoga is a restraint of the tendencies of consciousness.

--Maharshi Patanjali

RISHI ĀRYABHATTA
The Great Astronomer and Mathematician

Rishi Āryabhatta, the great astronomer and mathematician, was born in 476 **CE** in the state of Bihār in India. His intellectual brilliance remapped the boundaries of mathematics and astronomy. In 499 **CE,** at the age of 23, he completed writing a textbook on astronomy and an unparalleled treatise on mathematics called *"Āryabhattiyama,"* in Sanskrit. In this book he gave the exact year of the beginning of *Kali-Yuga** as 3102 **BCE.**

In this book he described, in a very concise manner, the important fundamental principles of mathematics only in 332 *Shlokas* (verses). The first two sections of *Āryabhattiyama* deal with mathematics. The last two sections are devoted to *'Jyotisha'* (Astrology). In the first section of the book, he described the method of denoting large decimal numbers. In the second section of the book, we find difficult questions from topics such as Numerical Analysis, Geometry, Trigonometry and *'Beejaganita'* (Algebra). He also worked on indeterminate equations of Beejaganita. He is also acknowledged for calculating the numerical value of pi (π) = 3.1416 and for developing the sine-table in trigonometry. Centuries later, in 825 **CE**, the Arab mathematician, Mohammed Ibna Musā, wrote that this value of π (pi) has been given by the Hindus.

He formulated the process of calculating the motion of the planets and the times of eclipses. Āryabhatta was the first to proclaim that the sun is stationary and the earth revolves around it. He also proclaimed that the earth is round; it rotates on its axis and is suspended in space. This bold declaration came 1000 years before Copernicus published his heliocentric theory in 1543 **CE**. His work in astronomy became an asset to the later scholars. And above all, his most spectacular contribution is the concept of zero without which modern computer technology would have been non-existent. Unquestionably, Āryabhatta was a giant in the field of mathematics.

---

* Āryabhatta writes :

षष्ट्यब्दानां षष्टिर्यदा व्यतीतास्त्रयश्च युगपादाः ।
त्र्यधिका विंशतिरब्दास्तदेह मम जन्मनोऽतीताः ।।१०।।

"When the three *yugas* (*Sata-Yuga*, *Tretā-Yuga* and *Dwāpara-Yuga*) have elapsed and 60 x 60 (3,600) years of *Kali-Yuga* have already passed, I am now 23 years old." It means that in the 3,601st year of Kali Era he was 23 years old. Āryabhatt was born in 476 **CE**. Thus, the beginning of *Kali-Yuga* comes to be in 3,601 - (476 + 23) = 3,102 **BCE**. This is the year when Lord Krishna ascended to His Divine abode at the end of the *Dwāpara-Yuga*, and immediately followed by *Kali-Yuga*.

Thus in the year 2,008 **CE**, 3,102 **BCE** means 3,102 + 2,008 = 5,110 or approximately 5,000, which is generally taken as the period of Mahābhārata war or of Shri Krishna's appearance on earth.

CE is the abbreviation of Current Era.
BCE is the abbreviation of Before Current Era

JAGADGURU ĀDI SHANKARĀCHĀRYA
The Greatest Exponent of the Advaita Vedānta

Ādi Shankarāchārya was born at a time when Hinduism was passing through a period of chaos, superstition and bigotry. An avalanche of non-Vedic religious practices threatened to taint and erode out the Sanātana Dharma. Ādi Shankara was born on the fifth day of *Vaishakha Shukla Paksha of Yugābda* 2593 (509 **BCE**) at Kaladi in Kerala, India. After some controversy, the consensus on this date was arrived at the conference "*Akhila Bhāratiya Itihāsa Sankalana Yojanā*" held in Mumbai in December 2002. However, many believe that Shankarāchārya's life span was 788 **CE** - 802 **CE**. It is believed that Shankara was a partial incarnation (अंश-अवतार) of Lord Shiva to eradicate *Adharma* and to redeem *Bhāratavarsha* (India) from the clutches of *non-Vedic* practices. In a short span of his life, he re-established the Vedic Dharma and advocated Advaita Vedānta and restored it to its pristine glory.

His parents, Shivguru Nambudri and Āryamba, were very pious and religious. His father died when he was a child and thus he was left to the care of his mother. Shankara was a prodigious child and was hailed as '*Eka-Sruti-Dāra,*' one who can permanently retain anything that he happens to hear or read just once. He mastered all the Vedas and the six Vedāngas and related Hindu scriptures by the age of sixteen. Soon after, he persuaded his mother to grant him permission to renounce the material world and became a Sanyāsi. Āchārya Govind Pāda was his Guru who instructed him to proceed to Vārānasi and assume the role of a peripatetic teacher of the Hindu Dharma. Shankarāchārya wrote commentaries on the "*Prasthantraya*" and the Geetā, the Upanishads and the Brahmasootras, and established himself as the greatest exponent of the Advaita Vedānta.

The Advaita doctrine propagates the views that the bodies are manifold but the separate bodies have the one Divine in them. The phenomenal world of beings and non-beings is not apart from *Brahman*, but ultimately One with *Brahman*. The gist of the Advaita philosophy is that *Brahman* alone is real, and the phenomenal world is relatively unreal or an illusion. Shankara spread the tenets of the Advaita Vedānta, the supreme philosophy of monism (non-dualism), to all corners of India.

In the words of Swāmi Vivekānanda, "In Shankarāchārya, we saw tremendous intellectual power throwing the scorching light of reason on everything." In the short span of his life, he traveled all over Bhārata, revived the Hindu Dharma and regenerated Hindu unity on a spiritual and cultural basis even when the socio-religious fabric of the country was falling apart. He established four "Mathas" (Spiritual Centers) in the four corners of Bhārata; namely, Jyotira-Matha at Badreenātha (north), Shāradā-Matha at Shringeree (south), Kālikā-Matha at Dwārakā (west) and Govardhana-Matha at Jagannāthpuri (east). Each Matha was assigned to become the center for excellence in one of the four Vedas : *Atharva-Veda* (Badreenātha), *Yajura-Veda* (Shringeree), *Sāma-Veda* (Dwārakā) and *Rig-Veda* (Jagannāthpuri). These "Mathas" are still symbols of our Hindu identity and unity. The heads of these Mathas are considered our foremost Dharmāchāryas. It is believed that Ādi Shankarāchārya attained *Nirvāna* in Kedārnātha at the age of thirty-two.

✳ ✳ ✳ ✳ ✳

श्रीकृष्णं वन्दे जगद्गुरुम्

RĀMĀNUJĀCHĀRYA
The Leading Philospher-Saint of the Vaishnava Sampradāya

Shri **Rāmānuja** was a leading philosopher-saint of the *Vaishnava Sampradāya* (sect) and is known as one of the most dynamic characters of Hinduism. He was also a social reformer, displaying a catholicity that once was unparalleled in Hindu religion. He revitalized philosophy so much that nearly every aspect of Hinduism has been influenced by his work. His life and work show a truly unique personality, combining contemplative insight, logical acumen, catholicity, charismatic energy, and selfless dedication to God.

Rāmānuja was born in the village Tirukunnoora, about twenty-five miles west of Chennai, in India. His father, Keshava Bhatta, and mother, Kāntimati, were pious and virtuous persons. His date of birth is believed to be April 13, 1017 **CE**. Quite early in life, he lost his father. He was married at the age of seventeen. But he longed to devote life to worship and meditation. Rāmānuja became a Sanyāsi.

Rāmānuja received his early education from his *Guru*, Yadavaprakāsh, a teacher of *Advaita philosophy*, at Kānchipurama. Rāmānuja was a very brilliant student. Often he disagreed with his teacher's interpretations of Vedic texts and presented his own interpretations, to the delight of his fellow-students. Later, he got initiated into *'Vaishnavism'* by Yamunāchārya, head of the Shrirangama Matha, one of the three centers of the *Vaishnava Sampradāya*, the other two being at Kānchipurama and Tirupati, respectively.

Mahātmā Nambi initiated him in Shri Nārāyana Mantra, which was supposed to be sacred and secret for his own well-being and salvation. But Rāmānuja recited that mantra to all people for their benefit. Such was his compassion for others. He wrote commentaries on the Upanishads, the Brahmasootra and the Bhagavad Geetā. He also wrote three other books —*Vedānta Sāra* (Essence of the Vedānta), *Vedānta Sangraha* (An Anthology of the Vedānta) and *Vedānta Deepa* (the Light of the Vedānta).

Rāmānuja was the exponent of the *Visishtadvaita* philosophy (Non-dualism Qualified). It is also known as *'Sri Sampradāya.'* It emphasizes the concept of Brahman with tributes, according to which Lord Nārāyana or Bhagawāna is the Supreme Being; the individual soul is ***Chita***; matter is ***Achita***. Rāmānuja regards the attributes as real and permanent, but subject to the control of Brahman. Lord Nārāyana is the Ruler of the Universe and the *Jiva* is His servant. The Oneness of God is quite consistent with the existence of attributes, as the attributes depend upon God for their existence.

After Ādi Shankarāchārya, Rāmānujachārya can be said to have exerted maximum influence on the Indian masses through his philosophical doctrine of *Vishishthadvaita* or Qualified Monism. His long life was devoted in removing social inequality. He re-established the tradition of righteous conduct supported by the Scriptures, and of devotion (*Bhakti*). He lived a long life of 120 years.

The essence of his teachings is best summarized by his own prayer at the beginning of his Sri Bhāsya: *"May knowledge transformed into intense love directed to Sri Nārāyana (VISHNU), the highest Brahman, become mine, the Being to whom the creation, preservation and dissolution of the Universe is mere play, whose main resolve is to offer protection to all those who approach Him in all humility and sincerity, and Who shines out like the beacon light out of the pages of the Scripture (Vedas.)"*

The physical body of Rāmānuja is preserved even today in a sitting posture in all its pristine state unostentatiously, without any fanfare or publicity and without using any of the chemical preservatives, in the Sannidhi (Sanctum Sanctorum) dedicated to him on the southwest corner on the fifth round within the Shrirangama Temple, as ordered by Lord Ranganātha himself.

BHĀSKARĀCHĀRYA
The Most Well Known Indian Mathematician

Bhāskarāchārya, often mentioned simply as Bhāskara II, is probably the most well-known Indian mathematician of the Twelfth century. Bhāskara was born in 1114 **CE**, as stated in one of his own works. He was born in the present-day Vijayāpura (ancient name: Bijjadā Bida) in Karanātaka State of India. He was the head of the Astronomical Observatory at Ujjaina, India, that is said to have been founded by Varahamihira and Brahmagupta.

Bhāskarā wrote 'Siddhānta Shiromani' in 1150 **CE**. It contains four sections, namely, *Leelāvati* (arithmetic), *Beejaganita* (algebra), *Goladhyāya* (sphere/celestial globe) and *Grahaganita* (astronomy). His work on algebra, translated in several languages of the world, is considered unparalleled and is the testimony of his profound intelligence and eminence. In his treatise, *'Siddhānta Shiromani',* he wrote on the positions of planets, eclipses, cosmography, mathematical techniques and astronomical equipments. In his other treatise, 'Soorya Siddhānta,' he wrote on the force of gravity : ***"Objects fall on earth due to a force of attraction by the earth. The earth, planets, constellations, moon and sun are held in orbit due to this attraction."*** Some of his work was an extension or improvement of Āryabhatta's work of the Fifth century.

Bhāskara, without question, was a mathematical genius. We cite two typical examples of his work, which are of great interest and importance. He derived a cyclic ('Chakraval') method for solving equations of the quadratic form

$$ax^2 + bx + c = 0$$

It is usually attributed to William Brouncker who 'rediscovered' it around 1657. Bhāskara also provided a method for finding the solution of the equation

$$y^2 = ax^2 + 1$$

It is now called Pell's equation. Bhāskara's work in the Twelfth century can be listed as of historic importance. Much of his work came to be known to the Arab Mathematicians, and through them in Europe.

It should be noted that Bhāskarāchārya was the first to discover the law of gravitation, and not Sir Issac Newton, who rediscovered it 500 years later and is commonly credited for its discovery.

NIMBĀRKĀCHĀRYA
An Exponent of Dvaita-Advaita Philosphy

Nimbārkāchārya was born in the eleventh century **CE** to the pious parents, Aruna Muni and Jayanti Devi, who lived in Vaiduryapattanam on the banks of the Godāvari river in Andhra Pradesha, India. At birth, he was named Niyamānanda. He was a genius and mastered the Vedas, Vedāngas, Darshanas, and other scriptures at an early age.

The legend has it that Brahmā, the Creator of the Universe, came to the Āshrama of Aruna Muni, disguised as a Sanyāsi. Niyamānanda was in his teens. The Muni had been out. The Sanyāsi asked the wife of the Muni for alms. The Muni's wife remained silent as there were no fruits or roots to eat. The Sun was about to set and there was not enough time to prepare food before sunset. The sanyāsis do not take their meals after sunset. The Sanyāsi was about to leave when Niyamānanda said to him, "I shall bring quickly roots and fruits from the forest. I guarantee that the Sun will not set till you finish your meals." Niyamānanda placed his Sudarshana Chakra on a Neem-tree in the Āshrama where it shone like the Sun. In a few minutes, Niyamānanda returned with roots and his mother served them to the Sanyāsi with devotion. As soon as the Sanyāsi finished his meal, Niyamānanda removed the Sudarshana Chakra from the Neem-tree. It became pitch-dark. The Sanyāsi, who was really Brahmā, conferred on the boy the name *'Nimbārka'* (*Nim*-Neem tree; *Arka*-Soorya or the sun). Since then he was called Nimbārkāchārya. Shri Nimbārkāchārya is considered to be an incarnation of Lord Hari's Sudarshana Chakra (celestial discus).

Under the classification of avatāras (Incārnations of Lord Vishnu), Nimbārkāchārya is considered as an *Ansha-ansha avatāra* (Part of a Part-Incarnation) — like Shankara, Rāmānuja, Bhāskara, and Vallabha. Other Classes of avatāras are *Ansha* (Part-Incarnation) — like Jada Bharata, Nara Nārāyana, etc.; *Kala avatāras* (Epochal Incarnations) — Matsya, Varāha, Koorma, etc.; and *Poorna avatāras* (Full Incarnations) — Rāma, Krishna.

Nimbārkāchārya was the embodiment of mercy, piety, love, kindness and other divine qualities. He performed rigorous austerities at Neemagrāma, considered to be a holy place. It is believed that Nimbārkāchārya had *Darshana* of Lord Krishna at this place. Vrindāvana, Nandgrāma, Barsānā, Govardhana and Neemagrāma are the chief *Kshetras* (holy places) of the followers of Nimbārkāchārya. Parikramā (going around) of the 168 miles of Vraja Bhoomi, including a visit of the Shri Nimbārka's Temple in Neemagrāma, two miles from Govardhana, is their foremost duty.

Nimbārkāchārya was the exponent of the *Dvaita-Advaita* philosophy. Followers of this sect worship Rādhā and Krishna as the Primal or Representative Elements of the Divinity. *Bhāgavata Purāna* is the most important scripture. In this philosophy, jeeva (living beings) and the world (represented by Rādhā) are separate from, and yet identical with, Brahman, the Ultimate Reality (God), represented by Krishna.

Shri Nimbārkāchārya wrote: *Vedānta Pārijāta Saurabha,* a commentary on the Brahmasootras; a commentary on the Bhagavad Geetā; *Sadāchāra Prakāsh,* a treatise on Karma Kānda; *Rahasya Shodasi,* an explanation of the Sri Gopāla Mantra in verses; *Prapanna Kalpa Valli,* an explanation of Shri Mukunda Mantra in verses; *Prapatti Chintāmani,* a treatise pertaining to Supreme refuge; *Prātah Smarana Stotram* (प्रातः-स्मरण स्तोत्रम्), a devotional hymn; *Dasa Shloki* or *Kāma Dhenu,* the ten nectarine verses; and *Savisesh Nirvisesh Shri Krishna Stavam.*

Salutations and Glory to the Āchāryas! May their blessings be upon us all!

Source: Swami Sivānanda; www.dishq.org

✢   ✢   ✢

MADHAVĀCHĀRYA
An Exponent of Dvaita Philosphy

Madhavāchārya, a great religious reformer and an accomplished commentator on the Hindu philosophy, was born in 1199 CE at Valali, a few miles from Udipi, in the state of Karanātaka, India. His childhood name was Vasudeva. Madhava is regarded as an incarnation of Vāyu the Wind-god.

Madhava studied the Vedas and other scriptures and became well-versed in them. He was initiated into Sanyāsa in his twenty-fifth year of age by Achyuta Prakāshāchārya and soon after was made the head of the Matha (monastery) and received the name Ānanda Teertha. Madhava traveled throughout India to preach his gospel of *Bhakti* (Devotion to God). He wrote commentaries on the Upanishads, the Brahmasootra and the Bhagavad Geetā. He built several temples at Udipi — the main center of the *Madhava Sampradāya*. The followers of the *Madhava Sampradāya* try to make a pilgrimage to Udipi at least once in their life-time.

It is believed that Madhava had superhuman powers. He performed many miracles. Once he rescued a boat carrying the image of Lord Krishna from being capsized. On another occasion he stilled the waves of the ocean when he went to take a bath.

Madhavāchārya was a great exponent of the *Dvaita* (dualistic) philosophy of Vedānta. His Vaishnava teachings are called the *Sad-Vaishnavism* in order to distinguish it from the *Vaishnavism* of Rāmānujāchārya. According to Madhava philosophy, the Supreme Being is Vishnu or Nārāyana. The followers of the *Sad-Vaishnavism* have a firm belief in the *Pancha-bheda* Five Eternal distinctions viz, the distinction between the Supreme Being and the individual soul, between spirit and matter, between one Jiva and another, between the Jiva and matter, and between one piece of matter and another. He taught that the phenomenal world is real and eternal. The worship of Vishnu includes rituals: ***Ankana***, marking the body with His symbols, ***Nāmakarana***, giving the names of the Lord to the children, and ***Bhajana***, singing His glories. Madhava laid great emphasis on the remembrance of God (*Smarana*). He said, "Form a habit of remembering God. Then only it will be easy for you to remember Him at the moment of death." He prescribed rigorous fasting to his followers.

According to him, renunciation, devotion and direct cognition of the Lord through meditation lead to the attainment of salvation. The aspirant should equip himself or herself with the study of the Vedas, control of the senses, and with dispassion and perfect self-surrender in order to have the vision of the Lord.

Main source : The life of Shri Madhavāchārya — Swāmi Sivānanda

❋   ❋   ❋

VALLABHĀCHĀRYA
An Exponent of Shuddha-Advaita Philosphy

Vallabhāchārya, the founder of the *Pushti Sampradāya* (sect), who propounded the philosophy of '*Shuddha Advaita*' (Pure Non-Dualism), was born on the 11th day of Vikram Samvat 1535 (1478 **CE**) *Chaitra Krishna Paksha* at Champāran near Raipur in the State of Chhatisgarh, India.

Vallabhāchārya was a scholar, philosopher and devotional preacher in the Vaishnava tradition who wrote sixteen '*stotras*' (tracts) and several commentaries on the Bhāgavata Purāna describing the Krishna Lilā (Life of Shri Krishna). He is especially known as a propagator of the '*Bhāgavata Dharma*.'

He was a brilliant student who could recite hundreds of mantras, not only from beginning to the end but also in the reverse order. He commanded the study of the Vedas at an early age. He acquired mastery over the books expounding the six systems of the Hindu philosophy. He also learnt philosophical systems of Ādi Shankarāchārya, Rāmānujāchārya, Madhavācharya, and Nimbārkāchārya, along with the Buddhist and Jain schools of thoughts. He was regarded as an embodiment of knowledge and thus applauded as Bāla Saraswati.

Once a philosophical Samvād (debate) was organized at Vijayanagar between the scholars of Madhava and Ādi Shankara philosophies on the question whether the nature of God is dualistic or non-dualistic. Vallabhāchārya participated in the discussion considering it as a divine call. The discussion continued for 27 days. The vaishnavaites lead by Vallabha expounded the nature of '*Brahman*' better than the other group and became victorious. Everyone regarded Shri Vallabha as a God-send missionary. Vallabha was honored as 'Āchārya' and a world-preceptor.

Āchārya, the leader of spiritual preceptors, is the one who has written commentaries on the 'Brahmasootra,' the 'Bhagavad Geetā,' and the 'Upanishads.' Ādi Shankarāchārya, Rāmānujāchārya, Madhavāchārya and 'Vallabhāchārya' are only four in the Hindu culture so honored.

He gave discourses on Bhāgavatam at 84 places and explained the subtle meanings of the Purānic text. These 84 places are referred to as "*Chaurāsi Baithakas* (Eighty Four Conferences)." He used to stay in Vraja Mandala for four months each year.

When in Gokul, Vallabhāchārya pondered on the question of restoring people to the right path of devotion. He meditated on Shri Krishna who appeared to him in a vision in the form of Shrināthaji. He heard the command of self-dedication or consecration of Self to Shri Krishna. He dedicated himself to preach the message of devotion to God and God's grace, called '*Pushti-Mārga*.' Vallabhāchārya performed three pilgrimages of India barefooted and performed the initiation ceremony of religious rite by conferring on many '*Nama Nivedana*' mantra or '*Brahma Sambandha*' mantra. Thousands of persons became his disciples but 84 devotees are famous and are cited as the '*Chaurāsi* Vaishnavas'.

He was to remain a life-long celibate, but his spiritual master Vitthalanātha commanded him to marry and live a life of householder. His sons and descendants are known as 'Goswāmi Mahāraja'.

Vallabhāchārya strictly adhered to three rules:

- Not wearing stitched clothes; wearing only a simple white '*dhoti*' and a white covering (known as '*Uparano*') to cover the upper part of the body;
- Always performing pilgrimages barefooted;
- Always residing at the outskirts of a village.

जय राधे कृष्ण ◆ जय राधे कृष्ण ◆ जय राधे कृष्ण

✳ ✳ ✳

CHAITANYA MAHĀPRABHU
A Great Saint of Vaishnava Sampradāya

Shri Chaitanya Mahāprabhu, believed to be an incarnation of Lord Krishna, was born on February 18, 1486 (*23rd Phālguna Shakābda 1409*) in Māyāpura, Bengāl, India. His father, Jagannātha Misra, and mother, Sachidevi, gave him the name Nimāi on account of the 'neema' tree near which he was born. The neighboring ladies called the child Gaurahari on account of his golden complexion. His mother's father, Pundit Nilāmbara Chakravarti, a renowned astrologer, foretold that the child would be a great person in time; and he, therefore, gave him the name Vishvambhara. He was admitted to the school when he was five year old and quickly learnt the Bengāli language.

Most of his contemporary biographers have mentioned certain anecdotes regarding Chaitanya which are simple records of his early miracles. We may mention one event that may be called a miracle: When he was an infant in his mother's arms, he wept continually; and when the neighboring ladies recited '*Haribol*,' he used to stop weeping. Thus, there was a continuation of utterance of '*Haribol*' in the house, foreshowing his future mission.

In his eighth year, he started studying the Hindu scriptures and in the next two years, he became well-read in Sanskrit, mastered the '*smriti*' and the '*nyāya*.' Thereafter, he continued studying other texts at home. His brother, Vishwaroopa, became sanyāsi when he was ten years old. His father passed away some time later. At the age of 14 or 15, Chaitanya was married to Lakshmidevi, the daughter of Vallabhāchārya. Even at this tender age, he became known as a renowned scholar of the '*nyāya*' philosophy and Sanskrit. His wife died a short time later and he was remarried to Vishnupriyā at the request of his mother.

At the age of 16 or 17, he traveled to Gayā and took his spiritual initiation from a Vaishnava sanyāsi, Ishwara Puri — a disciple of Mādhavendra Puri. On his return from Gayā he started preaching Vaishanvism to spiritualize people. The āchāryās of Nadia believed that Nimāi Pundit is not only a genius, but also a missionary and a Godman. From this time to his twenty-third year of age, Mahāprabhu preached his principles and sang '*samkirtana*' in Nadia and in all important towns and villages around the city. His followers of the town of Nadia commenced to sing the holy name of Hari in the streets and bazaars. This created a sensation and roused different feelings in different quarters.

In the houses of his followers, he showed miracles, taught the esoteric principles of '*bhakti*', and sang his *Samkirtana* with other devotees. The world was astonished at his spiritual power, and hundreds of heretics converted and joined the *Samkirtana*. In order to fulfill his mission, he resolved to renounce the worldly life and became Sanyāsi, under the guidance of Keshava Bhārati, at the age of 24 years. Then he left for Jagannāthapuri for the spiritual enlightenment as per the wishes of his mother, rather than going far away to Vrindāvana. He did go on a pilgrimage to Vrindāvana and returned via Prayāga and Vārānasi. During the sojourn, he had discussions with many learned scholars and sanyāsis, including the very well-versed Prakāshānand Sarswati, who also became his follower. From Vārānasi he returned to Puri where he lived until his death on June 14, 1533. During the eighteen years of his residence at Puri, he preached Vaishnavism and 'nāma-samkirtana.' He composed a series of verses known as the '*Sikshastaka*' — *the Eight Verses of Instruction, containing his teachings*. His life was one of love and piety.

He preached *'Vaishnavism'* and *'Nāma-samkirtana'* throughout his life.

★ ★ ★ ★ ★

HARIBOL ★ HARIBOL ★ HARIBOL

The partial text material was provided by Vineet Chander of ISKCON.

GOSWĀMI TULASIDĀSA
A Great Scholar and Rejuvenator of the Hindu Dharma

Goswāmi Tulasidāsa, the greatest devotee of Shri Rāma, was born on August 10, 1497 CE in Rājapura village in the Bāndā district of present-day Uttara Pradesha, India. His father, Pandit Ātmārāma Dubey, and mother, Hulsi, were very religious. His parents died in his childhood and he had to go through a lot of hardships. He received his education under Shri Narahariji who narrated the story of Bhagawāna Shri Rāma to him. Spiritually inspired, Tulasidāsa became a devotee of Maryādā Purushottam Shri Rāma. To him Shri Rāma was not only an incarnation of Lord Vishnu, who, out of compassion for the humankind, descended to earth in human form, taking upon himself the trials and tribulations of human existence, willingly suffering ordeals to protect the virtuous and to annihilate the wicked; but also his only 'Ishta Devatā' to be worshipped. It is said that when Tulasidāsa was in attendance of 'Shri Krishna Poojā,' rather than be a worshipper of Shri Krishna, he said :

क्या कहूं छबि आपकी भले बने हो नाथ।
तुलसी मस्तक तब नवे जब धनुष वाण लियो हाथ।।

What can I say to describe your image — you are so good, O Master ! However, I, Tulasidasa would bow only to the One who bears in his hands bow and arrow (i.e., Shri Rāma).

Such was his unshakable devotion to Shri Rāma. In fact Tulasidāsa wrote — and the Hindus believe — that the *Rāmāvatāra* (Incarnation as Rāma) is the most luminous incarnation of Vishnu.

Tulasidāsa was a great poet. Despite being a Sanskrit scholar, he wrote in the people's dialect (Avadhi) of Hindi which was easily understood by the masses. He wrote several well-known spiritual and religious works of poetry, but he is best known for his famous epic "*Rāmacharitmānasa*" (the Life of Shri Rāma) that took two years and eight months to complete. This Avadhi classic was kept in the sanctum sanctorum of Shri Kāshi Vishwanātha Temple when the dispute arose whether the book in Hindi was acceptable as the word of God, rather the one in Sanskrit, the norm at the time. It is believed Lord Vishwanātha wrote the words '*Satyam Shivam Sundaram*' on the cover of the book, and it was accepted as the blessed one. Besides *Rāmacharitmānasa*, he also wrote the '***Kavitāvali***' and the '***Vinaya Patrikā***'. He also composed verses in praise of Shiva, Ganesha and Devi. These are classic Sanskrit compositions. His composition of '*Hanumāna Chālisā*' in Hindi is recited by masses on every Tuesday, the birth day of Shri Hanumāna. Tulasidāsa recited the *Rāmacharitmānasa* and ***Hanumāna Chālisā*** during his extensive travel in North India. This gave a new life to the Hindu society. Thus, by using the language of the masses, Tulasidāsa was able to restore life, strength and a new sense of pride in Hindu society which was being ruthlessly oppressed by the alien Muslim rulers at that time. He left his mortal body at the age of 126.

* * * * *

नाम राम को अंक है सब साधन हैं सुन।
अंक गए कछु हाथ नहिं अंक रहें दस गुन।।

The name of Rāma is the essence (of life), all other means are naught. If this essence is gone, nothing remains; but with the essence, the effects are multiplied ten times.

- Goswāmi Tulasidāsa

SAMARTHA GURU RĀMADĀSA
A Great Saint-Philospher and Proponent of the Hindu Nation

Samartha Guru Rāmadāsa was the 17th Century saint from Central India. Known as Nārāyana in his childhood, he was born on the Ninth day of *Chaitra Shukla Paksha* (Rāmanavami) in the calendar year 1530 of the Shālivāhana Era (1608 **CE**), on the banks of the river Godāvari in Aurangābāda district of present-day Mahārāshtra, India.

It is said of him that he was fascinated with the stories of Shri Hanumāna, and also that he had a vision of Lord Pānduranga Vittala as Shri Rāma. He became a great devotee of Shri Rāma, just as Shri Hanumāna was. Shri Rāma's declaration that one's mother and one's Motherland were superior even to heaven ("*Janani Janma-bhoomischa swargādapi gareeyasi*") touched his heart. His love for his mother and motherland, Bhāratavarsha, overflowed his mind. He took the vow of 'celibacy-for-life' and to create an environment for the establishment of '*Dharma-Rājya.*' This resolve helped him in guiding Shivāji to bring back the lost glory to Hinduism.

With the vow of celibacy, he undertook penance for 12 years at Panchavati, a sacred place where in the *Tretā-Yuga*, Shri Rāmachandra, Seetā and Lakshmana had spent their days during the fourteen-year exile. He traveled throughout India, deeply observing the prevailing conditions of the people. He engaged himself in the task of social and religious upliftment. He conveyed the message of adopting the philosophy of '*Karma-Yoga*' to the Hindus, reeling under the attacks of the alien anti-Dharma forces, to become competent (समर्थ), agile (स्फूर्त) and brilliant (तेजस्वी).

Shivāji was at the time faced with similar situation. Guru Rāmadāsa happened to meet Shivāji, and became the guiding spirit (*guru*) to Kshatrapati Shivāji. He advised Shivāji for the establishment of Dharma in the service of God and the Hindu society. Shivāji followed this advice to the letter. Once, Guru Rāmadāsa advised Shivāji: "Put down mercilessly those who rebel against you. Leave no work half-done. What is the use of being a coward? One who cannot face danger is not a soldier. Courage is the stepping-stone to success. Go ahead with your task in the name of God." Another time his advice was: "Lead a pure life. First you owe a duty to your family and to your Motherland. Then alone should you turn your thoughts towards *Moksha.*"

Shivāji led formidable resistance against the iconoclastic tyrant, Aurangazeb, and thus helped to establish an Independent (free from Mughal dominance) Hindu self-government ('*Hindavi Swarājya*') based on the ideals of the Sanātana Dharma.

He popularized and gave new interpretation to the devotional worship by removing the dependency upon elaborate '*Brahmanical*' rituals. He inspired the Hindus to shun off their weakness by preaching the worship of the Bow-Arrow-Wielding Bhagawāna Shri Rāma and invoking the invincible strength of Shri Hanumāna as a part of mainstream culture throughout India. He established more than one thousand hermitages (*Matha*), each one having an *Akhārā* (wrestling-arena) for physical exercises, to make the people physically fit, strong and healthy with a view to inculcate the message of Shakti-Poojā (veneration to the goddess of righteous strength).

His poetic creation, *Dāsabodha,* provides guidance for achieving the spiritual goal as well as for living the worldly life rationally and effectively.

✳   ✳   ✳

Call of the Hindu Dharmāchārya : Establish Dharma - Rājya

KSHATRAPATI MAHĀRĀJA SHIVĀJI
A Foresighted General and Founder of the Hindu Nation

Shivāji founded the Hindu kingdom against all odds, fighting against the mighty power of the Mughals. At the age of 16, he took a pledge to establish a sovereign Hindu Nation dedicated to the high ideals of the Hindu Dharma. He inspired and united the common man to fight against the tyranny of the alien ruler Aurangzeb, by inculcating a sense of pride and nationality in them. He lived an exemplary life shaped by the principles of the Hindu Dharma and is thus respected by the entire cross-section of Indians. He matched cunning against cunning, courage against courage; he was one of the wisest rulers as he was one of the Greatest Generals.

He was born on February 19, 1630 at Shivaneri in the present-day State of Mahārāshtra, India. His father, Shāhaji, was serving in the court of Sultan of Beejāpura. His mother, Jijābai, was a very religious woman who taught Shivāji about Hindu Dharma and the predicament of the Hindu society under the foreign Muslim invaders, and prepared Shivāji to face what was to come. Shivāji thought ahead of times and was a true visionary. In his private life, his moral values were exceptionally high. His thoughts and deeds were inspired by the teachings of his mother Jijābai, teacher Dādāji Kond Dev, great saints like Jnaaneshwara and Tukārāma, and the valiancy and ideals of Bhagawāna Shri Rāma and Yogeshwara Krishna. Last but not the least; Shivāji was also given the requisite guidance by Samarth Guru Rāmadāsa.

Shivāji invented and used the technique of guerillā warfare and fought very effectively against the large armies of the Muslim rulers and thus expanded his kingdom. He captured most of South India and established "*Hindavi Swarāja*" (Hindu Rāshtra). This was the first Hindu Empire after the fall of Prithvirāja Chauhāna five hundred years earlier. He raised a strong army and navy, constructed and repaired forts, developed a strong intelligence network, gave equal treatment to the people of all religions and castes, based on merit, and functioned like a seasoned Statesman and General. He appointed ministers with specific functions such as Internal Security, Foreign Affairs, Finance, Law and Justice, Religious matters, and Defense. He provided the best of governance to his subjects.

He distributed the land for agriculture to those who were in need, and thus the ownership of land was transferred from the few to the many. This private ownership brought prosperity in the kingdom. Shivāji gave religious freedom to all. He gathered the views of his subjects on various matters concerning the administration of the State and used them to guide his rule which gained him the confidence and respect of the people. By providing an exemplary administration guided by the Hindu values, he established himself as an ideal king devoted to Dharma and the service of the people. Thus he saved the Hindu heritage and '*Hindu Rāshtra*' from the onslaught of the Mughals. Shivāji ruled until he passed away on April 3, 1680.

Shivāji has been a source of inspiration and pride to the past generations of Hindus, and will continue to inspire generations in future.

✶ ✶ ✶ ✶ ✶

PRICELESS JEWELS OF HUMAN LIFE
Obedience • Benevolence • Bravery • Honesty

GURU GOBIND SINGH
An Enlightened Teacher, Great Soldier and the Protector of Hindu Dharma

Guru Gobind Singh, like the previous Sikha Gurus, was an 'Enlightened' person who dispelled delusion and brought awareness among the masses. He was born on December 22, 1666 when his father, Guru Tegh Bahādura, the Ninth Guru, was touring the eastern provinces of India. His father was beheaded by the order of Aurangzeb, for refusing to accept Islāma. He was taken care of by his mother Gujariji. On November 18, 1675 he was anointed as the Tenth Guru. At such an early age, he accepted the responsibility of guiding the followers to the teachings of the previous Gurus: *Oneness of mankind, love and worship of God, self-awakening, freedom from temporal ties, glory to religion, welfare of others, and valor*. However, the Hindus were being forced to accept Islāma and those who refused were being tortured to death. Guru Gobind Singh faced the reality head-on and organized his followers into a new kind of army called '*Khālsā*' to face the oppressive tactics of the Muslim ruler. His life was devoted to fighting the evil forces of Aurangzeb. Wars and self-sacrifice for Dharma became the norms of his life. Even during this period of turmoil, he did not deviate from the mission of unity, equality, compassion, love, and virtuous deeds. In the Khālsā Pantha (meaning 'the Path of the Pious One) he created, all the members were soldiers motivated to follow the path of righteousness. Guru Gobind Singh declared the aim of his birth as follows :

या ही काज धरा हम जन्मे, समझ लेहु साध सब मनमें।
धरम चलावन, संत उबारन, दुष्ट सभी को मूल उबारन।।

Let all bear in mind that I am born on this earth for just one purpose : to extol Dharma, to protect the righteous, and to uproot all the wicked.

His first disciples in the Khālsā Pantha, the "Panja Piāre" (the Five Dear Ones), were the embodiment of national unity as they came from the five corners of the country: Lāhore, Meerut, Karnātaka, Dwārakā and Jagannāthpuri. Guru Gobind Singh initiated them and then himself initiated by partaking of a "Prasādam" (blessed food) he made by mixing raw sugar in water with his sword. He then declared: "The Khālsā is all set for the protection of the cow and the Vedas." Guru Gobind Singh again roared :

खालसा प्रगटयो प्रमातम की मौज। खालसा अकाल पुरख की फौज।।
'The Khālsā is taking birth with the grace of God and it is the army of God Himself!'

He also cautioned his disciples about the nature of Khālsā by saying

सकल जगत में खालसा पंथ गाजै। जगे धर्म हिन्दू सकल भण्ड भाजै।।

"May the Khālsā Pantha shine in the whole world; for, as the Hindu Dharma awakens, all the evils will be destroyed?"

The concept of Khālsā was universal. He cautioned his disciples, "Khālsā Pantha is not a new Dharma; Dharma is only Hinduism." He also declared that after him, there would be no more Gurus, but everyone would be guided by the wisdom of the preceding Gurus whose teachings were compiled in the "Guru Grantha Sāhib." However, the teachings of Guru Gobind Singh are contained separately in the "Dashama Grantha." He passed away in 1708.

* * * * *

OUR GOAL
Every one of us will have to be like Guru Gobind Singh to protect the 'Hindu Dharma'.

MAHARSHI DAYĀNANDA SARASWATI
A Great Reformer of Vedic Dharma and Founder of the Ārya Samāja

Maharshi Dayānanda Saraswati, rejuvenator of the ancient Vedic traditions, was born on February 12, 1824, in the present-day State of Gujarāta, India. His childhood name was Moolashankara. His father, Pundit Karsanji Tiwāri, was the priest of a Shiva temple. On a Shivarātri night, Moolashankara, then only fourteen years old, witnessed rats nibbling at the offerings around the Shivālinga. He lost faith in the deity-worship and developed an urge to understand the 'Truth' and to realize God. He tried to seek this knowledge from many known scholars and mendicants, but could not find satisfactory answer until he found Swāmi Virajānanda and became his disciple. He learnt Sanskrit and mastered all the Vedas. He was consecrated as a Sanyāsi. Inspired by his Guru, he laid down the basis to spiritually rehabilitate people worldwide, and to energize them to reach out to attain the level of the people of India's Golden Age again.

He wrote a book, *'Satyārtha Prakāsha'* (the Light of Truth), in Hindi to provide the Hindus concrete directions, to guide them onwards in a life aimed at regeneration and to show them how to worship and pray. In *Satyārtha Prakāsha* he had described the historical, doctrinal and ethical aspects of the Vedic life. This text embodied the sum-total of his message of reform that was meant to lead Hindus to a higher standard of life experience. Thereafter, Swāmiji sought to bring back into popular practice the Karmakānda traditions of Yajna and Samskāra. For this he wrote a text called the *'Samskāra Vidhi'* which explains how to perform Yajna and Samskāras. He preached the Vedic philosophy in India, but in reality the whole of humanity was his congregation.

On April 10, 1875, he founded the Ārya Samāja, an organization committed to reforms in Hinduism; and spearheaded India's Independence Movement long before the National Congress came into picture. In fact, the Ārya Samāja became synonymous with the independence of India.

He introduced many positive reforms, among them: the abolition of the practice of Sati; child-marriage and the dowry custom; the untouchability in the prevalent caste system; dispelling superstitions; introduction of women's education; and the right of every human being to read and teach the Vedic scriptures. In short, his goal was to give back to the world the Vedas, the ancient treasure-house of the Divine wisdom. He emphasized the concept of nationhood and importance of one national language.

It can be said that, since the time of Ādi Shankarāchārya, India never saw a more learned Sanskrit scholar, a deeper metaphysician, a more wonderful orator, and a more fearless denunciator of any evil, than Dayānanda Saraswati.

Poisoned by an assassin on September 26, 1883, he left for the Abode of God on October 30, 1883.

* * * * *

कृण्वन्तो विश्वमार्यम्
Let Us Ennoble the Whole World.
-Rig-Veda

MAHARSHI RAMAN
A Self-Realized Saint

Maharshi Raman, an exponent of the Advaita Vedātna, was born on December 30, 1879, in a village called Tirucculi near Madurai, India. He was named Venkataraman at birth. At the age of 12 years, his father passed away and he went to live with his uncle in Madurai where an event occurred in 1896 that changed his life forever. While alone, a violent and sudden fear of death overwhelmed him. He felt that he was going to die, and began thinking what to do about it. He felt that he had to solve the problem of fear itself. At age 16, he became Self-realized spontaneously. Then he decided to leave Madurai for good, and lived the rest of his life on the Arunāchala Hill near Tiruvannamalai in present-day Tamil Nadu. He had no human *'Guru.'* He often said that his guru was Arunāchala — the holy mountain. He was never initiated in the order of *'Sanyāsa'*, but he lived the life of one.

From the experience of fear of death, an inward enquiry about the nature of dying arose that led to the conclusion that— 'I' is the Spirit transcending the body. The body dies, but the spirit transcending it cannot be touched by death. 'I' is the deathless spirit. From this time onward the fear of death vanished for him. The ego was lost in the flood of Self-awareness. An absorption in the Self continued unbroken from that time onward like the fundamental *'shruti' — that which is heard.* The knowledge that he acquired became the core of his teachings — the practice of *'ātma-vichāra'* (Self-enquiry) in which the seeker continually focuses attention on the 'I' thought in order to find its source. In the beginning this would require effort, but eventually something deeper than the "small- self" would take over and the mind would dissolve in what Raman called the "heart-center." This was possible because the human personality is but a mental idea.

This system of philosophy endorses the view that the "true being" within each human is the ultimate, "sublime reality — the Brahman, or the one without a second, or simply the Self." What prevents humans from realizing this is the identification with the mind and the body. Therefore, these identifications — which make up the "ego" — must be transcended in order to realize the truth. However, from the Vedānta perspective, 'realize the truth' is a bit of a misnomer, because the Self in Vedānta-thought is the truth and is free. One needs merely to remove the false veil of wrong identification with the body and mind to see it.

Maharshi Raman recommended his followers to ask the question *"Whence am I ?",* which some of his devotees consider to be more relevant than : *"Who am I ?"* In this way they would try to trace the "I-thought" back to the "*source.*" The word "*source*" in this context is used synonymously with the words GOD or SELF. He used to answer questions from people from all walks of life and never considered himself a *'Guru'* of anyone.

For several years he stopped talking and spent many hours each day in *'samādhi.'* When he began speaking again, people came to ask him questions, and he soon acquired a reputation as a sage. In 1907, when he was 28, one of his early devotees named him Bhagawāna Shri Maharshi Raman : *Divine Eminent Raman the Great Seer;* and the name stuck. Eventually he became world-famous and an āshrama was built around him. He died of cancer on April 14, 1950 at the age of 70.

✳   ✳   ✳

RĀMAKRISHNA PARAMAHAMSA
An Exponent of Divinity in All

Rāmakrishna Paramahamsa, a Hindu religious teacher and an influential figure in the Bengāl Renaissance of the Nineteenth century, was born on February 18, 1836, in the village of Kamarpukur in the Province of Bengāl, India. His childhood name was Gadādhar Chattopādhyay. The best-known record of Rāmakrishna's teachings are compiled in 'Kathāmrita' in Bengāli language and translated into English by Swāmi Nikhilānanda as 'The Gospel of Shri Rāmakrishna.' From the very childhood, he was not interested in the pursuit of formal education or money. However, he was always eager to hear discourses of religious preachers.

When his elder brother, Rāmkumāra, retired as a priest of Kāli temple at Dakshineshwara, he succeeded him as the priest. There he used to pray to goddess Kāli, imploring, *"Mother, you've been gracious to many devotees in the past and have revealed yourself to them. Why would you not reveal yourself to me, also? Am I not also your son?"* He prayed intensely and is said to have become overwhelmed with his deep longing to have the vision of goddess Kāli, some times even falling unconscious on the floor. Finally, he began to have such transcendental experiences often and realized the ultimate goal of his life. He had the similar experiences later while practicing the tenets of Christianity and other religions. This led him to preach to have an attitude of harmonious respect for all religions.

At the insistence of his mother, Rāmakrishna married Shāradā Devi who later became his first disciple. She learnt quickly and realized the spiritual experiences known to Rāmakrishna. As a result, their relationship can only be understood on the divine spiritual plane. She began to be treated as the 'Universal Mother'. This was the role she played all her life. She showered her love to all his disciples as a mother to them all.

Rāmakrishna had little formal education. He was initiated in *Advaita Vedānta* (Vedic Philosophy of Non-Duality) by a wandering monk, Totāpuri, who directed him to attain the state of '*samādhi*' (transcendental state of meditative super-consciousness, with total detachment from the world and from any feeling of pain or pleasure, etc.). At Totāpuri's death, he reportedly remained in *samādhi* for six months.

Rāmakrishna's mystical realization is classified in Hindu tradition as the 'N*irvikalpa Samādhi*' (involuntary meditation). This experience led him to say that the various religions are different ways to reach the Ultimate Reality (God-Realization) that is beyond expression in an ordinary language, thus echoing the well-known dictum from the Rig-Veda: "*Truth is One, but the Pundits call it by many names.*" The key concepts in Rāmakrishna's teachings were :

(i)   The Oneness of experience;

(ii) Divinity in all living beings;

(iii) The unity of God and the harmony of religions;

(iv) The primal bondage in human life is lust and greed.

More generally, his teachings are based on the Vedas and the Upanishads. His example shows that Self-realization and great spiritual heights are accessible to any one even without conventional education.

Rāmakrishna became a self-realized soul by his own sincere and constant efforts. He developed throat cancer and attained Mahāsamādhi on 16 August, 1886, leaving behind a devoted band of 16 young disciples headed by Swāmi Vivekānanda, who would eventually become a well-known saint-philosopher and exponent of Hinduism as well as Indian nationalism, inspiring the people not only in India but around the world. Rāmakrishna's vision of life is the vision of humanity. If this vision is followed with sincere heart, peace and prosperity would prevail in the world.

✳   ✳   ✳   ✳   ✳

Main source: www.wikipedia— the free encyclopedia.

SWĀMI VIVEKĀNANDA
A Saint-Philospher and Exponent of Hindu Nationalism

Swāmi Vivekānanda, an embodiment of dedication, who gave a rousing call of underlying Hindu unity and social justice, and proclaimed the holy land of Bhārata a Hindu Nation, was born on February 12, 1863, in Bengāl, India, as the son of Vishwanātha Dutta and Bhavaneshwari Devi. His childhood-name was Narendra Nāth Dutta. He showed a precocious mind and very keen memory. He practiced yoga and meditation from an early age. Even when he was young, he questioned the validity of superstitious customs and discrimination based on caste and religion.

Swāmi Vivekānanda was one of the most famous and influential spiritual leaders of the Vedānta philosophy. He was the chief disciple of Shri Rāmakrishna Parmahansa and was the founder of the Rāmakrishna Matha and the Rāmakrishna Mission. Many consider him as an icon of modern Hinduism for his leadership, knowledge, revolutionary acts, and also for his fearless courage, his positive exhortations to the youth, and his broad outlook on social and national problems. He delivered countless lectures and discourses on the Vedānta philosophy. He is regarded by many Indians as well as by non-Indians as a Messenger of God, like Buddha.

In 1880, while studying the western philosophy and history of the European nations at the Scottish Church College, his urge to realize God intensified. It led him first to the Brahmo-Samāja and then to Shri Rāmakrishna. Narendra met Rāmakrishna in November, 1881. He asked Rāmakrishna the same old question, whether he had seen God. The instantaneous answer from Rāmakrishna was, *"Yes, I see God, just as I see you here, only in a much intense sense."* Narendra was astounded. He started visiting Rāmakrishna frequently. Rāmakrishna patiently and persistently taught him the Vedānata philosophy. In five years Narendra was transformed from a restless, puzzled, impatient youth to a mature man who was ready to renounce everything for the sake of God-realization. In August 1886, Shri Rāmakrishna passed away. Along with the fellow-disciples, Narendra took the vow of *Sanyāsa* and became known as Vivekānanda. On July 1890, Vivekānanda set out in search of his future-mission and reached the south-most part of India on December 24, 1890. During this long journey, Vivekānanda observed the imbalance in the society and tyranny in the name of caste. He realized the need for a national rejuvenation if India was to survive at all. He sat on a lonely rock (now called the Vivekānanda Memorial Rock) located in the Indian Ocean, meditated for three days and night about the past, present and future of India, and got the vision of his future mission. This led him to attend the first 'World Parliament of Religions' at Chicago in 1893, where he represented Hinduism. This illustrious son of Bhārata captivated the audience with his eloquent address. His mission was an instant success. Subsequently he was invited to speak all over America and Europe. He preached the gospel of the Vedānta with exemplary brilliance. However, his success was not without controversy, much of it from the Christian missionaries of whom he was fiercely critical. He returned to India in 1897 and devoted most of his time in rejuvenation of India, except for his short visit to the West from January, 1899 to December, 1900.

Swāmi Vivekānanda, moved by the spirit of America's Declaration of Independence, wrote tributes to a nation founded on the principle of democracy, on July 4, 1898, in a poem titled 'To the Fourth of July.'

He underlined the importance of nursing the poor and the sick as the foremost step towards understanding religion. Vivekānanda's vision of Bhārata is reflected in his own words: *"It is the same India which has withstood the shocks of the centuries, of hundreds of foreign invaders; it is the same land which stands firmer than any rock in the world, with its undying vigor, indestructible life. Its life is of the same nature as soul, without beginning and without end, immortal; and we are the children of such a country."* Swāmi Vivekānanda inspired India's freedom-struggle movement. His writings inspired a whole generation of freedom-fighters in India. Most prominent among them were Subhash Chandra Bose, Aurobindo, and countless others. He left his mortal body on July 4, 1902.

LONG LIVE THE HINDU NATION

SWĀMI RĀMA TIRTHA
An Illustrious Symbol of Indian Nationalism

Swāmi Rāma Tirtha, a descendent of Sant Tulasidāsa, was born on October 22, 1873, in a village called Murāriwālā, in the Gujranwālā district of Punjab (in undivided India, now in Pakistan). As a child, Rāma was very fond of listening to recitations from the Holy Scriptures. He was a brilliant student, especially in mathematics in which he obtained a Master's degree with distinction. He was perfectly at home in Persian, English, Hindi, Urdu and Sanskrit literatures. He served for a while as a Professor of Mathematics. But he loved solitude. It was at this stage that his spiritual life began to blossom. He began to read the Geetā and began delivering lectures on devotion (*Bhakti*) under the auspices of the *Sanātana Dharma Sabhā* of Lahore. He studied the Vedānta under the inspiration of Shri Mādhava Tirtha of the Dwārakā Matha. A great impetus was given to his spiritual life by Swāmi Vivekānanda, whom he saw for the first time at Lahore. The sight of the great Swāmi as a Sanyasin kindled in him the longing to don the same type of robe.

Rāma soon resigned from the teaching post and left for the forest in the Himālayas. He took Sanyāsa a few days before the passing away of Swāmi Vivekānanda. A few years later he returned to the plains to preach. The effect of his presence was marvelous. His infectious joy and his bird-like warbling of ॐ enchanted everyone.

Rāma Tirtha was a great ascetic and an enlightened mystic. Today, Rāma Tirtha is not present amongst us in person, but he is truly ever-alive, shining as a beacon-star in the spiritual world. He had the realization of the 'Satchidānanda' — the Truth-Consciousness-Bliss-Supreme. The ancient sages and modern saints have proved this ineffable nature of the Supreme, not by logical proofs of knowledge, but by actual experience which cannot be simply communicated to others.

He had a great love for India. He emphatically declared that if one has real patriotism, then one must deify the Motherland and behold Bhāratavarsha as a Living goddess. "If you must realize unity with God, realize first your unity with the Whole Nation. Let this intense feeling of identity with every creature within this land throb in every fiber of your frame," he said. His love for India was so profound that he identified himself with India. He declared: I am India. India is my body. (मैं भारत हूं, भारतवर्ष मेरा शरीर है।)

Swāmi Rāma Tirtha was a notable philosopher of Vedānta. His burning desire to spread the message of Vedānta made him leave for Japan and, later, for the USA. He spent about a year and a half in San Francisco under the hospitality of Dr. Albert Hiller. He started many Societies, one of them being the Hermetic Brotherhood, dedicated to the study of Vedānta. His charming personality had a great impact on the Americans. Many Americans even looked upon him as a Living Christ. He was among the first few to spread the Vedānta philosophy abroad, notably in the United States, Japan and Egypt.

On his return to India, Swāmi Rāma continued to lecture in various parts of India. He established Swāmi Rāma Tirtha Mission Āshrama at Kotal Gaon Rājpura near Dehrādun in Uttarānchal, India. The āshrama is engaged in spreading the vision of Swāmi Rāma to the humanity at large.

But his health began to break down. He went back to the Himālayas and settled at the Vasishtha Āshrama. His health did not improve. He gave up his mortal body at the bank of the Gangā River on 17 October, 1906, when he was only thirty-three.

* * * * *

मैं भारत हूँ, सत्य हूँ, शिव हूँ और सुन्दर भी।

I am Bhāratvarsha — Satyam, Shivam, Sundaram (Truth-Auspiciousness-Beauty Incarnate.)

–स्वामी रामतीर्थ

Source: www.ramatirtha.org ; www.dishq.org

KESHAVA BALIRĀMA HEDGEWĀRA
A Visionary of Hindu Unity and Social Justice

Keshava Balirāma Hedgewāra's life was best described by Shri Mādhava Sadāshiva Golwālkara in a glowing tribute to this Seer of Hindu Nation when he said: "Words fail to describe the depth of that pure and selfless love. The boundless affection of the mother's heart, the sleepless care and diligence of the father, and the inspiring guidance of the guru found their culmination in that single bosom. I for one feel it my proud privilege to worship him as my ideal. The worship of such a soul transcends the worship of an individual and becomes the worship of the ideal itself. He is verily my chosen deity." Today he lives in the hearts of millions of Hindus in India and abroad who gather regularly in the Shākhās of the Rāshtreeya Swayamsevaka Sangha (RSS) in India, and of the Hindu Swayamsevaka Sangha in other countries, to offer their prayers to keep the flame of the Hindu Dharma ablaze.

Keshava Balirāma Hedgewāra was born on April 1, 1889, in Nāgapura in the State of Mahārāshtra in India. His father, Balirāmpant, and mother, Revatibai, were pious persons. Right from the very childhood, Keshav's life was a glowing candle of patriotism. As a small boy he heard the story of Mahārāja Shivāji and was inspired by his patriotism and supreme dedication to the cause of Dharma. This spirit found expression in the acts of Keshava when, at the age of eight, he threw away sweets distributed in his school to celebrate Queen Victoria's Diamond Jubilee and questioned his teacher how a handful of aggressors came to rule over this Hindu land. On another occasion he could not bear the sight of Union Jack flying over Sitabuldi Fort in Nāgapura. He gathered his playmates to dig "an underground tunnel" from his master's house to the fort to pull down the Union Jack and hoist the Bhagavā Flag. Once, at the age of sixteen, he was expelled from the school for reciting '*Vande Mātaram.*' Such were his intense feelings about the nation. He joined another nationalist school and completed high school. Later, he joined National Medical College at Kolkata and received a degree in medicine. In Kolkata he came in touch with revolutionary movement trying to free India from the foreign yoke.

In June 1915, Keshava completed one-year apprenticeship in medicine and returned to Nāgapura as a doctor. But his mind did not accept practicing medicine and be content just earning a livelihood. He wanted to diagnose the disease that had afflicted the nation and to cure it. With this determination in his mind, he dedicated his life at the altar of the Motherland. He came in close touch with many revolutionaries and worked with the National Congress and the Hindu Mahāsabhā, and thus worked with national leaders like Mahātmā Gāndhi and Veer Sāvarkara.

Working with these leaders of independence, his ideas evolved and the vision for his future work developed. He concluded that without the Hindu unity and social justice, the future of India will remain clouded with uncertainty. For realization of this vision, and to shape the future of India, the nation needed honest, sincere and dedicated workers of great will. With this in mind, in 1925 he founded the *Rāshtreeya Swayamsevaka Sangha* (RSS) with the firm conviction that the will and dedication of "*Swayamsevakas*" (volunteers) would bring about the desired results. He introduced the unique "*Shākha*" method of training and inspired thousands of youths to become selfless "*Prachārakas*" (full-time volunteers) dedicated to spreading the work to all parts of India and many other nations where Hindus reside. The RSS is perhaps the largest voluntary organization in the world today. There are many off-shoots of this organization, dedicated to serving the many needs of the society. The Vishwa Hindu Parishad, a notable example, is working in many countries to preserve and upheld the Hindu culture and values. Dr. Hedgewāra breathed his last on June 21, 1940.

✶ ✶ ✶ ✶ ✶

Call of the Hindu Society : Hindu Unity and Social Justice.

MAHĀTMĀ GĀNDHI
An Advocate of Non-Violence

Mohan Dāsa Karamachand Gāndhi, rightly called a Man of the Millennia, who changed the course of history by introducing the concept of '*Satyāgraha*' (resistance through mass civil disobedience based upon the foundation of non-violence) against the tyranny of the oppressors — was born on October 2, 1869, in Porbandar in the State of Gujarāta, India. He is lovingly addressed as Mahātmā Gāndhi (Mahātmā meaning the 'great' soul). He was the son of Karamchand Gāndhi, the Minister of Porbandara Estate. At the age of 13, Gāndhi was married to Kasturbā Makhanji.

He joined University of Bombay in 1887. He was not happy at the college, because his family wanted him to become a barrister. He welcomed the opportunity to study in England, which he viewed as "a land of philosophers and poets, the very center of civilization." At the age of 18, on September 4, 1888, Gāndhi went to the University College, London, to train as a barrister. During his stay in London, he kept the vow he had made to his mother to observe the Hindu precepts of abstinence from meat, alcohol, and women.

On returning to India, he tried practicing law at Mumbai, with little success. Subsequently, he came to practice at Rājakota. In 1893, Gāndhi had an opportunity to go to South Africa in connection of a case of one of his clients. There he observed blatalant discrimination of the white against the non-white people, including Indians. He first employed his ideas of '*Satyāgraha*' — peaceful civil disobedience — in the Indian community's struggle for civil rights, with marked success. He was then inspired to return to India to join the Indian National Congress to lead the efforts for the independence of India. He pioneered an all-India campaign for alleviation of poverty, liberation of Indian women, brotherhood among different religious and ethnic communities, an end to untouchability and caste-discrimination, and the economic self-sufficiency of the nation. As a symbol of self-reliance, he adopted '*Charkhā*' (spinning wheel) as the means to produce clothing that opened the way to cottage industry. Above all, Gāndhi led the struggle for '*Swarāja*' — the Independence of India from the British rule. He led Indians in the Disobedience Movement. He organized a mammoth march through the 248 miles (**'Dāndi Salt March'**) in 1930 to protest against the Salt Tax imposed by the British Government. He made an open call for the British to quit India (**Quit India Movement**) in 1942. He spent many years of his life in jails as the British government in India tried to stop the Independence Movement by imprisoning leaders of the Movement. However, the Movement culminated in victory and the nation became free, albeit at a high cost of division of the country. He spent his final years in the quest of communal peace and harmony.

It is said that he was not a saint who retreated to the forest, but a saint in the political arena. He called himself a proud Hindu, but respected all religions. He firmly believed in *Ahimsā* (non-violence) and he tried to apply the instruments of *Ahimsā* to the problems of the world and to achieve the Independence of India. He was equally emphatic in his efforts to minimize the economic disparity and other kinds of discriminations existing in the society. He was the foremost champion of the oppressed. To fight injustice was his Dharma.

Gāndhiji worked relentlessly to remove untouchablility. He even gave a respectable name to the class of untouchables, "*Harijana*" (Children of God). In his life he followed a high standard of morality and described (Young India, 1925) seven sins afflicting the human society as: **1.** Politics without principles, **2.** Wealth without work, **3.** Pleasure without conscience, **4.** Knowledge without character, **5.** Commerce without morality, **6.** Science without humanity, **7.** Worship without sacrifice.

Gāndhiji was an ardent advocate of free and *"Akhanda Bhārata"* (Unified and Undivided India). But as a result of the partition, millions of people were uprooted from their homes and numberless people were massacred. Gāndhiji was engaged in efforts of reconciling the bitterness that followed the partition, when an assassin's bullet ended his life on January 30, 1948.

AUROBINDO GHOSH
A Scholar, Revolutionary and Saint

Aurobindo Ghosh was born on the 15th of August 1872, in Kolkata, India. His father wanted him to have a thorough western education. He sent him first to Loreto Convent School in Dārjeeling at the age of five, and then to England where he entered St. Paul's School in London in 1884 and King's College, Cambridge in 1890. His father was trying to make him a perfect English gentleman, with no touch of India's culture. But Aurobindo was destined to be a great Indian scholar, writer, poet, literary critic, philosopher, social thinker, revolutionary, patriot, visionary and yogi.

Aurobindo was a brilliant student. As per his father's wish he appeared and passed the Indian Civil Service (ICS), but purposely did not appear for the horse-riding test and was disqualified. By this time Shri Aurobindo was learning about the happenings back home and felt that a period of great upheaval for the Motherland was coming — in which he was to play a leading role. He began to learn Bengāli and joined a secret society `Lotus and Dagger,' where the members took an oath to work for India's freedom. After 13 years in England, Shri Aurobindo returned to India on February 6, 1893. He joined the Barodā State Service from 1897 to 1906 and taught French and English. Shri Aurobindo read the Mahābhārata, the Rāmāyana, the works of Kālidāsa, Bhavabhuti, Bankim Chandra as well as of Homer, Dante, Horace and many others. He started writing a series of fiery articles under the title 'New Lamps for Old' in the 'Indu Prakash,' a Marāthi-English Daily from Mumbai, strongly criticizing the Congress for its moderate policies for gaining Independence for India from the British rule. Wrote Shri Aurobindo: *"Our actual enemy is not any force exterior to ourselves, but our own crying weaknesses, our cowardice, our selfishness, our hypocrisy, our purblind sentimentalism."* The editors, fearing adverse reaction from the British government, discontinued his column. In 1901 Shri Aurobindo was married to Mrinālini Devi who had to go through all the joys and sorrows which are the lot of one who marries a genius and someone so much out of the ordinary as Shri Aurobindo.

In 1907, the freedom movement in India was gathering momentum. Shri Aurobindo felt, however, that passive resistance would not be adequate for achieving Independence for India. In a true spirit of a yogi, he called for following a path of active strife based on Dharma for opposing and battling the unjust enemy, as preached by Shri Krishna in the Bhagavad Geetā. To him, the greatest Dharma of every Indian then was the liberation of India from the foreign yoke, and an armed struggle against the British was well justifiable. He wrote, *"What India needs is the aggressive virtues, the spirit of soaring idealism, bold creation, fearless resistance, and courageous attacks."* Shri Aurobindo participated in many revolutionary activities and was promptly jailed by the British. In the prison, he underwent a profound change. In 1910, Shri Aurobindo had a vision that India was already free and he needed to go to Pondicherry, then a French colony, for continuing to serve the Motherland. He wrote all his masterpieces there.

Shri Aurobindo's spiritual collaborator was a French lady, Mirrā Alfāssā, who later came to be simply known as 'The Mother.' She joined him in 1920 and they together founded a spiritual center in Pondicherry, known as the Aurobindo Āshrama. It became a prominent seat of an enduring spiritual experiment for the transformation and perfection of human life. Shri Aurobindo affirmed that life itself was Yoga (Integration with God) and through a conscious aspiration, one could evolve into a higher being and open oneself to a new consciousness, which he referred to as the *Supramental.* The great political revolutionary-turned-sage passed away on December 5, 1950.

VINĀYAKA DĀMODARA SĀVARKARA
An Exponent of Oneness in Hinduism and Indian Nationalism

Vināyaka Dāmodara Sāvarkara, a great revolutionary, who was always ahead of his time in action and thought and who propounded the philosophy of 'Hindutva,' was born to Dāmodarpant Sāvarkara and Rādhābai on May 28, 1883, in Bhagurā, a small town in Nāsika district of Mahārāshtra, India.

After passing High School, Vināyaka was enrolled in the Fergusson College in Poona in 1902, where he declared in 'Abhinava Bhārata' that *"India must be Independent; India must be united; India must be a Republic; India must have a common language and common script."* In June 1906, Vināyaka left for London to study law and took India House in London for his residence. It was a center of revolutionary activists. In 1908, Sāvarkara completed his book entitled "The History of the War of Indian Independence." The book inspired revolutionaries like Bhagata Singh and Subhāsh Chandra Bose. In 1909, Madanlāla Dhingrā, a follower of Sāvarkara, shot Sir Wyllie of the India Office after failing in his attempt on the life of Lord Curzon, the Viceroy, for the atrocities committed on Indians. Vināyaka, under arrest for being a part of revolutionary activities, was being taken to India on a ship. He escaped by jumping from the ship and swimming across the English Channel to France. But luck did not favor him and he was arrested on the soil of France and brought to the Andaman's prison on July 4, 1911 to serve 50 years of rigorous imprisonments. Vināyaka was 27 years old at that time. His elder brother was serving a prison sentence in Andamans, too. In the history of India's Freedom Movement, no one else was subjected to as much inhuman physical and mental torture by the tyrannical British rule as Sāvarkara in the hellish conditions of the Andamans.

On May 2, 1921, the Sāvarkara brothers were brought back to India as demanded by Vithalbhai Patel, but remained imprisoned in Ratnāgiri Jail and then in Yeravadā Jail until January 6, 1924. Then he was freed under the condition that he would not leave Ratnāgiri district and abstain from political activity for the next five years. While in Ratnāgiri Jail, Sāvarkara wrote his famous book "Hindutva" that was smuggled out and published under the pen-name "A Marāthā."

India has the great distinction of having countless illustrious men and women whose services to the country are without parallel throughout the world; and the story of Sāvarkara is among the most inspiring and glorious ones. For his great courage and urge for freedom, he was called *Swātantrya-Veera*. Sāvarkara was a brilliant poet, powerful writer and an electrifying speaker, great patriot, dauntless revolutionary, embodiment of sacrifice, and true to his convictions. No power could dampen his boundless love for freedom. He was foremost among the revolutionaries who wanted to throw away the British rule, by an armed struggle if necessary.

He was also a champion in the movement for the removal of un-touchability and the caste system from the Hindu society. He was the first to declare that the uprising against the British in 1857, which the historians of that time called a 'Mutiny,' should be recognized as a 'War of India's Independence.' He was indeed always ahead of his time in thoughts and actions. He did not accept the partition of India as permanent. His writings are even now a source of profound inspiration for the youth of India. He propounded Hindu Cultural Nationalism, or Hindutva, and supported it with a strong logic. He left his mortal body on February 26, 1966. His life was a beacon of light and will inspire the Indians forever.

********** जय भारतमाता **********

Our Goal : *One God, one nation, one language, one race, one form, one hope.*
- Swātantrya Veera Sāvarkara

A.C. BHAKTIVEDĀNTA SWĀMI PRABHUPĀDA
A Great Teacher of Vaishnava Sampradāya

His Divine Grace A. C. Bhaktivedānta Swāmi Prabhupāda was born as Abhaya Charana De on September 1, 1896, in Kolkatā, India. His education was mainly at the Scottish Church College, Kolkatā. In his later years, as a Vaishnava mendicant, he became an influential communicator of Gaudiyā Vaishnava theology in India and then in the West by founding the International Society for Krishna Consciousness (ISKCON) in 1966.

In 1922 he met his spiritual master, Srila Bhaktisiddhānta Saraswati Goswāmi, who was a prominent religious scholar and the founder of sixty-four 'Gaudiyā Mathas' (Vedic Institutes) in India. Sirlā Goswāmi accepted Prabhupāda as his student, who later dedicated his life to teaching Vedic knowledge to English-speaking people. In 1933 Srilā Prabhupāda was formally initiated as his disciple. In the following years, Srilā Prabhupāda wrote a commentary on the *Bhagavad-Geetā*, and assisted the Gaudiyā Matha in its work. In 1944, he started 'Back to Godhead,' an English fortnightly magazine. The magazine is now continuing to be published by his disciples in the West.

In 1950 Srilā Prabhupāda retired from married life, assuming '*Vānaprastha,*' engaged in studies and writing. He moved to the holy city of Vrindāvana, where he lived in the Rādhā-Dāmodara temple and continued to devote his time in study and writing. He adopted the order of '*sanyāsa*' in 1959. At Rādhā-Dāmodara temple, Srilā Prabhupāda began work on his life's masterpiece: a multivolume commentated translation of the eighteen-thousand-verse *Shrimad Bhāgavatam*, the first three volumes of which were published in India.

In September 1965 Srilā Prabhupāda came to the United States to fulfill the mission of his spiritual master. Subsequently, His Divine Grace wrote more than fifty volumes of authoritative commentated translations and summary studies of the philosophical and religious classics of India. His commentated translation of *Shrimad Bhagavad Geetā* is the most profound one and translated in many world-languages. About one hundred million copies of this masterpiece have been distributed around the world. Before his passing away, he almost completed his work on *Shrimad Bhāgavatam* except three volumes which were completed by one of his disciples.

In July 1966, Prabhupāda established the International Society for Krishna Consciousness. In the following 12 years, he guided the Society and saw it grow into a worldwide confederation of more than one hundred '*āshramas,*' schools, temples, institutes, and farm communities — a gigantic achievement. Since then his disciples have established similar projects throughout the United States and the rest of the world.

Srilā Prabhupāda's most significant contribution, perhaps, is his writing. The Bhaktivedānta Book Trust, established in 1972, to publish the works of His Divine Grace, has arguably become the world's largest publisher of books in the field of Indian religion and philosophy, publishing more than 400 million copies of books and magazines, translated into over 50 languages — a staggering achievement in a short time of only 12 years! He left his mortal body on November 14, 1977, in Vrindāvana, India.

* * * * *

हरे कृष्ण हरे कृष्ण, कृष्ण कृष्ण हरे हरे।
हरे राम हरे राम, राम राम हरे हरे ॥

SWĀMI   CHINMAYĀNANDA
A World Renowned Exponent of Vedānta

Swāmi Chinmayānanda, one of the greatest exponents of the Vedānta — the foundation of Hindu religion and culture — and a great visionary and '*yuga-purusha*' (man of the Era), was born on May 8, 1916, as Bālakrishnana Menon in the State of Kerala; India. He took a degree in Law and English literature from Lucknow University before plunging into India's freedom struggle against the British rule. His nationalist activities led to his imprisonment. During this period he studied the works of Vivekānanda, Rāma Tirtha, Aurobindo, Maharshi Raman and others. However, he was profoundly influenced by Swāmi Sivānanda, who stressed: "Be good, do good, serve and love, purify, meditate, realize, and be free."

After he was released from prison, Bālakrishnana joined 'The National Herald' newspaper. While working for the newspaper, he decided to write an article 'exposing' pretentious sādhus (monks). For this he traveled to Swāmi Sivānanda's āshrama in Rishikesha. However, he was overwhelmed when he met Swāmi Sivānanda. A transformation took place within Bālakrishnana, and he started pondering over the eternal questions: What is the purpose of life? What is the secret of permanent happiness? He decided to become a sādhu himself. On February 25, 1949 (Shivarātri day), he was initiated into sanyāsa by Swāmi Sivānanda. Thus, Bālakrishnana Menon was reborn as Swāmi Chinmayānanda.

After some months at the āshrama, Swāmi Sivānanda guided him to the most renowned Vedānta master of the time, Swāmi Tapovanam, who lived in Uttarkāshi in the Himālayas. As Swāmi Tapovanam's disciple, Swāmi Chinmayānanda went through a rigorous study of the scriptures for eight years. After his studies, he traveled throughout India. He observed widespread spiritual and social degradation in the country, and felt the urge to share with others the knowledge that had brought fulfillment to his own life.

After obtaining Swāmi Tapovanam's blessings, Swāmi Chinmayānanda conducted his first '*Jnāna Yajna*' (spiritual discourse) in December 1951, in Pune, with only eight people in attendance. However, as he conducted more *Jnāna Yajnas* around India, orthodox priests were outraged. They felt that the Vedānta was their preserve and should not to be given out to the public. They complained to the Shankarāchārya of Kānchi, a senior Hindu saint. However, instead of restraining Swāmi Chinmayānanda, the Shankarāchārya advised the priests to go and listen to him!

From then on, there was no turning back. The Chinmaya Mission was founded in 1953. From public pulpits throughout India and the world, Swāmi Chinmayānanda spread the man-making knowledge of the Vedānta. His speeches were highly dynamic, logical and witty, appealing to young and old alike. Tens of thousands came to hear him. Chinmaya Mission Centers sprung up all over India and the globe. Hundreds of swāmis and *brahmachāris* were trained to teach Vedānta. Many social projects were initiated, such as schools, colleges, child and youth development programs, hospitals, old-age homes, training programs for village nurses, and rural environment projects. Swāmi Chinmayānanda authored more than 35 books, which include commentaries on the major Upanishads and the Bhagavad Geetā. He was the founding member and the elected President of the Vishwa Hindu Parishad, in 1964. In 1992, Swāmi Chinmayānanda gave an address in the United Nations titled "the Planet in Crisis." He was recognized as a world-renowned teacher of the Vedānta and Hindu religion. He passed away on August 3, 1993. By then the sage had created a renaissance, the pride and awakening in Hinduism.

✳   ✳   ✳   ✳   ✳

Jai Jai Jagadeeshwara

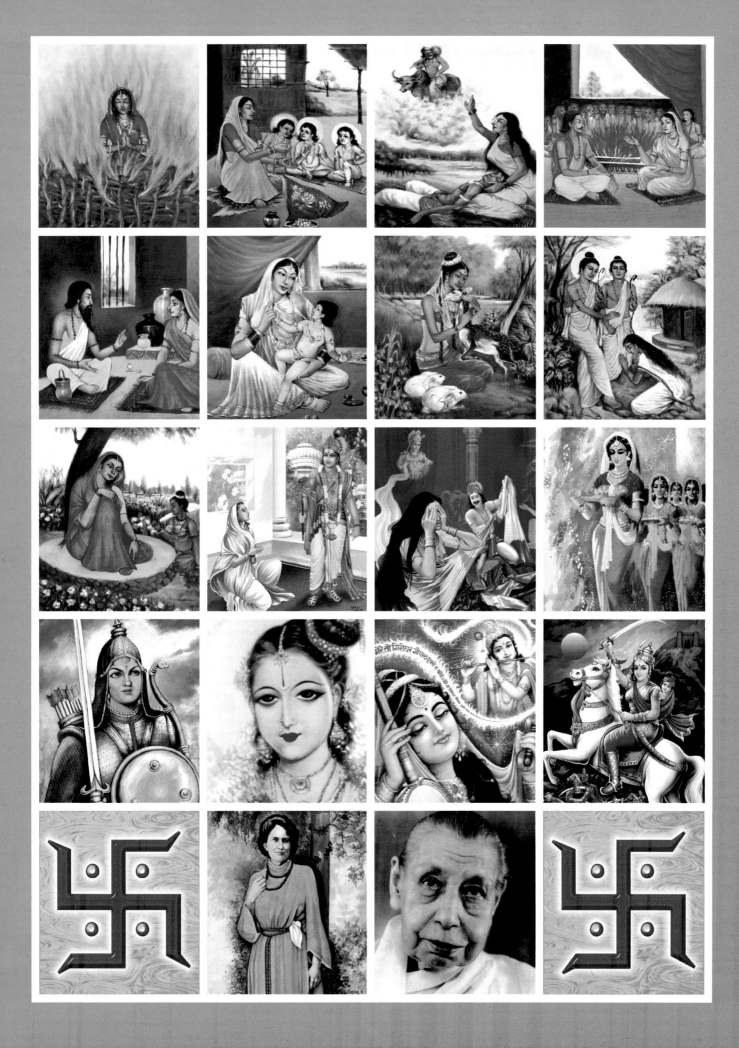

Part II

THE WOMEN ARCHITECTS OF SANĀTANA DHARMA

The position of women in a society is a true index of its cultural and spiritual distinction. The ideals of Hindu womanhood and the role of women in Hindu way of life have been a constant source of inspiration to all.

From time immemorial, Vedic culture has exalted the tradition of venerating women as the fountainhead of inner strength and divine power. Indian masses worship womanhood in the form of sacred goddess images such as Saraswati, Lakshmi, Pārvati, Durgā and Kāli, and in the form of the name of country as 'Bhārata Mātā.' The most sacred book is addressed as 'Geetā Mātā,' the most sacred river as 'Gangā Mātā,' and the whole earth is 'Dharati Mātā.' The personification of primal power of the universe (*Shakti*) in of the form of Mother and her worship is characteristic of Hindu thought and philosophy. In fact the 'Mother Image' is a symbol of all that is good and auspicious. According to the traditions evolved over the period of thousands of years, women enjoy the highest level of respect and freedom in India. This tradition has given rise to innumerable women throughout the history of India who exalted in all walks of life from spirituality to poetry, from government to the battlefield, representing the best of Vedic culture and heritage. In many cases, the greatness of a celebrated historic legend who happened to be a man was to a great extent the result of sublime greatness of his mother or wife. Well-known examples are Shakuntalā, the mother of Emperor Bharata in whose honor India was named Bhārata in ancient times; Jeejābāi, the mother of Kshatrapati Shivāji; and Shāradā Devi (the 'Holy Mother'), the wife of Shri Rāmakrishna Paramhansa.

In the Vedic period, many women contributed in the composition of hymns and in the development of philosophy and moral, cultural, social and family values; noted among them being Maitreyee, Gārgee, Lopmudrā. Shakuntalā, Anasooyā, Shabari, Ahalyā, and Seetā (preceding and during the Rāmāyana period); Draupadi, Damayanti and Sāvitri (during the Mahābhārata period); Devahuti, Satee, Umā and Bhāmini (during the Purānic period). Many of the women characters mentioned in the Sanskrit literature have inspired the thoughts and ideals of women of India and shaped their lives for untold centuries.

The ideals presented by *bhikshunees* (nuns) in Buddhism and Jainism are of great significance as well. The services and sacrifices of Mahāprajāpati Gautami, Kshema, Patachara, Vishākha and Āmrapāli in Buddhism; and Ārya Chandanā, Jayanti and Mrigāvatee in Jainism, are of historical importance.

Later history has recorded many women saints. The names of Meerābāi in the North and Āndāla in the South are household-names. Rich and poor alike sing their devotional songs in the praise of Lord Krishna. These songs are a source of inspiration to Hindus everywhere.

In more recent times, we remember the great contributions made by Shāradā Devi (the Holy Mother), Bhagini Niveditā, Mirrā Alfāssā ('The Mother'), Jeejābāi, Rāni Durgāvati, Rāni Lakshmibāi of Jhānsi, Ahilyābāi Holkara, Rāni Padmini, to name just a few.

The Indian culture has gained a high level of splendor from the aura of such great women. The life and legacy of these illustrious women will surely continue to inspire us all in times to come. A few of them are presented here.

SATEE

Satee was the daughter of the last Prajāpati (Principal Administrator of the universe created and appointed by Lord Brahmā) Daksha. She was the consort of Lord Shiva. There are many mythological legends related to Satee. Once upon a time when Lord Shiva and Satee were strolling in the woods, he had a vision of Rāma and Lakshmana wandering in the forest in search of Seetā; and he bowed his head in salutation to Lord Rāma. Satee became surprised to observe this act of Shiva, and asked him to explain the mystery behind it. Even after Shiva explained everything, however, Satee was not convinced and she resolved to test Lord Rāma. She assumed the appearance of Seetā and started to walk slowly in the same venue where Rāma and Lakshmana were moving around. Shri Rāma became aware of what the matter was. He paid homage to Satee and asked, "What is the matter: You are roaming around alone, without Lord Shiva?" Satee became embarrassed on hearing Rāma's words. Recognizing the power of Shri Rāma, Satee came back to Lord Shiva.

Upon Satee's return, Lord Shiva faced a dilemma, since Satee had assumed the appearance of Seetā. Shiva regarded Seetā as His mother and now accepting Satee would go against Shiva's feeling of devotion toward Seetā. How could He now regard Satee as His consort? Shiva resolved in His mind, "In this life, there can not be any meeting with Satee in this body."

After some time, Prajāpati Daksha, Satee's father, arranged to hold a Yajna (special religious observance) in his capital. In this Yajna, many kings, emperors and gods were invited, but Daksha did not invite Shiva. Satee expressed her wish to go to her father's house. Shiva tried hard to make her understand that it was not a good idea to go anywhere uninvited, as one may be insulted. But Satee stubbornly held her ground. She went to her father's house to participate in the Yajna even though she was not invited.

Having gone there, she found that her husband, Lord Shiva, was being insulted. She could not bear her husband's insult, and sitting in the altar of the Yajna, she left her mortal body of her own free will. Everyone became grief-stricken. When Shiva came to know about this, he sent Veerabhadra there and had the Yajna stopped.

Lord Shiva bore the dead body of Satee on His shoulders, and started roaming over the land, totally depressed. The universe came to the verge of deluge ('*Pralaya*'). To avert the impending universal catastrophe, Lord Vishnu devised a way to rid Shiva of the dead body and awaken Him into His normal Self. He used His '*Sudarshana Chakra*' (Divine Discus) that secretly followed oblivious Shiva and severed the dead body's limbs one by one. All the limbs of Satee's dead body dropped one after another. Wherever any limb of Satee's dead body fell down, the spot became a '*Siddhapeetha*.' According to '*Devee Bhāgavata*,' there are 108 such '*Siddhapeethas,*' but some other scriptures mention 51 '*Siddhapeethas*.' Among these, 42 '*Siddhapeethas*' are in current-day India, 2 in Nepāla, 1 in Tibet, 1 in Sri Lankā, 1 in Pakistan, and 4 in Bangalādesh. Worship of Shiva and Shakti takes place at these '*Siddhapeethas*.'

Satee reincarnated in the following life as the daughter of Himālaya Parvata, hence she became known by the name of 'Pārvati'. Pārvati observed great austerity and won Lord Shiva again as her husband. Kārtikeya and Ganesha were sons born of Shiva and Pārvati.

Anasooyā with her three sons — Soma, Dattātreya and Durvāsā

ANASOOYĀ

The legend of Anasooyā is unique in Indian mythological history. She was Sage Atri's wife. Her mother was the daughter of Sage Swāyambhuva, and her father was Sage Kardama. She was a great and illustrious woman of India. Her fame as a woman steadfastly devoted to her husband permeated not only the *Bhooloka* (the Earth) but also the *Devaloka* (the Heaven). According to the Mārkendeya-Purāna, once Sage Māndasya cursed a Brāhmana named Kaushika that he would die at the sunrise the following morning. When Kaushika's wife Kaushikee heard about the curse, she declared, "From now on, the sun shall never rise." When the sun did not rise for many days under the influence of Kaushikee's honor, lamentations filled all the Three Worlds (Earth, Heaven and Hinterland). Brahmā encouraged the gods to go in the shelter of Anasooyā saying that she alone could help them. The gods then went to Anasooyā and prayed to her that she bring about sunrise using the force of her austerity and moral power. Upon hearing the gods' entreaty, Anasooyā inspired Kaushikee to permit the sunrise to take place. Kaushikee did permit the sunrise to occur, but her husband Kaushika expired instantly on account of the curse. However, Anasooyā brought him back to life by the force of her austerity and devotion to her husband. The Mārkendeya-Purāna presents the illustration to us that one Indian woman, by virtue of her devotion to her husband, is capable of stopping the sun from rising, while another one, of imparting a new life to a dead person.

Because of the stoppage of the sunrise, the whole earth was about to be destroyed. It was saved when the sunrise took place again. All the gods were very pleased with Anasooyā for her act and asked her to seek any boon her heart desired. Anasooyā asked for the boon that she should have sons who were incarnations of Brahmā, Vishnu and Mahesha (Shiva). By virtue of this boon, Brahmā incarnated as her son Soma, Vishnu as Dattātreya, and Mahesha as Durvāsā. In time all three became great and illustrious sages.

When Shri Rāma arrived at Sage Atri's āshrama during His exile to the forest, then Sage Atri, introducing his wife Anasooyā to him, said, "She is a great lady following the path of austerity and deserves the salutations of all beings. She is like a mother to you, deserving your worship. She is completely free of anger." Anasooyā was a shining model among women devoted to their husbands, bearing a heavenly glow.

The word 'Anasooyā' means 'One free from all vices and shortcomings.' Seetā also saluted Anasooyā at her ripe old age. Anasooyā told Seetā, "A husband is like a highest god to his wife. You should continue serving your husband, Shri Rāmachandra, as you have been doing. Always follow your Satee-Dharma (being engaged in devotion and duty to husband). This would satisfy your Dharma (duty) and also give you good name and fame as well."

The prestige of Indian womanhood has been established in the world through the glorious character and illustrious personality of such women. *The Indian culture has gained a high level of splendor from the aura of such great women.*

SĀVITREE

According to the tales contained in the Mahābhārata and the 'Matsya-Purāna,' there lived a king of Madra-Desha named Ashwapati. He observed penance for years, to please Brahmā for the sake of being blessed with progeny. After some time, he had a daughter, whose name he chose to be Sāvitree. Sāvitree was Ashwapati's only child. She was a girl of incomparable beauty, illustrious personality, high character and all great qualities.

When Sāvitree grew up, Ashwapati could not find a worthy husband for her, and sent her to different provinces so that she could herself find a husband she liked. Sāvitree decided to marry Satyavāna, the son of Dyumatsena, the exiled and blind king of Shalya-Desha. They lived in a forest due to being in exile. Satyavāna also lived in the hermitage with his parents. His conduct was like a young sage, since Dyumatsena himself lived in the forest like a sage. Yet there was a glimmer of royalty in Satyavāna's countenance, which charmed Sāvitree's heart. Within her heart she started to regard Satyavāna as her husband. When she was narrating her decision to her father in this connection, Sage Nārada happened to come there. He had all the praise for Satyavāna, but he revealed the fact that Satyavāna was to live only for a short time. He would die exactly after one year. But Sāvitree had already selected him as her husband, once for all, and she insisted that she would not marry anyone but him. The king was obliged to have this marriage performed.

Satyavāna used to go every morning to the forest to chop woods, coming back in the evening. Exactly after one year, Satyavāna set out to chop woods as usual. Sāvitree was already observing penance for months. She also started after him. While chopping woods, Satyavāna suffered a headache and he fell down.

Just then Sāvitree saw a ferocious being coming closer. It was Yama (god of Death). He had come to fetch Satyavāna's soul, as his life span was over. Sāvitree started following him. Yama tried to dissuade her from following him, accepting to give her many boons one after another, except for Satyavāna's life; but Sāvitree continued to follow him.

Sāvitree asked Yama for eyesight for her blind father-in-law as the first boon; and regaining for him, his lost kingdom as the second boon. For the third boon, she asked for one hundred sons for her father. Then, for the fourth boon, Sāvitree said: "Let there be one hundred sons born to me also, all just as handsome, brave and wise as Satyavāna."

Yama, without minding much, just as before, uttered, "So be it." A moment later he realized his mistake but, bound by his words, he brought back Satyavāna to life again. He was full of praise for Sāvitree. In this manner, by virtue of her steadfast devotion to her husband, Sāvitree redeemed the families of her husband as well as of her father. *Sāvitree conquered even death through the power of her austerity, wisdom and devotion to her husband*. Sāvitree's name will forever remain immortal. The Hindus and India are proud of Sāvitree.

❑　❑　❑

SHAKUNTALĀ

Once the celestial nymph Menakā alighted to the earth and, by marrying the Sage Vishwāmitra, gave birth to a baby girl. However, Menakā left the baby in the forest where a swan protected her under its wings; hence the name 'Shakuntalā' was given to her by Sage Kanva who found her and adopted her as his daughter. His āshrama was nearby where Shakuntalā grew among the āshrama's folks as well as loving flora and fauna. She grew up to be the most beautiful young woman and spent time, with her female companions, Anasooyā and Priyamvadā taking care of the dears and creepers around the āshrama.

One day, King Dushyanta came near the āshrama while out on a hunting trip to the forest. Sage Kanva was away at that time. The king and Shakuntalā saw each other and instantly fell in love. The king, however, hid his true identity from Shakuntalā, just saying that he was an official of the king. He married Shakuntalā. After a few days, he had to return to his kingdom. He took leave of Shakuntalā, assuring her that he would send for her soon. He gave the royal ring to her as a parting gift and as an insignia of royalty.

Shakuntalā became very lonely and sad upon the departure of her beloved husband. She would sit by herself for hours, forgetting her surroundings, reminiscing about Dushyanta. One day Sage Durvāsā, renowned for his quick temper, came to the āshrama and called out for alms. No one was around except Shakuntalā who, as usual, was lost in Dushyanta's memory and, therefore, did not hear Durvāsā's call. Durvāsā, thinking that she was purposely ignoring him, became furious and cursed her, saying that whosoever she was thinking about would completely forget her. Shakuntalā's friends, Anasooyā and Priyamvadā, just back in the āshrama from their errands, overheard the curse and prayed to Durvāsā to nullify it. Durvāsā did not comply. However, he said that if the person Shakuntalā was thinking about sees some sign or object belonging to him, he would remember her just fine. The two friends became assured because they knew Shakuntalā had the ring given by Dushyanta, which would ward off any calamity. Shakuntalā remained oblivious to all this happenings.

After some time Sage Kanva returned to the āshrama and learnt everything about Shakuntalā's marriage with Dushyanta. Shakuntalā was carrying Dushyanta's child, and it was decided that she should best go to her husband's place to live with him, even though he had not sent for her or cared to inquire about her welfare so far. As ill luck would have it, in course of her journey to the kingdom with the āshrama troupe, Shakuntalā lost the royal ring while drinking water in a river. When Dushyanta saw Shakuntalā in his court, he refused to recognize her because of Sage Durvāsā's curse. Shakuntalā, following the premonition of her friends, wanted to show the king his ring to help the situation, but the ring was not to be found. Finally, she had to leave the court in humiliation and went to a forest to stay by herself. In time, she gave birth to a handsome and strong boy whom she named Bharata. Bharata was so strong that, when he was a little older, he played with the cubs of lions, counting their teeth.

By coincidence, a fisherman found the missing royal ring in the belly of a fish he caught in the river, and gave the ring to the king. As soon as Dushyanta saw the ring, he remembered everything about his meeting Shakuntalā, getting married to her, leaving her in the āshrama, and rejecting her when she came to see him in the court, pregnant. He became most dejected at his forgetfulness and folly, and searched for her everywhere, but of no avail. One time, he happened to be in the same forest where Shakuntalā lived, and met his forgotten wife and son Bharata. They all came back to the kingdom and lived happily ever after. Shakuntalā is regarded with the highest respect and love for her steadfast devotion for her husband. Her son, Bharata, became such a valiant emperor that the country, now known as India, was named as Bhārata after him.

⌘　⌘　⌘

AHALYĀ

Ahalyā was the wife of Sage Gautama. Of the five glorious women who are regarded as worthy of being remembered every morning, the name of Ahalyā comes first. The other four jewels of women are : Seetā, Draupadi, Tārā and Mandodaree. Ahalyā's name has been mentioned in the *Atharva-Veda* and other Vedic books as well.

Brahmā caused the origin of a beautiful baby girl who was called 'Ahalyā' for being free of '*Hala*' (sin). Brahmā kept this girl with Sage Gautama as a caretaker. After some time, when Ahalyā grew to be a beautiful young woman, Gautama went to Brahmā to return her to him. Brahmā, pleased with the sense of pious duty and self-control on part of Gautama, got Ahalyā married with him. They had a son named Shatānanda, who became the royal priest of King Janaka. Ahalyā's story is described in the Devee-Bhāgavata, the Brahmavaivarta-Purāna and the Vālmeeki Rāmāyana.

One episode that is famous is as follows: Indra, the king of gods, in cooperation with the Moon god, assumed the form of Sage Gautama and committed a sin with Ahalyā. Ahalyā, though she was devoted to her husband, could not recognize Indra incognito. On learning about this incident, Gautama became incensed with anger and cursed Indra to become *'Sahasrabhanga'*, and Ahalyā to turn into a stone. Later, becoming pleased with Ahalyā's entreaty, he said to Ahalyā that she would resume her original human form when, in the *Tretā-Yuga*, Lord Rāma would touch her with his feet. Due to the curse, Ahalyā continued lying in the form of a stone. When the time came, Shri Rāma, traveling to Janakapuri with his guru, Sage Vishwāmitra, emancipated Ahalyā, bringing her to resume her human form.

The reason for Indra's transgression was the fear the gods had of Sage Gautama and his severe austerities, which made him capable of gaining the kingdom of the heaven. The gods wanted to disrupt Gautama's *tapasyā* (austerities), which was possible only by raising fumes of rage in his mind. To disrupt Sage Gautama's *tapasyā* and to set his mind on extreme rage, Indra committed sin under permission from the Devatās. The enraged sage uttered the curse, and this damaged the effect of his penance and austerities.

Devoted to her husband, always absorbed in serving him, Ahalyā became a stone due to her husband's curse; and Lord Rāma himself brought her back to human life. Ahalyā is most certainly one of the greatest women of India.

❖ जय श्रीराम ❖

SEETĀ

Seetā was King Janaka's daughter. Janaka, the king of Mithilā, had to ceremonially plow the land due to a famine in the kingdom. While moving the golden plow, a pitcher full of human blood, buried in the ground was unearthed. Out of which Seetā appeared. The tip of the plow is called 'seetā.' Since the pitcher appeared through the plow's tip, so this baby girl's name was chosen to be Seetā. The blood was that of saints and sages who failed to pay the taxes levied by the demon king of Lanka, Rāvana. Out of fear, he had it buried in a field in Mithilā, far away from Lankā. Thus, Seetā was born out of the blood of those sages, and became the cause of Rāvana's destruction. In the previous life, Seetā's name was Devavatee, who was the daughter of Krishdhwaja, son of Vrahaspati. When Rāvana compelled Devavatee to marry him by force, she burned herself in fire to ashes and cursed him, saying, "In my next life, I would become the cause of your destruction."

Rāma, the son of Dasharatha, the king of Ayodhyā, broke the Bow of Lord Shiva (a precondition set by King Janaka in Seetā's *Swayambara*) and won Seetā's hand in marriage. By the order of Mother Kaikeyi, Rāma, Lakshmana and Seetā took exile in the forest. During the period of the exile, Rāvana abducted Seetā while Rāma and Lakshmana were away. Rāvana kept her in the *Ashoka-Vātikā* (garden of the Ashoka trees) in Lankā. He began to coerce her again and again to marry him. Rāma and Lakshmana kept wandering in many forests in search of Seetā. With the help of an army of the Devatās (gods) disguised as monkeys, Rāma attacked Lankā when he found the whereabouts of Seetā. A fierce battle followed in which Rāvana and his demon army was annihilated, and Seetā was freed from Rāvana's captivity.

Agni-Parikshā (witness by Fire-god to testify the truth) was arranged to protect Seetā's reputation as a devoted wife. Thereafter Lord Rāma, Lakshmana and Seetā returned to Ayodhyā. Rāma was crowned and he began looking after the people of the kingdom. One time a washerman expressed doubt about Seetā's plight as a prisoner of Rāvana. Following a king's dharma (duty) to put his subject first, Rāma made a supreme self-sacrifice; he exiled his beloved and devoted wife Seetā who was an expectant at that time. She gave birth to twin boys in the Āshrama of Sage Vālmeeki. They were named Lava and Kusha, respectively.

When the twin boys grew up to become young adults, Sage Vālmeeki came to Ayodhyā with Seetā, Lava and Kusha. There, the sage told the citizens of Ayodhyā that Seetā was as pure as the Gangā. Rāma wished to welcome Seetā back, but the Daughter of the Earth prayed to Mother Earth to open and let her take shelter within, thus ending her mortal life.

Seetā's entire life was full of self-sacrifice and struggle in order to observe her dharma as a daughter, a wife, a queen, and a mother. She gave up all the comforts of the palace and resolved to bear every adversity of the forest to accompany her husband. She always upheld the sanctity of the Indian Woman. Seetā holds the highest place among Indian women by bringing honor to women and by establishing a model of marital faithfulness and duty. Seetā epitomizes all that is good in womanhood to be emulated in real life. Seetā is looked upon by all Hindus as virtue incarnate; they worship her as a goddess.

Swāmi Vivekānanda once remarked: "Seetā is unique, that character was depicted once and for all. There may have been several Rāmas, perhaps, but never more than one Seetā! Here she stands these thousands of years, commanding the worship of every man, woman and child, throughout the length and breadth of Āryāvarta (the greater India). There she will always be glorious Seetā, purer than purity itself, all patience, and all suffering. All our mythology may vanish, even our Vedas may depart, and our Sanskrit language may vanish forever, but there will be the story of Seetā. Seetā has gone into the very vital of our race. She is in the blood of every Hindu man and woman; we are all children of Seetā. The women of India must grow and develop in the footprints of Seetā, and that is the only way."

❖ जय सीताराम ❖

KUNTI

Queen Kunti was one of the two wives of king Pāndu. She was gifted with great beauty and character. She gave birth to Yudhishthira, Bheema and Arjuna. Mādri, Pāndu's second wife, bore two sons, named Nakula and Sahadeva, respectively. These five sons of Pāndu were called the Pāndavas. Karna was another son of Kunti, elder to the Pāndavas, but the ill-fated hero was not to be called a Pāndava. Pāndu was the ruler of the kingdom of Hastināpura (present-day Delhi), since his elder brother, Dhritarāshtra, was blind from birth. Dhritarāshtra married Gāndhāri from the kingdom of Gandhāra (present-day Kandhāra in Afghānistāna) and fathered one hundred sons called the Kauravas. The eldest was the ambitious, wicked and cruel Duryodhana.

Yudhishthira, as the eldest son of king Pāndu, was designated as the future king when he came of age. But a smooth transfer of power was not to be. Although Dhritarāshtra at first recognized Yudhishthira as the rightful future king, he later allowed himself to be swayed by his eldest son, the power-hungry and wicked Duryodhana, who wished to ascend to the throne in place of Yudhishthira. Driven by jealousy and lust for power, Duryodhana plotted against the Pāndavas. He inflicted many sufferings upon them, including a plot to kill the Pāndavas. All the while, the Pāndavas were accompanied by their mother Kunti. She also suffered Duryodhana's atrocities in the company of her beloved sons. Miraculously, however, Kunti and the Pāndavas repeatedly escaped death. Ultimately Duryodhana cheated the Pāndavas out of their kingdom in a gambling game. As a result of the game of dice, Pāndavas' wife, Draupadi, was humiliated in the royal court by the Kauravas, and the Pāndavas themselves were forced to spend thirteen years in exile in the forest — to the great sorrow of Kunti.

On return from the exile, the Pāndavas sought to get their kingdom back. All their efforts failed, however, including the peace mission of Shri Krishna. The war became inevitable. The Mahābhārta war began and lasted for eighteen days in which all but a handful of the warriors were killed. The Pāndavas aided by Shri Krishna won the war.

Kunti always wished peace and welfare of all; but she was helpless to change much of what was happening. She saw grandsire Bheeshma's death and her grandson Abhimanyu killed by unfair means. Her eldest son, Karna, a great warrior in the Kaurava camp, was killed by Arjuna. When the war was over, Yudhishthira was crowned the emperor. Dhritarāshtra and Gāndhāri left to live in solitude for peace. Kunti and Vidura accompanied them.

Kunti was a steadfast devotee of Shri Krishna. He called her 'Buā' (father's sister), and accorded her the highest respect. She, on her part, loved Him as she did her own sons; though she was well-aware of the divinity in Him. Even facing calamities, she would exclaim to the Lord, "I do not mind my suffering at all, for suffering makes me remember you more."

DRAUPADI

Draupadi was the daughter of Drupada, the king of Pānchāla (the present-day Punjāb State of India). She was born from the fire of the Yajna, hence Draupadi was also called 'Yajnasenee.' As she was of dark complexion, she bore still another name — Krishnā. In accordance with the inadvertent words of Kunti, Draupadi became the wife of the five Pāndavas. In reality, Draupadi was the wife of god Indra who took five different forms to fulfill a boon granted to her by Lord Shiva in her previous birth. She was most devoted to her husbands and a great devotee of God. She had steadfast devotion and love for Lord Krishna. She regarded Krishna as her protector, great well-wisher and a close friend. When wicked Duhshāshana was trying to disrobe her in the court of the Kauravas, then Draupadi, becoming hopeless from all directions, beckoned Krishna for her protection. Krishna heard Draupadi's distress-call and protected her honor by magically imparting endless lengh to the robe, while He was in Dwārakā. During the exile of the Pāndavas, the quick-tempered sage Durvāsā invited himself along with hundreds of his disciples to test Draupadi's hospitality. She had been gifted a magic pot with inexhaustible supply of food, but only till she herself finished eating. As she had already done so for the day, she called upon Krishna to save the day. Krishna just tasted a tiny residual bit of vegetable still sticking in a corner of Draupadi's magic pot. This act of Krishna made the stomachs of Durvāsā and his entourage painfully full in order to save her and the Pāndavas from embarrassment and from Sage Durvāsā's curse.

Draupadi had the fire of a lady-warrior and yet she was forgiving as a devotee. She was steadfastly devoted to, and eager to serve, her husbands. She was extremely tolerant, truthful, sweet- spoken and free of jealousy and egotism. These qualities of Draupadi's character are apparent from many episodes of the Mahābhārata. She says to Satyabhāmā about herself, "I serve the Pāndavas day and night, tolerating hunger and thirst. I rise before anyone else, and go to bed after everyone else does." One can learn how a wife should conduct herself from the conduct Draupadi followed.

Draupadi gave birth to five sons who all became strong and brave warriors. But at the end of the Mahābhārata war, Ashwatthāmā of the Kaurava camp killed all of them when they were asleep.

When Lord Krishna was going to the Kauravas with a peace treaty, Draupadi said to him, "Shri Krishna, you are going to propose a treaty, which is just fine. But please do not forget about my vow (to avenge Duhshāshana). If the Pāndavas decline from waging a war, then my old father, together with his warrior sons, will fight the Kauravas. They will be joined by Abhimanyu and my five brave sons." This utterance of Draupadi shows her image of a self-respecting and brave Kshatriya (warrior) lady. Yet her illustrious and forgiving character is reflected by the fact that she forgave Ashwatthāmā because he was the son of the family guru and she had utmost respect for the guru.

Towards the end of their lives, the Pāndavas set out to the Himalayās. Eventually, they gained ascension to the Heaven. Draupadi was the last in the line, walking slowly. On the way, she was the first to fall down from fatigue. By God's grace she ascended to the Heaven after she died.

Draupadi was an ideal devotee to her husbands, a superb householder, and a devotee to Lord Krishna, second to none. Her entire life was full of terrible conflicts and struggles. She is one of the greatest women of the ancient India.

MADĀLASĀ

Madālasā holds a very high rank among the women of India who shine brilliantly like jewels. Indeed, the high place India holds in the world in the realm of spirituality and transcendental knowledge owes much to the brilliant light she, among other jewels of India, bore. The lore of Madālasā, famed for preaching spiritual knowledge to her children in the form of lullaby songs, is narrated in the Mārkandeya Purāna.

Madālasā was the daughter of the Gandharva-king Vishwavasu. She was married to Ritadhwaja, the son of the famed and powerful king Shatrujita. Her marriage took place in the absence of her parents. So, when Ritadhwaja came to see his father along with his new bride, the king Shatrujita became very happy and blessed the couple. After some time, when Shatrujita passed away, Ritadhwaja was crowned as the king and he started taking care of his duty of looking after his subjects as a king.

In due course, Madālasā gave birth to a son. He was named Vikrānta. Whenever the baby-boy cried, his learned mother used to sing a lullaby to pacify him, "O my son! You are really a soul. You have no name; this fictitious name has been assigned to you just recently. The body is constituted of five elements — the earth, water, air, fire, and space. Neither this body is yours, nor you are of this body. Why do you, then, cry." In this way, Madālasā imparted the spiritual knowledge to her son. By virtue of such knowledge and his *samskāras* (the inherent inclinations cultivated from previous birth and also imparted by parents, teachers and elders at an early age), Vikrānta became detached from worldly interests and royalty, etc., and left for the forest to pursue 'tapasyā' (austerity and meditation).

Similarly, her second and third sons, named Subāhu and Shatrumardana, respectively, inspired by their mother's preaching of spiritual knowledge, left home, renouncing the world. Madālasā preached about the mortality of the body and the immortality of the soul to her husband, Ritadhwaja, as well.

However, Ritadhwaja asked Madālasā not to preach the same knowledge to their fourth son, Alarka, so that there would be at least one prince who would choose the worldly path and take care of the kingdom as a future king. On being so instructed by Ritadhwaja, Madālasā sang a different lullaby to Alarka, "O son! You are blessed to look after and nourish the land for a long time to come, all by yourself, free from enemies. You would protect and nourish the land and attain immortality and thereby enjoy the bounty of life. Serve your family, kin, subjects and Brāhmans well; and never let your mind stray to other women," and so on.

In this way, Madālasā educated her son, Alarka, about the duties of a king. This is how great women offer truthful thoughts and good samskāras to their children so as to render their lives successful and meaningful, as Madālasā did so well. She is a mirror of the nobility and greatness of Indian womanhood endowed with the knowledge of high degree of spirituality as well as of the principles of good governance.

✳ ✳ ✳

In the Hindu Tradition, samskāras, the natural and inherent inclinations of a person resulting from his or her accumulated karma of previous births as well as from the teachings of the parents, teachers and elders at an early age, are considered as one of the most important elements of life. Indeed, development of the samskāras occurs as a part of the life-long-journey, beginning from the conception of the baby to the end of life, impacting one's own life as well as the lives of one's progeny.

GĀRGEE

Gārgee is very renowned in the Vedic literature. Her father's name was 'Vachaknu,' and so she came to be known as 'Vāchaknavee.' Because of being born in the Garga Gotra (community), she was also called Gārgee — a name that became well known. Nowhere one finds mention of her real name Vāchaknavee. From the questions she asked Sage Yajnavalkya, as mentioned in the Vrihadāranyak Upanishad, it is apparent that she was extremely wise and highly learned in the spiritual sciences.

King Janaka once organized a debate in his court to discuss spiritual scriptures. He wanted to know as to who was the best knower of *Brahman* in the world at that time. He arranged to present one thousand cows, their horns covered with gold, and announced in the court, "Whosoever is the best Knower of *Brahman* amongst you, can take these cows." None of the Brāhmanas (scholars, knowers of Brahman) dared to take the cows, since everyone knew that he would have to prove his knowledge in the debate to establish him as the best among the lot. Then the great sage, Yajnavalkya, asked his disciple, "You shepherd all these cows and take them away from here for me." This opened the debate. Many scholars asked many questions to Yajnavalkya, who patiently answered all their questions, allaying their concerns and doubts.

Now it was Gārgee's turn. She asked many difficult and complex questions to Yajnavalkya on the science of the *Brahman*, Cosmology, elements of immortality, language, etc. From these questions asked by Gārgee, it was obvious that she was a most learned lady and exponent of *Brahman*. Upon hearing from Yajnavalkya the answers of her last two questions, regarding *Brahman*, the Absolute Soul, Gārgee also bowed her head to the great sage Yajnavalkya. In that assembly of the learned, Gārgee pronounced the verdict, "There is no Knower of *Brahman* superior to Sage Yajnavalkya; no one can defeat him."

Gārgee was not only herself very studious and profoundly learned in the scriptures, but she also respected others who were learned. She had no bias to prove herself above others. That's why Gārgee generously praised Yajnavalkya. Gārgee was an ascetic lady and a learned one of the highest order — a luminous jewel among the women of India.

* * *

MAITREYEE

The great sage, Yajnavalkya, had two wives: Maitreyee and Kātyāyanee. Both were of high character and devoted to their husband. But Maitreyee possessed a greater degree of love for God; she took a deeper interest in Brahma-Vidyā (knowledge of God) and spirituality. Kātyāyanee's mind was more inclined toward worldly delights. At the time of opting for Sanyāsa (renunciation of the world), the great sage said to Maitreyee, "O Maitreyee, now I wish to follow the path of Sanyāsa, renouncing the stage of the householder. In order for you two to live happily after I am gone, I want to distribute the assets of the family between the two of you in equal shares."

Maitreyee was a very wise and farsighted lady. She thought that someone becomes ready to relinquish his possession only when he acquires something which is even more valuable. The great sage was leaving this household, so he must have gotten something in comparison of which this household started appearing of little value to him. The great sage must be renouncing this (householder's) life only to reach God, Who is the Symbol of Immortality and delivers from the bondage of birth and death. Thinking thus, Maitreyee asked the great sage, Yajnavalkya, "Lord, even if I get the whole earth full of all the riches, can I obtain immortality from that?" Yajnavalkya answered, "Not at all. Your life might enjoy all the happiness and conveniences upon getting riches; but that cannot lead you to immortality or to God."

Maitreyee said, "What would I do with the riches that are incapable of delivering me from the bonds of birth and death? Please tell me about immortality, about that Absolute Being, to achieve which you are happily giving up this life of a householder, now insignificant in your eyes."

Thereupon, Sage Yajnavalkya propounded to Maitreyee the precept of the Self. He said, "A woman is not dear to a man for her being a woman, but for being the Self. A son is not dear to the father for being the son, but for being the Self. The world is not dear for its worldliness but for being the Self. The Self or the Soul is the only basis of Absolute Love. In fact, only the Soul is worthy of philosophy, hearing, meditation and contemplation. All knowledge becomes accessible by witnessing, hearing of, meditating upon, and a direct experience of, the soul. This is the divine knowledge, and harbinger of immortality. Maitreyee, this is the precept for you, and this is the path for *Moksha* (liberation from the bondage of birth and death)."

This tale from the Vrihadāranyak Upanishad tells us that after this, Yajnavalkya adopted Sanyāsa and Maitreyee attained Absolute bliss upon hearing her husband's precept and by virtue of her powerful sense of renunciation and her thirst for knowledge. It is because of women dedicated to true spiritual knowledge, such as Maitreyee, that the great name of India is spread all over the world.

❋   ❋   ❋

Rāni Padmini

Rāni Padmini going for Jauhara

Rāni Padmini is the epitome of Indian womanhood, and saga of sacrifice and valor. This heroic episode of the Bhārtiya culture was repeated two-times more. Third time the Mughal army of Akabar plundered and destroyed all the buildings and monuments of Chittora, the capital moved to Udaipur. In Indian history, Chittora stands for the heroism, chivalry, valor and sacrifice.

Rāni Padmini's Palace and Jauhara Kund

RĀNI PADMINI

Rāni Padmini was the queen of Rānā Ratan Singh of Sisodia dynasty of Mewāra, with its capital Chittora, in Rājasthāna, India. It was a fiercely independent kingdom. Rāni Padmini was famous for her exquisite beauty. However, she also had an exalted place in the Rājaputa chivalry. No woman in the history can match what Padmini did to uphold the honor of Indian womanhood. Delhi had fallen to the relentless and savage attacks of Islamic invaders. Ala'uddin Khilji happened to be at the helm of power at the time. It is said that one reason for Ala'uddin Khilji's invasion of India, in particular Rājasthāna was his ardent lust for Padmini. The history records the chivalrous role of Padmini and a number of other women of Mewāra when the famous citadel of Chittora was besieged by Ala'uddin. The valiant Rājaputas offered a heroic resistance against his onslaught for about eight months, but they were no match to the large army of Delhi. Before the final battle of the citadel, however, on the 26th August 1303, the brave Rājaputa women, under the leadership of Rāni Padmini, plunged themselves into the fire of *'jauhara'* (self immolation) to escape captivity.

The historical records show, "The funeral pyre was lighted within the great subterranean retreat, in chambers impervious to the light of the day, and defenders of Chittora beheld in procession the queens, their own wives and daughters, to the number of several thousands. The queen Padmini closed the throng. Then they were conveyed to the cavern, and the opening was closed upon them, leaving them to the final security from dishonor in the devouring fire." Thus Padmini and other women of Chittora preferred heroic death rather than disgrace. Today Rāni Padmini is one of the epitomes of Indian womanhood and a saga of sacrifice and valor.

In continuation of this heroic episode, the fort at Chittorgarh was under siege thrice and each time the Rājaputas had to suffer heavily to uphold their honor. The second time the attack took place in 1535 by Sultāna Bahādura Shah when, Bikaramajeeta was on the throne. In this instance Rāni Karmavati undertook *jauhara* with other women of Chittora. The third attack was by Akabar during the rule of Mahārānā Udai Singh. This was the final attack on Chittora when the Mughal army looted and destroyed all the buildings and monuments. Thereafter, the capital was shifted to Udaipur. Chittora stands for the heroism, chivalry, valor and sacrifice — inherent characteristics of the Rājaputas. The *Victory-Stambha* (The Victory Tower) of Chittora speaks of the valor of men and women of Rājasthāna.

✻   ✻   ✻

RĀNI DURGĀVATI

Rāni Durgāvati was born on October 5, 1524, at Kalanjar in Bānda district of the Uttara Pradesha State of India. She was the daughter of the Rājaputa chief of Mahobā and descendent from the Chandela Emperor Vidyādhara — a man of great accomplishments. He was one of the few Indian kings who repulsed the attack of the Islamic invader, Mahmood Ghaznavi, in the closing years of the 12th Century. However, the Chandela Dynasty is best known for building 85 Khajurāho temples. Even today a few temples that survived are among the wonders of magnificence and architecture, especially the Kandariya Mahādeva Temple

In 1542 **CE**, Durgāvati was married to Dalpatashāha, the eldest son of the Gonda king Sangrāmashah. The marriage united the Chandela and Gonda dynasties. This enabled her father, the Chandela king Keerata Rai, to get help from the Gondas at the time Shershāha Suri invaded. A short time later, her husband became seriously ill and died in 1550 **CE**. She gathered her courage and began to rule as her only son, Bira Nārāyana, who was born in 1545 **CE**, was a minor. This kingdom was so well administered that it became full of wealth and thus became a target for conquest by other rulers.

Rāni Durgāvati of the kingdom of Gondwānā was a very brave lady who was inspired by a sense of genuine loyalty to the interests of her country. Endowed with loveliness and grace, fine accomplishments, unflinching determination and selfless heroism, she not only repulsed an attack on the kingdom of Gondwānā by Baz Bahādura of Malwā, but also made a gallant defense against the onrush of Mughal imperialism on it. She was a fearless hunter. It was her pledge that if a tiger had made an appearance, she didn't drink water till she had shot the tiger.

In 1564 **CE**, the Mughal emperor, Akbar, directed one of his commanders, Āsaf Khan, to conquer the kingdom of Gondwānā. On the advance of the huge imperial Mughal army, Rāni Durgāvati was cautioned by her counselors, to which she replied, "*It is better to die with glory than to live with ignominy.*" Her son, Bira Nārāyana, was seriously wounded and moved to safety. But she waged the war with great skill and bravery until she was disabled by two arrow-shots. That meant the inevitable defeat and surrender. Her faithful officers wanted to carry her from the battle-field to a place of safety. She rejected the proposal. In the true spirit of one of Rājaputa descent, Rāni Durgāvati preferred death to disgrace and stabbed herself to death. It was the 24th day of June in 1564 **CE**. Her son was later captured and killed.

Thus, her end was as noble as her life. She ruled the kingdom during her fifteen-year of regency with great ability and nobility. The memory of this brave queen is cherished even today. Rāni Durgāvati is famous in Indian history for refusing to submit to the Mughal emperor, Akbar, as he pushed ever deeper into Central India as part of his goal of dominating all of India.

❊ ❊ ❊

ĀNDĀLA

The dates of birth and death of Āndāla are not known. It is believed that she lived in the middle of Seventh or Eighth century **CE**. Periāzhwāra (henceforth referred here as Azhwara — one who dives deep into the ocean of Divine love) is known to be her father. One day Azhwara was working in the tulasi garden of Vishnu Temple in Shrivilliputtura when there suddenly appeared a baby girl. The childless Azhwara accepted the baby as divinely bestowed and named her Godā (born of Mother Earth).

Godā had intense love for God and accepted Him as her beloved consort. She used to adorn herself daily with the flower garland prepared for the Lord at the temple. After admiring her reflection and thinking of herself as His ideal bride, she would put the garland back for her father to take to the temple and offer to the Lord. One day, her father noticed a strand of Godā's hair on one of the garlands. Shocked and saddened by this desecration of what was meant only for the Lord, he scolded Godā for her misuse of the garland and discarded it. He carefully prepared a new one and offered it to the Lord, begging His pardon all the while. That night, the Lord appeared in his dream and told him that He missed the scent of Godā's body-hair-smell in the flowers, and that He preferred them that way. Her father realized that his daughter's love of God was so intense and pure that the Lord Himself wished to share her presence. From that day on, she became known as Āndāla, the girl who "ruled" over the Lord.

Tiruppāvai, by Āndāla is a most beautiful string of 30 verses giving expression to the purest love of God — equivalent to the love of the *gopis* of Vrindāvana for Lord Krishna. The story of Āndāla is a towering example of the purest love of God that any human could have. She wanted for herself nothing but God Himself, with absolutely no inhibition or doubt. She was certain that she belonged to the Lord and the Lord would accept her.

The two *Prabhandhāmas* (poetic creation) attributed to her are '*Tiruppāvai*' (30 verses) and '*Nāchiyāra Tiru-moli*' (143 verses), both included in the first thousand of the 4000 verses of the epic *Divya Prabhandhāma*. In 30 verses of *Tiruppāvai* she expressed her divine love in her immortal lyrics glowing with fervor. Her poems reflect the quintessence of the Upanishads. Her life was like her poem of the blossoming and fulfillment of that divine longing for her chosen Bridegroom. '*To see the Lord, to serve Him, and to be a part of Him,*' is the heart-rending theme of these immortal poems.

Āndāla is one of the most extraordinary personalities in religious history of India. She is known in the Tamil language as an '*Alvara*,' one who is immersed in the enjoyment of God, the omnipresent mysterious One. She is one of the twelve *Alvaras* of the *Vaishnava Sampradāya*, and the only female one (the others being Poykai, Bhutam, Pey, Tirumazhisai, Nammalvar, Periyalvar, Kulasekharan, Madhurakavi, Tondar-adi-podi, Tiruppaan and Tirumangai). Her significance in perfect spirituality, in Hinduism, is very unique. She was an example of perfection and purity. It seems that Meerā was her reincarnation many centuries later.

* * * * *

God Accepts Love : पत्रं पुष्पं फलं तोयं यो मे भक्त्या प्रयच्छति।
तदहं भक्त्युपहृतमश्नामि प्रयतात्मनः।।

Patram pushpam phalam toyam yo me bhaktyā prayachchhati;
Tadaham bhaktyupahritamshnāmi prayatātmanah.

—*Shrimad Bhagavad Geetā (Ch. 9, Shloka 26)*

Whoever offers even a leaf, or a flower, or a fruit or just water with devotion to Me, I accept that offering of love from my pure-hearted devotee.

✥ ✥ ✥

MEERĀBĀI

Meerābāi, the poet-laureate of devotional songs (*Bhajan*), and regarded as the incarnation of Rādhā, was born in 1498 **CE** in Mertā district of Rājasthāna, India. Her father, Ratan Singh, was the second son of Rāo Dudāji, a descendant of Rāo Jodhāji who was the founder of the city of Jodhapura. During her childhood, she was given a figurine of Lord Krishna by a wandering monk. She played, sang and always talked with it and developed an intense love for Lord Krishna. Meera's mother died when she was ten year old. She then came to live with her grandfather who died in 1515. Her father's brother, Vikrama Deo, who succeeded to the throne, arranged her marriage at the age of eighteen, with Prince Bhoja Rāja, the eldest son of Rānā Sāngā of Chittora. This marriage raised Meerā to a very high social status, as the ruler of Chittor was considered to be the leader of the Hindu princes. But luck didn't favor Princess Meerā. In January 1528 **CE** she lost her father in a battle with Mughal invader Bābar. Then she lost her husband and her father-in-law as well. Meerā, who dedicated her life to Lord Krishna, accepted these bereavements as a matter of course. Her love of Krishna was so absorbing that she neglected her social and royal responsibilities. She refused to offer worship to the family deity, Durgā. She sang and danced ecstatically in public temples and mingled freely with commoners. Her royal family members found this type of openness objectionable. Because of this, Meerābāi suffered great hardships, including being given a cup of poison to drink. Yet by Krishna's grace, she willingly accepted all such ordeals and she remained unscathed. On the advice of Sant Tulasidāsa, that *"the love of God alone is true and eternal; all other relationships are unreal and temporary,"* she left the palace for good at the age of 30, and went to the pilgrimage of Mathurā, Vrindāvana and finally to Dwārakā. Meerābāi spent most of her time in prayer and worship of Krishna.

She left behind a legacy of many soulful and prayerful songs, which are affectionately sung in India even today. Meerābāi is widely regarded as a saint in the tradition of the Bhakti (devotion) Movement. Meerābāi did not recognize social and caste-barriers and adopted Shri Ravidāsa, who belonged to a lower status in social order, as her Guru. She composed about 1300 devotional songs (*Bhajans*) that most passionately praised Lord Krishna. Most of them are in Hindi. Other saints belonging to this culture were Tukārāma, Kabir, Guru Nānaka and Rāmānanda.

Her love for Krishna is epitomized by the popular belief about her final disappearance in the temple of Krishna in Dwārakā. She is believed to have entered the sanctum of the temple in a state of ecstasy, singing. The sanctum doors are believed to have closed on their own and later, when people opened the door, the '*sārī*' of Meerābāi was seen wrapped around the statue of the deity, Lord Krishna, symbolizing the culmination of her union with her Lord, as if she came face-to-face with Krishna. She conversed with Krishna. She ate with Krishna — her Beloved. She drank the *Krishna-prema-rasa* (the nectar of love for Krishna). She sang from the core of her heart the music of her soul, the music of her Beloved, her unique spiritual experiences. On account of her renunciation of worldly attachments, including her royal status and a life of luxury, in preference to devotion to Lord Krishna, she will be remembered for ever. She spent her life dancing in trance and singing the attributes of her Beloved Krishna, till she left this mortal world in 1550 **CE** to be united with Him. She was a great Hindu woman-saint and will always be remembered as such.

Meerā and Sant Tulasidāsa were among the saviors who saved Hinduism from the ruthless onslaught of the Islamic imperialism and oppression in India perpetuated by Mughal emperors during the Sixteenth and Seventeenth centuries.

❖ जय गिरधर गोपाल ❖

RĀNI LAKSHMIBĀI OF JHĀNSI

Rāni Lakshmibāi of Jhānsi was a great heroine of the First war, in 1857, against the British imperialism, for Independence of India. A great symbol of the resistance against the British rule, she was born to Moropantha and Bhāgirathibāi on November 19, 1835, at Vārānasi, Uttara Pradesha, India. Her mother died when she was only four years old. In her father's care, she completed her education and learnt horse-riding, swordsmanship and target-shooting. She was married at an early age to Rājā Gangādhara Rāo of Jhānsi. She gave birth to a son who died at the age of 4 months. After this tragedy, Dāmodara Rao was adopted as a son. Mahārājā Gangādhara died on November 21, 1853, when Lakshmibāi was only eighteen years old. She did not lose her courage and took the responsibility of governing the estate. Dāmodara Rāo was a legal heir and successor of Mahārājā Gangādhara as per the Hindu tradition, but the-then Governor-General of British-India did not accept it as legal, and decided to annex the state of Jhānsi to expand the British Empire. In March 1854, the British ordered her to vacate the Jhānsi Fort. Rāni of Jhānsi was determined not to surrender the kingdom of Jhānsi to the British. She could not accept foreign domination on her soil and over the country. Her life thenceforth centered upon her resolve, *"I will not give up my Jhānsi."* As a true-born Marāthā princess, she took up a mission to fight the British. She was a symbol of patriotism and self-respect. The British were making every effort to destroy the freedom of the country, whereas Rāni was determined to rid the country of the British. Rāni Lakshmibāi assembled a volunteer army. The entire population of the kingdom was determined to fight with great enthusiasm for the cause of independence.

The War of India's Independence from the British was secretly organised by great revolutionary leaders of the country. However, by accident, it prematurely began at Meerut and Delhi on May 10, 1857. It rapidly spread to other parts of India. On June 5, 1857, it sparked in Jhānsi and on the 9th of June, Rāni Lakshmibāi's authority was proclaimed throughout the State. From this date to April 4, 1958, the Rāni stoutly defended the fort of Jhansi. She mobilized the people, organized the army by recruiting the Rājaputas and Rohillās, and joined the forces of Tāntia Tope against the British. The Rāni was always at the forefront of every battle, encouraging and directing her army and personally fighting the British forces. Ultimately, finding her position extremely precarious, she made her adventurous, lightening exit from the fort through the cordon of British troops, fiercely riding on her horse with her son, Dāmodara, strapped to her back. Her small fighting force with meager resources was no match to the well-equipped large army of the British. The Rāni fought valiantly, but lost her life in the battle at the age of 22, on June 17, 1858.

Rāni Lakshmibāi of Jhānsi was a national heroine, whose name conjures up visions of tremendous bravery and dauntless courage against overwhelming odds. In her, we find a symbol of unbreakable pride and utter fearlessness. The tales of this national heroine will be told to generations to come.

* * * * *

हमारा कर्त्तव्य

देश की सीमाएं माता के वस्त्रों के समान होती हैं, उसकी रक्षा करना पुत्र का प्रथम कर्त्तव्य है।

–भीष्म पितामह

BHAGINI NIVEDITĀ

To arouse the sleeping lion of India — to put the country on her glorious pedestal — was the life-mission of Swāmi Vivekānanda. For accomplishing this task, among many of his disciples, the name of Sister Niveditā is taken with great affection and respect. She was born on October 20, 1867, in Ireland, to parents Mary Isabel and Samuel Richmond Noble. Her childhood-name was Margaret Elizabeth Noble. Her father was a preacher to whom religion meant service to the poor. This had an imprint on Niveditā. She was very intelligent and hard-worker; and she loved music, art, and the natural sciences. After her education, she spent ten years, from 1884 to 1894, in teaching. She had a gift of being able to inspire her students. She was a proud, generous and ardent woman. By the age of eighteen, she came to understand that religion did not mean belief in the doctrines; it meant search of the Divine Light and Eternal Truth. She began to doubt the truth of the Christian doctrines. She started reading about Buddhism, but only with partial success in meeting her life-goal.

This was the time when she met a Hindu Monk, Swāmi Vivekānanda, who was visiting England in 1895. She attended all his lectures. In the question-answer sessions, she was an active and enthusiastic participant. Swāmiji's words — that selfishness, ignorance, and greed were the evils which brought suffering to the world — pierced through her mind and heart, and her life changed for ever. Swāmi Vivekānanda was very much impressed with her sincerity and urged her to help in his plans for the betterment of people, particularly underprivileged women. In response to the call of Swāmi Vivekānanda, Niveditā left England and arrived in Kolkata on January 28, 1898. Swāmiji initiated her to be a *Brahmachārini* (celibate women dedicated to austerity, studies and service) on March 25, 1898, and gave her the name 'Niveditā', meaning one who is dedicated to God. She started to study the 'Geetā' and to practice meditation. This helped her to cast-off her vain pride in the English culture. Salvation for oneself and to work for the welfare of others, were two ideas she pledged herself to pursue. For this, she lived a simple and pure life to realize God, and humbly served the people. By nature, she was optimist, but there were times she felt disheartened. At such moments, Swāmi Vivekānanda's words, *'Death for the cause is our goal, not necessarily success,'* inspired her. When Swāmi Vivekānanda passed away on July 4, 1902, she felt an added responsibility to her adopted land, India, and to her people.

She realized that political independence of India is a first essential step towards equality, progress and justice. In 1902, she addressed a meeting of the youth at Madras (now Chennai) and gave a rousing call to them to fight for the freedom of the country. She inspired the people in all walks of life through her lectures and writings. ***She always believed that India could not be great and powerful unless there was unity.*** She emphasized this in every possible way, and was never tired of speaking about it. Her hard work and lack of rest were having an adverse effect on her health. Nearing the end of her life, Niveditā said, "*The frail boat is sinking, but I shall yet see the sun rise.*" Chanting the prayer of the Upanishad — *Asato mā sad gamaya, tamaso mā jyotir gamaya, mrityor mā amritam gamaya* (From the truth, lead me to the Truth; from darkness, lead me to Light; from death, lead me to Immortality), Nivedita breathed her last. The dedicated daughter of Mother India went to sleep for ever, in her lap, on October 13, 1911.

The great offering, giving her life for Mother India, was like a song of love. Love is blind for it sees no faults of the beloved, and Niveditā never found faults with India. Such was her dedication to India.

ॐ शान्ति शान्ति शान्ति

MIRRĀ ALFĀSSĀ

Mirrā Alfāssā, lovingly called 'The Mother', the spiritual disciple and associate of Shri Aurobindo, was born in Paris on 21 February 1878. Her mother was Jewish-Egyptian and her father was Jewish-Turkish. Both of them were very materialistic. However, Mirrā had divine visions from her childhood. At the age of five, she realized that she did not belong in that surrounding, and right then, her spiritual discipline (*sādhanā*) began. She would lapse into a trance sometimes. Outwardly, she was brought up as an atheist, until she entered adulthood. In her early years, she had a good education in music (especially piano), painting, and higher mathematics. During this period, she used to have spontaneous spiritual experience, including that of coming out of her body, to discover the inner reality, even though she lacked an understanding of what all this really meant. As she was growing up, she began to have such experiences more often. Mirrā said that between nineteen and twenty years of age, she had achieved a conscious and constant union with the Divine Presence. Swāmi Vivekānanda's book on *Rāja-yoga* helped her. Thereafter, she studied the Bhagavad Geetā, taking Shri Krishna as a symbol of the Divinity. It put her on the path of a rapid progress.

One day, in 1912, she had a great vision of the future: "The advent of universal harmony, the realization of human unity, and the establishment of an ideal society." Shri Aurobindo had already visualized these ideas in his writings. She met Shri Aurobindo on 20 March 1914. He exactly resembled the man she used to see in her vision, since 1904. She went back to Paris, then traveled to Japan and other places and, finally, returned in 1920 to Pondicherry, India, where she remained for the rest of her life. Now the question for her was as to realize the ways and means by which this great vision of whole-being, whole-knowledge and whole-power could be attained for the whole society. Shri Aurobindo had recognized that this could be done through the processes of 'Yoga', many elements of which were known, while other ones had to be rediscovered, created, developed and perfected, in order to meet the needs of the modern man. She engaged herself with Shri Aurobindo in discovering a process of spiritual transformation totally different from that of the prevalent practices of yoga in order to attain *Moksha* (Liberation of the soul). It involved working on transforming and divinizing the consciousness of the entire planet — the spiritual transformation of humanity and life on earth as a whole. Shri Aurobindo considered Mirrā to be an incarnation (*Avatāra*) of the supreme power (*Shakti*). She came to be known by all 'The Mother'.

Shri Aurobindo was engaged in the same task since he came to Pondicherry. The Mother became an active participant in this endeavor. The result was what is known as the 'Integral Yoga,' developed jointly by Shri Aurobindo and the Mother. In the Integral Yoga, the Divine Power in us uses all life as the means of our upward evolution and then every experience becomes a step on the path toward achieving perfection. In this process, the Mother was to act as the '*Shakti*' in action. She accelerated this process with great vigor, even after Shri Aurobindo left his mortal body on December 5, 1950. She continued to expand that vision through education and counseling of the seekers of inner peace. Under her direction, Shri Aurobindo Āshrama (Spiritual Center) developed into a great spiritual-residential center where one could try to seek the Divine without having to worry about for food and shelter. In 1960, she also established a place where people from different parts of the world could live together in harmony and seek spirituality. She named this place Auroville. Her imprints can be seen in almost all aspects of the āshrama routine. She worked relentlessly till she passed away on November 17, 1973.

✳ ✳ ✳ ✳ ✳

The Divine is everywhere, in everything and if He is hidden, it is because we do not take the trouble to discover Him.
- The Mother

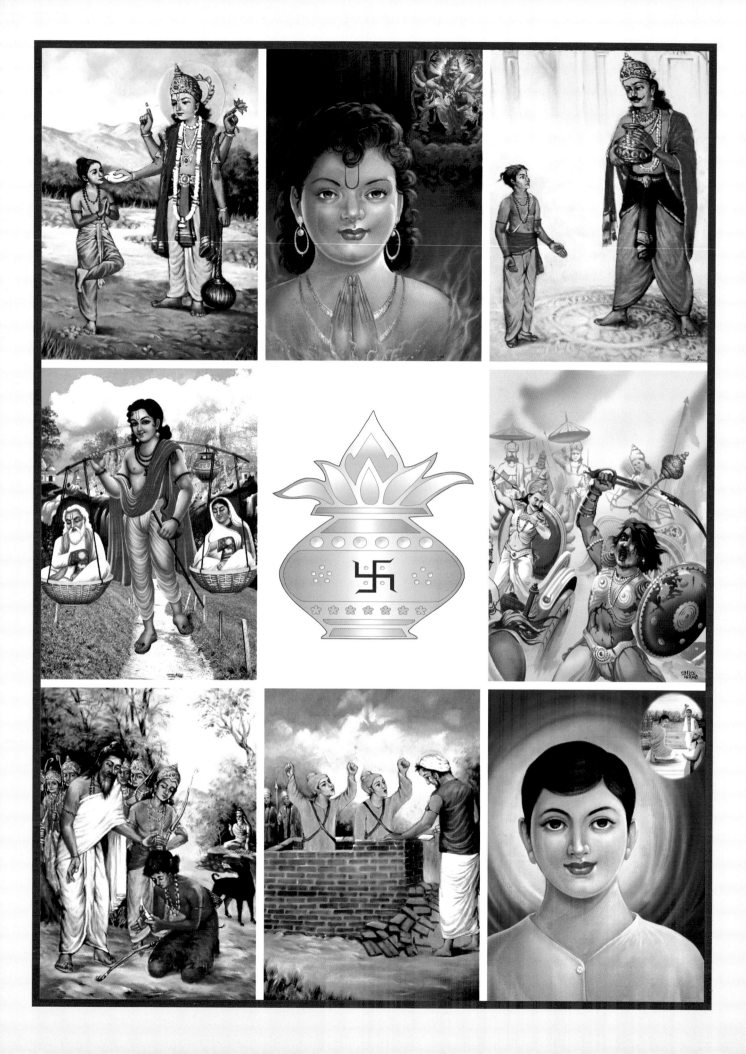

Part III

THE YOUTH ARCHITECTS OF SANĀTANA DHARMA

It is rightly said that the youth of today are the men and women of tomorrow and, hence, represent the future of the country. The character of the youth thus mirrors the direction and achievements of the society and the nation in days to come.

The children and youth may be ideally guided by the *Samskāras* of the Sanātana Dharma, by the simple, yet profound, principles such as: '*Mātri devo bhava*' (Mother is goddess); '*Pitri devo bhava*' (Father is god); '*Āchārya devo bhava*' (Teacher is god); '*Satyam vad*' (Speak the Truth); '*Dharmam char*' (Follow the Dharma — of humanity); and so on. The youth's adherence to such precepts would, and does, determine the destiny of their own lives as well as of their families, their nation, and, in no small measure, of the world at large.

What if the youth possess adult-like maturity and innate capability of performing superior feats, accomplishing outcomes far beyond the highest stretch of imagination, at a very tender age? There have been numerous examples in the landscape of ancient, and even more recent, India that come in this category, glorifying the Sanātana Dharma from which they all invariably draw strength and inspiration. Dhruva, Prahlāda, Shravana Kumār, Devavrata, Abhimanyu, Nachiketā, Ekalavya, Hakikata Rāi, Jorāvar Singh, Fateh Singh and many more are those illustrious names which illumine the pages of the history of India, ancient and modern. An endeavor to capture the glimpses of such immortal youths of India will surely benefit all readers, young and old.

Compassion, obedience, benevolence, bravery and honesty (दया, आज्ञापालन, परोपकार, वीरता, ईमानदारी), among other notable traits, are the priceless possessions of human life. These virtues make life elevated and are the essential part of a person's character to make one's life blissful and successful. Therefore, these values should be cultivated from childhood, so that the children become obedient to parents, teachers and elders, be always brave and honest, and may be benevolent to others.

The tales of such virtuous youth are inspiring. We hope that they will help in imbibing these virtues among children of coming generation, making them brave, honest, responsible and good citizens of the world, today and tomorrow.

DHRUVA
A Symbol of Firm Mind, Absolute Devotion, and Perfect Faith

King Uttanapada, of the Vedic Era, had two queens, Suneeti and Suruchi. Suneeti, the senior queen, had a son named Dhruva; while Suruchi had a son named Uttama. Once, when Dhruva was about five years old, he went to visit his father and saw Uttama sitting on his lap. When Dhruva approached the king, Queen Suruchi stopped him and exclaimed that if he wished to sit on his father's lap, he would have to be born as '*her*' son. The king had developed a partiality for Suruchi and, thus, he did not say a word. The dejected boy went to find his mother and explained what had happened. She advised him that, instead of craving for a mortal's lap, he should strive to gain a place in the lap of the Almighty. So his best recourse was to please Nārāyana (God). When Dhruva asked where he could find Nārāyana, Suneeti replied that strong penance was an established way to achieve the favor of God. At that instant, though he was very young, Dhruva made the decision to go to the jungle and perform strong austerities to please God. When he left the palace, Nārada, the wandering sage, devotee of Lord Vishnu, met him and tested his determination. Happy to see the young boy so resolute, Nārada told him to meditate in the Madhuvana forest on the banks of the Yamunā River. Dhruva innocently asked how he was to meditate, and Nārada instructed that he chant the mantra, "*Om Namo Bhagavate Vāsudevāya* (Om, Salutation to Bhagawāna Vāsudeva) ."

Dhruva began his austerities. As the months passed by, he first subsisted on fruits, then on water, and then just air, totally fasting. Eventually, he even gave up breathing! By the sixth month, Dhruva's concentration created such powerful vibrations that the inhabitants of the heaven and earth were unable to breathe. Then Nārāyana, pleased, descended on the earth to see his great devotee. Dhruva beheld in person the same vision of the four-armed Nārāyana he had in his heart. Nārāyana touched his conch on Dhruva's cheek and blessed him with divine knowledge. Dhruva delivered a prayer, and Nārāyana blessed him to go back to his kingdom and rule for many years, after which he would get a permanent place in the heaven as the '*Dhurva-Tārā*' (the Pole Star). While returning home, however, Dhruva felt remorse that though he had met Nārāyana, he did not achieve the ultimate goal of merging with Him.

ॐ

ॐ नमो भगवते वासुदेवाय !

ॐ नमो भगवते वासुदेवाय !

ॐ नमो भगवते वासुदेवाय !

ॐ नमो भगवते वासुदेवाय !

ॐ नमो भगवते वासुदेवाय !

PRAHLĀDA
A Devotee Par Excellence

The Hindu Mythology says that the *daityas* (demons) were the step-brothers of the *devatās* (gods) born of Diti and Aditi, respectively, the two wives of Sage Kashyapa. Both the demons and the gods were always at war with each other. Both ruled the three worlds (the Heaven or the Upper-Land, which is the abode of the gods; the Middle-Land where the mortals dwell; and the Nether or lower-Land, the abode of the demons) in their own way. But occasionally the demons gained control, seizing the thrones of the gods and usurping their power. Then the gods had to go to Lord Vishnu, the Preserver of peace and prosperity, and pray to Him to help them to regain their power. Lord Vishnu sometimes did it in a very curious way.

In such an epoch, there lived an atheist king, named Hiranyakashipu. He was powerful enough to defeat the gods. He crowned himself on the throne of the three worlds, declaring that nowhere in the universe there was any God. Therefore, being supreme in power, he ordered everyone to worship only him.

Hirnayakashipu had a son, Prahlāda, who was a great devotee of God. He refused to obey his father's command and, instead, prayed to Lord Vishnu. Hirnayakashipu became so angry that he ordered that Prahlāda be killed. However, all attempts to kill Prahlāda failed, including the attempt by Hirnayakashipu's sister Holikā who tried to burn Prahlāda in a pyre of fire but herself burned to ashes instead.

Hirnayakashipu was given a boon that no person or animal could kill him; that he would not die in the day or night, inside the palace or outside through the use of a weapon held in hand or thrown to him, and so on. Therefore, Lord Vishnu appeared at the time of dusk in the form of Half-lion and Half-man ('*Narasimha Incarnation*') and killed Hirnayakashipu at the edge of the door tearing him into pieces with His sharp nails. Thus, Lord relieved Prahlāda, His devotee, from all the sufferings being inflicted by his father. God-loving Prahlāda became the king and the subjects of the kingdom became God-loving. Peace and prosperity prevailed thereafter.

*   *   *   *   *

यदा यदा हि धर्मस्य ग्लानिर्भवति भारत।
अभ्युत्थानमधर्मस्य तदात्मानं सृजाम्यहम्॥
Yadā yadā hi dharmasya glānirbhavati Bhārata;
Abhyutthānamdharmasya tadatmānam srijāmyaham.
-Shrimad Bhagavad Geetā (Ch. 4, Shloka 7)

***O** Arjuna! Whenever there is a decline of righteousness, then I manifest Myself for emancipating and glorifying Dharma.*

NACHIKETĀ

The tradition of the teachings of Sanātana Dharma has long been in the format of dialogue and questions and answers. Such narrations are very productive and inspiring in passing the Hindu values to the younger generations. This ancient tradition is continuing even to this day.

There is an inspiring story in the *Kathopanishad* about a little boy named Nachiketā. He was the son of a great Rishi (Sage) Uddalaka and mother Vishwavaradevi. Following the usual tradition, Uddalaka organized a *Yajna* to please the gods. It was customary to donate cows to Brāhmanas at the end of the *Yajna*. Uddalaka was a miser and he donated old and weak cows to the Brāhmanas. None of the cows yielded any milk. This disturbed Nachiketā. He questioned his father about it. Not receiving a satisfactory answer, Nachiketā felt indignant and asked in despair, "Father, to whom would you give me in charity?" His father first ignored him so the boy repeated his question. This made his father lose his temper, and he said, "I give you to *Yama* (the god of Death)." Unhesitatingly obeying his father's command, Nachiketā went to *Yama's* kingdom. He reached *Yama's* house and was told that Yamarāja had gone out. Nachiketā decided to wait at his doorsteps till Yama returned. Nachiketā had waited for three days without any food or water. Yama returned on the fourth day and saw little Nachiketā at his doorsteps. He felt pained for keeping a Brāhmana boy waiting without the customary hospitality, without even food and water. It was a sin not to accord a proper welcome to an *atithi* (the guest). Yamarāja and his wife accorded Nachiketā a fitting welcome and hospitality. Yamarāja still did not feel completely satisfied. So he told Nachiketā, "Dear child, I have offended you by keeping you waiting for three days. As an atonement of my sin, I request you to ask for three boons."

Nachiketā asked, "My first wish is that my father become peaceful and free from anger; and when I return home, may my father welcome me lovingly. My second wish is to grant me the knowledge by which I can be worthy of living in the Heaven. My third wish is to grant me *Ātmajnāna* — the knowledge of the *ātman* (soul) *or the Self*." Yama granted the first two boons immediately, but tried to convince Nachiketā to give up his third wish. He offered him gold, pearls, coins, horses, elephants and all the happiness of 'Swarga' (heaven) instead. "No, I do not wish for anything else," replied Nachiketā firmly. Finally, Yamarāja granted him the third boon too, and Nachiketā was enlightened with the knowledge of the *ātman*. Nachiketā spread the knowledge of *ātman* — the ultimate mystery of life and death and the soul immortal that is really a part of the Ultimate Reality, the Absolute Soul (Paramātama) to all and became a great Rishi.

* * * * *

कामक्रोधविमुक्तानां यतीनां यतचेतसाम् ।
अभितो ब्रह्मनिर्वाणं वर्तते विदितात्मनाम् ।।

Kāmakrodhavimuktānām yateenām yatachetasām;
Abhito brahma nirvānam vartate viditātmanām.

-Shrimad Bhagavad Geetā, (Ch. 5, Shloka 26)

Those who have no desire or anger, whose minds are under control, and who have realized the Self, have liberation even here, not to mention hereafter.

SHRAVANA KUMĀRA
A Son Most Devoted to His Parents

Long ago, in the *Tretā-Yuga*, there lived a boy whose name was Shravana Kumāra. He was a very devoted son. He loved his parents very much. Unfortunately his parents were blind and old. Shravana took great care and did everything for them with sincerity and love. He used to fulfill every wish of his parents. Once they expressed their wish to go out on pilgrimage. But they were unable to see or walk. Therefore, he made a *bahangi* (a device like a large weighing balance with two baskets on the two sides of the sturdy bar, to be balanced in the middle upon his soldiers; so that each parent could sit on one of the baskets) to carry them on his shoulders. His parents were quite pleased. During the journey Shravana managed to get roots and fruits from the forest, and water from streams for them to eat and drink.

While on pilgrimage, they arrived in a forest near Ayodhyā. His parents were thirsty. Shravana Kumāra took a vessel to fetch water from the nearby Sarayu river. Coincidently, in the same forest Dasharatha, the king of Ayodhyā, was out on a hunting trip. Dasharatha was so proficient in the art of archery that he could shoot his target only by hearing a sound from it. While Shravana Kumāra was filling his pitcher with water, Dasharatha heard the gurgling sound of water entering the pitcher. He thought that the sound was coming from a deer drinking water. He shot his arrow aiming it by the sound, and it pierced Shravana Kumāra's heart. It was a fatal mistake. Shravana was killed. Before dying, Shravana Kumāra narrated the story of his parents who were thirsty and waiting for the water at a distance from the river bank. Dasharatha was very sad at what had happened. When Dasharatha asked Shravana Kumāra what the king could do for him, Shravana's last wish was that the king should take the water for his thirsty parents. Dasharatha did accordingly, repenting greatly for his hasty action. Shravana's parents cried and told the king to take them to their dead son. The king carried them on his shoulders to the place where Shravana had died. Dasharatha found that in place of Shravana's dead body, there was a Muni (*ascetic*) sitting on a high ground.

Just then, Shravana Kumāra, as the Muni, spoke to his parents, "Through my services to you, I have attained a place in the heaven. Do not worry about me. I shall wait for you both and render my services to both of you when you come to me." They both had a dip in the river Sarayu. But they died on the spot because of the unbearable shock. Before dying, they cursed Dasharatha, "Just as we are dying because of our son's departure, you would also die one day for the same reason, O King."

The curse became a reality when Rāma was exiled for fourteen years in order to fulfill the promise he made to queen Kaikeyi. King Dasharatha died pining for his beloved son, Rāma. Shravana Kumāra is remembered even today, as one of the most devoted and ideal sons ever born !

* * * * *

मातृ देवो भव • पितृ देवो भव
आचार्य देवो भव • अतिथि देवो भव

ABHIMANYU
A Matchless Warrior

Abhimanyu was the son of the great warrior, Arjuna. His mother was Subhadrā, the sister of Shri Krishna. He is renowned for the valor displayed in the Mahābhārata war that took place in India about five thousand years ago. It was an epic-battle fought between the forces of evil and righteousness. In the eighteen-day Mahābhārata war, the thirteenth day would be remembered by all, when sixteen-year old Abhimanyu showed his bravery in warfare and phenomenal valor against the mighty warriors of the Kauravas. He wreaked such havoc in the enemy camp that they resorted to the most treacherous and cowardly means to kill the young warrior.

When Grandsire Bheeshmapitāmaha was completely disabled and made to lie on the bed of arrows in the hands of Arjuna, Dronāchārya became the Commander-in-Chief of the Kauravas army, starting on the eleventh day of the war. At dawn on the thirteenth day, the Kauravas army was arranged in a special, invincible battle-formation known as the *Chakravyuh*. 'Chakra' means circular. At the center was kept Duryodhana, to be guarded through the complex seven circular formations radiating outwards. At the entrance of each *'chakra'*, Drona placed formidable warriors: Dushāsana, Karna, Kripāchārya, Ashwatthāma, Shakuni, Shalya, Bhurishrava and Jayadratha, respectively. When the Pāndavas and their leader, Yudhishthira, saw the Chakravyuh, their spirits drowned in despair. Nobody among them knew how to break the *Chakravyuh*. It was impregnable. Only Arjuna and his son Abhimanyu knew the secret. But Arjuna was, by Kaurava's cunning and wicked game plan, tied up in another battle far away.

Therefore, Yudhishthira reluctantly agreed that their sixteen-year old nephew, Abhimanyu, help smash the *Chakravyuh*. However, though Abhimanyu knew the secret of entering the battle formation, he did not know how to exit from the *Chakravyuh*. The Pāndavas then formed a battle strategy. When Abhimanyu broke through, the Pāndavas and their army would immediately and closely follow him to create a wider opening and protect him. Abhimanyu started the battle of his life. However, Jayadratha effectively stopped the Pāndavas and their army at the very first entrance. The Pāndavas could not help Abhimanyu, who had entered the enemy formation speedily alone. At the center, a terrible battle ensued. Abhimanyu, fighting all alone, but most valiantly, smashed and destroyed the hundreds of arrows shot at him.

The many Kaurava Mahārathis (warriors), acting collectively, all at once, succeeded in destroying Abhimanyu's chariot, and all his weapons. Abhimanyu started using the wheel of his broken chariot for his weapon. Finally the Kauravas, attacking the weaponless boy, killed him mercilessly. Arjuna was despondent to learn of his untimely death, and outraged at the Kauravas, especially at Jayadratha, who was mainly responsible for his death. Yet he was proud of his young son who had fearlessly fought for the Dharma (righteousness) and sacrificed his life at the altar of duty. Indeed, the sixteen year old child was the supreme hero of the thirteenth day of the war and perhaps of even the whole of the Mahābhārata war!

EKALAVYA
The Greatest Archer

Ekalavya was an ideal disciple, an excellent archer, and a steadfast keeper of his promise. Ekalavya wanted to learn the art of archery from Āchārya Drona, the royal teacher of the Pāndavas and the Kauravas, and the best teacher of archery at the time. Since Ekalavya's father, Hiranyadhanu, was the king of an aboriginal hunter tribe, considered as belonging to a low stratum of the society, Ekalavya was denied admission in Āchārya Drona's school. Ekalavya's desire of learning archery from Drona was so intense that he made a statue of Dronāchārya and, regarding it as his virtual preceptor (*Guru*), started learning the art of archery, and became the best archer by virtue of shear determination and relentless practice for years.

One day, the young Pāndava and Kaurava princes were out hunting in the forest with their teacher Drona. Their dog wandered to the place where Ekalavya was practicing archery. On seeing Ekalavya, the dog began to bark, disturbing Ekalavya. Furious, Ekalavya shot arrows into the dog's mouth in such a way that it did not hurt him, but merely stopped him from barking. Ekalavya resumed his practice without any more trouble from the dog.

When Dronāchārya came to know about this incident, he realized that Ekalavya had really become the best archer, excelling even Arjuna, his most favorite disciple. Dronāchārya had promised Arjuna to make him the greatest archer ever. Drona was in a fix. Finally, he decided to play as the devil for Arjuna's sake. To disable Ekalavya, Dronāchārya asked Ekalavya to cut off his right thumb to offer it to him as his *gurudakshinā* (ceremonial offering to the Guru upon completion of the course of study). Ekalavya willingly cut his right thumb and offered it to Dronāchārya as his gurudakshinā, knowing fully well that it will end his career as an archer. Ekalavya's career effectively ended, but he established a great ideal of devotion to the Guru. He is remembered as an ideal disciple even today.

ॐ   ॐ   ॐ

JORĀVAR SINGH AND FATEH SINGH
The Symbols of Ultimate Sacrifice

Jorāvar Singh and Fateh Singh, aged 13 and 11, respectively, were the sons of the great Sikha Guru, Guru Gobind Singh who was a great warrior, spiritual teacher, and the protector of the Sanātana Dharma. To understand the motive behind the supreme sacrifices of Jorāvar Singh and Fateh Singh along with those of their two elder brothers, Ajit Singh and Jujhār Singh, one has to know the life and the teachings of Guru Gobind Singh, the Tenth Guru of Sikhism. Like Buddhism and Jainism, Sikhism originated in India as a branch of the Sanātana Dharma and subsequently attained the rank of a world religion by itself.

Ajit Singh and Jujhār Singh laid down their lives fighting against the Mughals. Fateh Singh and Jorāvar Singh were too young to fight. They were sent with their mother to live out of sight of the Mughals. Later, they were captured and tortured to force them to accept Islam. They refused to do so. They were threatened that they would be entombed alive unless they accepted Islam. They still refused to relinquish their own faith. They ultimately sacrificed their lives by preferring to be killed by being laid alive inside, while a brick wall was built around them, on the orders of the Nawāb of Sirhind, rather than yield to the pressure of conversion into Islam. What a sacrifice it was!

What was it that sustained them as they suffered tortures and chose to make the ultimate sacrifice of their lives? For this, one has to understand the life of their grandfather, the Ninth Guru, GuruTegh Bahādur, and of their father, Guru Gobind Singh. When Guru Gobind Singh was just nine years old, Guru Tegh Bahādur became a martyr as he was beheaded by Aurangzeb for refusing to accept Islam. Also, let us briefly look at the life and teachings of Guru Gobind Singh, the great master who inspired and created a regiment of citizens, called the Khālsā, that took up arms against the tyranny of the Muslims on the Hindu populace with great distinction. He had mentioned about his mission in his autobiography called '*Vichitra Nātaka*' : "Let the virtuous understand that I was born to advance Dharma and to destroy the evil." For twenty years, he trained his followers in martial arts to liberate the 'Motherland' from the clutches of the Muslim invaders. He established the 'Guru Granth Sāhib' as the last and Eleventh Guru for the Sikha religion, and said that, from that point onward, the teachings of all the Gurus inscribed therein would guide and inspire the followers.

He realized that he and his followers were unable to achieve the goal of driving the invaders out of the country. Then, this lone survivor of the family of martyrs, Guru Gobind Singh, left for South India to seek the cooperation of Kshatrapati Shivāji. Shivāji was also relentlessly fighting the Mughals and succeeded in establishing a Hindu Kingdom. Unfortunately, on 7 October 1708, Guru Gobind Singh was treacherously assassinated by two Muslims while he was asleep. Had he succeeded in meeting Shivāji, the history of India and of the Hindu Dharma would, perhaps have been different. In this family of valiant keepers of the Dharma, the supreme sacrifice of Jorāvar Singh and Fateh Singh is written in golden letters in the history of India. They are the symbols of conviction, of ultimate sacrifice, and an enduring source of inspiration to all.

● जय हिन्दुस्थान ●

HAKIKAT RĀI
A Proud Hindu Boy, Who Was Executed for Refusing to Accept Islam

Hakikat Rāi was born in 1724 **CE** at Sialkot (now in Pakistan). At that time, the rampant tyranny of the Muslim rulers in the Punjāb province was ubiquitous and unabated. The province was ruled by the religious decree of Islam. Hakikat Rāi was studying in a school where majority of the student-body was Muslim, and for all purposes the school was governed by the Islamic laws. Also, it was the time when Zakaria Khan, a Muslim, was the Governor of Lahore. Muslim boys used to harass and tease Hakikat Rāi and even abused the Hindu gods and goddesses. It was becoming unbearable to Hakikat. Once, in response to the abusive language used against the Hindu gods, Hakikat returned the abusive language in reference to the Prophet of Islam. He was barely 12 years old. He was taken to the Qāzi, a Muslim judge, who sentenced him to be executed for daring to abuse the Prophet of Islam. The case was appealed to the Governor who reaffirmed the Qāzi's sentence, declaring, however, that should the boy embrace Islam, the sentence would be revoked. Hakikat Rāi, true to the faith of his ancestors, rejected the offer to embrace Islam, and was executed.

The Hindus had built a Samādhi (a monument) at Lahore (now in Pakistan) — in honor of Hakikat Rāi. The Hindus used to flock in multitudes to bow before it and held his tomb in great reverence. The annual fair of 'Basanta' was held at this Samādhi in the spring season prior to Partition of India. The memorial has since been demolished. However, there is a memorial to Hakikat Rāi at Batālā at the spot that marks the samādhi of Lakshmi, the wife of young boy Hakikat Rāi.

All through the history, there are innumerable such cases of atrocities committed in the name of Islam to terrorize the Hindu masses in order to force them to accept Islam. .

＊　＊　＊　＊　＊

जो बोले वह अभय ☆ हिन्दू धर्म की जय।

*This process of Islamic imperialism and atrocities is continuing even today. One only needs to open one's eyes. 'Islam stands for peace,' is the standing slogan by many Muslims, especially after September 11, 2001. But one has to ask the question **'Where is the peace'** as the world continues to suffer terrorism in the name of Islam?*

Vedāntic Wisdom

कुर्वन्नेवेह कर्माणि जिजीविषेच्छतं समाः।
एवं त्वयि नान्यथेतोऽस्ति, न कर्म लिप्यते नरे।।

Kurvanneveha karmāni jijeevishecchatam samāh,
Evam tvayi nānyatheto'sti, na karma lipyate nare.

- Yajurveda (40/2)

One should desire to live up to one hundred years, doing good work. If one remains active in this manner, he will guide others and there will be no attachment with the work.

कृतवैरे न विश्वासः कार्यस्त्विह सुहृद्यपि।
छन्नं संतिष्ठते वैरं, गूढोऽग्निरिव दारुषु।।

Kratavaire na vishvāsah kāryastviha suhrdyapi,
Chhannam samtishthate vairam, goodho'gniriva dārushu.

- Mahābhārata / Shāntiparva (139/44)

One, who had been an enemy and now has become a friend, should not be trusted. Enmity remains hidden in such a manner as a fire quietly remains hidden in wood !

योऽमित्रं कुरुते मित्रं वीर्याभ्यधिकमात्मनः।
स करोति न सन्देहः स्वयं हि विषभक्षणम्।।

Yo'mitram kurute mitram veeryābhyadhikamātmanah,
Sa karoti na sandehah svayam hi vishabhakshanam.

–पञ्च./लब्धप्रणाश/२२

One, who makes friendship with a person who is more powerful than him and who also had been his enemy, is eating poison himself, undoubtedly.

Chapter 7

MISCELLANEOUS

In the preceding chapters, we have briefly introduced the subject-matter related to certain aspects of the Sanātana Dharma without elaboration. In this section, an attempt has been made to slightly elaborate on some of these and other subjects; namely,

(1) The story of the spiritual relationship between Rādhā and Krishna;

(2) The significance of the symbol Swastika;

(3) The Divine Incarnations of Bhagawāna Vishnu;

(4) A brief description of the Hindu Samskāras;

(5) A brief introduction of the system of 'Yoga';

(6) A glimpse of the science of Āyurveda; and

(7) A concise description of the Hindu system of time measurement and calendar.

The last topic (including introduction of the 'Shaka Calendar') provides the glimpses of the great achievements of the Hindu scholars in understanding and explaining the laws of Nature. These were the landmark discoveries in the field of Cosmology and Astronomy.

THE THEME OF VEDĀNTA PHILOSOPHY

"The one theme of the Vedānta philosophy is the search after unity. The Hindu mind does not care for the particular; it is always after the general, nay, the universal. 'What is it that by knowing which everything else is to be known ? That is the one search.

Look upon every man, woman, and everyone else as God. You cannot help anyone, you can only serve: serve the children of the Lord, serve the Lord Himself, if you have the privilege."

- Swāmi Vivekānanda

RĀDHĀ AND KRISHNA

Shri Krishna, believed to be an Incarnation in the human form of Lord Vishnu, was born in the city of Mathurā, North India, about 5000 years ago. From His birth to the end of His earthly lifetime, His life was full of astounding feats and miracles, as befitting a godly Incarnation. But the account of His life would remain incomplete without a mention of Rādhā and her spiritual love for Him. Among all other playmates — the gopas (cowherd boys) and gopis (cowherd girls) who were greatly devoted to Him, the love of Rādhā for Krishna was that of a perfect devotee to the Almighty. Rādhā's life-journey was unique and can be visualized only on the spiritual plane. Later in the Hindu history, Meerābāi (1504-1550 **CE**) came to compose and recite songs in praise of Lord Krishna, singing them with '*Ekatārā*' (one-string musical instrument) and dancing in ecstasy, expressing her love for Lord Krishna as her beloved husband. Meera's songs are sung by devotees even today. Rādhā and Krishna mutually enjoyed spiritual love for each other, while Meerā worshipped the mental image of her Lord. Rādhā and Meerā were both absorbed in the love of their beloved Krishna, as if they were the incarnation of pure love — free of any expectation.

Krishna's foremost devotee and beloved, Rādhā, is worshipped by the Hindus as is Krishna Himself, the divine pair of Rādhā-Krishna symbolizing the eternal love of humans for God. When Krishna played His flute in the forests of Vrindāvana, gopis danced with Him in ecstasy, Rādhā-Krishna occupying the helm of the entire gathering.

As the renowned author, Bansi Pandit, explains, the gopis represent the individual souls assuming physical bodies, whereas Rādhā symbolizes the enlightened individual soul awakened in the love of God and absorbed in it. The sound of Krishna's flute represents the call of the divine for the individual souls. The gopis' love for Krishna signifies the eternal bond between the individual soul and God. The dance of the gopis and Krishna (*Rāsa-Lilā*) signifies the union of the human and the divine, the dance of the souls. This dance illustrates that when an individual soul responds to the call of the divine, the soul enjoys union with the Lord and becomes absorbed in the divine ecstasy. Krishna, an incarnation of God, to eliminate the evil with the use of force, if necessary, was also love-incarnate, playing flute to spread the melody of love among the gopis, symbolic of the devotees — the people.

When Krishna left Vrindāvana to visit Mathurā on His mission to slay the tyrannical Kamsa, He stated that no matter where He resided physically, His spirit would always remain with Rādhā. He promised Rādhā that she would forever dwell in His heart. Krishna pledged to Rādhā that her name would always precede His own when devotees chant their names. Thus, people chant 'Jai Rādhe-Krishna.' Rādhā is the 'manifested universe' that emanates from the Un-manifest God. The young Krishna is described by devotee-poets, such as Soordāsa and others, to steal butter — symbolic of our minds and hearts. Milk, when churned, turns into butter; mind when churned by various experiences of life, turns purer and wiser. It is the mind and hearts of the gopis that Krishna 'steals' and charms. Even today the devotees recite melodious love songs and dance in ecstasy in remembrance of Rādhā -Krishna, an experience, for the participants and observers alike, hard to describe.

When Krishna had accomplished His life's mission of eradicating the evil, His departure from the earth became imminent. His wife, Rukmini, thought that her husband appeared dejected because He missed His flute that He had given away to Rādhā. Therefore, Rukmini set out for Vrindāvana to meet Rādhā to urge her to return the flute. On her arrival, Rādhā washed Rukmini's feet, making the water purer with the dust from the land where Krishna was residing. Rādhā loved Krishna's flute and believed that Krishna resided in it. Hence she repeatedly enquired whether Krishna had asked for it to be returned. When Krishna was leaving Vrindāvana, Rādhā did not complain about her being left behind. She knew that Krishna had incarnated to fulfill a grand mission of destroying the evil. She believed that her place lay in Vrindāvana to look after her Krishna's footprints, left behind! Knowing this, Rukmini conceded that Krishna without Rādhā was incomplete. Thus, while we pronounce in devotion and prayer: Seetā-Rāma, we offer our prayers and remembrance with 'Rādhe-Shyām' rather than 'Rukmini-Shyām.'

In the *Sri Sanatkumāra-samhitā*, from the *Skanda Purāna*, we find a dialogue between Sage Nārada and Lord Shiva. We present below an extract of the same, providing an insight into the relationship between Rādhā and Krishna:

Sage Nārada asked, "O master! Please tell what method the people of *Kali-Yuga* might adopt to easily attain the transcendental abode of Lord Hari (Shri Vishnu or Krishna) without any kind of austerities?"

Lord Shiva answered, "O fortunate one, I will tell you the secret *chintāmani* (wish-fulfilling) mantras; namely, the following two peerless Krishna mantras:

First : *Gopijana-vallabha charanau sharanam prapadye* (गोपीजन-वल्लभ चरणौ शरणम् प्रपद्ये)

I take shelter of the feet of He who is the gopis' beloved; and

Second : *Namo gopijana-vallabhābhyām* (नमो गोपीजन-वल्लभाभ्याम्)

Obeisance to the divine couple, who are dear to the gopis.

Elaborating on these Mantras, and emphasizing the importance of Rādhā's place, Lord Shiva continued, "Please hear, O Nārada, the meaning of these mantras. The material world is manifested by the Lord's '*māyā*' potency and other external potencies. The spiritual world is manifested by the Lord's '*chita*' potency and other internal and everlasting spiritual potencies. The protector of these potencies is Rādhā, who is Lord Krishna's beloved. The transcendental goddess Rādhā is the direct counterpart of Lord Krishna. She is the central figure for all the goddesses of fortune. She is the pleasure potency of Lord Krishna. She is goddess Mahā-Lakshmi and Lord Krishna is Lord Nārāyana. O Greatest of Sages, there is not the slightest difference between Rādhā and Krishna. O Best among the Sages, what more can I say? Nothing can exist without Them. This universe made of spirit and matter together is Their potency. She is Durgā and Lord Hari is Shiva. Lord Krishna is Indra and She is Shachi. She is Saraswati and Lord Hari is Brahmā. She is Dhumorna and Lord Hari is Yama. O Nārada, please know that everything is Their potency. Even if I had many hundreds of years, I could not describe all Their glories."

जय राधे-श्याम ॐ जय राधे-श्याम ॐ जय राधे-श्याम

* * * * *

A post-script to the present day youth : *Many naughty young men exclaim, "Why can't we have as many girlfriends as Krishna had gopis, and get away with it like He did?" Yes, you can! If you can pick up the Govardhana mountain with your little finger; if you change the poison that was offered to Meerā and turn it into nectar; if you can dance on a thousand fanged cobra; and above all, if you are a spiritually transcendent young lad of 9, you may dance with as many gopis as you please.*

स्वस्तिक

THE SWASTIKA
A Symbol of Great Veneration

The Swastika is an ancient symbol signifying auspiciousness. It is a reminder of the path for human endeavor to realize 'Brahman' — the Ultimate Reality (God). It has been used since the Vedic times, in the Indus Valley Civilization and also in ancient Troy and by the Native Americans. In recent years, around 1900, the symbol was very popular in Europe until it was adopted by the Nazis and became associated with their war-mongering and atrocities.

Originally, 'Swastika' is a Sanskrit word composed of two words: "su" meaning "good," and "asti" meaning "is." Thus 'swastika' means "that which brings good luck and well-being." It is mentioned in one of the most frequently used mantras of the Rig-Veda, the oldest scripture known to mankind:

स्वस्ति न इन्द्रो वृद्धश्रवाः स्वस्ति नः पूषा विश्ववेदाः।
स्वस्ति नस्ताक्ष्र्यो अरिष्टनेमिः स्वस्ति नो बृहस्पतिर्दधातु।।

Swasti na indro vriddhashravāh swasti nah pooshā vishwavedāh,
Swasti nastākshryo arishtanemih swasti no brihaspatirdadhātu.

ऋग्वेद संहिता (१.८६.६)

May the Widely Respected, the Resplendent God, guard our welfare! May the All-knowing Nourisher guard our welfare! May the Creator of the cyclic universe ceaselessly guard our welfare! May the Sovereign Protector, with unblemished weapons, guard us for our prosperity!

It also has a symbolic visual representation consisting of a cross with extensions of each arm at a right-angle in a clockwise direction ["right-handed swastika"] — used as a sacred symbol, with positive attributes, by Hindus, Buddhists and Jains. In contrast, an anti-clockwise swastika ["left-handed swastika"] denotes negative attributes.

Because the swastika has been so widely used for so long, it has been interpreted in a variety of ways by practitioners of the Eastern Religions.

In **Hinduism**, the swastika has multiple symbolic interpretations, including:

- A solar symbol, spreading light in all directions;

- The Four Goals of Human Endeavour : The line from the bottom left to the top right represents the pursuit of *Artha* [material security] and *Kāma* [sensual pleasure]; the line from the bottom right to the top left represents the flow from *Dharma* [Righteous Action] to *Moksha* [Liberation];

- Lord Ganesha, the Remover-of-Obstacles and the Repository-of-Wisdom, who is invariably invoked at the start of any religious ceremony.

The symbol drives its auspiciousness from the Four-fold Principles of the Divinity, as Lord Brahmā is said to be Four-Faced (as being the Originator of the Four *Vedas* — *the Rig-Veda, the Sāma-Veda, the Yajura-Veda* and *the Atharva-Veda*). The swastika is also associated with the Four *Āshramas* (*Brahmacharya, Grahasthya, Vānaprastha and Sanyāsa*); the Four *Varnas* (*Brāhmana, Kshatriya, Vaishya* and *Shoodra*); and the Four *Purushārthas — Dharma, Artha, Kāma and Moksha.* These elements are the heart of the Hindu Way of Life. It also represents the World-Wheel, the continuously changing world, revolving around an Eternal Center — God.

It has been used as a symbol of the Sun spreading out light or radiation in all four directions. More generally, it symbolizes the Cosmos and the progress of the Sun through space. In the Hindu astronomy, the swastika represents the celestial transition of the sun into the Tropic of Capricorn.

The *Vāyu Purāna* states that the Lord of serpents, who lives on the *Devakuta* Mountain, has one hundred hoods, each marked with the swastika symbol, representing the *Chakra* of Lord Vishnu. According to the *Matsya Purāna* and the *Shiva Purāna,* respectively, the swastika is one of the eight types of yogic postures referred to in the *Vayaviyasamhitā.*

The symbol is commonly engraved on sacred objects of worship as well as on doorways of temples and homes. It forms a part of religious ceremonies to celebrate weddings, consecration of new homes, embarking on new ventures, and similar other auspicious undertakings. In many Asian countries, especially India, it is used to decorate books, vehicles, cash registers in stores, and similar other objects in daily use.

In **Buddhism**, the four arms of the swastika are interpreted to represent the Four Noble Truths taught by Lord Buddha:

- 'There is suffering in life';

- 'The origin of suffering is Desire';

- 'Suffering can be made to cease';

- 'The Eight-fold Path is the Way out of suffering'.

In **Jainism**, the swastika symbol is the primary holy symbol. It is a symbol of the Seventh Jina (Saint), the Teerthankara Supārsva. All Jain temples and holy books invariably contain the swastika and ceremonies usually begin with marking multiple swastika symbols with rice around the altar. The four segments of the swastika represent the Four Destinies of living beings:

- 'Life as a human being';

- 'Life as a celestial being';

- 'Life as a fish, bird or animal';

- 'Life as living in the lower world.'

卐　　卐　　卐

THE TWENTY-FOUR DIVINE INCARNATIONS OF BHAGAWĀNA VISHNU

God is Infinite. He is Almighty, Omniscient, Omnipresent and Most Compassionate. Even though He has no need to do so, He incarnates for the deliverance of the good and the meek, for preserving righteousness, and for bestowing mercy on all creatures, and for vanquishing the evil. His Incarnations and characters thereof are also beyond count. Sage Sootji said in Shrimad Bhāgavatam :

अवतारा ह्यसंख्येया हरेः सत्त्वनिधेर्द्विजाः।
यथाविदासिनः कुल्याः सरसः स्युः सहस्रशः।।

Avatārā hyasankhyeyā hareh sattva-nidherdvijāh;
Yathāvidāsinah kulyāh sarasah syuh sahasrashah.

- Shrimad Bhāgvatam (Canto 1, Ch. 3, Shloka 26).

"Just as thousands of streams emerge from an inexhaustible body of water, and flow in all directions; in the same way, innumerable Incarnations arise from God, Who is an ocean of Truth and Existence."

There are many different kind of Incarnations of '*Parmeshwara*' (God): Purushāvatāra (Incarnation as a Human), Gunāvatāra (Incarnation as a Virtuous Attribute), Kalpāvatāra (Incarnation at the transition of the Kalpas), Yugāvatāra (Incarnation at the transition of the Yugas), Poornāvatāra (Whole Incarnation), Anshāvatāra (Part Incarnation), Kālāvatāra (Epochal Incarnation), Āveshāvatāra (Fierce Incarnation), etcetera. God's character differs according to the 'Kalpa.' In the Bhāgavad Purāna and in many other scriptures, there appear detailed descriptions of Twenty Four Incarnations of the Almighty and All-Auspicious Bhagawāna Vishnu, the Supreme Godhead. The names of these Incarnations are given below :

1.	Kumāra	(कुमार)	14.	Narasimha*	(नरसिंह)
2.	Varāh*	(वराह)	15.	Vāmana*	(वामन)
3.	Nārada	(नारद)	16.	Hayagreeva +	(हयग्रीव)
4.	Nara-Nārāyana	(नर-नारायण)	17.	(a) Shri Hari	(श्रीहरि-ध्रुव पर कृपा)
5.	Kapila	(कपिल)		(b) Shri Hari +	(श्रीहरि-गजेन्द्र उद्धार)
6.	Dattātreya	(दत्तात्रेय)	18.	Parashurāma*	(परशुराम)
7.	Yajna	(यज्ञ)	19.	Vyāsadeva	(व्यासदेव)
8.	Rishabha	(ऋषभ)	20.	Hansa +	(हंस)
9.	Prithu	(पृथु)	21.	Rāma*	(राम)
10.	Matsya*	(मत्स्य)	22.	(a) Balarāma	(बलराम)
11.	Koorma*	(कूर्म)		(b) Krishna*	(कृष्ण)
12.	Dhanvantari	(धन्वन्तरि)	23.	Buddha*	(बुद्ध)
13.	Mohini	(मोहिनी)	24.	Kalki*	(कल्कि)

- Asterisk (*) marked are 'Dashāvatāra,' the Ten prominent Avatāras of Bhagawāna Vishnu.
- Kalki Avatāra is foretold — to be at the end of the Kali-Yuga (present-epoch) in about 43,000 **CE**.
- Asterisk (+) marked are not cited as the prominent Avatāras in the Shrimad Bhāgavatam.
- Among many Avatāras, only Twenty-two are mentioned including Lord Balarāma.

|| ओ३म् शान्तिः शान्तिः शान्तिः ||

Source: "Kalyāna Avatāra-Kathānka", Gita Press, Gorakhapur, India, January 2007.

THE HINDU SAMSKĀRAS

It is culture that distinguishes man from fellow creatures. It took a very long time for the human beings to evolve certain norms considered necessary for a civilized society. With the passage of time, these social norms were assimilated into socio-religious rites. In the Hindu tradition, these rites (referred to as the sixteen Hindu samskāras) were described elaborately in the Hindu religious texts. These *samskāras* help to unify and purify the Hindu society as they also deeply influence every individual's life.

The sixteen *samskāras* are:

1. Garbhādhāna (गर्भाधान)   : Conception
2. Pumsavana (पुंसवन)   : Birth
3. Seemānta (सीमांत)   : Hair-parting at birth
4. Jātakarma (जातकर्म)   : Ceremony on birth
5. Nāmakarana (नामकरण)   : Naming ceremony
6. Karnavedha (कर्णबेध)   : Ear-piercing ceremony
7. Nishkramana (निष्क्रमण)   : Taking the child out
8. Annaprāshana (अन्नप्राशन) : First-time eating of solid food by the child
9. Kshudakarana (क्षुदकरण)   : Removing impure hair
10. Vidyārambha (विद्यारंभ)   : Initiation of learning
11. Upanayana (उपनयन)   : Initiation as a student with wearing of the sacred thread (जनेऊ)
12. Vedārambha (वेदारंभ)   : Higher studies of the Vedas etc.
13. Keshānta (केशांत)   : First shave of beard for male
14. Samvarttana (संवर्तन)   : Completion of studies
15. Vivāha (विवाह)   : Marriage
16. Antyeshti (अंत्येष्टि)   : Last rites

The *samskāras* vary in ceremonial details from one community to another. Not all the sixteen rituals are necessarily observed now-a-days except among highly conservative families.

A noted writer, Sānkhya, commented, "Refined by the *samskāras*, a person, who is able to cultivate the eight noble qualities — mercy, forbearance, freedom from envy, purity, calmness, right behavior, freedom from greed and freedom from coveting — would rise up to the level of '*Brahman*' from where there is no fear of fall." Sage Atri wrote, "By birth, every one is a *shoodra* (the lowest stratum of the social structure); by *samskāras* he or she becomes a *Dvija* (twice-born). By learning (studying Vedas), he or she becomes a *Vipra* and by realizing *Brahman*, he or she attains the status of a Brāhmana." Kumārila summarized the significance of the samskāras, "Samskāras are those rites which impart fitness and eligibility to perform certain actions."

In short, '*Upanayana*,' the Eleventh *samskāra*, is for the beginning of formal education; *Vivāha* (marriage), the Fifteenth *samskāra*, is considered a house-holder's duty and social obligation for a stable society. According to Sage Manu also, *Vivāha* is the most important samskāra, as it makes one responsible for undertaking one's social obligations.

Presently, most of the *samskāras* have lost their religious significance. In the above list, some of the *Samskāras* have almost disappeared. Even when performed, they are merely superficial rituals. *Upanayana* and *vivāha* have become events for socialization, and flaunting of the status-symbols with feasting and exchange of gifts have assumed priority activities. But it is worthwhile to know and to understand the true purpose and significance of the *samskāras* to appreciate how our ancient social and spiritual thinkers instituted ways to guide an individual's passage and behavior in society at the specific milestones of life.

* *Source: Dr. Jyotsna Kamat*
  First Online: December 16, 2004; Last Updated: November 05, 2006

> Yoga is the physical, mental and spiritual discipline to control our body, mind and soul so that we may realize the Self.
> *-Maharshi Patanjali*

YOGA
A Science of Healthy Living

Yoga literally means unification. It is a union of breath to the body, of the mind to the muscles, and most important, of the self to the Divine. In the Hindu spiritual system, Yoga refers to unification of the individual's inner self or soul (*Ātmā*) with the Ultimate Reality (*Pārabrahman*) that is God, also called the Absolute Soul (*Parmātmā*).

To achieve this goal, one needs a robust body, fearless attitude and sound mind that has acquired knowledge and is free from stress. *Yogāsana is a way to physical discipline involving bodily postures to relieve stress, as a pre-requisite for uniting the body and mind, and for understanding the nature of the soul that would lead to better integrated living.* It ensures greater efficiency in work, better control of mind and emotions. Through yoga, one can achieve both physical fitness and mental harmony. Therefore, the practice of *Yogāsana* is the first requirement.

YOGĀSANA

Before undertaking the practice of **Yogāsana**, we pray to Maharshi Patanjali who perfected this unique system for good health and longevity.

Maharshi Patanjali

योगेन चित्तस्य पदेन वाचा, मलं शरीरस्य च वैद्यकेन।
योऽपाकरोत्तं प्रवरं मुनीनां, पतञ्जलिं प्राञ्जलिरानतोऽस्मि।।

Yogena chittasya padena vāchā, Malam shareerasya cha vaidyakena.
Yo'pākarottam pravaram muneenām, Patanjalim pranjalirānato'smi.

I offer my salutations with folded hands to Patanjali, the renowned amongst the sages, who removed the impurities of the mind by (explaining) yoga, of the speech by (commenting on) grammar, and of the body by (expounding) medicine.

The technique of *Yogāsana* has two facets. **First** the *āsanas*, which deal with physical exercises for all parts of the body making, muscles strong and joints flexible. This also helps in developing poise and peaceful mental attitude. Āsanas mainly work on the endocrines and the nervous system, which are interrelated with other systems of the body. The beneficial effects produced by these two systems are also reflected on other systems. Thus, they rectify the imbalance of the physiological system. At a glance, complete Yoga Cycle may be expressed as

- Yoga-āsana (physical postures and exercises)
- Prānāyāma (breathing exercises)
- Dhyāna or Sādhanā (meditation)

The attention to the following instructions is necessary for the performance of the āsanas :

- Assume posture of āsana slowly and steadily;
- Retain the āsana-posture comfortably;
- Increase the time of retaining posture slowly;
- In case of inability to retain the posture, repeat again several times with ease;
- Avoid all jerks while assuming and releasing the posture;
- Ensure that the correct posture is assumed and retained;
- Know the purpose of each āsana, so that while retaining the posture, you may concentrate on the particular part of the body that is intended to be exercised;
- Always start from a simple posture and then take up the advanced ones.

Second, the *Prānāyāma* refers to regulating and controlling the breathing rhythms. This technique employs both the slow and the fast inhaling and exhaling of the breath, holding the air inside the body for an appropriate duration. The union of *āsana* and *prānāyāma* is known as *Yogāsana*. We present below one of the most effective and important *Yogāsanas*. It is called Sooryanamaskāra and is beneficial for all ages.

SOORYANAMASKĀRA

The practice of Sooryanamaskāra early in the morning, before breakfast is very useful for a healthy living. The complete cycle of ten poses constitutes one cycle of the Sooryanamaskāra. It is considered an important Yogāsana. One should start with a few sets of postures comprising the Sooryanamaskāra, and then increase the number. It gives combined benefits of āsanas, prānāyāma and exercise. By regular practice of Sooryanamaskāra, the body will be active and the functions of organs will improve.

There are thirteen *mantras* to be recited when performing the Sooryanamaskāra. One *mantra* is recited before the beginning of each Sooryanamaskāra in the posture of readiness. One needs to undergo through ten postures to complete one cycle, which is one Sooryanamaskāra. As in any *yogāsana*, breathing is very important while performing Sooryanamaskāra. In each posture, one has to **inhale** *(pooraka)* or **exhale** *(rechaka)* or **hold** *(kumbhaka)* the breath. It is recommended that one should practice a minimum of 12 Sooryanamaskāras daily for good health. The specific steps involved are summarized below :

SOORYANAMASKĀRA
WORSHIP EXERCISES

ध्येयः सदा सवितृ-मण्डल-मध्यवर्ती ।
नारायणः सरसिजासन-सन्निविष्टः ।।
केयूरवान् मकर-कुण्डलवान् किरीटी ।
हारी हिरण्मयवपुर्धृत-शंख-चक्रः ।।

ॐ मित्राय नमः ।
ॐ रवये नमः ।
ॐ सूर्याय नमः ।
ॐ भानवे नमः ।
ॐ खगाय नमः ।
ॐ पूष्णे नमः ।
ॐ हिरण्यगर्भाय नमः ।
ॐ मरीचये नमः ।
ॐ आदित्याय नमः ।
ॐ सवित्रे नमः ।
ॐ अर्काय नमः ।
ॐ भास्कराय नमः ।
ॐ श्री सवितृसूर्यनारायणाय नमः ।

अकाल-मृत्युहरणं सर्व-व्याधिविनाशनम् ।
सूर्य-पादोदकं तीर्थम् जठरे धारयाम्यहम् ।।

Salutation Mantra
for
Sooryanamaskāra

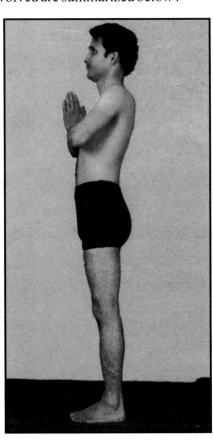

Readiness Posture
Feet touching each other from toe to heel; body erect; chest out forward; neck straight; eyes fixed on the nose-tip; palms and fingers together and perpendicular to ground in the posture of namaskāra; thumbs pressed on chest hollow; forearms in a straight line.

Posture I *(Pooraka)*
Folded hands; fingers closed upwards (above head); arms and elbows stretched; eyes fixed on wrists; head bent backward; spine strung backward in a curve; legs and knees straight and body above hips bent backward.

Posture II *(Rechaka)*
Arms down; palms resting on both sides of feet on the ground; palm and feet in a straight line; front-distance between palms equal to that between shoulders; chin touching chest and forehead touching knees; legs (shin, knee and thigh) straight and vertical to the ground.

Posture III *(Pooraka)*
Left leg thrown backward; knee and toe touching ground; right foot firm; right shin, thigh and the last rib close together; palms resting on ground; elbows straight; chest out; shoulders and head strung back; body curved.

Posture IV *(Rechaka)*
Right leg thrown backward; both legs and knees straight; feet close together; arms and elbows straight; body supported on palms and toes; body from head to feet in a straight-line; eyes fixed on the ground at right angle to body.

Posture V *(Kumbhaka)*
Arms bent at elbows; body in prostrate position; forehead, chest, palms, knees and toes touching the ground. Pelvic region slightly up, elbows strung towards each other and chin drawn towards chest.

Posture VI *(Pooraka)*

Arms and elbows straight; chest out; head and shoulders strung back; eyes up; pelvis drawn towards palms; knees on the ground; toes firm (as in postures III and IV) and feet close together.

Posture VII *(Rechaka)*

Palms and toes as in posture VI; pelvic strung upwards; heels touching ground; arms and elbows straight; chin touching chest; head stretched towards knees; heels, pelvis and wrist forming a triangle.

Posture VIII *(Pooraka)*

Left leg forward in between palms. Right knee and toe touching ground; left shin, thigh and the last rib close together; rest of the body as in posture III.
Note: Position of feet alternating with each namaskāra.

Posture IX *(Rechaka)*

It is the repeat of posture II. Arms down; palms resting on both sides of feet on the ground; palm and feet in a straight line; front-distance between palms equal to that between shoulders; chin touching chest and forehead touching knees legs (shin, knee and thigh) straight and vertical to the ground; body fully balanced.

Posture X *(Kumbhaka)*

Body erect as in readiness posture. Chest out; neck straight; eyes fixed on nose; palms fingers closed and perpendicular to the ground in the namaskāra posture; thumbs pressed on hollow part of the chest; elbows in a straight line.

PRĀNĀYĀMA

The most popular part of Yoga is doing the **āsana**. But, since ancient times, Prānāyāma has been practiced to control the body and the mind and to make it steady and peaceful for achieving pure consciousness, called Samādhi. It is called the gateway to meditation, as it strengthens the nervous system. Through the proper practice of Prānāyāma, the body is purified and one can maintain good health.

Technically speaking, Prānāyāma is the controlling of the breathing process. Inhalations and exhalations are the complementary phases of Prānāyāma. Controlled inhalations are called *Pooraka* and exhalations, *Rechaka*. Each round of Prānāyāma consists of one *pooraka* and one *rechaka*. Applying a break in the speed of inhalations and exhalations is the process of Prānāyāma. After attending the morning calls, we should do Yogāsana, but before meditation we must practice Prānāyāma as a daily routine. This will keep one steady and peaceful throughout the day.

For Prānāyāma, sit in Padmāsana or Vajrāsana (see postures below) or in any other comfortable meditative pose, arms stretched over the knees; and back, neck and head erect. If necessary, use right ring finger and right little finger together on the left side of the nostril and right thumb on other right side while inhaling and exhaling. While practicing Prānāyāma, the ratio of inhaling to exhaling should be approximately **1 : 2**. The time of inhaling and exhaling may vary from person to person. We present below a few simple techniques of Prānāyāma for the beginners.

Padmāsana Posture

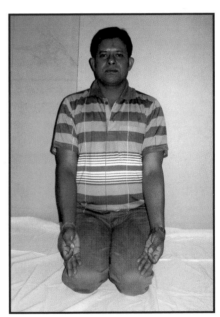

Vajrāsana Posture

Kapālabhāti: Kapālabhāti means that sequence (of breathing), which brightens the brain and stimulates the brain cells. Sit in any comfortable meditative pose as discussed above (keeping the spine erect and balanced). One may even sit on a chair if so required. Then, keep the left hand on the left knee and right hand on the right knee and be relaxed. Exhale through both nostrils by contracting the lower and middle portions of the abdomen. Release the contraction of the abdominal muscles quickly and follow at once by another forcible expulsion of breath. Repeat this a number of times in quick succession at a frequency of about 60-120 strokes per minute. Start with lower number of strokes and gradually increasing as the days pass. After completing the rounds, take a deep breath and exhale slowly. Then breathe freely and relax.

Kapālabhāti Posture

Bhāstrikā: Bhāstrikā means 'bellows'. It is performed by instant and quick expirations of breath. Sit in a comfortable position keeping the spine erect and balanced. Do 20 strokes of Kapālabhāti. While inhaling and exhaling, one produces rapid sounds. It is a good exercise for abdominal viscera and lungs.

Bhāstrikā Posture

Anuloma-Viloma (Nādishuddhi): Sit in any comfortable meditative pose as discussed above (keeping the spine erect and balanced). One may even sit on a chair if so required. Then, keep the left hand on the left knee and right hand on the bridge of the nose as described above. Put the thumb on the right side of the nose and the 4th and 5th fingers on the left side of the nose. Fold the index and middle fingers. Do not twist the nose, only press it on the bony region to control the breathing. First exhale through the left nostril, then inhale through the same nostril by closing the right nostril. Then, exhale through the right nostril while keeping left nostril close. Then, inhale through the right nostril and exhale through the left nostril. Have inhalation and exhalation for the same duration (about 20 seconds each). Both the chest and abdomen expand during this rhythmic breathing. One should have 10-15 rounds to begin with, and may go 30 rounds. This completes one round of Anuloma-Viloma Prānāyāma. In this type of Prānāyāma, the inhaling and exhaling are done very slowly.

Anuloma-Viloma Pose

Anuloma-Viloma Pose

There are two types of Anuloma-Viloma Prānāyāma :

a) **Chandra Anuloma** : Here inhalation and exhalation are through the left nostril (Chandra Nādi) only. Right nostril is closed all the time. All other steps of Anuloma-Viloma are applicable.

b) **Soorya Anuloma** : In this case, inhalation and exhalation are carried out through right nostril (Soorya Nādi) only, keeping the left nostril closed all the time. All other steps of Anuloma-Viloma are applicable.

Ujjāyi : The sitting position is the same as in Anuloma-Viloma. In this case, during inhalations and exhalations, one produces some sound (hissing sound) by partially closing the glottis and, therefore, it is called *Ujjāyi*. Inhale through both nostrils with a low uniform sound through the glottis. Hold the breath after inhaling; exhale with sound again, only through the left nostril by closing the right nostril. Complete the desired number of rounds. It helps in improving the thyroid gland and respiratory disorders, specially bronchitis and asthmā.

Sooryabhedana : The sitting position is the same as in Kapālabhāti. In this Prānāyāma, one always uses right nostril for inhalation. Inhale through the right nostril. Hold the breath and then exhale through the left nostril. Continue to complete these rounds up to a comfortable number. Then increase the number each day, to about 40-50.

Once one is accustomed to these simple kinds of Prānāyāma, other kind may follow. These Prānāyāma are to introduce one to the steady and peaceful environment of healthy living.

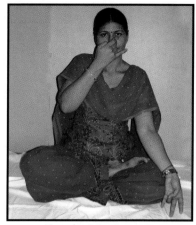

Sooryabhedana Pose

MEDITATION

Meditation is a specialized technique. One should learn it from an expert. We give a very brief account so that one may familiarize oneself to meditation. It alongwith Prānāyāma and āsana completes the process of **Yogic Practice.** The meditation is the technique of controlling mind by focusing inward, curtailing the extraneous distractions as completely as possible. In the present, fast-moving, world of stress-filled environment, it is playing an important role in minimizing the tension and achieving peace of mind for a large number of practitioners. The salient features are given below.

- Sit in any comfortable meditative pose keeping the spine straight and close the eyes. Then follow the instructions step by step as given below.

- Relax your body, let there be no movement. Moderate your breathing.

- Keep yourself away from outer noises and draw in.

- Control your thoughts and let nothing disturb your concentration.

Meditation Pose

Slowly draw attention on your breathing. Think that the oxygen that you are inhaling is purifying your body and mind and is cultivating pure and noble thoughts in you. Think that with air you are breathing out, you are throwing out the dirt, impurities and bad tendencies of the body and the mind.

Keeping all outside thoughts away, fix your attention on your favorite object or symbol, which is pure and holy to you. The symbol ॐ is recommended as it is identified with purity of thoughts, and used by the ancient practitioners. Relax and try to forget the body and the mind. You are now fully integrated physically and mentally. Keep yourself in this position and you will feel the bliss — an atmosphere of peace, calm and happiness inside as well as outside.

For regular practice one should sit in meditation for about 45 minutes or whatever time one can spare. The practice should be repeated every morning and evening. Meditation helps to absorb the daily strength derived through āsana, Prānāyāma and other exercises. Moreover, it changes the attitude, behavior and actions of the person. It is the best way to reduce tension.

The Science of Yoga is a tool for holistic living.

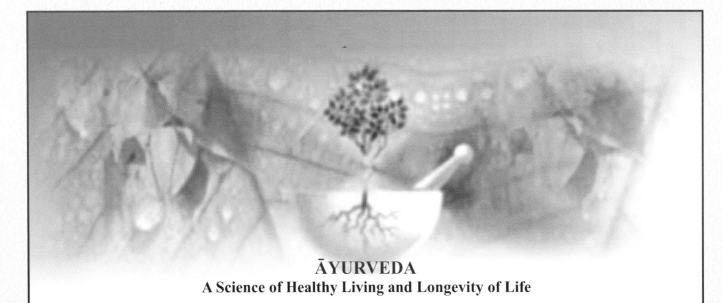

ĀYURVEDA
A Science of Healthy Living and Longevity of Life

The Hindu civilization evolved in India over a long period that may be traced back to the earliest prehistoric period. It is this land of Bhārata where it was proclaimed that entire world is 'One family,' giving the message to humanity of universal love and friendship, harmony and peace, non-violence and tolerance and respectful acceptance of diverse cultures and creeds. The Rishis, the seers and seekers of true knowledge, searched relentlessly for the ultimate purpose of life and for the realization of the Self and the Divine. In the process they discovered the identity of the nature of the Self within and the Divinity manifesting in, among other things, the physical laws of nature that govern the material world around. All this was achieved through a unique and holistic way of living. For this a traditional holistic health-care system, the science of 'Yoga' and a special branch thereof called the 'Āyurveda' were invented and developed that helped one to live a life that is free from ailments and day-to-day stress. Based on the principle of eternal life, this system of health-care has a vast body of knowledge covering eight sub-branches discussed later. Its major premise involves the symbiosis of mind, body and spirit. Any imbalance in this synthesis results in physical ailments. This ancient Indian system of medicine seeks to establish a harmony between the body, mind and spirit by creating an optimum health environment. Thus, these holistic health approach and benefits of Āyurveda encompass the physical, mental as well as the spiritual aspects of a person.

The history of Āyurveda can be traced to the Vedic period (about 5000 years **BCE**). The *Atharva-Veda* contains passages devoted to medicine. In the Hindu mythology, Dhanvantri is considered as the divine physician who discovered the medical science of Āyurveda, along with the Ashwini Kumar twin brothers. This system of medicine is rooted in the Vedic culture as a science of healthy and long life using medicines mostly extracted from herbs and minerals. However, a comprehensive use of the Āyurvedic system was developed between 1000 **BCE** to 500 **BCE**, and is used even today.

The current knowledge about this ancient Indian medicine is primarily from the *Charaka Samhitā* (though there are a few earlier versions as well). *Charaka Samhitā* in its present form is estimated to date from 1st century **CE**. Vāgbhatta's *Ashtānga Hridaya* (approximately 500 **CE**), and the *Shushruta Samhitā* is believed to have originated in the last centuries **BCE**. But the date of its present version is fixed by researchers at 7th century **CE**. These three classic texts describe the basic principles and theories from which this system of medicine has evolved. They reflect an overwhelming wealth of clinical as well as surgical information, enriched further by later research, on the management of a multitude of diseases and ailments.

Dhanvantri

Maharshi Charaka is credited to have written a treatise, *'Charaka Samhitā,'* in 500 **BCE** for the use of the physicians. It details the anatomy of the human body, notes on pathology, diagnosis and treatment of various diseases, and recipes for their remedies.

> "Life (*āyu*) is the combination (*samyoga*) of body, senses, mind and reincarnating soul. Āyurveda is the most sacred science of life, beneficial to humans both in this world and in the world beyond."
> —*Charaka Samhitā, Sutrasthana*, (1.42-43)

Charaka

Āyurveda believes that three main elements determine the state of health of a person and these — termed as the '*dosha*' (fault), the '*dhātu*' (tissue) and the '*mala*' (impurity), respectively — should be in proper balance.

सम दोषः, समाग्निश्च, समधातु मलःक्रिया ।
प्रसन्न आत्मेन्द्रिय मनः स्वस्थ इत्य मिधीयते ।।

Sama doshah, Samāgnishcha, Samadhātu Malahkriyā,
Prasanna ātmendriya manah swastha itya midheeyate.

–चरक संहिता

A person who possesses **Dosha** *(vāta, pitta, kapha)*, **Agnis** *(Dhātwāgni & Jatharāgni etc)*, **Dhātu** *(rasa, rakta, mānsa, meda, āsthi, majjā, shukra)*, *and* **Mala** (perspiration, urine & stool) in normal state — neither in excess nor in shortage; and whose mind, spirit and sense-organs are also felicitous — (only) such a person can be said to be healthy.

Any deviation in this balance due to external or internal causes is a cause for concern. These are basically therapeutic measures taken either to prevent diseases or to cure them. Thus, the Āyurvedic procedures are often applied to detoxify the body as a prelude to strengthening the immune system. '*Panchakarm*' (the five procedures) is the most commonly followed procedure for detoxification therapy, leading to an Āyurvedic treatment or healing, called '*Kāyā Kalpa*' — a rejuvenation of the body.

Also, for the diagnosis of the imbalance that causes the disease, the Āyurvedic system postulates that the constitution of a person can be divided into three categories —*Vāta* (ether/air), *Pitta* (fire) and *Kapha* (water/earth). According to this system, *Vāta* rules mobility; *Pitta* governs digestion and assimilation of food, and *Kapha* governs the substance within the body responsible for weight, cohesion and stability. These three, in combinations of two, create six more sub-types, known as *dwidoshaj*. A seventh sub-type also exists, which is a combination of all the three categories known as *tridoshaj*. Thus, the Āyurvedic medicines, extracted mainly from herbs and minerals for possible treatment of the diseases, are used to restore the balance between *Vāta, Pitta* and *Kapha*. Maharshi Charaka knew the characteristic medicinal properties of over 100,000 different herbs. He mentioned 341 special plant substances, 64 mineral substances and 177 substances of animal origin for preparation of the medicines. The *Charaka Samhitā* defines the eight major divisions of Āyurveda as follows :

1. शल्य चिकित्सा (Shalya Chikitsā)   :   Surgery
2. शालाक्य चिकित्सा (Shālākya Chikitsā)   :   Surgery and treatment of head and neck, Ophthalmology and Otolaryngology etc
3. काय चिकित्सा (Kāya Chikitsā)   :   Internal medicine
4. भूतविद्या तंत्र (Bhutavidyā Tantra)   :   Mental and supernatural diseases (Psychiatry)
5. कौमारभृत्य चिकित्सा (Kaumārabhratya Chikitsā)   :   Pediatrics
6. अगद तंत्र (Agada Tantra)   :   Toxilogy — treatment against venoms
7. रसायण तंत्र (Rasāyana Tantra)   :   Pharmacology — preparation of medicines from organic and inorganic substances
8. वाजीकरण तंत्र (Vājeekarana Tantra)   :   Virilification — Science of fertility

The oldest treatise available on this codified version is *Atreya Samhitā*.

300 DIFFERENT OPERATIONS

Sushruta describes the details of more than 300 types of surgical operations and 42 surgical processes. In his compendium on surgery, '*Sushruta Samhitā*', he minutely classifies surgery into 8 categories :

Sushruta

1.	आहार्य (Āharya)	:	extracting solid bodies
2.	भेद्य (Bhedya)	:	excision
3.	छेद्य (Chhedya)	:	incision
4.	एष्य (Eshya)	:	probing
5.	लेख्य (Lekhya)	:	scarification
6.	वेध्य (Vedhya)	:	puncturing
7.	विश्राव्य (Vishrāvya)	:	evacuating fluids
8.	सीव्य (Seevya)	:	suturing

The ancient Indians were also the first to do amputation, caesarean operation, and cranial surgery. The Bhāgavata Purāna recites sage Vashishta as cutting the womb of a pregnant woman with *Kusa Sastra*. Kautalya's Arthashāstra deals with postmortems. Jeevaka, the personal physician of Lord Buddha, is said to have practiced brain surgery. The 'Bhoja Prabandha' describes a cranial operation performed in 927 **CE** on King Bhoja, where two surgeons made the king unconscious (by administering anesthesia material), opened the skull, removed a tumor-like growth from the brain, stitched the head, and restored him to consciousness. The art of anesthesia and cataract surgery was also known.

125 TYPES OF SURGICAL INSTRUMENTS

The Hindus were so advanced in surgery that their instruments could cut a hair longitudinally."

-Mrs. Plunket

Sushruta worked with 125 kinds of surgical instruments, which included scalpels, lancets, needles, catheters, and rectal speculums, mostly conceived after jaws of animals and birds to obtain the necessary grips. He also defined various methods of stitching with the use of horses' hair, fine thread, fibers of bark, goat's gut and ants' head.

EXCEPTIONAL ACHIEVEMENTS

- Charaka described the functions of the heart and the circulatory system, 2000 years before the English physician Dr. Harvey who is said to have discovered the system in the 16th century in Europe.
- अग्नि कर्म विधि (Agni Karma Vidhi) — A process devised by Sushruta, where treatment was given through rays and heat without surgery.
- जलौका प्रयोग (Jalaokā Prayoga) — A system for purifying blood through 18 different methods.
- There were instances of eye surgery, artificial limbs, and treatment for tumors and even of hair loss.

PLASTIC SURGERY IN INDIA 2600 YEARS AGO

Sushruta, known as the Father of Surgery, had practiced his skill as early as 600 BCE. He used cheek skin to perform plastic surgery to restore or reshape the nose, ears and lips with incredible results. Modern plastic surgery acknowledges his contributions by calling this method of rhinoplasty as the Indian method. "The whole plastic surgery in Europe has taken its new flight when the devices of the Indian workmen became known to us."

-Dr. Hirschberg

The science of Āyurveda, holistic health system, encompasses the physical, mental as well as the spiritual aspects of a person.

THE COSMIC TIME SCALES : CREATION OF THE UNIVERSE
THE HINDU VIEW

Poetic, philosophical and scientific expositions of the Creation of the universe are cited in the Vedas and the Purānas.

The Vedic Concept of Creation

Qualitative concept of Creation enunciated in the Vedas, the oldest Hindu scriptures, is very similar to the present 'Big Bang' theory accepted by modern scientists. The famous creation hymns in the *Rig-Veda* are :

नासदासीन्नो सदासीत्तदानीं नासीद्रजो नो व्योमा परो यत् ।
किमावरीवः कुह कस्य शर्मन्नम्भः किमासीद्गहनं गभीरम् ।।१।।

न मृत्युरासीदमृतं न तर्हि न रात्र्या आह्न आसीत्प्रकेतः ।
आनीदवातं स्वधया तदेकं तस्माद्धान्यन्न परः किं चनास ।।२।।

तम आसीत्तमसा गूल्हमग्रेऽप्रकेतं सलिलं सर्वमा इदम् ।
तुच्छ्येनाभ्वपिहितं यदासीत्तपसस्तन्महिनाजायतैकम् ।।३।।

कामस्तदग्रे समवर्तताधि मनसो रेतः प्रथमं यदासीत् ।
सतो बन्धुमसति निरविन्दन्हृदि प्रतीष्या कवयो मनीषा ।।४।।

तिरश्चीनो विततो रश्मिरेषामधः स्विदासी३दुपरि स्विदासी३त् ।
रेतोधा आसन्महिमान आसन्त्स्वधा अवस्तात्प्रयतिः परस्तात् ।।५।।

Rig-Veda (Vol. XIII, Kānda 10, hymn 129/1.5)

Gist of the above Vedic Shlokas (verses) :

In the Beginning there was neither nought nor aught
Then there was neither sky nor atmosphere above
What then enshrouded this entire universe?
In the receptacle of what was it contained?
Then was there neither death nor immortality,
Then was neither day, nor night, nor light, nor darkness,
Only the Existent One breathed calmly, self-contained.

Pundit S. Vidyālankara, writing in *The Holy Vedas — A Golden Treasury,* explains that in the beginning of the present order of things the whole universe existed in a state which was invisible, subtle and un-manifested. That which we now know as the earth, the sun, the moon and the stars was then, in the beginning of the *Kalpa*, formless matter in its most elemental state. Hindu philosophers called it *'Asat'*, meaning non-being. *Asat* proceeded the state of being. That single point, which present-day scientists call 'singularity,' where all the mass and energy of the entire universe was stored, is called in the Vedic language *'Hiranyagarbha'* the Womb of Energy. 'In the Beginning was *Hiranyagarbha*, the Seed of elemental Existence.'

हिरण्यगर्भः समवर्तताग्रे भूतस्य जातः पतिरेक आसीत् ।
स दाधार पृथिवीमुत द्यां कस्मै देवाय हविषा विधेम ।।

Hiranyagarbhah samavartatāgre bhootsya jātah patireka āseet;
Sa dādhāra prithveemuta dyām kasmai devāya havishā vidhema.

Atharva-Veda (Vol. II, Kānda 4, hymn 2.7)

God, the Master of luminous planets, existed before the creation of the world. He is the One Lord of all created objects. He sustains the earth, the sun, and the created world. May we worship with devotion, Him, the Illuminator and Giver of eternal Bliss.

At the Beginning of Time ("singularity"), all known physical laws of science break down. The Hindu view is that eternal laws (called *Rita* in the Vedas) always exist and one God, without a Second, governs these laws to create the world and all forms of life.

आपो अग्रे विश्वमावन्गर्भं दधाना अमृता ऋतज्ञाः ।
यासु देवीष्वधि देव आसीत्कस्मै देवाय हविषा विधेम ।।

Āpo agre vishwamāvangarbham dadhānā amritā ritajnāh;
Yāsu deveeshvadhi deva āseetkasme devāya havishā vidhema.

Atharva-Veda (Vol. II, Kānda 4, hymn 2.6)

The immortal forces of Matter, the physical cause of the animate and inanimate world, imbibing all the germs of life, before the beginning of the universe, preserve the entire world in their womb. God rules over all these divine material forces. May we worship with devotion, Him, the Illuminator and Giver of eternal Bliss.

This view is also illustrated in the Yajur-Veda:

सहस्रशीर्षा पुरुषः सहस्राक्षः सहस्रपात् ।
स भूमिम् सर्वत स्पृत्वाऽत्यतिष्ठद्दशाङ्गुलम् ।।

Sahasrasheershā purushah sahasrākshah sahasrapāt;
Sa bhoomim sarvata spritvā'tyatishthaddashāngulam.

Yajur-Veda (Vol. III, Ch. 31, hymn 1)

God is the 'Purusha' (the Cosmic Man) with a thousand (i.e. innumerable) heads, eyes and feet because in Him, the all-pervading Supreme Being, there exist innumerable heads, eyes, and feet of all living beings. The Supreme Lord fills the earth and the 'Prakriti' (the Nature, the Universe) from all sides.

It is important to mention that there is no mention of the division of time, *Chaturyugi* cycle etc. in the Vedas. This is described in the Purānas.

The Purānic Concept of Creation

The Primeval and Eternal Divine Power (identified by Poet-Sage Vedavyāsa with Bhagawāna Shri Krishna) creates the Universe 'for His pleasure-play'. In His own potency, Brahmā, Vishnu and Mahesha are manifested. This trio is known as *TRIMOORTI (the Hindu Trinity)*. Lord Brahmā creates the physical universe, Lord Vishnu sustains, and Lord Mahesha (Shiva) dissolves it. This period of existence is called *Janma Kalpa* (Cosmic Period of Creation), or a 'Day of Brahmā' (i.e., one Divine Day), which the Purānas determine to be 4.32 billion years long in terms of the current (Sun-Earth motion-based) measure of time by humans. This means that Lord Vishnu sustains the universe for this period (4.32 billion years). At the end of this *Kalpa,* Lord Mahesha dissolves it and the entire Existence transitions into a dormant state, for an equal period of cosmic Time. This period is, therefore, called *Pralaya Kalpa* (Cosmic Period of Dissolution) — one Divine Night of Brahmā. Then Brahmā arises from His (4.32 billion-human-years long) sleep, His next (4.32 billion-human-year long) Day — the next *Janma Kalpa* begins, and the Universe is reborn. This cyclic Cosmic process — of the Birth and Death of the Universe with a fixed periodicity — is repeated for one hundred Brahmā-Years (making one "Brahmā's Life"), each Brahmā-Year consisting of 360 Brahmā-

Days plus, of course, 360 Brahmā-Nights. The cosmic Time-period of one Brahmā-Life is also called *Mahā Kalpa.* After one *Mahā Kalpa*, there is a complete Dissolution of the *Brahmānda* (the primordial Seed of the Universe) itself. This grand cosmic episode is called *Prakrati Pralaya of the Brahmānda* [The Shrimad Bhāgavatam (12/4/2-6)]. The cosmic time-scale indicated above can thus be summarized in terms of the familiar human-years as follows :

According to the Hindu scriptures (e.g., the *Shrimad Bhāgavatam)*, a basic unit of cosmic Time (denoted here by the symbol *U*), is 432,000 (human) years. Four distinct 'Yugas' — specific cosmic eras — are mentioned: *Sata-Yuga, Tretā-Yuga, Dwāpara-Yuga* and *Kali-Yuga*, with progressively decreasing length of Time (in terms of human-years). Indeed, as pronounced in the Shrimad Bhagavad Geetā, each *Yuga* is marked by a new Incarnation of Lord Vishnu, to protect the righteous, to vanquish the evil-doers, and to re-establish Dharma (Righteousness). One set of the Four *Yugas, taken in chronological order,* is called a *Chaturyugi* :

Sata-Yuga	*1,728,000 years*	*(= 4 U)*
Tretā-Yuga	*1,296,000 years*	*(= 3 U)*
Dwāpara-Yuga	*864,000 years*	*(=2 U)*
Kali-Yuga	*432,000 years*	*(= 1 U)*
One Chaturyugi	**4,320,000 years = 4.32 million years (= 10 U)**	

Brahmā's One Day spans (as does Brahmā's One Night) a cosmic period equal to 1,000 cycles of *Chaturyugi*s, the combination covering a period of (4.32 + 4.32) x1000 million human-years, that is, 8.64 billion human-years. A set of 360 such Brahmā-Day-Night periods (i.e., One Brahmā-Year) define One *Kalpa;* while *100 Kalpas* constitute one *Mahā Kalpa*, of cosmic Time:

Kalpa = (One Divine Day + One Divine Night) x 360 (Divine Days in One Divine Year)
= 1000 **x** (4.32 + 4.32) x 360 billion years =311, 040 billion years
= 311.04 trillion (human-years)

Mahā Kalpa = One Life-Time of Brahmā = 100 Kalpas
= 31, 104 trillion (human-years)

The above cyclic pattern of *Mahā Kalpa*s is then repeated indefinitely.

Lord Brahmā has completed 50 Brahmā-Years of His life and is in the 1st Day of the 51st Year of the current *Mahā Kalpa.* Therefore, Brahmā's Age, or the elapsed time in the *Mahā Kalpa* in terms of man's time scale is
= 50 x 720 (Days and Nights in one Year of Brahmā) x 4.32 billion years (One Day of Brahmā) + Time elapsed in the 51th Year
= 155.52 trillion years + time elapsed in 51st year.

For the calculation of the elapsed time in 51st year, let us consider the following:

There are three cycles of time:
- The smallest one is called *Chaturyugi* and is of 4.32 million years.
- The second one is called *Manvantara* (मन्वन्तर) and is of 4.32 million x 1000 divided by 14 = 308.57142 million years.
- The third one is called *Kalpa* (or a Day of Brahmā) and is of 4,320 million years.

Manvantara is the time-span in which position of one *manu* ends and the position of next *manu* begins. These are swāyambhuva, swārochina, auttama, tāmas, revata and chākshusha manvantaras. At present, we are in the vaivasavata manvantara. Vivasawana — being the son of Sun God is called Vaivasavata manu.

There are 14 *Manvantara* (*manus*) in One *Kalpa* or the Day of Brahmā. For the same length of time there is One Night of Brahmā. As far as the present universe (the time elapsed in the 51st Year of Brahmā's Life) is concerned, it has already completed six out of fourteen *Manvantara*, Twenty-seven out of Seventy-two *Chaturyugi*s in the seventh *Manvantara*, three *Yugas* in the Twenty-eighth *Chaturyugi*, and by the (human) year 2008 would be completing 5110 (human) years in the Fourth *Yuga*, known as *Kali-Yuga.*

The present cosmic cycle consists of

6 *Manvantara* = 6 x 308.57142 million = 1,851.4285 million years
27 *Charuryugi* = 27 x 4.32 million = 116.64 million years
3 *Yugas (Sata-Yuga, Tretā-Yuga & Dwāpara-Yuga)* = 3888000 years = 3.888 million years
Kali-Yuga by year 2008 = 5110 years = 0.005102 million years
Total = (1,851.4285+116.64+3.888+0.005110) million years = 1971.9624 million years. This is the cosmic Time-epoch in the 51st Year of Brahmā's Life. *This is, therefore, the life of present universe.*
The life of Brahmā in the present *Maha Kalpa* = (155.52 trillion + 1.972 billion) = 155.521972 trillion years.

Conclusion

The age of the present universe based on the calculations given above as per Hindu scriptures is approximately 1.972 billion years. The Big Bang theory estimates the age of the solar system in the range 2 to 4 billion years and the age of the universe to be in the range of 10-20 billion years. These figures are being constantly revised as more of the data are obtained.

According to Purānas, on 20 March 2007 (Chāitra Shukla 2 - Vikrama Samvat 2064) the age of the present universe is 1,97,29,49106 years.

To recapitulate :

Janma Kalpa (one day of Brahmā or one cycle of creation) = 4.32 billion years
Pralaya Kalpa (one night of Brahmā or one cycle of dissolution) = 4.32 billion years
Mahā Kalpa (100 years-age of Brahmā) = 311.04 trillion years
Elapsed time in the present Mahā Kalpa (age of Brahmā) = 155.52197 trillion years
Creation & Dissolution cycle (Janma Kalpa + Pralaya Kalpa) = 8.64 billion years
Number of creation & dissolution cycles = (311.04 trillion/8.54 billion) = 36,000
Mānvāntara: 14 in one *Janma Kalpa* = (4.32/14) billion years = 308.5714 million year
One Mānvāntara = 72 Chatuyugis
Number of Chatuyugis in one cycle of creation & dissolution = (8.64 billion/4.32 million) = 2000
Chaturyugi (Mahāyuga): Total period of 4 *yugas* = 4.32 million years
One Kalpa (Janma or Pralaya) = 1,000 *Chaturyugi (Mahāyuga)*
According to Hindu view as outlined in the Shrimad Bhāgavatam the physical universe is created and dissolved periodically and then is reborn. The above cosmic cycle is repeated indefinitely.

- In the context of modern science, presently, the universe is expanding. All galaxies are receding with respect to one another. One view supported by the presently available data is that the universe may expand forever. The other view is that this universe is restored to its original (beginning) state of very dense mass as postulated in Big Bang theory. However, according to Hindu view the universe is created from a point called बिन्दु-विस्फोट (*Bindu Visphot* — the dot of explosion) that essentially is in agreement with the modern Big Bang theory of cosmology. According to the Hindu view, the universe will revert back to the dense mass referred to as the Big Crunch in the terminology of modern Cosmology.

- *The Hindu view of the formation of cosmos is described in the Purānas, which are more than 5000 year old, while the theory of Big Bang has been proposed only recently. The above astounding agreement between the estimates of the age of the universe speaks volumes about the depth of knowledge, on part of the ancient Hindu scholars, about the cosmic time scales and phenomena. A few other facets in this connection are briefly mentioned below.*

MEASUREMENT OF TIME

In *Soorya Siddhānta*, Bhāskarāchārya calculates the time taken for the earth to orbit the sun to 9 decimal places and is given equal to 365.258756484 days. It can be compared to the value of 365.2564 days given by Astronomer W.M. Smart and currently accepted measurement of 365.2596 days. Between

Bhāskarāchārya's ancient measurement 1500 years ago and the modern measurement the difference is only 0.00084 days, i.e. only 0.0002%.

LONGEST TIME MEASURE

The longest measure of time in the history of humanity is the *Kalpa* in Hindu Chronology. In astronomy a cosmic year, the period of rotation of the sun around the center of the Milky Way Galaxy, is 0.225 billion years, while the *Kalpa (Janma + Pralaya)* is equivalent to 8.64 billion years. From the largest to the *Krati*, which is a measure of 34,000th of a second, Bhāskarāchārya gives details about the different measures of time.

THE HINDU CALENDAR
A Concise System of Time Measurement

The Gregorian calendar is the most widely used one in the world. It is based on the movements of the earth relative to the sun. It is a modification of the Julian calendar, decreed by Pope Gregory XIII, for whom it was named, on 24 February 1582 **CE**. The years in the calendar are numbered from the birth year of Jesus Christ, which has been labeled the "Anno Domini" (AD) era and is also labeled the "Common Era" or the "Christian Era" (**CE**); some also label it as the "Current Era." The main aim of this calendar was to fix the date of the 'Easter' so that it could be celebrated by the Christian populace on the same day.

However, in India, two systems of calendars were prevalent before the Gregorian calendar was introduced.

(1) The Vikrama Samvat, named after King Vikramāditya, based on the relative motions of the earth and the moon (Lunar system); and

(2) The Shaka Samvat, named after King Shālivāhana, based on the relative motions of the Earth and the Sun (Solar system). These two systems of Calendar were introduced 57 years before and 78 years after, respectively, the birth of Jesus Christ, whereas the Gregorian calendar came into practice after 425 years (in 1582 **CE**).

Among the two Indian systems of calendar, the Shaka Samvat is the most accurate and simple. It shows that the scientists of India were far ahead in the field of Astronomy even before the birth of Christ. It is the official calendar of India adopted in 1955 **CE**. The highlights of the Shaka Samvat are given below.

THE SHAKA SAMVAT
The National Calendar of India

In 1757 **CE**, the British introduced the Gregorian calendar in India. However, it is inconvenient. In November 1952, the government of Free India appointed a 'Calendar Reform Committee' chaired by Prof. M.N. Saha. On November 10, 1955 the Committee submitted its report and recommended the adoption of the *Shaka Samvat* based on the findings of 'Hindu Astronomy' and 'Solar System' for all official and civil use in India, and, possibly worldwide. The Government of India adopted the recommendation of the Committee. It uses the *Shaka Samvat* for all official purposes along with the Gregorian calendar. The campaign for its adoption worldwide was, and remains, dismal. We present the important conclusions of the report.

● The *Shaka* era should be used in the unified national calendar. The year 1954-55 **CE** corresponds to 1876 *Shaka*. In other words, the year 1954 **CE** corresponds to 1875-76 *Shaka*. The difference between the two systems is 78 years.

● The year should start from the day following the vernal equinox.

● A normal year would consist of 365 days, while a leap-year would have 366 days. After adding 78 days to the *Shaka* era, if the sum is divisible by 4, then it is a leap-year. But when the sum becomes a multiple of 100, it would be a leap-year only when it is divisible by 400, otherwise it would be a common year.

Examples: The years *Shaka* 1878, 1882, 1886, 1890, 1894 etc. are leap-years consisting of 366 days each. But the years *Shaka* 2022, 2122, 2222 and again 2422, 2522, 2622 are not leap-years, while *Shaka* 1922, 2322, 2722 are leap-years.

● Chaitra should be the first month of the year, and the lengths of the different months would be fixed as follows :

Chaitra	30 days (31 days in a leap-year)	Āshwina	30 days
Vaishākha	31 days	Kārtika	30 days
Jyeshtha	31 days	Mārgasheersa	30 days (Agrahāyna)
Āshādha	31 days	Pausha	30 days
Shrāvana	31 days	Māgha	30 days
Bhādrapada	31 days	Phālguna	30 days

Corresponding dates:

The dates of the 'Indian Calendar' would thus have a permanent correspondence with the dates of the Gregorian calendar. The corresponding dates are as follows :

Indian Calendar (Shaka Samvat)		Gregorian Calendar		
Chaitra	1	March	22	in a common year
		March	21	in a leap-year
Vaishākha	1	April	21	
Jyeshtha	1	May	22	
Āshaadha	1	June	22	
Shrāvana	1	July	23	
Bhādrapada	1	August	23	
Āshwina	1	September	23	
Kārtika	1	October	23	
Mārgasheersa	1	November	22	
Pausha	1	December	22	
Māgha	1	January	21	
Phālguna	1	February	20	

The Indian seasons would thus be permanently fixed with respect to the Shaka Calendar as follows:

Seasons		Calendar Months		
Greeshma	(Summer)	Vaishākha	&	Jyeshtha
Varshā	(Rainy)	Āshādha	&	Shrāvana
Sharata	(Autumn)	Bhādrapada	&	Āshwina
Hemanta	(Late Autumn)	Kārtika	&	Mārgasheersa
Shishira	(Winter)	Pausha	&	Māgha
Vasanta	(Spring)	Phālguna	&	Chaitra

*　*　*　*　*

BIBLIOGRAPHY

Shrimad Bhagavad Geetā - A.C. Bhaktivedānta Swāmi Prabhupāda, The Bhaktivedānt Book Trust, Mumbai, India, 1971

Shrimad Bhāgavatam - A.C. Bhaktivedānta Swāmi Prabhupāda, The Bhaktivedānt Book Trust, New York, 1982

Manusmriti - Rameshwar Bhatt, Chaukhambā Sanskrit Pratishthān, Delhi, India, 1985.

Yoga in Daily Life - Institute of Naturopathy and Yogic Sciences, Bangalore, India, 1995

Chaitanya Bhārati - Publication of VHP of America, Inc, 2000, 2001, 2004

Sri Rāmacharitmanasa - Tulasidāsa, Geetā Press, Gorakhpur, India

Kalyāna Upanishad Anka - Gita Press Gorakhpur, India, Vikram Samvat, 2055.

What Religion Is? In the Words of Swāmi Vivekananda - Vidyatmananda, Advaita Āshrama, Kolkata, India, 1991.

Lives of Saints - Sivananda, The Divine Life Society, Sivānanda Āshrama, Rishikesha, India, 1943.

Shrimad Vālmeeki Rāmāyana - Vālmeeki, Gitā Press, Gorakhpur, India, 1998.

Spiritual Import of Religious Festivals - Krishnānanda, The Divine Life Society, Sivānanda Āshrama, Rishikesha, India, 1980

Lectures from Colombo to Almora - Vivekānanda, Advaita Ashrama, Kolkata, 1992.

Kautileeya Arthshastra - Chowkhambā Vidyābhawan, Vārānasi, India, 1984.

The Hindu Mind - Bansi Pandit, B.& V Enterprises, Inc., Glen Ellyn, IL, USA.

Pātanjalayogadarshanam - Swāmi Hari Harananda Aranya, Motilal Banārsidās, Delhi, India.

Kalyāna Avatāra-Kathānka - Gitā Press, Gorakhapur, India, January 2007

and the following websites :

www.DharmicScriptures.org
www.hinduism.co.za
www.religionfacts.com
www.wikipedia -the free encyclopedia
www.hindunet.org
www.rudraksha-ratna.com
www.csuohio.edu
www.hinduism.about.com
www.lotussculpture.com
www.sanatansociety.org
www.koausa.org
www.lotussculpture.com
www.gsbkerala.com
www.acharyaonline.com

www.swstemple.org
www.webonautics.com
www.ayyappa.com
www.exoticindiaart.com
www.freeindia.org
www.luckymojo.com
www.meditationiseasy.com
www.group.yahoo.com
www.Rama.avatara.org
www.hinduism.8k.com
www.Ramayana.com
www.boloji.com
www.Krishna.avatara.com
www.Krishna.com

Note : The first Website, www.DharmicScriptures.org, due to Niraj Mohanka, contains an exhaustive list of the Hindu Scriptures.

www.haryana-online.com

www.yogausa.com

www.dishq.org

www.angelfire.com

www.whc.unesco.org

www.sidharthnagar.nic.in

www.poetseers.org

www.jagannathpuri.blessingsonthenet.com

www.indiatravels.com

www.indiantemples.com

www.pilgrimage-india.com

www.odissa.com

www.madurai.com

www.maduraimeenakshi.org

www.templenet.com

www.india-travel-agents.com

www.lifepositive.com

www.maavaishnodevi.org

www.Journeymart.com

www.kamat.com

www.mydivineplanet.com

www.mahashivratri.org

www.answers.com

www.dreamersden.com

www.rajasthaninforline.com

www.incrediblerajasthan.com

www.indiatourism.com

www.rajasthan-tourism.org

www.rajasthantours.co.in

www.bharatonline.com

www.art-and-archaeology.com

www.tourtravelworld.com

www.sawf.org

www.stupa.org.nz

www.lineone.net

www.orientalarchitechure.com

www.geocities.com

www.culturalindia.net

www.travelmasti.com

www.indianngos.com

www.indiasite.com

www.sacredsites.com

www.sgpc.net

www.Mandir.org

www.Swaminarayan.org

www.austin.about.com

www.retreats.barsanadhama.org

www.jkp.org

www.incredibleindia.org

www.infoindiatours.com

www.kumbh-mela.Pilgrimage-india.com

www.kumbh.org

www.Hardwar.com

www.divinerevelation.org

www.lonelyplanet.com

www.indialine.com

www.nashik.nic.in

www.headlines.sify.com

www.gosai.com

www.krishnascience.com

www.hinduismtoday.com

www.hinduwisdom.info

www.sringeri.net

www.mangalore.com

www.onlinebangalore.com

www.ayodhya.com

www.flex.com

www.mathuravrindavan.com

www.indiayogi.com

www.varanasi.nic.in

www.varanasionline.com

www.members.tripod.com

www.somnath.org

www.kamakoti.org

www.kanch.nic.in

www.advaita-vedanta.org

www.bstdc.bih.nic.in

www.indiaprofile.com

www.amritsar.com

www.spiritualjourneys.net

www.indiaprofile.com

www.Kurukshetra.com

www.haryanatourism.com

www.hindubooks.org

www.balmikiramayan.net

www.bharatadesam.com

www.hinduism.com
www.members.rediff.com
www.is.wayne.edu
www.mythfolklore.net
www.sacred-texts.com
www.Jainworld.com
www.indhistory.com
www.infoplease.com
www.sify.com
www.stephen-knapp.com
www.sankaracharya.org
www.iloveindia.com
www.geometry.net
www.hinduwebsite.com
www.india_resource.tripod.com
www.religiousbooks.net
www.yogamovement.com
www.saranaathati.wordpress.com
www.Samartharamadas.com
www.hindutva.org
www.buddhist-temples.com
www.Buddhanet.net
www.allaboutsikhs.com
www.sikh-heritage.co.uk
www.sikhpoint.com
www.sikhnet.com
www.sikh-history.com
www.sikhphilosophy.net
www.sikhiwiki.org
www.salagram.net
www.vedicculturalcentre.com
www.aryaspiritualcenter.com
www.meta-religion.com
www.lifepositive.com
www.bluedove.com
www.swargarohan.org
www.vivekananda.org

www.Ramakrishna.org
www.Ramakrishnavivekananda.info
www.hssworld.org
www.countercurrents.org
www.mkgandhi.org
www.lucidcafe.com
www.sriaurobindosociety.org
www.liveindia.com
www.india-today.com
www.krishna.com
www.Prabhupada.krishna.org
www.webcom.com
www.chinmaya-chicago.org
www.chinmayamission.com
www.sacred-texts.com
www.suite101.com
www.tamilstar.com
www.stutitmandal.com
www.mythfolklore.net
www.moralstories.wordpress.com
www.swami-krishnananda.org
www.chittorgarh.com
www.tribuneindia.com
www.rdunijbpin.org
www.orbat.com
www.ramanuja.org
www.womenhistory.about.com
www.womeninworldhistory.com
www.Jhansi.nic.in
www.hinduwomen.org
www.auroville.org
www.hinduonnet.com
www.astrouniverse.com
www.kids.swaminarayan.org
www.thecolorsofindia.com
www.hinduism.iskcon.com

SHARING IS CARING

One should be benevolent and ready to serve those in need. But merely being benevolent is not enough. One should be benevolent for some worthy cause.

SELECT THE WORTHY CAUSE WISELY !

Acknowledgements

This publication is financed in part by the courtesy of the following sponsors. Our sincere appreciation and thanks to all.

Bhutada Family Foundation
Houston, Texas

Vivek Welfare and Educational Foundation
Orlando, Florida

DBM Family Foundation
Houston, Texas

Shaila Bala and Late Raj Kumar Jain
New Delhi, India

Aruna and Jagdish C. Sharma
Gaithersburg, Maryland

Srivalli and Shivaram Sitaram
Germantown, Maryland

Anupama and Sudhir Sekhsaria
Potomac, Maryland

Kusum and V.S. Raghavan
Potomac, Maryland

Saraswathi Devi and C.K. Hiranya Gowda
Nashville, Tennessee

Rekha and Mohan Goyal
Columbia, Maryland

Geeta and Vijay Pallod
Houston, Texas

Renu and Vinod Mahajan
Fairfax Station, Virginia

Veena and Sharad Gandhi
Voorhees, New Jersey

Late Indrawati and Late Nathumal Jain
Ambala Cantt, India

Pushpa and Ram Sewak Goswami
Orchard Lake, Michigan

Adarsh and Suresh C. Gupta
Potomac, Maryland

Meera and Ravi K. Jain
Palo Alto, California

Sundresh and Sant Kumar Jain
Ambala, India

Get up and set your shoulder to the wheel — how long is the life for? As you have come into this world, leave some mark behind. Otherwise, where is the difference between you and the trees and stone? They too come into existence, decay and die.

-Swāmi Vivekānanda

GLORY TO SANĀTANA DHARMA : GLORY TO PUNYABHOOMI BHĀRATA

हरि बोल

* * *

हरे कृष्ण हरे कृष्ण
　　　कृष्ण कृष्ण हरे हरे।
हरे राम हरे राम
　　　राम राम हरे हरे।।

* * * * * * * * * *

Hare Krishna Hare Krishna
　　　Krishna Krishna Hare Hare
Hare Rāma Hare Rāma
　　　Rāma Rāma Hare Hare.

About the Authors:

The authors of this publication, Dr. Shardanand and Dr. Ashok K. Sinha, have Ph.D. degrees in Physics, and have retired after successful professional careers. Their present mission is to create and enhance awareness, especially among the Hindu youth born in the United States of America, of the universal and eternal tenets of Sanātana Dharma — the mother-religion of Buddhism, Jainism and Sikhism, and the intertwined relationship with India — the birth-place of these religions. It is hoped that, with the help of this introductory book and other similar publications, the young readers can gain familiarity with, and closely relate themselves with, the spiritual, cultural and socio-political aspects of the country of their origin, and perhaps find themselves better equipped to even contribute to the same in times of need.

ॐ त्वमेव माता च पिता त्वमेव, त्वमेव बन्धुश्च सखा त्वमेव। त्वमेव विद्या द्रविणं त्वमेव, त्वमेव सर्वं मम देव देव॥

Om ! Tvameva mātā cha pitā tvameva, tvameva bandhushcha sakhā tvameva;
Tvameva vidyā dravinam tvameva, tvameva sarvam mama deva deva.

*Om ! Thou art my mother and Thou art my father also; Thou art my brother and my friend; Thou art
Knowledge and wealth unto me; Thou art my all-in-all, O Lord of Lords.*